Zionism and the State of Israel

Zionism and the State of Israel
A moral inquiry

Michael Prior

London and New York

First published 1999
by Routledge
11 New Fetter Lane, London EC4P 4EE

Simultaneously published in the USA and Canada
by Routledge
29 West 35th Street, New York, NY 10001

Routledge is an imprint of the Taylor & Francis Group

Typeset in Garamond by Routledge
Printed and bound in Great Britain by MPG Books Ltd, Bodmin

British Library Cataloguing in Publication Data
A catalogue record for this book is available from the British Library

Library of Congress Cataloguing in Publication Data
Prior, Michael (Michael P.)
Zionism and the State of Israel: a moral inquiry / Michael Prior.
 p. cm.
Includes bibliographical references and index.
1. Zionism–History. 2. Zionism–Moral and ethical aspects.
3. Israel–History. 4. Christian Zionism. I. Title.
DS149.P74 1999   99–10921
320.54'095694–dc21   CIP

ISBN 0–415–20462–3

Cats

Maurice Harmon

The cats patrol the fields
the tips of their arched tails
flick to and fro, their claws
flex and unflex, every step indicative of power,
they march along the walls,
or stalk in single file
between the trees, sometimes
they pace upon the roofs
to get a better view,
sometimes they gather in groups
to share the latest news.
The birds are terrified.
They have their lives to live,
they know the cats can kill,
they know they want control,
but still they scratch the earth,
still perch and sing in trees,
still make their nests in walls,
still teach their young to fly,
as their ancestors did.
As far as they're concerned cats should live somewhere else.
Clashes occur. Bird flocks
attack, harass, disrupt.
The cats retaliate.
The birds they catch they put
in cages out of sight.
No one quite knows why cats have such a hate for birds.
Some say that they themselves were once controlled by dogs,
had fruitful fields to sow
until the dogs appeared.
That may explain why cats
make life so hard for birds.

Contents

Preface

This study of the Zionist conquest and settlement in Palestine pays particular attention to biblical, theological and moral considerations. The theme of 'land' was neglected in Western biblical scholarship prior to the State of Israel's conquest of the Occupied Territories in 1967, and subsequent biblical research was stimulated by that event. However, as Walter Brueggemann has noted in his Foreword to W. Eugene March's study, while the scholastic community has provided 'rich and suggestive studies on the "land theme" in the Bible they characteristically stop before they get to the hard part, contemporary issues of land in the Holy Land' (March 1994: vii). I am confident that readers will acquit me of that charge.

The subject-matter demands that the discussion engage with several disciplines. The modern proliferation of academic disciplines has ensured that few deal with any subject in a way which respects its complexity, with the result that each element functions in isolation from the others and reflects only a portion of the fuller picture. Moreover, the specialization of scholarship intimidates outsiders, and even the most versatile scholars scarcely ever move beyond the limits of their own discipline. There is a tendency to escape into specialization, and evade the responsibility of engagement with the wider world, with the excuse that even critical moral questions must be left to the specialists.

Every relevant discipline which deals with the question of the land of Canaan–Palestine–Israel falls victim to the affliction of specialization. Biblical scholars, in their concentration on questions of historical and literary criticism, pay virtually no attention to the ethical dimensions of the discussion. In general terms, scholars of human rights eschew any reference to the God-question, while acknowledging perfunctorily the link between God and the land, and historians and political scientists frequently discuss the issue purely in terms of political power and interests. What results is a series of truncated discourses, each peddling its own grasp of wisdom, with none respecting the complexity of the total question.

This study includes discussion of the Bible and modern biblical hermeneutics, post-biblical Jewish and Christian cultures, the history and development of Zionism, the international law of war and of occupation, and human rights. If the task of dealing competently with virtually every aspect of the problem is so formidable as to intimidate even the most versatile and gifted academic, the concerned individual nevertheless is left with the moral imperative of deciding on the matter. While a committee of competent and versatile scholars is likely to do better than one person, it does not have a unified conscience. Responsibility for moral judgement and action rests with the individual and cannot be exercised vicariously. Moral responsibility may not be shifted even to others more gifted, learned, and morally upright than oneself.

Paradoxically, theological and biblical reflection frequently evade moral considerations, and in the specific case of Palestine academic discussion of them is not welcomed. The novel perspective of this study is the moral question which arises on consideration of the impact which the Zionist conquest and settlement have had on the indigenous population of Palestine. The scope of the study is wide. I begin with the founder of political Zionism, Theodor Herzl who outlined his programme for a state for Jews (*Der Judenstaat*) in 1896, tracing the history of the movement down to the present (Chapter 1). Chapter 2 considers the antecedents to Herzl's utopian vision. Chapter 3 illustrates how the secular programme of political Zionism initially was rejected out of hand by virtually all strata of religious Judaism. It tracks the different stages of its acceptance in those quarters, to the consequence that today the most vibrant supporters of Jewish conquest come from the ranks of the religious establishment whose leaders initially regarded Zionism as sinful and heretical. Chapters 4 and 5 consider the attitudes of the Christian Churches and theologians to Zionism and the State of Israel. Some reflect a particular Zionist reading of Jewish History and a certain naïveté with respect to the intentions and achievements of the Zionist enterprise.

Chapter 6 attends to how the biblical narrative of the promise of the land of Canaan to Abraham and his posterity, and realised in the account of the conquest of Joshua, has been used to justify the Zionist enterprise. It subjects the traditions of the Bible, which is customarily viewed as a yardstick of moral excellence and as 'the soul of Theology', to an ethical evaluation which derives from general ethical principles and criteria of human decency, such as are enshrined in conventions of human rights and international law. Such an enterprise is not only legitimate, but necessary. When people are dispossessed, dispersed and humiliated, not only with alleged divine support, but at the alleged express command of God, one's moral self recoils in horror. Any association of God with the destruction of people must be subjected to an ethical analysis.

Biblical studies and theology should concern themselves with the real conditions of people's lives, and not satisfy themselves with comfortable survival in an academic or ecclesial ghetto. This book examines the use of the Bible as a legitimisation for the implementation of the ideological, political programme of Zionism and its consequences. The recognition of the suffering caused by the Zionist enterprise requires one to re-examine the biblical, theological and moral dimensions of the question. This study addresses aspects of biblical hermeneutics, and informs a wider public on issues which have implications for human well-being as well as for allegiance to God. While such a venture might be regarded as an instructive academic contribution by any competent scholar, to assume responsibility for doing so is for me, who has seen the situation for myself, of the order of a moral imperative.

Chapter 8 considers a number of critiques of the Zionist aspiration and achievement from Jewish intellectuals, both inside Israel and in the diaspora. While some of these argue in terms of the perceived self-interest of Jewry, others do so in broader, universalist terms. Most of the criticism, however, comes from secular quarters.

My treatment of the subject reflects ongoing engagement with the region since my first visit to Israel and the Occupied Territories. The experience of seeing things on the ground gradually required me to interrogate my very favourable dispositions towards Israel and the Zionist enterprise. The television pictures and reports of the Arab–Israel war of June 1967 conveyed to me that I was observing a classic David versus Goliath conflict, with diminutive, innocent Israel repulsing its rapacious Arab predators. The startling, speedy, and comprehensive victory of Israel produced surges of delight in me. Later that summer in London, I was intrigued by billboards in Golders Green, with quotations from the Hebrew prophets, assuring readers that those who trusted in biblical prophecy would not be surprised by Israel's victory.

During my first postgraduate biblical study visit in 1972, enquiring into the remains of ancient civilisations, I sensed something wrong in the obvious *Apartheid* of Israeli–Arab society. Nine years later I began to see the reality of land expropriation, and the sufferings of the inhabitants of the Occupied Territories. Yet, I had no doubt that Israel's occupancy was justified in terms of its own security needs, a position I only began to question during the course of my sabbatical year in Jerusalem (1983–84). The aggressive programme of Jewish settlement in the territories during that period, and the religious fervour of the terrorist group caught in the act of attempting to blow up the Dome of the Rock and the Al-Aqsa Mosque raised for me questions about the role of the biblical narrative of promise and possession of land in the expansionist activity of the Jewish settlers.

I can date to that period also my first voicing of my perceptions that the land traditions of the Bible appeared to legitimise/mandate the maltreatment/genocide of the indigenes of 'Canaan'. While at that time it was common to construct a Theology of Liberation with strong dependence on some of the traditions of the Hebrew Scriptures, I began to realise that it would be no more difficult to construct a Theology of Oppression on the basis of other biblical traditions. I was thinking of the narratives of Israelite origins, and of the traditions that mandate the destruction of other peoples. My *The Bible and Colonialism* is the fruit of my reflection on the subject (1997).

Frequent and extended study visits throughout the 1980s and 1990s, culminating in my tenure as Visiting Professor in Bethlehem University and Scholar-in-Residence in Tantur Ecumenical Institute, Jerusalem (1996–97) provided a lively context in which to engage in my biblical studies.

The public reception of my *The Bible and Colonialism* (1997a) has encouraged me to deal in a more focused way with Israel–Palestine, a region where the narrative of the Bible is particularly apposite. Fundamentally, the Jewish claim to return rests with the Bible which is a *sine qua non* for the provision of alleged moral legitimacy. While it is not the only one, it certainly is the most powerful moral one, without which Zionism is a discourse virtually entirely in the conquest mode. The Bible read at face value provides not only a moral framework which transposes Jewish claims into a divinely sanctioned legitimacy, but postulates the taking possession of the Promised Land and the forcible expulsion of the indigenous population as the fulfilment of a biblical mandate. For the last ten years I have read widely on the subject of Zionism and the State of Israel in an effort to construct an ideological framework into which I could integrate my thoughts and provide some context for my experiences.

I have come to realise that the philosophy of Zionism has penetrated virtually all relevant discourses, and has succeeded in refracting the whole history of the Israelite–Jewish people through its lens. Moreover, conventional Eurocentric historiography has distorted our view of 'ancient Israel', and virtually silenced the wider history of the region. Political Zionism, a child of the nineteenth-century European colonial age, has successfully portrayed all Jewish aspirations since the biblical period in its terms, and has seduced the mainstream of Western thought also along those lines. I have discovered how the Zionist ideology, detested from the beginning by virtually all shades of religious Jews, has been embraced by the establishment of virtually all sectors of Jewish religious opinion.

The situation within the Christian Churches and mainstream Christian Theology is even more alarming. They, too, have been seduced into accepting a Zionist rendering of all Jewish history. I am disturbed that some sectors of these agencies concur, either by direct support or silence, in the ongoing humiliation of an innocent people, and I am convinced that the prevailing theological, biblical and religious assessments of Zionism and the State of Israel should be subjected to a critique which reflects the concerns of justice, human rights and international legality. That is what I have been struggling to do over the last decade, and my book represents my current understanding of the matter.

I am very grateful to David McDowall and Julia Head for making many helpful comments on chapters of the book, and to Duncan MacPherson who read the whole manuscript and made many helpful suggestions. I am grateful to Professor Maurice Harmon for permission to include his poem, 'Cats', which he wrote during his tenure as Visiting Professor in Bethlehem University, which happened to coincide with the *intifada*. I am grateful to many others who encourage me in my research.

I am very grateful to the staff at Routledge for their efficiency and expertise in preparing the book for publication.

Part I

The achievement of Zionism

1 From Zionism to the establishment of the State of Israel

As will become clear, several streams converge to issue in the broad and complex ideology of 'Zionism', a term used in its modern sense for the first time by Nathan Birnbaum in 1890 (Bein 1961: 33). Whether one approaches the question from a strictly secular perspective, or from one which takes account of religious considerations, the role of the biblical narrative is a critical element in any discussion of Zionism.[1] However, overt appeal to the Bible and its interpretation in underpinning Zionist nationalism was not prominent in the beginning, and only assumed a critical role when the religious settler movement collaborated with the new phase of Zionist expansionism which was inaugurated by the conquests of the 1967 War.

Since theological discourse should aspire to familiarity with unfolding realities, it is desirable to situate the Zionist movement within the social and political contexts in which it arose and progressed. I divide the history of the movement into five phases, beginning with Herzl's programmatic statement calling for the establishment of a state for Jews, and bringing the discussion up to the present day. I trust that this survey will be illuminating for those not familiar with the aspirations of the Zionist movement and its planned programme to realise its ideal to establish a state for Jews. Antecedents of Herzl's vision, and the sacralisation of the Zionist project will be examined in succeeding chapters.

The early phase of Zionism (1896–1917)

While Theodor Herzl (1860–1904) was not the first to suggest the establishment of a state for Jews, he was the one who most systematically

---

1 I have shown elsewhere how the Bible has been deployed in support of different forms of colonialism emanating out of Europe (Prior 1997a). If the European settlers could deploy its narrative as a legitimating charter for their enterprises, the case for Jews doing so appears to require less justification.

planned the elevation of his vision into a programme of action. He interested himself in the Jewish Question as early as 1881–82, and while in Vienna had considered mass Jewish conversion to Catholicism as a solution to the problem of being a Jew in European society. By 1895 he judged the efforts to combat antisemitism to be futile (Herzl 1960, vol. 1: 4–7).[2] He composed the first draft of his pamphlet, *Der Judenstaat*, between June and July 1895.[3]

On 17 January 1896 the editor of the London *Jewish Chronicle*, although decidedly unsympathetic to Zionism, invited Herzl to summarise his scheme, and published his article, 'A Solution of the Jewish Question'. Herzl called for the establishment of a model and tolerant, civil, Jewish state, which, while not a theocracy, would 'rebuild the Temple in glorious remembrance of the faith of our fathers'. He summed up, 'We shall live at last as free men, on our own soil, and die peacefully in our own home'. The editorial was sceptical: 'We hardly anticipate a great future for a scheme which is the outcome of despair'. The response to the article was lukewarm, and for several more years, despite the *Jewish Chronicle* giving lavish space to Zionist activities, its editor continued to view Zionism as 'ill-considered, retrogressive, impracticable, even dangerous'. Matters changed in 1906, when Leopold J. Greenberg, a leading figure in English Zionism bought the paper (in Finklestone 1997: xiii–xiv). In February 1896, Herzl published the full statement of his programme.

It is commonly held that the public degradation of Captain Alfred Dreyfus, an Alsatian Jew on the French General Staff, wrongly convicted of selling military secrets to the Germans (5 January 1896), signalled for Herzl the impossibility of Jews ever assimilating into European society, and confirmed him as a Zionist. Nevertheless, Herzl's journalistic dispatches from Paris were by no means 'Zionist'. It was only after the second guilty verdict of September 1899 that he publicly declared that Dreyfus' fate was essentially that of the Jew in modern society, and he suggested for the first time, in an article for the *North American Review* (1899), that the original Dreyfus trial had made him into a Zionist (Wistrich 1995: 17). There is no word about the Dreyfus affair in the early part of his diaries, and nothing in *Der Judenstaat*.

2　Herzl began his Diaries in 1895, and continued until shortly before his death. Seven volumes of the Letters and Diaries have been published, vols 1–3 edited by Johannes Wachten *et al.* (1983–85), and vols 4–7 by Barbara Schäfer (1990–96). Raphael Patai edited an English translation of the diaries in five volumes. In general, I quote from Patai's edition (rendered Herzl 1960), which I have checked against the original in Wachten and Schäfer. Where I judge it to be important, I give the original German (or other language) from the latter (rendered Herzl 1983–96).

3　Invariably, the items of Herzl's affairs I note are described fully in his Diaries, at the appropriate date, e.g. in this case in the complete German edition, Vol II: 277–78.

Herzl's vision and its underpinning

Herzl insisted that Jews constituted one people (Herzl [1896] 1988: 76, 79), and spoke of 'the distinctive nationality of Jews' (p. 79).[4] Wherever they were, they were destined to be persecuted (pp. 75–78). Antisemitism was a national question, more than a social, civil rights or religious issue, and could be solved only by making it a political world-question (p. 76). The solution to the Jewish Question could be achieved only through 'the restoration of the Jewish State' (p. 69), in which sovereignty would be granted over a portion of the globe large enough to satisfy the rightful requirements of a nation (p. 92). Jews could rely on the governments of all countries scourged by antisemitism to assist them obtain that sovereignty (p. 93), and on the Powers to admit Jewish sovereignty over a neutral piece of land. The creation of a Jewish state would be beneficial to both the present possessors of the land and to adjacent countries (p. 95). Concerning whether the state should be established in Argentina or Palestine, he said, 'Palestine is our ever-memorable historic home. The very name Palestine would attract our people with a force of marvellous potency' (p. 96).

Reflecting typical nineteenth-century European colonialist attitudes, Herzl presented the proposed Jewish state as 'a portion of the rampart of Europe against Asia, an outpost of civilisation [Herzl's term was 'Kultur'] opposed to barbarism' (p. 96). Elsewhere he reflects the world-view of European racist superiority. He assured the Grand Duke of Baden that Jews returning to their 'historic fatherland' would do so as representatives of Western civilisation, bringing 'cleanliness, order and the well-established customs of the Occident to this plague-ridden, blighted corner of the Orient' (Herzl 1960, vol. 1: 343).

On the religious aspect, 'The Temple will be visible from long distances, for it is only our ancient faith that has kept us together' (Herzl [1896] 1988: 102). He appealed for the support of the rabbis (p. 129), and asserted, 'Our community of race is peculiar and unique, for we are bound together only by the faith of our fathers' (p. 146). But the Jewish state would not be a theocracy: 'We shall keep our priests within the confines of their temples in the same way as we keep our professional army within the confines of their barracks' (p. 146). Herzl's final words were:

> A wondrous generation of Jews will spring into existence. The Maccabeans will rise again. ... The Jews who wish for a state will have it. We shall live at last as free men on our own soil, and die peacefully in our own homes. The world will be freed by our liberty,

---

4   Quotes in what follows are from *The Jewish State*, New York: Dover (1988).

enriched by our wealth, magnified by our greatness. And whatever we attempt there to accomplish for our own welfare, will react powerfully and beneficially for the good of humanity.

(pp. 156–57)

Herzl's proposal met with considerable opposition, not least from Chief Rabbi Moritz Güdemann of Vienna, who maintained that the Jews were not a nation, and that Zionism was incompatible with the teachings of Judaism.[5]

Herzl acknowledged that the notions of 'Chosen People', and 'return' to the 'Promised Land' would be potent factors in mobilising Jewish opinion, despite the fact that the leading Zionists were either non-religious, atheists or agnostics. However, Rabbis representing all shades of opinion denounced Zionism as a fanaticism and contrary to the Jewish scriptures, and affirmed their loyalty to Germany. On 6 March 1897 the *Zionsverein* decided upon a Zionist Congress in Munich for August, but the Munich Jews refused to host it. Moreover, the executive committee of the German Rabbinical Council 'formally and publicly condemned the "efforts of the so-called Zionists to create a Jewish national state in Palestine" as contrary to Holy Writ' (Vital 1975: 336). On the Zionist side, Herzl's critics found little specifically Jewish about the state he envisaged.

In addition to the challenge his programme proposed to traditional Orthodox Messianic eschatology – the Almighty alone would bring about the Jewish 'return' – Herzl's insistence on unredeemable antisemitism was a source of considerable annoyance to the Jewish leadership in several Western countries. In England, for example, Chief Rabbi Herman Adler judged Herzlian Zionism to be radically divergent from the main core of Judaism, which it would undermine. He regarded the First Zionist Congress as an 'egregious blunder' and an 'absolutely mischievous project'. No less seriously, where the Jewish leadership of the Rothschilds, Montagus, Cohens, Montefiores and others had honours bestowed on them by government and crown, there was no enthusiasm for the Herzlian dogma that life in the diaspora was inherently unnatural (see Finklestone 1997: xi–xxi).

Herzl convened the First Zionist Congress (29–31 August 1897) in Basle. On the day before the Congress, though non-religious, he attended a synagogue service, having been prepared for the reading of the Law (Vital 1975: 355). The purpose of the Congress was, in three days, to lay the foundation stone of the house to shelter the Jewish nation, and advance the interests of civilisation. The civilised nations would appreciate the value of establishing a cultural station, Palestine, on the shortest road to Asia, a task Jews were ready to undertake as the bearers of culture. Zionism, he

---

5   (1897) *Nationaljudentum*, Leipzig and Vienna, p. 42, quoted in Laqueur 1972: 96.

summarised, seeks to secure for the Jewish people a publicly recognised, legally secured (*öffentlich-rechtlich*) home in Palestine for the Jewish people.[6]

The Congress also founded the World Zionist Organisation, and adopted the motion to establish a fund to acquire Jewish territory, which 'shall be inalienable and cannot be sold even to individual Jews; it can only be leased for periods of forty-nine years maximum' (in Lehn 1988: 18), the forty-nine years reflecting the divine provenance of land-possession (Lev 25).[7] Herzl envisaged that the European powers would endorse Zionism for imperialist self-interest, to rid themselves of Jews and antisemitism, and to use organised Jewish influence to combat revolutionary movements. After the Congress, Herzl wrote in his diary (3 September),

> If I were to sum up the congress in a word – which I shall guard against pronouncing publicly – it would be this: At Basle I founded the Jewish state. If I said this out loudly today, I would be greeted by universal laughter. Perhaps in five years, and certainly in fifty, everyone will know it.
>
> (Herzl 1960, vol. 2: 581)

Herzl's tactics would combine mobilising the Jews with negotiating with the imperial powers, and colonisation. Realising that intensive diplomatic negotiations at the highest level, and propaganda on the largest scale would be necessary (11 May 1896, Herzl 1983–96, vol. 2: 340–41), he obtained audiences with key international figures, including the Sultan, the Kaiser, the Pope, King Victor Emmanuel, Chamberlain and prominent Tsarists. During his first visit to Palestine (1898) he was received by the German emperor, Wilhelm II, at his headquarters outside Jerusalem (2 November) after which he realised that the Zionist goal would not be achieved under German protection. Jerusalem, with its musty deposits of two thousand years of inhumanity, intolerance and uncleanness lying in the foul-smelling little streets, made a terrible impression on Herzl (31 October, 1983–96, vol. 2: 680). In a series of meetings with Sultan Abdul Hamid (May 1901 to July 1902), Herzl promised that Jews would help him pay his foreign debt, and promote the country's industrialisation. The Sultan promised lasting

---

6 (1911) *Protokoll des I. Zionistenkongresses in Basel vom 29. bis 31. August 1897*, Prag: Selbstverlag – Druck von Richard Brandeis in Prag, p. 15.

7 The Fifth Zionist Congress in Basle (29–31 December 1901) established the Jewish National Fund (JNF), which from the beginning was an instrument for the realisation of a Jewish state. The JNF, legally established in 1907, with the 'primary object' to acquire land for exclusive and inalienable Jewish settlement, purchased its first Arab-owned land in 1910 from absentee landlords. So difficult was it to purchase land from small holders that by 1919 it had obtained only 16,366 dunums (a dunum being 1,000 square metres, i.e. about one quarter of an acre; see Lehn 1988: 30–39). The Director of its Palestine Office, Arthur Ruppin (1876–1943), promoted 'economic segregation', as signalled in the axioms of 'self-help' or 'self-labour'.

protection if the Jews would seek refuge in Turkey as citizens. However, Herzl, unable to raise a fraction of the money, decided to open negotiations with Britain. As we shall see, Britain would have its own interests in supporting the Zionist enterprise.

Herzl explained to Joseph Chamberlain, Britain's Colonial Secretary, that in patronising the Zionist endeavour the British Empire would have ten million agents for her greatness and her influence all over the world, bringing political and economic benefits (October 1902, 1983–96, vol. 3: 469). In this *quid pro quo*, England would undertake to protect its client Jewish state, and world Jewry would advance British interests. In August 1903, Herzl discussed with the Tsarist government the speeding up of the emigration of Russian Jews, and argued that the European powers would support Jewish colonisation in Palestine not only because of the historic right guaranteed in the Bible, but because of the European inclination to let Jews go.

Chamberlain had raised already the option of Jews settling in Uganda, rather than Palestine, which was hotly debated, and finally carried at the Sixth Zionist Congress at Basle (22–28 August 1903), with 295 for, 175 against and 90 abstentions. Herzl emphasised that Uganda would only be a staging post to the ultimate goal of Palestine, but fearing that the issue might split the Zionist movement, lifting his right hand, he cried out, '*Im Yeshkakhekh Yerushalayim* ... ' ('If I forget you, O Jerusalem, may my right hand wither'), quoting Psalm 137.5 (Laqueur 1972: 129). The Seventh Congress, at which Herzl was not present, officially buried the Uganda scheme.

With failing health, Herzl visited Rome on 23 January 1904, and met King Victor Emmanuel III and Pope Pius X. To Herzl's request for a Jewish state in Tripoli, the king replied, '*Ma è ancora casa di altri*' ('But it is already the home of other people') (Herzl 1983–96, vol. 3: 653). Neither Pius X nor the Secretary of State, Cardinal Merri del Val, considered it proper to support the Zionist intentions in any way (Herzl 1960, 4: 1602–1603), opposing it on religious grounds. Herzl made the last entry in his Diaries on 16 May 1904, and died in Edlach on 3 July. On the day of his burial Israel Zangwill, the Anglo-Jewish writer and propagandist, compared him with Moses, who had been vouchsafed only a sight of the Promised Land. But like Moses, Herzl 'has laid his hands upon the head of more than one Joshua, and filled them with the spirit of his wisdom to carry on his work' (Zangwill 1937: 131–32).

Evaluation of Herzl

That Herzl provided the inspiration, the leadership and the organisation of the Zionist movement is reflected in David Ben-Gurion's proclamation of the State of Israel (14 May 1948) under his portrait, and in the transfer of his remains to Jerusalem in 1949. His genius lay in elevating his vision and plan into action, through remarkable organisational and diplomatic skills. While others who advocated the establishment of a Jewish state hoped that someone else would lead the march, Herzl organised practical means to advance it, most significantly the convening of the First Zionist Congress in 1897. He was very much a man of action, a 'Tatmensch', as Martin Buber put it. To have dealt with the Kaiser, the Sultan, a king and the Pope, as though he were the leader of a state was no mean achievement. Moreover, his early death ensured that he could be embraced by all factions within the broad Zionist and Israeli camp:

> This iconisation of Herzl has been a useful and unifying force for Zionism, transcending the gulf between Right and Left, liberals and conservatives, secular and religious Jews. There is potentially something for everybody in Herzl's rhetoric of unity, in his visionary 'third way' between capitalism and socialism, in his enlightened, optimistic liberalism.
>
> (Wistrich 1995: 3)

Although Herzl's motivation was not dictated by a religious longing for the ancient homeland, nor by appeal to biblical injunctions, e.g. to go to the Promised Land in order to observe the Torah, at various times people referred to him as the Messiah, or King of Israel, and as the fulfilment of the prophecies of the Jewish Scriptures. At his graveside, Buber did not hide the fact that Herzl had no sense of Jewish national culture, and no inward relationship to Judaism or to his own Jewishness. Moreover, he had the soul of a dictator (in Wistrich 1995: 30–31). Indeed, Herzl's Zionism had much in common with 'Pan-Germanism', with its emphasis on *das Volk*: all persons of German race, blood or descent, wherever they lived, owed their primary loyalty to Germany, the *Heimat*. Jews, wherever they lived, constituted a distinct nation, whose success could be advanced only by establishing a Jewish nation-state.

Moreover, Herzl's claim to construct a separate state 'like every other nation' amounted to special pleading. The basic assumption of European nationalisms was the indigenous nature of a specific community, and its desire for independence from the imperial power. Moreover, reflecting stereotypical colonialist prejudices, he gave little attention to the impact of his plans on the indigenous people. Notwithstanding, he knew what was needed to establish a state for Jews in a land already inhabited. An item in his diary entry for 12 June 1895 signals Herzl's plans. Having occupied the land and expropriated the private property, 'We shall endeavour to expel the poor population across the border unnoticed, procuring employment for it in the transit countries, but denying it any employment in our own country'.[8] He added that both 'the process of expropriation and the removal of the poor

---

8 I offer this translation of 'Die arme Bevölkerung trachten wir unbemerkt über die Grenze zu schaffen, indem wir in den Durchzugsländern Arbeit verschaffen aber in unserem eigenen Lande jederlei Arbeit verweigern' (Vol. II: 117–18), in preference to Zohn's translation, 'We shall try to spirit the penniless population ... ' (Herzl 1960, 1: 87–88).

must be carried out discreetly and circumspectly'.

In public, however, he showed a different face. In a letter of 19 March 1899 he assured a concerned Jerusalem Arab: 'But who would think of sending them away? It is their well-being, their individual wealth, which we will increase by bringing in our own' (in Childers 1987: 167). This kind of duplicity, as we shall see, was a characteristic of Zionist discourse, which masked true Zionist intentions. Moreover, after Herzl's death in 1904, his private diaries were held by the Zionist movement, and until 1960 only edited versions were released, carefully omitting his 'population transfer' plans.

Furthermore, the modern, secular Jewish state of Herzl's novel *Altneuland* (1902), set in 1923 and for European consumption, was a haven of the liberal spirit and a blessing for the natives. To the visiting Christian, Mr Kingscourt, who had asked, 'Don't you look upon the Jews as intruders?', the Palestinian Rashid Bey, replied, 'The Jews have enriched us, why should we be angry with them. They live with us like brothers. Why should we not love them?' But in 1902 also, Herzl's general disdain of natives was obvious from his response to Chamberlain's protest that Britain could not support the Zionist proposal for a joint Anglo-Zionist partnership, since it was against the will of the indigenous population of Cyprus (Herzl's diary of 23 October 1902). Earlier in the entry for the same day, we read: 'Not everything in politics is disclosed to the public – but only results of what can be serviceable in a controversy'.

Zionism and European Imperialism

The early Zionists realised the necessity of winning the support of at least one of the major Europeans powers, whose own agenda might favour the creation of a Jewish state in Palestine. Reflecting international political interests in the controversies surrounding Jerusalem and the Holy Places throughout the Ottoman period Britain stationed a Consular Agent in Jerusalem in 1838, after which a Protestant (Anglican) Bishopric in Jerusalem was established in 1841. Moreover, Britain sought to ensure safe and speedy overland communication with its newly acquired territories in India, and wished to protect her trade with the Persian Gulf region, as well as to keep Mohammed 'Ali of Egypt in his place.[9]

Having already occupied Egypt in 1882, Britain set its sights on Iraq in the years before the outbreak of the First World War, while the French, in

---

9 'The Jewish *people*, if *returning* under the sanction and protection and at the invitation of the Sultan, would be a check upon any future evil designs of Mohammed Ali or his successor' (my emphasis; Viscount Palmerston to Viscount Ponsonby, 2 August 1840, Foreign Office 79/390 [No. 134] Public Record Office).

anticipation of the break-up of the Ottoman Empire, invested heavily in Syria. Dr Chaim Weizmann (1874–1952), the Zionist leader and, later, the first President of Israel, reflected the prevailing colonialist attitudes of the European powers:

> We can reasonably say that should Palestine fall within the British sphere of influence, and should Britain encourage Jewish settlement there, as a British dependency, we could have in twenty to thirty years a million Jews out there, perhaps more; they would develop the country, bring back civilization to it and form a very effective guard for the Suez Canal.
>
> (Letter to *Manchester Guardian*, November 1914, in Weizmann 1949: 149)

The Zionist enterprise would resemble the struggle between progress, efficiency, health and education, on one side, and stagnation on the other: 'the desert against civilization' (Weizmann 1929–30: 24–25). Weizmann considered it self-evident that England needed Palestine for the safeguarding of the approaches to Egypt, and that if Palestine were thrown open for the settlement of Jews, 'England would have an effective barrier, and we would have a country' (letter to Zangwill on 10 October 1914, in Stein 1961: 14–15).

The entry of the Ottoman Empire into the War in October 1914 had a profound impact on future developments in the Middle East. The British Government, fearing a hostile Pan-Islamic opposition led by the Ottoman sultan-caliph, looked to the Sharif of Mecca, Husayn ibn 'Ali to advance its interests. The Sharif agreed, on condition that when the Turks were defeated, the British would support Arab independence in the whole of the Arabian Peninsula (with the exception of Aden), Syria, Lebanon, Palestine, Trans-Jordan and Iraq (Ingrams 1972: 1–2). Sir Henry McMahon, the British High Commissioner in Egypt, with certain important reservations, agreed on 24 October 1915, 'to recognise and support the independence of the Arabs within the territories included in the limits and boundaries proposed by the Sharif of Mecca', i.e. from Cilicia in the north to the Indian Ocean in the south, and from the Mediterranean to Iran (Letter to the Sharif, in Laqueur 1976: 16–17).

Yet, in the Sykes–Picot Agreement 3 January 1916 France and Britain agreed on how to carve up the Middle East: France would control Cilicia, coastal Syria and Lebanon, and Britain would acquire Basra, Baghdad, the southern region of the Middle East, and Haifa and Acre, with the rest of Palestine being placed under an undefined international administration. Among the differences between the terms of the Sykes–Picot Agreement and the letter from McMahon to Husayn were the status of Iraq, the degree of independence of the Arab state(s), the position of Haifa and the status of Palestine. The absence of reference to Palestine in the McMahon letter suggests that it would presumably fall within the Arab state(s), whereas in the Sykes–Picot Agreement it was to be internationalised. However, new

British Prime Minister, Lloyd George decided on an advance into Palestine, and British forces captured Jerusalem on 9 December 1917 under General Allenby, and had penetrated into Aleppo by September 1918. Britain was on the way to becoming the dominant *Entente* power in the region.

Meanwhile, the Zionists had made little progress in winning international support for the creation of a Jewish state in Palestine, or in settling large numbers of Jews there before the outbreak of the War. Estimates of the number of Jews in Palestine at the outbreak of the War vary from 38,000 to 85,000, constituting some 5–10 per cent of the total population, of whom only about half were political Zionists.[10] Realising that Palestinian Arabs would not acquiesce in the Zionist dream, it was clear that British support would be necessary to ensure its realisation. For its part, however, Britain considered Palestine to be vital to its strategic interests, being a buffer against Egypt and a means of protecting the Suez Canal as its route to India, and a link with Iraq. Towards the end of the War, then, there was a convergence of interests between the Zionists and Britain. A Jewish Palestine would serve as a local garrison to defend British interests in the Suez Canal, and at the same time be a loyal political island for the British in a sea of newly established independent Arab states.

The second phase of Zionism (1917–48)

I shall trace here only the most significant developments in political Zionism during the thirty years between the end of the War and the establishment of the State of Israel. These include the Balfour Declaration, and its elevation into an internationally supported programme in the Mandate of the League of Nations, and developments in Palestine leading up to the UN Partition Plan of 1947.

Balfour Declaration

Chaim Weizmann, elected president of the English Zionist Federation on 11 February 1917, quickly sought to have a declaration of support for the

---

10 There are no exact figures for the number of Jews in Palestine before the First World War. Justin McCarthy's analysis of the demographic situation in Palestine (1991) concluded that in 1880 Palestine's population was c. 450,000, of which some 15,000 (less than 5 per cent) were Jews, and by 1914, after the first and second aliyahs (English plural of the Hebrew aliyah, literally 'ascent', referring to a movement of Jewish immigration into Palestine–Israel), it was c. 710,000, of which some 38,000 (still only 5 per cent) were Jews. According to studies based on Zionist sources there may have been 80,000–85,000. However, as many as half of the immigrants may have departed again, while others retained their nationalities rather than become Ottoman subjects (see R. Khalidi 1988: 213, 231). Ingrams gives the figures for 1914 as 500,000 Muslims, and 60,000 each of Jews and Christians (1972: 1).

Zionist goal from the British Government, which was finally given on 2 November. Between July and 31 October there were four main drafts. The Secretary of State for Foreign Affairs, Arthur James Balfour, acknowledged that, at his request, the first draft (of July) was drawn up by Rothschild and Weizmann (PRO FO371/3058, in Ingrams 1972: 9), and this was followed by the Balfour Draft of August, the Milner Draft of August; and the Milner-Amery Draft of 4 October. The first two drafts reflected a strident Zionist perspective, promoting the *reconstitution* of Palestine as *the* national home of the Jewish people, making no reference to the indigenous Arab population, and alluding specifically to the government's reliance on the Zionist Organisation as to the details of its implementation. It is only the final draft that mentions the commitment that nothing shall be done which might prejudice the civil and religious rights of existing non-Jewish communities in Palestine, or the rights and political status of Jews elsewhere.

In the War Cabinet meeting of 4 October, Edwin S. Montagu, the only Jew in the Cabinet, argued against a declaration of British support, and insisted that the project of creating a Jewish state would end by driving out the current inhabitants (Minutes, in Ingrams 1972: 11). Indeed, he regarded Zionism as 'a mischievous political creed', untenable by any patriotic citizen of the United Kingdom (Mayhew, in Adams and Mayhew 1975: 50). At that meeting also, Lord Curzon wondered 'how was it proposed to get rid of the existing majority of Mussulman inhabitants and to introduce the Jews in their place?' He proposed securing equal rights for Jews already in Palestine as a better policy than repatriation on a large scale, which he regarded as 'sentimental idealism, which would never be realised' (Ingrams 1972: 12). The War Cabinet decided that a draft declaration should be submitted confidentially to President Wilson, leaders of the Zionist Movement, and representative persons in Anglo-Jewry opposed to Zionism (PRO.CAB. 23–4, in Ingrams 1972: 13). There was no need to canvass Arab opinion.

Chief Rabbi J.H. Hertz, the first Zionist sympathiser appointed to the post (1913), had 'feelings of the profoundest gratification' on hearing that His Majesty's Government was to lend its powerful support to the re-establishment of a national home in Palestine for Jews. He welcomed the reference to the civil and religious rights of the existing non-Jewish communities in Palestine, which, he assured the Cabinet, was 'but a translation of the basic principle of the Mosaic legislation: 'If a stranger sojourn with thee in your land, ye shall not vex (oppress) him. But the stranger that dwelleth with you shall be unto you as one born among you, and thou shalt love him as thyself' (Lev 19.33,34). Lord Rothschild considered the proviso a slur on Zionism, as it presupposed the possibility of a danger to the rights of the other inhabitants of the country. Weizmann requested 'one or two alterations', and suggested three, including that 're-establishment' replace 'establishment', so that 'the historical connection with the ancient tradition would be indicated', and that 'Jewish people' be substituted for 'Jewish race'. Nahum Sokolov assured the Government that,

'The safeguards mentioned ... always have been regarded by Zionists as a matter of course' (in Ingrams 1972: 13–15).

Other prominent Jews replied, opposing the Zionist programme. Sir Philip Magnus, M.P., insisted that 'the great bond that unites Israel is not one of race but the bond of a common religion', and that 'we have no national aspirations apart from those of the country of our birth'. He found the reference to 'a national home for the Jewish race' both undesirable and inaccurate. C.G. Montefiore, President of the Anglo-Jewish Association, observed that the emancipation and liberty of the Jewish race in the countries of the world were a thousand times more important than a 'home'. Mr L.L. Cohen, Chairman of the Jewish Board of Guardians denied that the Jews are a nation, and repudiated the implication that Jews are a separate entity unidentified with the interests of the places where they live (in Ingrams 1972: 15–16). Indeed, the leadership of British Jewry, perceiving Zionism to be a threat to the well-being of British Jews, opposed it so strongly that it might prevent a British declaration.

But Britain had its own interests to promote. Balfour assured the War Cabinet on 31 October that a declaration favourable to Zionism would promote extremely useful propaganda in Russia and America, and should be made without delay.[11] An independent Jewish state would follow only after some form of British, American, or other protectorate, as a 'gradual development in accordance with the ordinary laws of political evolution' (in Ingrams 1972: 17). The Cabinet authorised Balfour to take a suitable opportunity for making the declaration, which he did in his letter to Lord Rothschild. The so-called *Balfour Declaration* promised the longed-for imperial patronage which was required for a Jewish national home:

Foreign Office
November 2nd, 1917

Dear Lord Rothschild,
I have much pleasure in conveying to you, on behalf of His Majesty's Government, the following *Declaration* of sympathy with Jewish Zionist aspirations which has been submitted to, and approved by, the Cabinet.

---

11 According to the Duke of Devonshire, Churchill's successor as Secretary of State for the Colonies, 'The Balfour Declaration was a war measure ... designed to secure tangible benefits which it was hoped could contribute to the ultimate victory of the Allies', by enlisting international Jewish support for the Allies, and bringing forward the date of the USA entry into the war (PRO.CAB.24/159, in Ingrams 1972: 173).

'His Majesty's Government view with favour the establishment in Palestine of a national home for the Jewish people, and will use their best endeavours to facilitate the achievement of this object, it being clearly understood that nothing shall be done which may prejudice the civil and religious rights of existing non-Jewish communities in Palestine, or the rights and political status enjoyed by Jews in any other country.'

I should be grateful if you would bring this *Declaration* to the knowledge of the Zionist Federation.

Yours
Arthur James Balfour

Jewish opposition to Zionism continued after the publication of the declaration, and led to the founding of The League of British Jews, incorporating all the leading anti-Zionists. Moreover, despite the excitement of the declaration, British Zionism diminished, and fewer than 500 British Jews settled in Palestine during the first decade of the Mandate. Indeed, Jewish opposition to the establishment of a state continued right up to its foundation, but since then support for it is the central focus of British Jewry's identity (Finklestone 1997: xxvi–xxx). Britain's undertaking to honour both its guarantee of Arab independence at the end of the War and the terms of the Sykes–Picot Agreement would be matched in incompatibility by its determination both to support the goal of Zionism and to guarantee the rights of the indigenous Palestinians. Both were cynical compromises by a Britain that was determined to see to its own benefit.

Understandably, the Arabs saw the declaration, which mentioned neither their name nor their political rights, as a betrayal, but petitions protesting at the injustice of settling another people on the Arab homeland were brushed aside (Mayhew, in Adams and Mayhew 1975: 40–41). 'The process of nullification had already begun' (Cragg 1997: 36). Manifestly, to support the intention to establish a Jewish homeland (state), without the consent of the indigenous population, was an audacious undertaking, especially when the Jews in Palestine in 1919 constituted no more than 9.7 per cent of the population, and owned only 2.04 per cent of the land (W. Khalidi 1992: 21). The nomenclature of defining the 670,000 Arabs as the 'non-Jewish communities in Palestine', that is, the non-60,000 Jews, is both preposterous and fraudulent, with the intention of concealing the demographic realities (see Jeffries 1976: 177–78). Moreover, the Zionists who arrogated to themselves the right to speak for 'the Jewish nation' constituted, at that time, only a tiny percentage of World Jewry.

But such arrogance was consistent with the culture of nineteenth century European racist imperialism in which Zionism was born. Its theoreticians, e.g. Weizmann[12] and Arthur Ruppin,[13] could not be expected to transcend the prevailing culture of European settler colonialism, which was driven by assumptions of European superiority based on theories of biological, racial and cultural supremacy. This unchallenged superiority permitted the wholesale exploitation of indigenous populations, sometimes under the guise of civilising them. Indeed, by 1918 some 85 per cent of the globe was in the hands of European colonising powers. Hence the dismissive attitude of Balfour and the Powers towards the indigenous population of Palestine:

> In Palestine we do not propose even to go through the form of consulting the wishes of the present inhabitants of the country. ... The Four Great Powers are committed to Zionism. And Zionism, be it right or wrong, good or bad, is rooted in age-long traditions, in present needs, in future hopes, of far profounder import than the desires and prejudices of the 700,000 Arabs who now inhabit that ancient land. In my opinion that is right. ... Whatever deference should be paid to the views of those living there, the Powers in their selection of a mandatory do not propose ... to consult them. In short, so far as Palestine is concerned, the Powers have made no statement of fact which is not admittedly wrong, and no declaration of policy which, at least in the letter, they have not always intended to violate.
>
> (Balfour memo to Lord Curzon, 11 August 1919,
> PRO. FO.371/4183, in Ingrams 1972: 73)

The Foreign Office set up a special branch for Jewish propaganda, and propaganda materials were distributed to virtually every Jewish community in the world. After Allenby's capture of Jerusalem, leaflets were dropped over German and Austrian territory, and pamphlets in Yiddish were distributed to Jewish soldiers in Central European armies, with the message, 'The hour of Jewish redemption has arrived. ... Palestine must be the national home

---

12 Weizmann wrote to Balfour (30 May 1918) of the treacherous and blackmailing nature of the Arab, whose Oriental mind was full of subtleties and subterfuges, compared with the enlightened and honest, fair and clean-minded English official (Weizmann PRO. FO.371/3395, in Ingrams 1972: 31–32).

13 Arthur Ruppin was pleased to be assured that Jews resembled the races of Europe rather than semites (Ruppin 1913: 213, 217). Further, 'The spiritual and intellectual status of [oriental] Jews is so low than an immigration *en masse* would lower the general cultural standard of the Jews in Palestine' (pp. 293–94). However, Ruppin conceded that a small number would be beneficial, as they would accept the low wages paid to Arab workers, which European Jews would not, and, since employing Arab labour was against the core value of separatist Zionism, the oriental Jew provided the perfect solution in ensuring purity of work-force at Arab rates of pay (p. 294). Years later, Abba Eban declared that, rather than consider oriental Jews as a bridge towards integration with the Arab-world, 'our objective should be to infuse them with Occidental spirit, rather than to allow them to draw us into an unnatural orientalism' (Eban 1957: 76).

of the Jewish people once more. ... The Allies are giving the Land of Israel to the people of Israel', with the intention of encouraging them to stop fighting the Allies (in Ingrams 1972: 19).

At the suggestion of its Middle East Committee, the War Cabinet dispatched to Palestine a Zionist Commission led by Weizmann, who, somewhat ingenuously, assured Arabs that,

> it was his ambition to see Palestine governed by some stable government like that of Great Britain, that a Jewish government would be fatal to his plans and that it was simply his wish to provide a home for the Jews in the Holy Land where they could live their own national life, sharing equal rights with the other inhabitants.
>
> (Memorandum of Major Cornwallis, 20 April, in Ingrams 1972: 29)

Weizmann assured Arabs and Jews in Jaffa that, 'It is not our aim to get hold of the supreme power and administration in Palestine, nor to deprive any native of his possession' (in Ingrams 1972: 30).

Weizmann displayed his versatility at the Foreign Office on 4 December 1918, assuring Balfour that, 'A community of four to five million Jews in Palestine could radiate out into the near East and so contribute mightily to the reconstruction of countries which were once flourishing.' This would require a Jewish National Home in Palestine, not mere facilities for colonisation to settle about four to five million Jews within a generation, and so make Palestine a Jewish country (PRO.FO.371/3385, in Ingrams 1972: 46). The attraction of such a proposal for British interests was considerable: 'The creation of a buffer Jewish state in Palestine, though this state will be weak in itself, is strategically desirable for Great Britain' ('The Strategic Importance of Syria to the British Empire', a memorandum by the General Staff at the War Office, 9 December 1918, PRO.FO.371/4178, in Kayyali 1979: 16–17).

As Lloyd George made clear, the British government, including himself and Balfour, always understood 'a national home for the Jewish people' to mean a Jewish state, and that it used the circumlocution merely to deflect Arab opposition is clear from a memorandum of Herbert Young, a Foreign Office official in 1921: The problem of coping with Palestinian opposition is 'one of tactics, not strategy, the general strategic idea ... being the gradual immigration of Jews into Palestine until that country becomes a predominantly Jewish state. ... But it is questionable whether we are in a position to tell the Arabs what our policy really means' (cited in Lehn 1988: 326–27 note 101).

While Herzl himself at the First Zionist Congress in 1897 had defined the aim of Zionism to be the creation of a home for the Jewish people in Palestine, he recorded in his diary of 3 September 1897: 'At Basle I founded the Jewish state' (Herzl 1960, 2: 581). Similarly, Max Nordau wrote in 1920: 'I did my best to persuade the claimants of the Jewish state in Palestine that we might find a circumlocution that would express all we meant, but would say it in a way so as to avoid provoking the Turkish rulers of the coveted land. I suggested *Heimstätte* as a synonym for state. ... It was equivocal, but we all understood what it meant. To us it signified *Judenstaat* then and it signifies the same now' (Sykes 1953b: 160 note 1). So also Zangwill in February 1919: 'The Jews must possess Palestine as the Arabs are to possess Arabia or the Poles Poland' (1937: 342), and Weizmann: 'We, not less than Herzl, regarded it as the Jewish state in the making' (1949: 68).

The *Balfour Declaration*, by which 'one nation solemnly promised to a second nation the country of a third' (Koestler 1949: 4), had no validity in international law, since Palestine was within the crumbling Ottoman Empire. Nevertheless, the support of Britain, whose foreign policy was not governed by altruism, immediately revolutionised the Zionist project. The creation of a client Jewish settler state in Palestine would serve Britain's purposes, prevent the growth of pan-Arab nationalism, and solve the problem of Jewish immigration at home, to which Balfour was so opposed.[14] Moreover, the creation of a Jewish state in Palestine, financed by Jews, and supported by interested Western bodies, would be an ideal and inexpensive resolution to Britain's designs. For Sir Ronald Storrs, Britain's military governor of Jerusalem and later of Palestine, Zionism 'blessed him that gave as well as him that took by forming for England "a little loyal Jewish Ulster" in a sea of potentially hostile Arabism' (*Memoirs* 1937: 364, in Quigley 1990: 8).

The King-Crane Commission, dispatched by President Wilson in 1919 confirmed that a Jewish state could not be accomplished without the gravest trespass upon civil and religious rights of existing non-Jewish communities, and recommended a greatly reduced Zionist programme for the 1919 Paris Peace Conference. It endorsed the programme announced by the General National Syrian Congress, the first Arab Parliament with representatives from all parts of Syria, including Palestine, which convened in Damascus on 2 July: the establishment of a united Syria as a constitutional monarchy under Faisal, the son of Sharif Husayn, who would be King. The Commission also warned of the intensity of the widespread anti-Zionist feeling in the region. Alas, President Wilson allowed the publication of the King-Crane Commission report only in December 1922, three years after its submission, and some months after Congress had supported the Zionist programme (30 June 1922). The turbulent history of the region since the break-up of Greater Syria into the national states of Syria, Lebanon, Jordan

14 Defending the Aliens Bill in 1905, Balfour, the then Prime Minister, noted that 'it would not be to the advantage of the civilisation of this country that there should be an immense body of persons, who, however patriotic ... remained a people apart, and not merely held a religion differing from the vast majority of their fellow-countrymen, but only inter-married among themselves' (quoted in W. Khalidi 1992: 23).

and Israel makes one question the wisdom of ignoring the wishes of the indigenes at that critical moment.

Immediately after the end of the First World War the victors embarked upon the division of the spoils. The Zionist Organisation's memorandum to the Supreme Council at the Peace Conference stipulated the boundaries of Palestine: 'Starting on the North at a point on the Mediterranean Sea in the vicinity of Sidon', moving east to include the Golan Heights, and that portion of the east bank of the Jordan, and 'in the East a line close to and West of the Hedjaz Railway terminating in the Gulf of Aqaba'. In the South, 'a frontier to be agreed upon with the Egyptian Government'.[15] The memorandum offered essentially economic arguments for these boundaries, with special attention to water (Hurewitz 1956: 46–50), making no reference to security considerations, nor appeal to any biblical mandates (Berger 1993: 14). We shall discuss later the petition from mostly Reform Jews presented to President Wilson on 4 March 1919, for transmission to the Peace Conference, which denounced Zionist efforts to segregate Jews as a political unit, in Palestine or elsewhere. It noted the minority status of Zionists in American Jewry, and warned against Zionist demands to reorganise Jews as a national unit with territorial sovereignty in Palestine, a demand which misinterpreted the history of the Jews, who ceased to be a nation 2000 years ago. Nevertheless, the Eleventh Zionist Congress (London July 1920) was devoted to the development of Palestine as *the* Jewish national home. Land purchased would remain solely in Jewish hands, and contrary to the claims of the Jewish National Fund, this required the displacement of the Arab peasants before the sale (Lehn 1988: 57).

The League of Nations entrusted to Britain the responsibility for the establishment of the Jewish national home, and for safeguarding the civil and religious rights of all the inhabitants of Palestine, irrespective of race and religion – the designation 'Arab' is not used (The Mandate for Palestine, Article 2, 24 July 1922). The *Balfour Declaration* was incorporated into the Mandate (preamble; articles 2, 4, 6, 7, 15, 22 and 23).

Arab opposition

There was immediate Arab opposition to the Zionist enterprise. It reached a climax in August 1929, after serious rioting broke out in Jerusalem which quickly spread, leaving some 240 Jews and Arabs dead. Not altogether surprisingly, a British commission discovered that the underlying cause of the riots was Arab opposition to the establishment of a Jewish state at their expense. A second commission in 1930 confirmed that Arabs were evicted

15 Much of the projected territory is currently under the control of the State of Israel, including the self-declared security zone in southern Lebanon, the Golan Heights, as well as most of the West Bank.

from land bought by Jews. The Passfield White Paper (October 1930) reminded all concerned that Britain's support for the national home of the Jewish people was conditional upon the rights of the indigenous community being safeguarded.

Between 1932 and 1937, 144,093 Jews immigrated to Palestine, and Jewish ownership of land more than doubled, but was still only 5.7 per cent of the total in 1939. In all, between 1922 and 1939 the Jewish population rose from 10 per cent to 30 per cent of Palestine (450,000) (W. Khalidi 1992: 31–33). Arab alarm led to the establishment of the Arab Higher Committee in April 1936, which called for a general strike to last until Zionist immigration and land purchases were stopped, and steps were taken to establish independence for Palestine. By way of response to more violence, the British sent a Royal Commission in November 1936. The Peel Commission reported in July 1937, acknowledging that the mandate was unworkable, since it involved two irreconcilables, a Jewish homeland, and Palestinian Arab independence. Resorting to Solomonic wisdom it recommended partition.

The partition plan proposed to give Jews, who owned only 5.7 per cent of the land, some 40 per cent of Palestine, wherein the Jewish state would embrace hundreds of Arab villages, and the solid Arab bloc in Galilee, from which, if necessary, there would be a forcible transfer of Arabs. The plan rekindled the flames of Arab rebellion, to which the British responded with massive repressive measures, resulting in 5,000 Arabs killed and 15,000 wounded, of a population of one million, in the period 1936–39 (W. Khalidi 1992: 34). This was followed by systematic disarming of the Arab population, and the breaking-up of Arab political organisation.

Ben-Gurion and Weizmann were jubilant in that the Peel partition plan was the first admission that the national home would be a state. Nevertheless, Vladimir (Zeev) Jabotinsky (the founder of revisionist Zionism in 1925), the leader of the Zionist opposition, regarded partition as a betrayal of the vision of a Greater Israel on both sides of the Jordan. Even though it had to be shelved, the partition plan elevated the Zionist aspiration, and became a benchmark against which to measure what could be achieved later. In November 1937, the Jewish Agency formed a special Population Transfer Committee, to whose deliberations we shall turn in Chapter 7.

Britain, recognising that partition would not work, outlined its goal in the White Paper of 17 May 1939: 'the establishment within ten years of an independent Palestine state ... in which Arabs and Jews share in government in such a way as to ensure that the essential interests of each community are safeguarded.' The White Paper required restrictions on land acquisition and Jewish immigration. Realising that British interests might conflict with Zionist ones, Ben-Gurion began to activate American Jewry, and gain more USA support, while Weizmann continued his diplomatic work in war-time London. Ben-Gurion's strategy was to define the Zionist objectives in maximalist terms and persuade the American Zionist leaders to endorse them openly. He regarded the Biltmore Programme, whose goal was the establishment of a Jewish Commonwealth in the whole of Palestine, as a benchmark in his strategy:

> The Conference urges that the gates of Palestine be opened; that the Jewish Agency be vested with control of immigration into Palestine and with necessary authority for upbuilding the country ... and that Palestine be established as a Jewish Commonwealth integrated in the structure of the new democratic world.
>
> (in Laqueur 1976: 79)

The boldness of this programme, adopted by 600 American Jews in New York on 11 May 1942, is reflected in the fact that Jewish land ownership in Palestine stood at only 5.9 per cent of the area, and that Jews accounted for only 31.2 per cent of the population. While it perfunctorily expressed the desire of the Jewish people for full co-operation with their Arab neighbours, the immigrant Jews, largely devoid of religious conviction, were animated by a spirit of political nationalism, determined to secure domination in Palestine, and made no effort to coalesce with the existing population (in Lilienthal 1982: 34).

Brigadier General Patrick J. Hurley, dispatched to the Arab Middle East to report directly, informed President Roosevelt that the Zionist Organization in Palestine was intent on establishing a Jewish state, embracing Palestine and probably Transjordan, and transferring the Arab population to Iraq. Meanwhile, Roosevelt planned to have some 500,000 Jews rescued from Hitler's genocide: Britain and the USA were ready to receive up to 150,000 each, and, with such a start, it would not be difficult to rescue half a million world-wide. His envoy, Morris Ernst, enquiring as to whether there might be Zionist opposition to the President's plan, was 'thrown out of parlours of friends of mine who very frankly said, "Morris, this is treason. You are undermining the Zionist movement" ' (Ernst 1964: 170–77; see Lilienthal 1982: 35–36). The President had to abandon the plan.

The death of Roosevelt in April 1945 brought Vice-President Harry Truman to the White House, and immediately he proved to be an ardent supporter of Zionist intentions. He wrote to Churchill on 24 April 1945, urging 'the lifting of these restrictions which deny to Jews who have been so cruelly uprooted by ruthless Nazi persecutions entrance into the land which represents for so many of these their only hope of survival'. Truman might have received, at America's expense, some of the 300,000 survivors of the Nazi barbarism who were in various relief centres. But his tactic gave him a double victory, winning the support of the Zionists, and allaying all fears that the USA might bear the brunt of Jewish immigration. In October 1945, he explained to Arab diplomats, 'I am sorry, gentlemen, but I have to answer to hundreds of thousands who are anxious for the success of Zionism; I do not have hundreds of thousands of Arabs among my constituents' (in W. Khalidi 1992: 48, 50–51). Although Truman's letter was addressed to

Churchill, by 26 July the British election had brought the Labour Party and Prime Minister Attlee to power. By that time, sympathy for Zionism was widespread in the British Labour Party, whose Annual General Conference of 1944 had approved of the solution, 'Let the Arabs be encouraged to move out, as the Jews move in' (in Mayhew 1975: 34, in Adams and Mayhew 1975).

Zionist opposition to the British presence increased in ferocity. In addition to blowing up the King David Hotel on 22 July 1946, which killed twenty-seven British, forty-one Palestinian Arabs, seventeen Jews and five others, the Irgun blew up bridges, mined roads, derailed trains and sank patrol boats, robbed pay vans and in a single night blew up twenty warplanes.[16] Irgun and *LEHI* blew up the British Embassy in Rome, dispatched letter-bombs to British ministers, and sent an assassination squad into Britain, with the mission – which was not accomplished – of executing General Evelyn Barker, the former commanding officer in Palestine.[17] Its members included Weizmann's nephew, Ezer Weizman, the current President of Israel. They captured and flogged British officers, and, on 30 July 1947, hanged two sergeants from a tree and booby-trapped their dangling corpses, an action which stirred the greatest anger in England (see Hirst 1983: 121 and Tastard 1998: 19–34). The British made the disbanding of the Zionist military establishment a condition for the admission of 100,000 Jewish immigrants, as recommended by a joint Anglo-American Committee.

In August 1946, the Zionist leadership proposed a plan which envisaged partition. It proposed a Jewish state consisting of all of Galilee, the Negev, the Golan Heights, with a corridor to the sea at Jaffa for the Arab state. Significantly, the Zionists awarded Jerusalem to the Arab state (see Hurewitz 1956: 260), or envisaged a special status for Jerusalem. Although Palestine was divided into sixteen sub-districts, in only one of which (the Jaffa-sub-district) was there a Jewish majority, the Zionist map envisaged the incorporation of nine of the sixteen into the Jewish state, as well as the bulk of others.

On 4 October 1946 (*Yom Kippur*), Truman sponsored a Zionist map giving 75 per cent of Palestine to the Jews, who owned less than 7 per cent of it.

16 The *Irgun Zvai Leumi* (National Military Organisation) was a Jewish underground armed group formed in 1931 by revisionist Zionist leaders, who were committed to the establishment of a state with a Jewish majority in the whole of Mandated Palestine, including Transjordan. Already at its World Congress (Prague, February 1938), the Revisionists passed a resolution which declared opposition to any plan that would deprive the Jewish people of their right to establish a Jewish majority on both sides of the Jordan. They judged the Jewish Agency to be traitors who had abandoned the ideals of Zionism as propagated by Herzl.

17 LEHI (Lohamei Herut Yisrael), better known as the Stern Gang, after its founder Avraham Stern, broke from the Irgun in June 1940. It called for the compulsory evacuation of the entire Arab population of Palestine, and advocated an exchange of Jews from Arab lands.

While only ten Jewish settlements (2,000 inhabitants) would come under Arab rule, about 450 Arab villages (700,000 inhabitants) would come under Zionist rule. Moreover, the Arabs would lose their richest lands and access to the sea, except for a corridor leading to Jaffa. Truman's support for the plan effectively killed off the proposal of the Arab delegates to a conference in London (September 1946) that there be a unitary Palestinian state, wherein Palestinian citizenship would be acquired through ten years' residence, and Jewish rights would be guaranteed.

White House support for the Zionist plan was critical, and the Jewish Agency set about constructing 'the Jewish vote', projecting the idea that Zionism was a blessing of enlightenment for the backward Arabs. While the Department of State resisted the partition of Palestine in its internal memoranda, the political advisers to the President responded positively to the Zionist propaganda. The Arab side was no match for the Zionists in winning American support, especially in the wake of Hitler's attempts to eliminate European Jewry (Berger 1993: 17–18).

In Britain, the Attlee government was under considerable pressure from the USA, whose ambassador conveyed the President's request for Britain to admit 100,000 Jews into Palestine immediately. To the objections of Christopher Mayhew, the Under-Secretary at the Foreign Office, that that would be a prescription for war,

> The Ambassador replied, carefully and deliberately, that the President wished it to be known that if we could help him over this it would enable our friends in Washington to get our Marshall Aid appropriation through Congress. In other words, we must do as the Zionists wished – or starve. Bevin surrendered.
>
> (Mayhew 1975: 18–19, in Adams and Mayhew 1975)

The United Nations Partition Plan 1947

Because Britain failed to make any progress towards an agreed settlement, His Majesty's Government declared (18 February 1947) that, 'The only course now open to us is to submit the problem to the judgement of the UN'. In April 1947 the General Assembly agreed to send a commission of inquiry. After a tour of the region, the United Nations Special Committee for Palestine (UNSCOP) recommended partition along the lines of the Truman *Yom Kippur* map, conceding the Negev to the Jewish state, although some 100,000 Bedouin cultivated a vast area of it, while only some 475 Jews lived in four settlements there.

In the UNSCOP recommendation, the Zionists stood to gain 57 per cent of the land, including most of the best arable land which was already home to a substantial Arab population, against 43 per cent for a Palestinian Arab state, even though by 1948 Jews had still reached only 6.6 per cent of the total ownership of Palestine (see Khoury 1985: 18, and Lehn 1988: 70–80). Moreover Jews constituted only one-third of the population (some 500,000–600,000 Jews against some 1.4 million Palestinians) – many of them recent arrivals – having risen from the 11 per cent (83,794 of 757,182) in the British census of 1922. Moreover, the plan left 509,780 Arabs against 499,020 Jews in the part allocated for a Jewish state (Hirst 1983: 133). On 29 November 1947 the UN General Assembly, by a vote of thirty-three to thirteen, with ten members abstaining, endorsed the UNSCOP partition plan (with minor modifications) and recommended the partition of Palestine into independent Arab and Jewish states, with Jerusalem and its carefully delineated surroundings a *corpus separatum* under a special international regime administered by the United Nations.

Not unreasonably, the partition plan was unacceptable to the Arabs, a people in place for centuries with no appetite to approve of the transfer of their birthright to recent arrivals. Their delegates at the General Assembly tested opinion as to the UN's competence to enforce such a plan on an unwilling Arab population. Moreover, their draft resolution that the members of the UN, in proportion to their resources, take in 'the distressed European Jews' did not win sufficient support.

For pragmatic reasons, and reflecting their tactical suppleness, the Zionists were not unprepared for compromise. The partition plan which led to the declaration of the State of Israel (*Medinat Yisrael*), however, envisaged less than the Eretz Yisrael (Land of Israel) desired by Ben-Gurion and others, including both the Mapai (Mifleget Po'alei Eretz Yisrael – The Party of the Workers of the Land of Israel, the forerunners of Labour, established in 1930) and Herut (Freedom, founded in 1948 by Menahem Begin, becoming part of the Likud bloc in 1973) parties.

Between the Partition Plan and the end of the Mandate

Following the Partition resolution, and with inter-communal strife and anti-British activity increasing to an unacceptable level, Britain announced its intention to terminate the Mandate (on 15 May 1948) and leave hastily. The UN would be free then to supervise the interregnum leading to the partition arrangements. Its failure to provide for an international force to supervise matters was an invitation to strife between the contending parties, which, given the superiority of Zionist resources, was bound to end in a Zionist victory.

The period 1947–49 falls into two distinct phases. The first period between the UN Declaration and the expiry of the mandate (29 November 1947 to 15 May 1948) can be described as the civil war phase. The second, the regular war phase, lasted from 14 May 1948, the date on which the State of Israel was declared, until the various Arab–Israeli armistices were concluded in 1948–49. Although, in general, Western historiography concentrates on the second phase of the conflict, and portrays Israel as a tiny, poorly armed and pacific new-born nation being attacked in its cradle and without provocation by the overwhelming force of the regular armies of the surrounding Arab countries, the first phase would be critical for Zionist possession of its bounty, and was, in fact, the more decisive.

The available evidence confirms that the *Yishuv* (the Jewish community in Palestine before and during 1948) was militarily and administratively vastly superior to the Palestinian Arabs, being far better armed, organised and led. The Arab or Palestinian national movement lagged behind its Jewish counterpart in cohesion, organisation, motivation and performance. It was too divided, too poorly organised and too politically inexperienced for the complexity of the challenge ahead (Mo'az 1992: 153). Nevertheless, throughout most of the period, Arab resistance was such that by mid-March 1948 the USA State Department reconsidered its position, and spoke of the need for a special session of the UN General Assembly to discuss the possibility of UN trusteeship over Palestine.

In the period leading up to the expiry of the Mandate, the relative strength of the contending parties was altogether unbalanced, a fact well realised on the Arab side. On 23 March 1948, General Ismail Safwat, the Commander in Chief of the Palestine Forces (General Officer Commanding the Military Committee of the Arab League), reported to the Prime Minister of Syria that in terms of armed forces (of all complexions), weapons, capabilities and morale, military plants, transport, reserves, etc., the Arabs were no match for the Jewish forces. Moreover, he concluded that unless the deficiencies of the regular Arab armies were addressed promptly there would be no hope of success when the Mandate expired (see the report in W. Khalidi 1998: 62–72).

The critical part of the first phase began in the first week of April 1948, with the execution of the two new operational plans, Plan Gimmel, and Plan Dalet, with the Yishuv taking advantage of a disintegrating British presence. Plan Gimmel aimed at buying time for the mobilisation of forces to carry out Plan Dalet. Plan Dalet was the master plan for establishing by force of arms Jewish control of the areas assigned to it by the UN Partition plan, for expelling as many Palestinian Arabs as possible, and for conquering as much additional Arab territory as possible, and, in addition, Jerusalem.

Ben-Gurion and the Haganah General Staff on the night of 31 March to 1 April decided that all Arab villages along the Khulda-Jerusalem axis were to be treated as enemy assembly or jump-off points. Those which resisted would be destroyed and their inhabitants expelled. Villages fell in quick succession (Al Qastal, Qaluniya, Khulda, Saris, Biddu and Beit Suriq). The strategy was one of massive surprise attack against the civilian populations, softened by continuous mortar and rocket bombardment. Clandestine Haganah radio stations broadcast threats of dire punishment in Arabic, and advised on modes of escape. Benny Morris puts the best possible face on the programme, suggesting that it was governed by military considerations and goals, rather than ethnic ones. He adds, that in the face of a life and death struggle, the gloves of the Yishuv had to be, and were taken off (1987: 62–63, 113).

A more sinister operation was enacted, with what Morris calls the reluctant, qualified consent of the Haganah commander in Jerusalem (1987: 113). On the night of 9 April 1948, the combined forces of approximately 132 members of the Irgun (led by Menachem Begin from 1943–48) and Stern (of which Yitzhak Shamir was a co-commander) organisations, supported by Haganah mortars, attacked the Palestinian village of Deir Yassin, on the western outskirts of Jerusalem. By noon of the following day, some 254 inhabitants including more than 100 women and children – the numbers are disputed – had been slaughtered, some of their bodies were thrown into a well, doused with kerosene and set alight.[18] There were also cases of mutilation and rape. Morris opines that the troops did not intend committing a massacre, 'but lost their heads during the battle'. He does concede that their intention probably was to expel the village's inhabitants. In any event, the massacre at Deir Yassin promoted terror and dread in the surrounding Arab villages, whose inhabitants abandoned their homes immediately (Morris 1987: 115).

The execution of Plan Dalet had devastating effect on the Palestinian population, and is the principal explanation for the departure of most of the Arabs of Palestine (Pappé 1992: 93). Hundreds of thousands were driven over the borders by the victorious Jewish brigades. By 23 April Plan Dalet had achieved its purpose. President Truman sent a message to Weizmann that if a Jewish state were declared, the President would recognise it immediately. On 14 May, the last day of the Mandate, the Chief Secretary of the British administration called a press conference in his office in the King David Hotel in Jerusalem. To a journalist's question, 'And to whom do you intend to give the keys of your office?' the Chief Secretary replied, 'I shall put them under the mat' (W. Khalidi 1992: 76). On the same day, the *Yishuv* declared the establishment of the State of Israel, and immediately Truman authorised its recognition by the USA.

The third phase of Zionism (the State of Israel 1948–67)

On 15 May 1948, the day after Ben-Gurion declared the establishment of the State of Israel, units of the regular armies of the surrounding Arab states went into Palestine. Amounting to some 14,000 troops, they were no match for the Zionist forces which prevailed in the ensuing conflict and ultimately conquered 78 per cent of Palestine. At the end of the war, Israel controlled

---

18 A former Stern Gang intelligence officer, a participant in the massacre, wrote of some of the brutality involved (*Ha'aretz*, 25 April 1993). His testimony and that of a Mossad intelligence officer on the scene are summarised by Norman Finkelstein (1995: 189 note 16).

all of Mandatory Palestine, with the exception of the West Bank and Gaza. The Palestinian *Catastrophe* can be measured in a number of ways, whether in terms of Palestinians killed (13,000, mostly civilians) (W. Khalidi, ed., 1992 Appendix III: 581–82), the families dispersed, the surrounding countries damaged, etc., or the financial cost (Hadawi 1988: 183).[19]

Flight of Palestinian 'refugees' in 1948[20]

The flight of the Palestinians is a sombre measure of the extent of the catastrophe. The great majority of the displaced fled or were expelled from the area of the newly-created state. With few exceptions, the major urban centres, including substantially Arab towns, were emptied of their Palestinian residents, with their assets falling to the Zionists. Moreover, hundreds of Arab villages were depopulated and destroyed. Some 156,000 Palestinian Arabs remained in their towns and villages, while some 25 per cent of the Arab population were driven from their villages but settled elsewhere in Israel, becoming 'internal refugees' (or, in terms of rights to their property, 'present absentees'). The estimates of the number of Palestinian Arabs displaced in 1948 fall between 700,000 and 800,000.[21] This constituted 54 per cent of the total Palestinian population of Mandatory Palestine, and has grown to create a diaspora in excess of five million.[22] Moreover, about six million dunums of land (a dunum being 1,000 sq. m., i.e. about one quarter of an acre) were summarily divided among the old and new Jewish colonies (W. Khalidi ed. 1992: xxxiii).

The destruction of the villages

That the international community has paid little attention to the wilful

---

19 The term *Al-Nakba* (The Disaster) was coined by Constantine Zreiq in 1948 to describe the events of 1948–49.

20 The UN Security Council's Resolution 242 refers to the displaced Palestinians as 'refugees'. The term 'refugee' is not satisfactory, since in international practice, and in the UN convention on refugees, it refers to one who seeks refuge in a foreign country. Palestinian 'refugees', on the contrary, want only to reside in their own country, and more properly should be referred to as 'displaced persons' (Quigley 1998: 84).

21 Elia Zureik surveys the estimates, showing that they fall within the range, 700,000–800,000 (1994: 11, Table 3), but more recently Abu-Sitta argues for a total figure of 935,000 (1998: 14). Janet Abu Lughod puts the number at around 770,000–780,000 (1987: 161).

22 According to the 1994 report of the United Nations Relief and Welfare Agency's commissioner general, there were 504,070 'refugees' in the West Bank, 42 per cent of the population, and 643,000 in the Gaza Strip, 75.7 per cent of the population (Sabella 1996: 193). The UNRWA 1995 Report estimated that there are now some 4,645,248 Palestinian displaced persons in camps throughout Syria, Lebanon, Jordan and beyond. Abu-Sitta calculates that the maximum estimate of Palestinians in 1998 is 8,415,930, of which 5,477,745 are refugees (1998: 15).

destruction of hundreds of Palestinian villages is a tribute to the determination of the State of Israel to preserve one of its best guarded secrets. Until recently no publication gave either the number or location of these villages, and the fact that they were completely destroyed helps perpetuate the claim that Palestine was virtually an empty country before the Jews entered.[23] Edward Said's criticism of the 'collective incompetence' of Palestinians in failing to provide a substantial Palestinian narrative of 1948 and after to challenge the dominant Israeli one no longer holds. A number of substantial publications (e.g. W. Khalidi, ed. 1992; Masalha 1992 and 1997, and most recently, Abu-Sitta 1998), together with the testimonies of individuals, have broken the silence.[24]

By the end of the 1948 war, hundreds of villages had been completely depopulated, and their houses blown up or bulldozed. Some one hundred Palestinian villages were neither destroyed nor depopulated, and survive to this day. However, over 80 per cent of the lands of those who never left their homes have been confiscated since 1948, and are at the exclusive disposal of the Jewish citizens of the state (W. Khalidi, ed. 1992: xxxii; see Geraisy 1994: 50–51). The exhaustive study by the research team under the direction of Walid Khalidi gives details of the destruction of each village, supplying statistical, topographical, historical, architectural, archaeological and economic material, as well as the circumstances of each village's occupation and depopulation, and a description of what remains. *All that Remains* is 'a kind of *in memoriam* ... an acknowledgement of the suffering of hundreds of thousands of men, women and children. It is a gesture of homage to their collective memories and their sense of ancestral affiliation' (W. Khalidi, ed. 1992: xviii-xix, xvii, xxxiv).

There is an inconsistency in the determination of the number of Palestinian localities destroyed. Morris lists 369 villages and towns, and gives the date and circumstances of their depopulation, relying mostly on recently released Israeli files (1987: viii–xviii). Khalidi's figure of 418 is based on the villages or hamlets (only) which are listed in the Palestine Index Gazeteer of 1945 falling inside the 1949 Armistice Line. Abu-Sitta's register of 531 includes the localities listed by Morris and Khalidi, and adds those of the tribes in the Beer Sheba District.

Some 414,000 inhabitants of 213 villages, more than half of the total

23 As late as September 1987 a document was distributed in Switzerland appealing for 6,000,000 Swiss Francs to plant a *Swiss Forest* in the region of Tiberias. The Jewish National Fund thanked its benefactors in anticipation, assuring them that their contributions would transform a desert into a green land. Forests frequently cover over the remaining traces of the destroyed Palestinian villages (Aldeeb 1992: 8).

24 For example, Toubbeh 1998, and the earlier ones of Chacour (1985), Rantisi (1990), the theological analysis of Ateek (1989) and the ongoing field work of individual scholars, such as May Seikaly, who are recording the memories of the distress of the Palestinians in 1948 (see Seikaly 1999). Moreover, the Washington-based Institute of Palestine Studies and Oxford University's St Anthony's College are sponsoring programmes on Palestinian historiography.

number of displaced persons, had become homeless before the expiry of the British Mandate on 15 May 1948. According to Morris' designation of the reason for the exodus from the 330 villages he assessed, forty one (12 per cent) left because of expulsion by Jewish forces, 195 (59 per cent) because of military assaults, and forty six (14 per cent) because of imminent Jewish attack after the fall of a neighbouring village, giving a total of 282 (85 per cent) villages depopulated as a result of direct military action. Abu-Sitta's equivalent method leads him to conclude that 441 villages (89 per cent) were depopulated as a result of direct military action, with fifty (10 per cent) succumbing as a result of fear of attack, and five villages (1 per cent) responding to the orders of the local Arab leader (1998: 8).

Khalidi's figure of 418 amounts to half the total number of Arab villages in Mandated Palestine. His research team visited all, except fourteen sites, made comprehensive reports, and took photographs, recording all the detail that remains (W. Khalidi, ed. 1992: xix).[25] While Abu-Sitta adds to that list, Khalidi's account is the most comprehensive. Of the 418 villages, 293 (70 per cent) were totally destroyed, and ninety (22 per cent) were largely destroyed. Seven survived, including 'Ayn Karim, but were taken by Israeli settlers. While an observant traveller can still see some evidence of these villages, in the main all that remains is 'a scattering of stones and rubble across a forgotten landscape' (W. Khalidi, ed. 1992: xv).[26] The profanation of sacred places adds to the offence.[27]

The depopulation and destruction of the Arab villages displaced some 383,150 inhabitants, plus some 6,994 from the surrounding villages, giving a total of at least 390,144 rural displaced persons (W. Khalidi, ed. 1992: 581). The total population of urban displaced persons is at least 254,016. Moreover, it is estimated that the 1948 war created between 70,000 and 100,000 Bedouin displaced persons. Yet, despite the evidence, some people still believe that the Palestinian displaced persons of 1948 left voluntarily. But, even if there were no evidence of expulsions and massacres to counter Israeli propaganda, Israel's persistence in not allowing Palestinians to return

25 Earlier, Israel Shahak compiled lists of the destroyed villages (1975). The nearest the Israeli government came to providing a list is in the map, originally produced by the British Mandate, and re-issued with Hebrew overprint in 1950, on which the destroyed villages are stamped with the word *harus*, Hebrew for 'demolished'. The efforts to quantify the destroyed villages range from 290 (from the Israeli topographical maps) to Abu-Sitta's 531.

26 The photographs include some village sites on which theme parks or recreation grounds have been constructed, e.g. the sites of al-Tantura, Zirin, and the cemetery of Salama (p. xxxix), as well as the remains of shrines, mosques and churches and cemeteries (pp. xliii–xliv).

27 See Geraisy 1994: 49. An Orthodox Church in 'Ayn Karim was converted into public toilets, the mosque in Safad into an art gallery, and one in Caesarea and 'Ayn Hud into a restaurant and bar. Moreover, the Hilton Hotel in Tel Aviv and the Plaza Hotel in Jerusalem, and the adjacent parks, both called Independence Park, were constructed over Muslim cemeteries (U. Davis 1987: 24). The case of the Christian village of Biram is particularly poignant (see Chacour 1985: 36–38, 71 and Aldeeb 1992: 9). The remains of Deir Yassin were converted into a mental hospital for Israeli patients.

to their homes is revealing.[28] Furthermore, Israel's refusal to allow the 1967 displaced persons also to return consolidates the judgement that Zionism in its essence required Jewish supplanting of the indigenous Palestinian population.

With respect to the critical question of land, while prior to 1948 Jews had purchased only 7 per cent of Arab land, the newly created Jewish state obtained much more land, to be exploited exclusively for Jewish use, through the enactment of a series of laws.[29] The result today is that 92 per cent of the area of the State of Israel is totally closed to non-Jews. But Zionist conquest was to lead to even further gains.

The fourth phase of Zionism (1967–93)

It was the 5–11 June 1967 War, which resulted in the capture of the West Bank (including East Jerusalem) from Jordan, the Golan Heights from Syria, and Gaza and the Sinai from Egypt, that stimulated my first curiosity in the Arab–Israeli conflict. The sources available to me portrayed innocent Israel defending itself against its rapacious Arab predators, in a war initiated, one was assured, by the Egyptians. The Israeli representative misled the emergency meeting of the UN Security Council (the morning of 5 June) with fabricated details that Egypt had initiated the conflict with the shelling of Israeli villages and the bombing of towns (UN Doc. S/PV 1347). International media repeated the false information, and on the following day the Israeli Foreign Minister, Abba Eban, a party to the decision to launch a pre-emptive attack on Egypt, repeated the deceit (UN Doc. S/PV 1348).

Eventually, in 1972, Israel conceded that its pre-emptive strike against Egypt initiated the war, attempting to justify its action by appealing to the imminence of Arab aggression which 'threatened the very existence of the state', and for which it had no responsibility. We shall examine these claims in Chapter 7. It is clear that Israel did not consider itself to be under threat of destruction in June 1967. Israeli General Mattityahu Peled later designated the claim as a 'bluff', and Chief of Operations Ezer Weizman (currently President) acknowledged that there was no threat to Israel's destruction, and

28 On 16 June 1948, the thirteen members of the 'Provisional Government' agreed to bar a refugees' return. The decision was never published, and the statements of Ben-Gurion and Sharett had to undergo successive rewritings to conform to accepted international political norms (Morris 1995: 56).

29 The 1948 Land Law stipulated that any land not in active cultivation for three years was considered 'neglected' and, upon the authority of the Ministry of Agriculture, its ownership could pass to another party. The 'Law of Abandoned Property' of 14 May 1950 made some 20 per cent of the Arabs in Israel into 'absentees', regardless of their citizenship. The re-activation of the 1945 British Defence Emergency Regulations permitted lands to be designated as 'security areas' for Jewish development. The 1953 'Land Acquisition Law' enabled Israel to expropriate all the lands temporarily in its hands since 1948.

that even if the Egyptians had attacked first they would have suffered a complete defeat. Former Foreign Minister Abba Eban considered such confessions by generals to be a 'sabotage of the moral basis of our political position' (see N. Finkelstein 1995: 136, 219). Yet, the revelations are no deterrent to Martin Gilbert's *apologia*: 'Israel would take the military initiative against those who were threatening her annihilation' (1998: 383).

In the light of subsequent events, Israel's intent to reap the fruits of victory, which the war certainly would bring, must be considered a likely explanation for her military aggression. Top of the list of such inevitable fruits was the neutralisation of the Arab states, and, most particularly, the undermining of Egyptian president Gamal Abdel Nasser's capacity to unify and modernise the Arab nation. Hence Israel's determination to rout Egypt before any diplomatic solution might be reached, which would frustrate its designs to cut Nasser down to size. But there were other motives also.

Ethnic cleansing in 1967

With victory in the war, Zionism finally had achieved its goal of controlling the whole of Palestine west of the Jordan. The speed with which Israel proceeded to benefit from its victory suggests that 'the territorial fulfilment of the Land of Israel', only partly achieved in 1948, and frustrated by Israel's requirement to withdraw after the Suez War of 1956, was one of the central aims of its aggression. Its long-term territorial intentions were signalled by evicting the some 1,000 inhabitants of the ancient Maghrebi Quarter of Jerusalem, and destroying 135 houses and historic religious sites, just two days after the capture of East Jerusalem, to make way for a plaza in front of the Wailing Wall. A further 4,000 Arabs were expelled from Jerusalem's Jewish Quarter and its surroundings, to enlarge and 'purify' it. Moreover, within days of the occupation the Knesset passed the law extending the boundaries of East Jerusalem to include villages close to Bethlehem in the south and Ramallah in the north. This action, judged by the UN and almost all states as illegal, was confirmed in 1980 when the Knesset declared 'Jerusalem in its entirety' (i.e. West and East) to be its 'eternal capital'.

Moreover, 10,000 Palestinians were expelled from the villages of Bayt Nuba, 'Imwas, and Yalu in the Latrun salient, which army bulldozers razed to the ground, making way for 'Canada Park', created on the destroyed villages and their land, and funded by the Canadian Jewish National Fund. Later in the year, four more Arab villages, Bayt Marsam, Bayt 'Awa, Habla and Jifliq were cleansed and razed to the ground.

But Israel's new 'demographic problem' became clear with the realisation that the total Arab population of Israel (some 400,000) and the Occupied Territories came to over 1.3 million, which, mindful of the relatively higher Arab birth rate, could lead to the Zionist nightmare of Palestinians equalling the number of Jews in the land. Immediately after the war, talk of '(compulsory) population transfer' and 'organised emigration' came to the fore for a second time, not behind closed doors nor among fringe groups only, but among several veteran army commanders, leading *literati*, Members of the Knesset, and prominent public figures.[30] Moreover, a public opinion poll three weeks after the war showed that 28 per cent of the Israeli Jewish electorate favoured the expulsion of the Palestinian citizens of Israel, and 22 per cent favoured the expulsion of the Palestinians from the conquered territories (Masalha 1997: 77–80).

Indeed, in the immediate aftermath of the war, the Israeli government discussed plans for solving the 'demographic problem', albeit in secret, information that has come to the surface only gradually, largely due to the research of Meir Avidan and the tenacity of some Israeli journalists, for example, Yossi Melman and Dan Raviv, who published articles to that effect in 1987 and 1988. They reveal that Premier Eshkol convened secret meetings of the cabinet between 15 and 19 June to discuss the demographic problem arising from the fact that, unlike the situation in 1948, the majority of the Palestinians remained *in situ*, even though some 320,000 fled or were expelled.[31]

Although the official transcripts of the meetings remain secret, the diary and notes of Ya'acov Herzog, brother of Haim and at the time Director-General of the Prime Minister's office reveal that Finance Minister Pinhas Sapir and Foreign Minister Eban called for settling the Palestinian refugees in neighbouring countries. Deputy Premier Yigal Allon proposed that the refugees be transported to the Sinai Desert, and that the others be persuaded to move abroad. Minister without portfolio Menahem Begin recommended the demolition of the 1948 refugee camps and the transfer of their inhabitants to El Arish, captured from Egypt, a proposal supported by Premier Eshkol and Minister of Transport, Moshe Carmel. Moreover, the Ministerial Committee for Defence decided on 15 June that Israel demand from the Arab countries and the Super Powers that arrangements be made for the settlement of refugees in the neighbouring Arab countries. Moshe Dayan favoured transfer to Jordan and in subsequent years continued to propose that the Arab states take in the Palestinians. Haim Herzog, the first Military Governor of the West Bank, revealed in November 1991 when he was President, that, in the immediate aftermath of the June 1967 War, he, in collaboration with Shlomo Lahat, the commander of Jerusalem, organised

---

30 These include military men, Meir Har-Tzion, Ariel Sharon, Raphael Eitan, Aharon Davidi, poet Natan Alterman, novelist Haim Hazaz, author Yigal Mossenson, novelist Moshe Shamir, politicians Eli'ezer Livneh, Haim Yahil and Tzvi Shiloah and Dov Yosefi (details in Masalha 1997: 62–77).

31 See Masalha 1999 for a discussion of the background to, and the actual evictions carried out by the Israeli army during and after the 1967 War.

the transfer of 200,000 Palestinians from the West Bank, including some 100,000 inhabitants of the refugee camps near Jericho, a fact that had escaped the attention of historians up to that time (see Masalha 1997: 84–88).

Premier Eshkol established a secret unit to encourage the departure of Palestinians for foreign shores, offering one-way tickets to various South American countries, and financial assistance to settle there – a scheme which had limited success, and ended dramatically when an aggrieved former resident of the Jabilya camp in the Gaza Strip shot dead the secretary of the Israeli ambassador in Paraguay in May 1970. All the while, Ariel Sharon was pressing for the total elimination of the refugee camps and the 'transfer' of their populations, mainly to Arab lands. He evicted the Bedouin communities in the Rafah salient, establishing Jewish settlements in their place. He assured his critics that he was implementing government policy, and reminded the complaining kibbutzniks that they themselves were occupying land abandoned by Arab refugees in 1948. Dayan, likewise, reminded the younger generation at the Technion in Haifa in 1969 that 'There is not one single place built in this country that did not have a former Arab population' (see Masalha 1997: 90–100).

William Wilson Harris' detailed investigation of the 1967 Exodus (1980) estimates that about 430,000 of a pre-war population of some 1.4 million left the territories occupied by Israel, including the Golan Heights and Sinai between June and December 1967, and mostly in June. Israel ethnically cleansed the Golan Heights of the 100,000 Syrians who had lived in 143 communities before 1967, leaving only four villages inhabited to this day by some 16,000 Druze.

The Israeli expulsions in 1967 and various deportations since, carried out with that unique form of 'legality' practised in Israel, but altogether in contravention of a range of human rights' conventions, emphasised the essential link between the fulfilment of the Zionist dream and the concomitant requirement to deport the Arab population. Israel has remained largely impervious to international criticism. As Michael Adams, London's *Guardian* Middle East correspondent, put it on 19 February 1968, 'No Israeli when he deals frankly with you (and many do) will deny that he would prefer to accept "the dowry without the bride", meaning that from Israel's point of view, the ideal solution to the problem of the occupied territories would be their absorption by Israel but without their Arab population'.

The Israeli Occupation

There was virtual unanimity in the General Assembly of the UN, that there should be a withdrawal of forces to the borders obtaining on 4 June 1967. On 22 November, the Security Council passed Resolution 242, emphasising 'the inadmissibility of the acquisition of territory by war and the need to work for a just and lasting peace in which every State in the area can live in security,' called for the 'withdrawal of Israeli armed forces from territories occupied in the recent conflict.' All parties, other than Israel, understood the indefinite, 'from territories occupied' (rather than 'from *the* territories occupied'), to require Israel to withdraw from all the territory occupied, allowing for the possibility of minor rationalisations of the pre-5 June 1967 borders (see Neff 1991: 17 for Lord Caradon, Dean Rusk, Presidents Carter, Reagan, and Bush). Israel has consistently refused to conform to the resolution 242, despite further votes in the General Assembly in 1971 and 1972, and in the Security Council in July 1973, when thirteen votes were cast, deploring Israel's continuing occupation of *the* territories. However, the USA delegate vetoed the resolution, thereby dashing the last hope for a peaceful resolution of the situation.

On 6 October 1973 (*Yom Kippur*), Egyptian planes targeted Israeli airfields and army bases deep in the Sinai, and at the same time the Syrian front attacked the Golan Heights. Initially the assault petrified the Israelis, but after surrounding the Egyptian army a cease-fire was declared on 22 October, and a cessation of hostilities on 24 October. After the War, which dented Israel's self-confidence and raised Arab morale, there was a return to the demands of Resolution 242, with Resolution 338 (22 October 1973) calling for the implementation of Resolution 242. The following year at the Rabat Summit, the Arab states designated the Palestine Liberation Organisation (PLO) as 'the sole legitimate representative of the Palestine people', and PLO Chairman Yasses Arafat made his first visit to the United Nations in November 1974.

All Israeli governments since 1967 have pursued a policy of confiscation of Arab land in the West Bank and Gaza. During the period of the Labour-led Governments of 1967–77, East Jerusalem and one third of the West Bank were seized. Gush Emunim, the chief colonising group founded in 1974, set about settling all of *Eretz Yisrael*. The process of Judaisation accelerated with the advent of the Likud-led Governments of 1977–84, and the Gush Emunim aim in a modified form (the Drobless Plan) was adopted as government policy (Benvenisti and Khayat 1988: 64, 102). Its intention was to ensure through a process of comprehensive Jewish settlement that Arab control could not be re-established (see Harris 1980; Benvenisti 1984; Aronson 1987).

Ever since the reinforcements of Palestinian positions in Lebanon at the end of the 1960s, Israel had assumed the right to police the region. It attacked Beirut airport in 1968, and invaded Southern Lebanon with 20,000 troops in 1978. Following the UN Security Council Resolution 425 (19 March 1978) calling upon Israel to cease immediately its military action and withdraw forthwith from all Lebanese territory, Israel did withdraw, but has retained a 'security zone' in some 10 per cent of the territory of Lebanon. In September Israel and Egypt signed the Camp David Accords.

Israel bombarded Lebanon again in 1981, and, using the pretext of the attempt on the life of the Israeli Ambassador to Britain (4 June 1982), Israeli jets and gunboats struck at Palestinian positions in southern Lebanon and East Beirut. The Security Council demanded a cessation of Israeli hostilities (Resolution 508). The figures for the dead (17,825) and injured (30,203) are likely to be underestimates. Estimates of Palestinian and Lebanese displaced persons are between 500,000 and 800,000. The International Commission of Inquiry into Israel's conduct concluded that Israel violated the laws of war in several respects (MacBride 1983: 34–35, 38, 40–42, 99, 108, etc.). The purpose of the Israeli invasion is obfuscated by its title, 'Operation Peace for Galilee', since Galilee had been peaceful for eleven months before the invasion. Moreover, the attempted murder of Ambassador Argov was the work of the fiercely anti-Arafat group led by Abu Nidal which was never part of the PLO. Israel's motivation was to exterminate Palestinian nationalism, and to curb the power of the PLO (see MacBride 1983: 65 and Shahak 1994: 18–19).

During the period of the 'National Unity' Coalition (Likud and Labour) Government (1984–88) there was an acceleration in the settlement programme. By 1988, land confiscation had resulted in Jewish control of over 52 per cent of the West Bank, and over 40 per cent of the Gaza Strip was declared to be 'state land', and hence under exclusively Jewish control (Matar 1992: 444–48 – for a complete analysis, see Halabi 1985). By early 1988, there were 117 Jewish colonies in the West Bank, with a population of over 67,000, built on seized land. This was in addition to the eight large Jewish residential colonies, with a total population of 100,000, built in fortress style in annexed East Jerusalem. In the Gaza Strip there were fourteen Jewish colonies, with a population of 2,500. Polls showed that approximately a quarter of the Palestinian population of the West Bank and the Gaza Strip had been dispossessed of all or parts of their lands (Matar 1992: 448).

Since 1967, the water-resource of the West Bank has been developed preferentially for Jews, both in the Occupied Territories and in Israel itself. By 1987, the Jewish water company, *Mekorot*, had drilled more than 40 deep-bore wells, and was pumping some 42 million cubic metres per year from West Bank underground water supplies, exclusively for Jewish colonies. By contrast, Palestinians pump only 20 million cubic metres from their pre-1967 shallow wells. It is estimated that pre-1967 Israel pumps one-third of its annual needs of 1.8 billion cubic metres from underground West Bank basins. Hence, Israelis exploit the water both for Israel proper, and for the Jewish colonies in the Occupied Territories. Meanwhile, the Palestinians are prevented from developing their own water resources (Matar 1992: 454).

Resisting the Occupation

Having enjoyed widespread popularity in the 1970s the fortunes of the secularist Palestinian resistance movements declined drastically following the Israeli invasion of Lebanon in 1982. The late 1970s brought to prominence specifically Islamic solutions to the Palestinian problem. The abject failure of the Arab nations in the 1967 War had already provided an opportunity to publicise the view that Islam was the only path to victory for the Arab nation (Ahmad 1994: 11). Moreover, the failure of secular options, together with the inspiration provided by the Iranian Revolution of Ayatollah Khomeini in 1979, and the Islamic resistance to Israeli control of South Lebanon, enhanced the popularity of Islamic groups within the Occupied Territories, especially in the refugee camps of Gaza. Islamic resistance movements in the Occupied Territories, then, were beginning to offer a serious challenge to the dominant nationalist trends of the PLO.

The Israeli occupation inevitably prompted an explosion of resistance, for which the catalyst was the incident on 8 December 1987 when an Israeli vehicle ploughed through a truck in Gaza killing four Palestinians, and injuring seven others inside who were returning from work in Israel. The following day some four thousand inhabitants of the Jabaliah refugee camp protested at the killings, and youths began to throw stones. Within a short time virtually the whole population of the West Bank and Gaza erupted in protest against the twenty year old occupation. The word *intifada* (from a root meaning 'to shake off, to recover, to recuperate, to jump to one's feet') entered international discourse, denoting the Palestinian eruption to shake off the occupation. The Israeli efforts to restore the *status quo* shocked the international community, and precipitated serious self-doubts among sections of the Israeli public. Moreover, the *intifada* politicised the Christian churches, both in the Holy Land and abroad (see Prior 1990; 1993), and gained widespread international sympathy for the Palestinians, and condemnation of the Israeli occupation.

The *intifada* also precipitated a significant development in specifically Muslim opposition to the occupation, since up to then religion was perceived to be the way to a more personal security only. But on that same 9 December, the leaders of Gaza's Muslim Brotherhood, including its spiritual leader, Sheikh Ahmad Yassin, met to discuss how the situation could be used to promote wider demonstrations. On 14 December, the group issued a statement calling for resistance to the occupation, which retrospectively was the first official leaflet of Hamas, although the group did not assume that name until January 1988. Hamas (an acronym for Harakat al-Muqawama al-Islamiya, the Islamic Resistance Movement) quickly leapt into the limelight. Within a year, it had distributed some thirty three leaflets, with religious slogans and imagery, quite unlike the secular ones distributed by the Unified Leadership of the Uprising, a coalition of Palestinian factions, Fatah, the Popular Front for the Liberation of Palestine, Democratic Front for the Liberation of Palestine, and the Palestinian Communist Party.

Hamas was determined not only to establish a Palestinian state and remove the Israelis from the Occupied Territories, but also to establish an Islamic state in all of Palestine: 'Let every hand be cut off that signs a relinquishment of a grain of the soil of Palestine to the enemies of Allah who have usurped the blessed soil' (Leaflet of March 1988, in Ahmad 1994: 52). It released its Covenant in August 1988 (English translation in Ahmad 1994: 129–59). In the introductory page we find, 'Israel will be established and will stay established until Islam nullifies it as it nullified what was before it'. Later, 'There is no solution to the Palestinian question except by *Jihad*' (Art. 13). Hamas' theocracy would tolerate the followers of other religions, but only under the shadow of Islam (Art. 6). Hamas' Covenant stresses the universality and unity of the Islamic nation, and demands open borders for the *mujaheddiin* of the Arab and Islamic countries 'so that they can take their role and join their efforts with their Muslim brothers of Palestine' (Art. 28). For their part, Arab countries strongly support Hamas.[32]

In a significant move from its goal of establishing a Palestinian state throughout Mandated Palestine, *The Palestine National Council* declared that the State of Palestine should exist side-by-side with the State of Israel (15 November 1988, in Algiers). Chairman Arafat confirmed the PLO's acceptance of Israel, its renunciation of violence, and its willingness to negotiate a peaceful settlement based on UN resolutions. Hamas rejected the Algiers Declaration, regarding it as an act of treason and a heinous crime, since the whole land of Palestine was an Islamic *Waqf* (holy trust) for all Muslim generations until the day of Resurrection (see Ahmad 1994: 41). Its criticism of the PLO's vision of a secular Palestinian state intensified. Initially, Israel's attitude to the activities of Hamas was relaxed, and it was only in May 1989 that it began to arrest some of its leadership. By September, however, Hamas, to the creation of which Israel had contributed, was declared illegal.[33] By 1992, slogans in Gaza promoted Hamas as 'the sole legitimate representative of the Palestinian people', and in July of that year armed Hamas–PLO clashes occurred in Gaza, leaving three Palestinians dead. Hamas regarded the PLO leadership, 'strutting around the world in a lavish style, while people lived in poverty in the camps', with disdain. Moreover, it had failed to liberate Palestine. Hamas'

32 Sudan provides training for activists. Algeria's Islamists are the role models of Hamas, and Saudi Arabian funds, previously channelled to the PLO now come to Hamas. Hamas needs the support of the Arab states to advance its goals, and the Arab states need Hamas to assist in the weakening of the PLO which did not always succumb to the dictates of Arab leaders (Ahmad 1994: 93).

33 The Israelis in 1973, seeing him as the ideal counter to the more popular PLO, issued a permit to Sheikh Ahmed Yassin to found a non-militant Islamic group which he named the *al-Mujii al-Islamiyaj* (The Islamic Centre). His organisation, with ongoing financial support from the Israeli government via its Military Governor in Gaza, grew in the refugee camps. Yassin's aim was to turn Palestinians away from the secular nationalist option, establish a Muslim Palestine, firstly in the Occupied Territories and subsequently throughout historical Palestine. Islamic resistance took on a more activist role with the outbreak of the *intifada*, leading to the founding of *Hamas*, and its military wing. By the time Israel tried to curb Yassin it was already too late.

strength among the Palestinians was estimated to be between 25 and 40 per cent, which encouraged it to demand 40 per cent of the seats in the Palestine National Council. But soon other events would transform the Israel–Palestine debate.

The fifth phase of Zionism (1993–)

The Peace Process which went public in 1993 (the Oslo Accords) inaugurated a new phase in the development of Zionism. The post-Gulf War 'new world order' promoted the Madrid Conference peace talks in November 1991, and later in Washington, Moscow, Ottawa, Tokyo, Vienna, and Brussels, raising hopes for a better future. However, the disintegration of the USSR, a co-sponsor of the talks, deprived the Palestinians of superpower support, and left the USA unchallenged. Premier Shamir acknowledged later that his only intention in attending was to gain time for Israel to consolidate its control of the Occupied Territories.

Islamists attributed the collapse of the USSR to its disavowal of the Islamic way of life. Moreover, the victory of the *mujaheddiin* in Afghanistan was presented as a paradigm of Islamist power, and boosted Islamic movements everywhere. Hamas could enter the stage like a long awaited Messiah, and substantial funding came, not only from Arab states but from Europe and the USA (Ahmad 1994: 48–49).

The Israeli election of June 1992 allowed Labour (forty-four seats) to form a coalition with Meretz (an amalgam of left-wing parties, with twelve seats), Shas (the Sephardi religious party, with six seats) and the Arab Democratic party (two seats), ending the almost unbroken fifteen years of Likud (32 seats) ascendancy. Labour Leader Yitzhak Rabin committed the government to pursue peace-making 'with a fresh momentum', and promised Palestinian autonomy within nine months. In his inaugural speech to the Knesset as Prime Minister (13 July 1992), he reminded the Palestinians and the Arab states that while wars have their victors and their vanquished, everyone is a victor in peace, ending with, 'Our entire policy can be summarised by a single verse from the Book of Books: "May the LORD give strength to his people! May the LORD bless his people with peace!" ' (Psalm 29.11). He ordered a freeze in the settlement of the Occupied Territories, and won the $10 billion loan guarantees from the USA (10 August). However, the Rabin freeze was mere casuistry, since his government initiated the most intensive phase of settlement ever, concentrating on Jerusalem and the extension ('thickening') of existing settlements.

By December 1992, five years into the *intifada*, there was a significant increase in tension in the region. *Izz al-Din al-Qassam* Brigades, the military wing of Hamas, ambushed four Israeli military personnel in Gaza and Hebron, and abducted Sergeant Nissim Toledano, all in the same week. After Sergeant Toledano's body was discovered near the *Inn of the Good Samaritan* on 15 December, Israeli troops arrested nearly 2,000 men in Gaza and the West

Bank, and the Israeli cabinet decided to deport 418 alleged Hamas supporters, in conformity with plans discussed within the politico military establishments (see Masalha 1997: 127–28). The portrayal of the 418, expelled by Israel and unwelcome in Lebanon, praying and studying on the icy hills of Marj al-Zuhour in southern Lebanon, was an ongoing international embarrassment to Israel. The protracted incident gained an unprecedented level of respect for the Islamists, internationalised the Palestinian crisis considerably, and constituted a public relations coup for Hamas.

The Oslo Accord

Nevertheless, by 20 January 1993 secret talks were taking place near Oslo between 'unofficial representatives' of Israel and PLO officials. By the summer the PLO's fortunes had fallen to the lowest point in its history, financially and administratively. In addition to problems posed by fatigue and routinisation, its collapse was affected by external factors, including the demise of the USSR and the rout of Iraq in the Gulf War, which had catastrophic consequences for the organisation. The PLO's belated support for Saddam Hussein led to its supply of money from the Gulf states being cut off, and the expulsion of many Palestinians. From being a state in the making it was struggling to keep open its missions around the world. By contrast, Hamas was rising in popularity, due both to its ideological purity and the success of its social work in the territories. The PLO's betrayal of its pledge to suspend negotiations with the Israelis until the deportees had been repatriated further alienated Hamas.

The secret negotiations in Oslo continued with the approval of the Israeli leadership, and Israeli withdrawal from Gaza first, and the stimulation of economic activity between Israel and the Palestinians were on the table. Nevertheless, Israel bombarded Lebanon, forcing some 400,000 persons north, killing some 130, mostly civilians, and badly damaging at least fifty five towns and villages (*Operation Accountability*, 25–31 July 1993). In the end Israel had to settle for an unwritten 'understanding' that Hizbullah would cease firing Katyushas into northern Israel. By August the mood amongst Palestinians was decidedly pessimistic, yet, by 20 August, Shimon Peres had put his signature to the Declaration of Principles emanating from the secret Oslo talks.

Meanwhile, the official Palestinian negotiators, frustrated with the lack of progress in the Madrid Process, threatened to boycott the tenth round of talks scheduled for early September. Arafat, aware of the progress of the secret Oslo track, prevailed upon them to continue. At the end of August, news of the secret Oslo contacts suggested that there might be an historic compromise. When the details were made public, Gaza-and-Jericho would be the first fruits, giving the Palestinians self-rule for the interim five-year period, after the third year of which discussions would begin on the permanent status, including the future of Jerusalem, the settlements, and the fate of the displaced Palestinians.

The preamble to the *Oslo Accord* (Declaration of Principles) stated the readiness of both parties 'to put an end to decades of confrontation and conflict, recognise their mutual legitimate and political rights, and strive to live in peaceful co-existence and mutual dignity and security and achieve a just, lasting and comprehensive peace settlement and historic reconciliation through the agreed political process.' The 13 September 1993 White House lawn handshake between Premier Rabin and Chairman Arafat promised a new beginning. It also marked the formal termination of the ailing *intifada*, which, however brief its duration, demonstrated that the Palestinians utterly rejected the occupation. Part payment of Rabin's 'peace dividend' followed on 12 November, when President Clinton yielded a cornucopia of economic, technological and military gifts, renewing 'America's unshakeable pledge to maintain and enhance Israel's qualitative security edge'.

For Hamas the Gaza-Jericho-First option was an historic act of treason, and it judged the PLO to be too inept and weak to pursue any real resolution. Nevertheless, the PLO persisted in its intentions, and despite the massacre of twenty-nine worshipping Muslims in Hebron (25 February 1994), and Hamas-inspired suicide bombings in early April, 4 May saw the signing of the agreement on Palestinian self-rule in Gaza and Jericho. On the Israeli side also, religious opposition to the 'Peace Process' was developing. Former Chief Rabbi Schlomo Goren called on soldiers to disobey any orders they might receive to dismantle settlements in the Occupied Territories, while at an anti-Rabin rally outside the Israeli Embassy in London on 9 August 1995, the president of Jerusalem's Great Synagogue described Rabin as heading a 'Nazi Jewish government'.

By the Taba agreement of 24–28 September 1995, Israel would deploy from six towns (amounting to 4 per cent of the West Bank area), inhabited by 250,000 Palestinians. The Palestinian Authority would have partial control of Hebron, and responsibility for 'public order' in the 440 villages of the West Bank, inhabited by 68 per cent of the Palestinian population, and occupying 23 per cent of West Bank territory. Israel would retain control of 73 per cent of the territory of the West Bank. The Palestinian Authority would have effective control over only 4 per cent of the land, and limited administrative responsibility for 98 per cent of the Palestinian population of the West Bank. The agreement reflected the Israeli victory of retaining control of most of the territory, while conceding the highly populated areas to the Palestinian Authority which would be responsible for controlling its own population. Short of total transfer of the Arab population, the Israelis could hardly hope for more. Yet some were not satisfied.

The agreement, derided by Palestinian dissidents as 'catastrophic' and a 'negotiated surrender', reflected the asymmetry of the negotiating parties. It remains to be seen whether the functional autonomy which the agreement offers will ever inaugurate 'a true start for a new era in which the Palestinian people will live free and sovereign in their own country', as Arafat promised. Although modest, the Israeli restitution does amount to some dilution of the Zionist dream of a Greater Israel. Redeployment began from Jenin on

25 October. Some days later (4 November) Rabin was assassinated by a religious Jew, and was replaced by Shimon Peres.

After the Israel army deployed from Tulkarm, Nablus, Qalqilya, Bethlehem and Ramallah in December 1995, President Arafat visited each town, promising that at the end of the peace 'tunnel' would stand 'the minarets, walls and churches of Jerusalem.' However, the 'Peace Process' suffered a severe blow after the extra-judicial execution on 5 January 1996 of Yahiya Ayash, one of the instigators of bomb attacks against Israel. The long-awaited Palestinian elections were duly held on 20 January without the participation of Hamas and of the other Palestinian rejectionist parties. Arafat won 88 per cent in the presidential contest, while his party, Fatah won fifty of the eighty eight seats on the Council. However, the euphoria of the election yielded almost immediately to Hamas-inspired suicide bombings in Jerusalem (which left twenty four dead, 25 February) and elsewhere. Israel imposed draconian collective punishment in the Occupied Territories, this time supported by the Palestinian police. The 'internal closure' of both Gaza and the towns and villages of the West Bank confirmed the fears of many that the Oslo Accord prefigured merely a Zionist corralling of natives into what in South African were called *Bantustans.* Peres threatened Arafat that his troops would re-occupy the Palestinian Authority's areas of Gaza if Hamas were not suppressed, and Arafat's troops opened fire on Hamas supporters in Gaza on 18 November, killing thirteen. Although it considered the Palestinian Authority to be behaving like a handmaiden or subcontractor of Israel, Hamas had no appetite to get embroiled in a contest with it.

In response to the violence in southern Lebanon and Hizbullah shelling inside Israel's northern border, Peres unleashed *Operation Grapes of Wrath* on 11 April 1996. The sixteen days of merciless bombing – 'an unhappy bombing campaign' according to the editor of *The 1997 Jewish Year Book* (Massil 1997: vi) – killed over 150 civilians, created up to half a million displaced persons, and wreaked havoc on the infrastructure of civilian life. The killing of more than 100 displaced civilians in the UN's headquarters at Qana (18 April) went beyond what could be tolerated even by a generally forgiving, pro-Israeli West. Israel's offensive against mainly civilian targets – the report commissioned by UN Secretary General Boutros Boutros Ghali, which the USA tried to persuade him to drop, dismissed Israeli claims that the shelling was an accident – violated the 1949 Geneva Convention, for which the perpetrators might be brought before tribunals for war crimes and crimes against humanity.[34] Rabbi Yehuda Amital, a member of Peres'

---

34 Ironically, during the period of Israel's incursion (15 April), Szymon Serafinowicz, an 85-year-old refugee was committed for Britain's first war crimes trial, charged with murdering three Jews during the winter of 1941–42. Sixteen witnesses came from far afield, and the Chief Executive of the Board of Deputies of British Jews applauded the action in recognition of the fundamental principle that justice must be done, however much time may have elapsed.

cabinet, called the Qana killings a desecration of God's name (*chilul hashem*) (*Jewish Chronicle*, 3 May 1996, p. 1).

The uncritical support which Israel received from President Clinton and Secretary of State Christopher betrayed that administration's disregard for international law and civilised behaviour when its own foreign policy interests were at stake, and when a Presidential election was on the horizon. The murderous ruthlessness of Peres, a Nobel Peace Prize winner, towards Lebanese civilians proved to be a monumental political miscalculation: he was beaten narrowly in the 29 May elections for the post of Prime Minister. With Binyamin Netanyahu's victory, 'the politics of delusion and fear had triumphed over those of hope and promise inherent in the Peres approach', according to Israel's retired ambassador to Britain (Raviv 1998: 260). He was supported not only by the Likud/Gesher/Tzomet list, but by Shas and the Lubavich religious movement (whose banners proclaimed that 'Bibi is good for the Jews'), and in general by the Orthodox Jewish community. In the USA, however, President Clinton was re-elected.

Netanyahu's period as Prime Minister has been characterised by a reluctance to advance on the peace front. The 23 September 1996 opening of the exit from an ancient tunnel under the Old City of Jerusalem precipitated widespread violence, resulting in the killing of fifty-six Palestinians and fifteen Israeli soldiers (25 and 26 September). After months of prevarication, the Hebron Agreement was finally signed on 17 January 1997, leaving 80 per cent of the city under the control of the Palestinian Authority. The next serious challenge to progress on the peace track was the decision of Netanyahu's government on 26 February 1997 to convert Jabal Abu Ghneim (Har Homa), an afforested hill, just opposite my residence in Tantur, to the north of Beit Sahour, into a Jewish settlement to house some 32,000 Jewish settlers. The project would close Israel's ring around Jerusalem, and cut off the last contiguous land corridor between Jerusalem and the southern West Bank. The Israeli Labour government had agreed the project before it lost the election, and in opposition threatened Netanyahu with a no confidence vote in the Knesset, should he not adopt a resolution to build an exclusively Jewish settlement on the site without delay.

President Clinton voiced his disapproval on 3 March, but after the USA had vetoed a European Union-sponsored resolution at the UN Security Council on 6 March – the USA's seventy-first veto since 1967, to be followed a fortnight later by its seventy-second – condemning Israel's intentions in Jerusalem as 'illegal', the General Assembly was authorised to take up the matter, and 130 nations supported the resolution condemning the Israeli settlement as illegal, with only the USA and Israel against, and Micronesia and the Marshall Islands abstaining.

Nevertheless, Netanyahu commenced work on the hill on 18 March, with bulldozers cutting ruthlessly through the trees. Soon roads were prepared for the infrastructure of the settlement. Predictably, sporadic violence erupted throughout the West Bank. The ritual of Palestinian youth throwing stones in the direction of Israeli troops, who responded with tear-gas, rubber-bullets, and sometimes live ammunition, resumed. During that period living in Jerusalem I judged that Netanyahu had thrown away his last real chance for making Israel acceptable in the region, and that Arafat had almost totally capitulated. The Oslo Accord had given the Israelis more than they could have hoped for, and yet they were not satisfied. With no advance in the 'Peace Process', and the behaviour of the Netanyahu government seriously undermining Palestinian confidence in any return from the Oslo Accords, 30 July brought to fourteen the number of serious bombing incidents since 13 September 1993. USA Secretary of State, Madeleine Albright's visit to the region in September 1997, and subsequent efforts at mediation, failed to breathe life into the 'Peace Process'.

Hopes that the Clinton administration would put pressure on Netanyahu, on his visit to Washington in January 1998, to advance the 'Peace Process' were frustrated by a number of domestic factors. The administration was reluctant to alienate the Jewish constituency in the USA, a major constituent of Democrat support. Opposition from the Republicans in Congress, as well as from the Christian fundamentalist camp, helped to steer the administration away from forcing the issue of an Israeli withdrawal from a further 13.1 per cent of the Occupied Territories. Moreover, the President was under pressure from allegations of sexual impropriety with Monica Lewinsky, hailed with tedious regularity by right-wing Jews as a latter-day Queen Esther, prepared to give herself to save her people.

Hopes that the 'Peace Process' might make progress after the Arafat-Netanyahu meeting in London, and Clinton's 'summoning' the two leaders to Washington on 11 May to begin final status talks, were quickly frustrated when Netanyahu insisted on seeking clarifications of the USA's proposal for a 13.1 per cent Israeli withdrawal. He was given a rapturous reception in Congress on 14 May, being treated like a conquering hero resisting the administration's efforts to 'bully Israel'. Altogether, by August it was clear that the USA would seek refuge in leaving the matter to the contending parties, which, of course, were altogether unequal contestants in what had been hailed in 1993 as a peace process of partners.

Eventually, the Wye Memorandum of 23 October 1998, with Israel committing to withdraw from 13.1 per cent of the Occupied West Bank, and the Palestinian Authority committing himself to suppressing Hamas, was signed by Arafat, to the annoyance of Iran's supreme leader, Ayotollah Khamenei, Syria's President Asad, and Egypt's President Mubarak. The agreement was accompanied by a series of five letters, one from Secretary of State Albright to Netanyahu, and four from the USA ambassador to Israel's Cabinet Secretary. These guarantee the USA's 'iron-clad commitment to Israel's security', and promise not to interfere with the extent of Israel's next deployment, allowing it to define its security needs. Moreover, the USA will oppose any unilateral declaration of Palestinian statehood. For his part, Arafat consented to CIA surveillance of his administered territories.

Secretly, in the wings of the Wye agreement, the USA and Israel negotiated another defence pact guaranteeing that the USA would protect Israel from missile attack by Iran, Iraq, or Syria, and would enhance Israel's deterrence capabilities, upgrading the military co-operation between the two sides (31 October). Furthermore, it would pay Israel $500 million to defray the expenses of Israel's promised withdrawal. Meanwhile, Israel continues to advance the USA influence in the region with its pact with Turkey. There are, however, signs that the Arab states are finally realising the implications of the new geopolitical map which is being drawn, and may collaborate to protect their interests.

The role of the USA

Israel's foreign interest has shifted firmly to the USA. The relationship between the two, measured both in terms of the extent of the USA's foreign aid to, and unique support of Israel in the face of criticisms from the rest of the world merits the designation 'special'.[35] This 'special relationship' has developed over the years in response to the changing political scene, and will continue to change, particularly after the collapse of the USSR, which ensured even greater USA influence in the region. Since international relations between two countries are seldom expressions of altruism one must assume that the USA's support of Israel is a function of its global, regional Middle Eastern, and domestic policies (see Sheffer 1997). It is recognised that the Clinton administration's support for Israel has been greater than even that of his predecessors, but that, too, must been seen against the background of the USA's interests.

Although the USA's attitude to Israel was relatively cool at the time of the formation of the state, its 'special relationship', exemplified by massive military, economic and political aid, arose in response to changing geopolitical and domestic factors, with domestic matters customarily playing a supporting, rather than a controlling role. The geopolitical elements could be measured most especially in the efforts to ensure Western influence in the highly volatile Middle East region, and particularly in curbing the expansion of Soviet influence in the area. Israel could be relied

---

35 The fact and extent of USA aid to Israel suggests either self-interest or a unique degree of philanthropy. Of the $12 billion total of USA foreign aid world-wide, Israel, with a population of five million, receives $3.5 billion grants and $2 billion in USA loan guarantees, and Egypt, with a population of some sixty million, receives $2.1 billion, in return for its peace agreement with Israel. The 1996 total of $5,505,300,000 grants and loan guarantees amounts to some $15 million per day, 365 days a year. Meanwhile, the USA owes the UN some $17 billion. Since the vast majority of members of Congress either take donations from pro-Israeli lobbies, set up by the American–Israel Public Affairs Committee, or fear that AIPAC might fund a rival candidate, hard questions are never asked.

on to act virtually as a USA proxy with respect to the pro-Soviet Arab states, and to be a testing-ground for USA weapons. Moreover, it was particularly close to the great oil-fields of the Middle East, and could help guarantee American access to them.

On the home front, domestic factors ensured that the USA would be a staunch supporter of Israel. Various factors have secured this: the powerful 'Jewish lobby', the 'Jewish vote' and the 'Jewish money' which finances various politicians; the importance of Israel to the military and security communities; as well as such factors as the perception in many Christian circles of the religious significance of Israel. Other contributory factors include Western guilt concerning the *Shoah*, and the success of the 'court historiographers' of Israel in portraying the fledgling country as an innocent victim of Arab predatorship, and as 'one of our own', a democratic 'island' in a sea of dictatorships.

In a sense, Israel's 'pioneering spirit' replicates that of some of the founding fathers of European settlement in North America. Indeed, history has encouraged white Americans also to consider themselves to be a chosen people with a universal mission. Their Puritan forebears also were motivated by an aspiration to create a religious Utopia, a Bible Commonwealth. They saw themselves as God's Chosen People, who had come to America in obedience to his command, like Israel of old. They were to be a city set on a hill, for everyone to see the wonders of God's covenant with his people. The native Americans, however, would become strangers in their own land, an alien presence to be pushed back before the waves of 'civilisation', in imitation of the Israelites' treatment of the Amalekites.

In a sermon delivered in Boston in September 1689, Cotton Mather charged the members of the armed forces in New England to consider themselves to be Israel in the wilderness, confronted by Amalek: pure Israel was obliged to 'cast out [the Indians] as dirt in the streets', and eliminate and exterminate them (in Niditch 1993: 3). The eighteenth-century preacher, Herbert Gibbs, thanked the mercies of God for extirpating the enemies of Israel in Canaan (i.e. Native Americans) (Bainton 1960: 168). Like the Israelis, citizens of the USA will have to come to terms with the reality that the establishment of their homeland came about only with the expropriation of the land of the indigenous peoples, and the importation of aggressive European cultural imperialism. Perhaps their failure to do so adequately provides one reason why they find barbarous colonialist behaviour by others less repulsive, and why, with such a history, the USA could never be a credible broker in a dispute between colonisers and colonised.

In the USA-sponsored negotiations between Israel and the Palestinians, scheduled to deal with the substantial issues leading to a comprehensive peace settlement, the demands of justice and conformity with the requirements of International Law and the conventions on Human Rights will have to yield to the reality of the political imbalance of power. The partners in the negotiations enjoy an asymmetric bargaining relationship. Israel is unlikely to conform to UN Resolutions and to respect the rights of the Palestinian people as enshrined in a range of Human Rights conventions. Indeed, it is almost the case that the only relevant UN Resolution it subscribes to is the UN Partition Plan of 1947, and only that half of it which suits its interests.

Conclusion

Although himself fully assimilated, Herzl eschewed a constitutional and civil rights' solution to antisemitism which he judged made Europe incapable of tolerating Jews. Within fifty one years of the First Zionist Congress, the State of Israel became a reality. The success of the enterprise is a measure of the imbalance of power between the contending parties: the determination and dedication of the Zionists, on the one hand, and the relative impotence of the indigenous population, on the other. The leaders of the Zionist movement from Europe could draw on political, diplomatic and capitalist skills unavailable to the indigenous Arab population.

It was the *Shoah* above all that elevated Zionism from minority to majority status among Jews world-wide, and which gained international sympathy for a Jewish state. Moreover, the Zionists had constructed a government in waiting, a largely self-reliant economy, state-building institutions, and a considerable defence force, which nothing on the Arab side could match. Although there was a number of Arab political parties, they lacked the cohesion required for a determined national movement. Prior to the foundation of the PLO in the late 1960s, the *hamula* ('extended family', or 'clan'), rather than the nation was the focus of group self-identity. Palestinian society was altogether ill-equipped to confront the organised European-based colonialist enterprise of Zionism.

The Israeli conquest of 1967 brought its own problems. The obvious barbarism of the occupation had to be defended in some way, characteristically by recourse to the pretence that the state's security demanded it. Moreover, the discourse of jurisprudence perverted itself in order to legitimise the theft of land, collective punishments, torture, and administrative oppression. But, Zionism, being a political ideology sharing much in common with nineteenth-century European nationalisms and colonialisms, predicated inferiority of all native peoples, determined to improve the lot of international Jewry at others' expense. Its conquest took place after the heyday of European colonisation, and at a time when the European nations were beginning to respect the right to self-determination of indigenous populations, and when the very notion of colonisation was beginning to break down.

Having reviewed significant stages in the development of Zionism, which was an essentially non-, if not directly anti-religious ideology, we now turn to the antecedents of the movement, paying attention to religious questions which, justifiably, have not featured in our discussion so far. The biblical narrative is critical for any understanding of Zionism, whose denigration of the diaspora focused almost exclusively on Palestine as the *Eretz Yisrael* of the Hebrew Kings and the Maccabees, rather than the Palestine of historical periods before or since those epochs. The relegation of the historical events of Palestine which intervened between the loss of Jewish independence and the ideology of return to a matter of no relevance is directly related to the biblical witness to Jewish identity.

Part II

An assessment of Zionism

2 From Zion to Zionism

Having traced the development of Zionism from its formulation to the establishment of the State of Israel, and its fifty years of existence since, it is fruitful to enquire into the antecedents of the programme. The term 'Zionism' was used for the first time towards the end of the last century, and has been used with a variety of meanings: Labour Zionism, revisionist Zionism, religious Zionism, cultural Zionism, political Zionism, humanistic Zionism, the Zionism of the right, and the Zionism of the left, the Zionism of the diaspora, and the Zionism of the State of Israel, and so on.

Although the term is modern, it is related to 'Zion', a revered concept of Judaism. The evidence for the desire to return to Zion (a symbol for Jerusalem, and, by extension for the whole land) is, as we shall see in this chapter, abundant in both Israelite and Jewish history. It appears in texts from the Hebrew prophets, in the exhortations of the Karaites of the Middle Ages,[1] in the Zion poetry of Halevy, in the various aliyahs associated with the Kabbalists and others,[2] in the Jewish opposition to emancipation and assimilation in the eighteenth and nineteenth centuries, and in the aspirations in the prayer-book presented afresh to each new generation of Jews.

Zion and the Bible

Within the Hebrew Scriptures, which mention 'Zion' no less than 192 times,[3] several texts express Yahweh's choice of it as his dwelling (e.g. Psalms 9.11; 48.2; 50.2; 74.2; Isa 8.18; 12.6; 24.23; Joel 3.17, 21; Zech

---

1 The Karaites, a group of Jewish sects who rejected the talmudic tradition and rabbinic authority, urged its members to come to Jerusalem, mourning, fasting, weeping, etc., to hold vigils until the day when Jerusalem shall be restored (Nemoy 1952: 36–37).

2 In Kabbalistic literature, the spiritual unity of the people and the land made it natural to accept the people's physical separation from it until the end of time (see Schweid 1987: 539).

3 In addition, 'Jerusalem' appears in 972 verses of the Bible.

8.3). Zion is 'the Holy habitation of the Most High. God is in the midst of her, she shall not be moved' (Psalm 46.4–5). From it would come deliverance (e.g. Psalm 14.7; 20.2; 53.6). After its destruction, Yahweh would rebuild it (e.g. Psalm 51.18; 69.35; 102.16; 126.1). Zion/Jerusalem, then, was no ordinary city, but became a symbol which pointed beyond itself, and contributed to keeping Judaism alive as a faith immersed in the imagery and longing for the Holy Mountain.

However, in some prophetic traditions, continued residence in Zion, and the very existence of the city, would be possible only if its inhabitants practised justice and equity (e.g. Micah 3.9–12; quoted in Jer 26.18). In traditional Judaism also, in line with this perspective, separation from the land was considered to be the consequence of infidelity to the Covenantal relationship (e.g. 2 Esd 14.31–32). Pining for Zion was typical for those separated from it, as in the case of the exiles in Babylon: 'If I forget you, O Jerusalem, let my right hand wither!' (see Psalm 137).

Zion had a profound theological significance, becoming a visible sign of the relationship between Yahweh and his people. In the diaspora also the symbolism and 'reality' of Zion remained vibrant in people's hearts. However, the perspective of those Jews living in the land was not shared by all diaspora Jews. Much to the annoyance of the Hasmoneans in Judaea, the Jews in Egypt considered their religion to be transportable, and manifested this dramatically in their erection of a temple in Leontopolis. The accompanying offerings of animals and vegetables in a foreign land gave expression to a view which regionalised the institutions of temple, priest and land itself. The practice challenged the victorious tradition that sacrifice should be offered in only one place, that which God would choose (Deut 12.4). The Samaritans, also, built a rival temple, on Mount Gerizim near Shechem, sealing their ongoing conflict with Jewish exclusivism.

Restoration of the people to the land

The promise of restoration to the land occurs frequently in the biblical material. At the end of the book of Amos we read,

> The time is surely coming, says Yahweh, when ... I will restore the fortunes of my people Israel, and they shall rebuild the ruined cities and inhabit them ... I will plant them upon their land, and they shall never again be plucked up out of the land that I have given them.
>
> (Amos 9.13–15)

Jeremiah also transmits Yahweh's word of assurance of raising up for David a righteous Branch, who shall reign as king and execute justice and righteousness in the land. In his days Judah will be saved and Israel will live in safety. Yahweh would lead the offspring of the house of Israel out of all the lands where he had driven them. 'Then they shall live in their own land' (Jer 23.5–8). Second Isaiah also reflects confidence that Yahweh would restore his people (Isa 49.14–26; 54.1–17). Zechariah, too, keeps the hope of future prosperity alive (Zech 2.10–12). But perhaps the most eloquent prophecy of a return is contained in Ezekiel's vision of the dry bones (Ezek 37). After the prophecy to the bones that Yahweh would 'cause flesh to come upon you, and ... you shall live' (verse 6) was fulfilled, another promise followed:

> I will bring you back to the land of Israel. ... I will take the people of Israel from the nations among which they have gone, and will gather them from every quarter, and bring them to their own land. ... Then they shall be my people, and I will be their God. My servant David shall be king over them. ... I will make a covenant of peace with them; it shall be an everlasting covenant with them. ... My dwelling place shall be with them. ... Then the nations shall know that I Yahweh sanctify Israel, when my sanctuary is among them forevermore.
>
> (Ezek 37. 12–28)

In the biblical traditions, restoration to the land was the prerogative of Yahweh alone (e.g. Jer 28.3–6; 29.10; Ezek 34.16; 37.12), since only he could adjudicate on the people's worthiness to return, and determine the means to effect it (e.g. Jer 3.14; Lam 4.22). The unquestionable authority of Yahweh to disperse and to gather in is emphasised particularly in Jeremiah's letter to the elders of the exiles in Babylon (Jer 29.4–14; cf. Jer 30.3; 32.37; 34.22). The fruits of restoration also are at the divine disposal, as recorded in Tobit's final counsel given in Nineveh (Tob 14.4–7). Some consider these prophecies to have been fulfilled already in Cyrus' permission to the exiles to return to their land in 538 BC.

It is clear that Jewish perspectives on the land and on Jerusalem as the location of God's presence reflects perspectives which relate to specific historical circumstances. Later use of the Bible, especially in the liturgy, invites new generations of hearers into the world-view of those perspectives. However, the traditions enjoy a currency in subsequent, quite different historical periods, only if one accords it to them. We shall see that subsequent generations reacted to these traditions in ways which reflected new social and religious realities, both of theology and practice.

Land in the New Testament

'The land' occupies a peripheral place in early Christian self-definition. The term occurs only forty-one times in the New Testament, and not once in a sense implying theological significance. It is used simply as a geographical indicator in the four gospels. Far from it being the case that the form of Judaism we call Christian discipleship required residence in the land, the climax of Matthew's gospel has the injunction to go from Galilee, and make disciples of all nations (Matt 28.19). Correspondingly at the end of Mark's gospel, we have the Risen Jesus addressing the disciples, 'Go into all the world and proclaim the good news to the whole creation' (Mark 16.15–20). For Luke also, disciples were to remain in Jerusalem only until they were empowered from on high (Luke 24.49), after which they were to preach forgiveness to the ends of the earth (Acts 1.8), which is symbolised by Paul preaching in Rome (Acts 28). In John's gospel, there is no significance attached to land. On the contrary, true worshippers will worship the Father neither on Mount Gerizim (for the Samaritans), nor in Jerusalem (for the Jews), but in spirit and truth (John 4.20–23).

The Acts of the Apostles is no more fruitful for developing 'land' as an element of self-definition for Christians.[4] Moreover, Paul never mentions 'land'. The term occurs four times in Hebrews: Heb 8.9 refers to the land of Egypt, and 11.29 to the 'dry land' at the crossing of the Red Sea; its author prefers the notion of a heavenly country (11.15–16) to the earthly one promised to Abraham (11.9). Jude 1.5 refers to the saving of the people from the land of Egypt. The three references to 'land' in the book of Revelation use the term in contradistinction to the 'sea' (Rev 10. 2, 5, 8). It is clear that the New Testament attaches no particular significance to the land.

By way of contrast, 'the land' is a key theological theme in the Old Testament, and its significance perdures in various expressions of Jewish piety since.[5] Moreover, since its establishment in 1948 the State of Israel has become a critical element in the self-definition of most Jews, even in the diaspora. Much of the theological emphasis in the New Testament, however, suggests a critique of a theology of land, and an universalisation of the concept, so that the Good News of Jesus Christ can be brought to the ends of the earth. In New Testament terms, the mountain comes to the believer. 1 Peter provides a striking reinterpretation of Jerusalem and its Temple for Christians in Asia Minor. They themselves were a spiritual house and a holy priesthood (2.5), offering spiritual sacrifices acceptable to God (see Walker 1996: 309–18). Walker concludes his study of Jerusalem by saying, 'If ... Jerusalem was to some extent demoted in their [the NT writers] thinking, it was only because something greater had now been revealed' (p. 326).

---

4 After the two references to Ananias' land (property), the author narrates Stephen's speech (Acts 7) with reference to the promise of land to Abraham (v. 3), and to the land of Midian (v. 29), and the land of Canaan (v. 40). In his word of encouragement to the synagogue in Antioch of Pisidia (Acts 13), Paul refers to the land of Egypt (v. 17) and land of Canaan (v. 19).

5 See the tracing of the theme in the biblical, hellenistic, tannaitic, mediaeval and modern periods in Hoffman 1986.

The land in other Jewish traditions

In the Deuterocanonical Old Testament and the Apocrypha (the Apocrypha and Pseudepigrapha), one finds some of the same attachment to the land that one encounters in the Old Testament, although notably less frequently.[6] One finds also the promise that God would restore his people to the land (*Psalms of Solomon* 17.26–28). He will protect only those who live in Israel (2 Baruch 9.2). The land will aid redemption (2 Baruch 1.1), and becomes 'holy' because God draws near it (4 Ezra 9.7–9). Finally, it is in the pleasant land of Israel that the throne of God will be erected (1 Enoch 90.20).

In the Dead Sea Scrolls we detect the persistence of the attitudes to the land we find in the biblical books. It is in the land that the members of the community practise truth and righteousness (1QS 1.5; 8.3). Part of the task of the Qumran community was to cleanse the land and render it acceptable to God, which the Temple sacrificial system had sought in vain to accomplish (1QS 9.3–5). Sin leads God to hide his face from the land (CD 2.9–11), and causes it to be desolate (CD 4.10). In the final war, the sect would occupy the land, and fight a holy war against the Gentile lands (1 QM 2).

After the devastation of the land in AD 70, so many Jews were leaving that the Rabbis feared it would be depopulated, and, consequently, began to extol its virtues. For them, the land was simply *Ha'aretz* ('the land'), and elsewhere was 'outside the land'. It required only the application of a rigid reading of the biblical text to recognise that an authentic Jewish life would be possible only in the land of Israel, centred on the Temple. Many of the *mitzvot* (commandments, e.g. the laws of sabbatical and jubilee years, and the rituals dealing with the Temple) could be observed only in the Land of Israel, and a fully Jewish life was possible only in the land. Hence a Jew living among the *goyim* (Gentiles) 'is like one who has no God' (Babylonian Talmud, *Ket*. 110b).

After the failure of the Bar Kochba revolt, movement from the land increased. The Jewish sages faced a dilemma. On the one hand, they had to try to prevent the total abandonment of the land, while on the other they had to devise a *modus vivendi* with the diaspora, which would authenticate Jewish living outside the land. The rabbinic exaltation of the land had its roots in the Old Testament, and since so much of the Torah dealt with the land, it would feature prominently even after dispersal. The sages repeated the biblical themes of the land of Israel, and tended to idealise them.

---

6 The term 'holy land' appears in a number of texts (e.g. Wisdom of Solomon 12.3; 2 Macc 1.7; Sibylline Oracles 3.266–67). The land is good/beautiful (e.g. Tobit 14.4, 5; Jubilees 13.2, 6), a pleasant and glorious land (e.g. 1 Enoch 89.40), extensive and beautiful (Letter of Aristeas, line 107). It is the land of promise (e.g. Sir 46.8; Jubilees 12.22; 13.3; 22.27). One notes other reflections of earlier biblical values: failure to observe the demands of Yahweh is incompatible with occupation (Jubilees 6.12–13); the circumcised will not be rooted out of the land (Jubilees 15.28), and the original Israelite conquest was due to sins of the Canaanite inhabitants.

About one third of the Mishnah treats of the land. Most of the first division, *Zeraim* (Seeds), of the fifth, *Kodashim* (Holy Things), and of the sixth, *Toharoth* (Purities) deal with laws concerning the land, and there is much else besides. Rabbi Simeon b. Yohai (140–65) said that the Holy One gave Israel three precious gifts: the Torah, the land of Israel, and the World to Come (Babylonian Talmud, *Berakoth* 5a). While 'the land of Israel is holier than all land', the tenth degree of holiness is the sanctuary: 'The Holy of Holies is still more holy' (Mishnah *Kelim* 1.6–9). The degree of holiness of the land derives from the extent of its association with the enactment of the Law. A fundamentalist reading of the Torah legislation on land matters would suggest that complete Jewish sanctity was possible only in the land, and that exile was an emaciated life (see W. Davies 1991: 26). However, such attitudes to religion and morality reflect a failure to adjust to radically changed circumstances.

Although the Jewish sages of the Tannaitic (*c*. first century BC–second century AD) and Amoraic (second–sixth century AD) periods were wary of political attempts to re-establish the kingdom of Israel on its own land, devoted and intense religious concern for the land/Temple remained part of the communal consciousness of Jews. The last revolt of Jews in the Roman Empire in the hope of re-establishing a Jewish state occurred after the anti-Jewish statutes of Emperor Justinian (AD 483–565). Later, Nehemiah, a Messianic figure, reigned in Jerusalem in the period 614–17. With the Arab Conquest in 639, and the building of the Mosque of Omar on the site of the Temple (687–91), Jewish devotion to the land was reflected in voluntary individual pilgrimages and immigrations, rather than in political activity for the establishment of a state.

The Law demanded that every male should make pilgrimage to Jerusalem at the Feasts of Passover, Weeks, and Tabernacles (Exod 23.14–17; see Deut 16.1–17). During the Second Temple period even diaspora Jews, in numbers we have no means of estimating, sought to observe the pilgrimage (e.g. Acts 2.5–11; 6.9; Mishnah *Taanit* 1:3), ensuring also the safe passage of the half-shekel tax from their communities. Philo of Alexandria has left a record of his attachment to the Temple, and describes world-wide pilgrimage to it (*Spec. Leg.* I, The MSS insert *Of the Temple* 67–70). Even after its destruction in AD 70, Jewish pilgrims worshipped at the site of the Temple, and invariably in a mood of lamentation. However, it is likely that the Jerusalem Temple had more symbolic than practical significance for Jews of the diaspora, since little changed in diaspora Jewish life with its destruction.

The polarity of the relationship of diaspora Jews to the land is reflected in the two contrasting standpoints of the poet Jehuda Halevi (*c*. 1075–141) and the great post-Talmudic spiritual leader, Moses Maimonides (1135–204). In his *Kuzari*, Halevi showed how exile had severed the links between the Torah, the people and the land, which would be mended only with the coming of the Messiah. He lamented his separation from Zion: 'My heart is in the East, and I am at the edge of the West ... it would be glorious to see the dust of the ruined Shrine' (*Libbi bemitzrach*, in Carmi 1981: 347). Invariably his lament is related to the devastation of the land and of Jerusalem in particular (see his Zion poems, and in particular 'Sion, halo tishali', which was included in the liturgy of *Tisha be-Av*, in Carmi 1981: 347). For Halevi, the land of Israel marked the threshold between the human and the divine spheres. He considered that every Jew must endeavour to go to the land of Israel to observe the commandments. In 1141, he left for the Levant (see his *Hava mabbul*, in Carmi 1981: 352), and whether he visited Jerusalem or not, we do know that his tomb in Lower Galilee was seen within some twenty years of his death by Benjamin of Tudela, the first mediaeval Jewish writer of whose travels we have a detailed record (Adler 1894).

By contrast, for Maimonides the land of Israel was of itself no different from other lands. However, it was distinctive because it was sanctified by the commandments and by events of Israelite history. Maimonides passed through the land on his way to Egypt but lived his entire life in the diaspora. Similarly, Benjamin of Tudela spent an extended period away from Spain, which he left in 1160, going as far as Syria, Palestine and Persia, and returning to Spain in 1173. His account reflects his interest in what we might call inquisitive journeying, rather than in what religious people call pilgrimage.

The fate of those living in several parts of the Jewish diaspora assumed dreadful proportions during the period of the Crusades. In an anonymous poem, 'Come with us', the smitten daughter of Zion is invited to join in the march to the Holy Land (Carmi 1981: 368–70). David bar Meshullam of Speyer called on God to avenge the mass suicides in Speyer during the First Crusade (1096) (Carmi 1981: 374–75), and the poems of Ephraim of Regensburg (1110–75) reflect the horrors of the Regensburg massacre of 1137, and of the Second Crusade (1146–47). The *Sefer Zekhira* of Ephraim of Bonn (1132–1200) records the decrees and persecutions of the Second and Third Crusades, and his lament for the massacre of Jews at Blois (1171) ends with the hope of being rescued and paying homage to God in Jerusalem (Carmi 1981: 385).

Shalem Shabazi (d. after 1681), the foremost Yemini poet, reflects on the Messianic expectations of Jews, especially in the wake of the persecutions of 1679–81: 'When will He give me leave to go up and make home within the extolled gates of Zion? Morning and evening I call to mind the Princess (the *Shekinah*)' (Carmi 1981: 487). And again, 'My Beloved ... will assemble all my kind and righteous tribes, and Israel will rise to greet the dawn in Zion's gates' (Carmi 1981: 488).[7]

---

7   The extant poetry, of course, also reflects the themes of poets of all periods, especially those dealing with love.

With regard to Jewish religious settlement in the land, Rabbi Moses Ben Nahman (Ramban, 1194–270), the highest religious authority of his time in Spain, emigrated to Palestine in 1267, and was active in founding *yeshivot* (rabbinic seminaries) and synagogues in Acre and Jerusalem. In 1286, Rabbi Meir of Rothenburg sought to lead a number of Jews from the area of the Rhine to Palestine. In 1523, a Messianic movement led by David Reuveni aimed at a return to the land, and attracted the interest of communities in Egypt, Spain and Germany. In 1772–80, Rabbi Nahman of Bratzlov journeyed to the land, considering that simply by direct contact with the land, 'he held the Law whole'. He achieved this merely by stepping ashore at Haifa. He desired to return immediately, but under pressure went to Tiberias, but never to Jerusalem. For the Maharal of Prague (Rabbi Yehuda Liwa of Loew – Ben Bezalel, 1515–1609) God would gather in the Jews in his own good time. Under the influence of Rabbi Elijah Ben Solomon Salman of Vilna (the Vilna Gaon), a number of groups went to Safed in 1808 and 1809, seeing themselves as representatives of all Jews, and considering themselves justified in appealing to other Jews for help. Some, such as Rabbi Akiba Schlessinger of Pressburg (1837–1922), were driven to go to the land, it being more and more difficult to live according to the Torah in an increasingly secular Europe. No Jewish sage, however, was inspired to establish a Jewish polity in Palestine, not to speak of expelling the non-Jewish inhabitants as a pre-requisite. Indeed, much of the longing and nostalgia for the lost trappings of Temple worship was fuelled by the frequent recurrence of such emotion in the cycle of Jewish prayers.

The Siddur

The promise of land to Abraham and his descendants, the Exodus and conquest and the centralisation of the Israelite cult in the Temple, etc., are singular eruptions into human history in the biblical narrative, appropriated by every generation of Jews, especially through the *Siddur* (prayerbook). One of the 'Eighteen' Benedictions (*Shemoneh Esreh*) incumbent on all adult males, appeals

> Sound the great *shofar* (horn) for our freedom; raise the banner to gather our exiles, and gather us together from the four corners of earth. Blessed are you, YHWH (the unpronounced divine name), who gathers in the dispersed of his people Israel.

While the rabbis prescribed the recitation of the Benedictions, the emphasis was on the Temple, rather than just the land: 'Zion the abiding place of Thy glory, and towards Thy temple and Thy habitation' (Benediction 14; see also 16, 18). The prayers were to be said facing Jerusalem, or at least while orienting the heart towards the Holy of Holies (Mishnah *Berakoth* 4.5).

The grace after meals contains the second blessing, 'We thank you, YHWH our God, because you have given to our forefathers as a heritage a desirable, good and spacious land ... '. The third blessing contains the petition:

> Have mercy YHWH our God, on Israel your people, on Jerusalem your city, on Zion the resting place of your glory, on the monarchy of the house of David your anointed (Messiah), and on the great and holy house upon which your name is called ... [with the addition on the Sabbath] And show us, YHWH our God, the consolation of Zion, your city, and the rebuilding of Jerusalem, the city of your holiness.

The wedding blessing contains the request, 'Bring intense joy and exultation to the barren one through the ingathering of her children amidst her in gladness.' Another blessing adds the hope: 'YHWH, our God, let there soon be heard in the cities of Judah and the streets of Jerusalem the sound of joy and the sound of gladness, the voice of the groom and the voice of the bride'.

In the *Kaddish* after a burial we have the eschatological hope: 'He will resuscitate the dead and raise them up to eternal life, and rebuild the city of Jerusalem and complete His Temple within it, and uproot alien worship from the earth, and return the service of heaven to its place and where the Holy One, Blessed is He, will reign in his sovereignty and splendour, in your lifetimes and in your days, and in the lifetimes of the entire house of Israel, swiftly and soon'.

The Jewish liturgy played a critical role in keeping alive the attachment to the land. The annual Liturgy of Destruction commemorates the devastation of the land, Jerusalem and its Temple. On the ninth day of Ab (*Tisha be-Av*), the prayer begins, 'O Lord God, comfort the mourners of Zion; Comfort those who grieve for Jerusalem', and ends with, 'Praised are You, O Lord, who comforts Zion; Praised are You, who rebuilds Jerusalem' (see also Mishnah *Rosh-ha-Shanah* 4.1–3 for the centrality of Jerusalem). That Jerusalem established the time for world-wide celebration of the Jewish festivals, and that all synagogues faced it added to its importance. Finally, the Passover Seder concludes with the formula, 'Next year in Jerusalem'.

However,

> For all of its emotional, cultural and religious intensity, this link with Palestine did not change the praxis of Jewish life in the diaspora: Jews might pray three times a day for the deliverance that would transform the world and transport them to Jerusalem, but they did not emigrate there; they could annually mourn the destruction of the Temple on *Tish'ah be-Av* and leave a brick over their door panel bare as a constant reminder of the desolation of Zion, but they did not move there.
>
> (Avineri 1981: 3)

As Yonatan Ratosh noted, 'Next year in Jerusalem' does not obligate Jews to do anything: 'In the last analysis any Jew can carry Zion in his heart

wherever he is, just as generations upon generations of Jews have carried it
... Slogans can be changed every morning' (in 'The Opening Discourse',
1944, in Diamond 1986: 74). Nevertheless, constant reference to the ritual
patterns endowed the land of Israel with almost mystical significance. It
became an imagined place, and longing for it took the form of that 'nostalgia
for Paradise' that one finds in many diaspora communities. However,
changes were taking place in Western Europe which would have profound
effects on Judaism and the self-definition of Jews.

Antecedents of Herzl's vision and plan

The scientific spirit promoted by Descartes, Locke and Newton in
seventeenth century Europe inaugurated a new approach to knowledge and
truth, issuing in the following century in the Enlightenment. It championed
a new wisdom, based on autonomous, critical, historical enquiry, pursuing
truth through reason, observation and experiment (reflecting Francis Bacon's
scientific method), unhindered by dogma, tradition or a hierarchy higher
than autonomous reason. The movement, summed up in Kant's phrase,
Sapere aude! ('dare to think'), was, in general, suspicious of, and often hostile
to the claims of religion, and challenged at its core every religious system,
including Judaism.

While one might expect that its promotion of tolerance and the equality
of peoples would have advanced the interests of Jews, its widespread disdain
of religion, with its innate respect for revealed truths and unchallenged
authority, adversely effected the status of Judaism and its adherents. Voltaire,
the most trenchant critic of Christianity, considered the Jews to be more
fanatical than even the Christians, and blamed them for giving Christianity
to the world. Diderot castigated them for their lack of reason and
philosophy, and for their blind obedience to authority (see Byrne 1996: 22).

In many respects, however, the new spirit was to be particularly fruitful
for Jews in Europe. Moreover, a Jewish version of the Enlightenment
(*Haskalah*), mostly associated with Moses Mendelssohn (1729–86), co-
existed alongside more traditional religious practice. It sought to enable
Jews to come to terms with modernity. Since the French National Assembly
voted for the recognition of Jews as citizens and the removal of existing
restrictions (28 September 1791) their lot changed for the better. By 1860,
their equality was generally accepted in Europe (Halpern 1969: 4). Indeed,
the nineteenth century was the best century they had experienced,
collectively and individually, since the destruction of the Temple: from
being a marginal community in the early part of the century, Jews had
become the great beneficiaries of the Enlightenment, emancipation and the
industrial revolution within a hundred years (Avineri 1981: 5–6).

The danger, however, was that European Jews would be assimilated.
'Assimilation', a term frequently used with overtones of xenophobia and
superiority, signifies a high level of 'social integration', becoming like one's

neighbours through various social contacts, interactions and modes of behaviour. It implies a more radical social affinity than the process of 'acculturation', which usually refers to forms of linguistic, educational and ideological association (see Sharot 1976: 3). In the more fearful religious circles, whether in antiquity or today, assimilation and acculturation were perceived as threats to Jewish continuity.[8] The Enlightenment and Emancipation provided a climate in which some Jews discarded some of the practices which were the 'mortar keeping the building together'. Western Jews insisted that they were not a separate nation, but a religious body, which denied any intention to 'return to Zion' (Halpern 1969: 10).

But as well as the Enlightenment, there were also dark clouds on the horizon for Europe's Jews, especially in the east. Wilhelm Marr, the first to use the term 'antisemitism',[9] complained that Jewish influence had already penetrated too far into European economic life (Laqueur 1972: 28–29). While the 1850s and 1860s were a happy period for Jews in Germany, hostility increased by the 1870s. The mood in Russia was assimilationist in the 1860s and 1870s, and Jewish pride in Russia was very strong, but the pogroms of the 1880s dealt a severe blow to the hopes for total assimilation.

Already in Germany in 1840, an anonymous pamphlet accepted the idea of a Jewish state, but rejected Palestine for practical reasons. The author proposed Arkansas, or Oregon, in which $10,000,000 would buy a territory the size of France, where Jews could show their full potential.[10] Another anonymous piece, in *Orient* (27 June 1840) argued that the best solution to the plight of Jews in Europe was an early return to Palestine, where the Sultan and Mehmet Ali could be persuaded to protect them.

One detects a development of ideas for which the establishment of a nation state could be the logical outcome. Heinrich Graetz (1817–91) contributed more than most to the view of Jews as a nation.[11] He insisted that Judaism required concrete expression, and that its interwoven religious

---

8 Others, however, were less insecure in their unique Jewish culture, and could, like Philo of Alexandria, be 'Jewish to the core and Hellenised to the same core', as in modern times, some Moroccan Jews were 'Moroccan to the core and Jewish to the same core' (see Barclay 1996: 91).

9 In popular usage 'antisemitic' is applied with little discrimination to a perpetrator of any form of perceived anti-Jewishness, covering the spectrum from Hitler's 'Final Solution', to a human rights' critique of the behaviour of the State of Israel. The term is problematic. The eighteenth-century division of peoples into racial categories reflected patterns of similarity between languages. One group of languages was clustered within a category of 'semitic languages'. On that basis, a specific people (race?), 'Semites', was designated, introducing the terms 'semitic' and hence 'antisemitic'. Arabs also are designated Semites, and are victims of a distinctive Occidental phobia. The terms 'Judaeophobia' or 'Jew-hatred' are more apposite. The Nazi hatred for Jews is more appropriately conveyed by the German terms, *Judenhass*, or *Judenfeindschaft*.

10 *Neujudäa. Entwurf zum Wiederaufbau eines Selbständigen jüdischen Staates von C.L.K.*

11 In the period 1853–76 Graetz published his eleven-volume *Geschichte der Juden von den ältesten Zeiten bis auf die Gegenwart*, which was translated into several European languages.

and political nature would require territorial manifestation. If the Law was the spirit of Judaism, and the Jewish people its historical subject, the Holy Land was its material foundation, giving the triad, the Torah, the Nation of Israel and the Holy Land. He regarded these three elements as standing in a mystical relationship to each other, inseparably united by an invisible bond. Without corporate, national life in the land, Judaism, he asserted, could never be more than a shadow of its reality (see Avineri 1981: 28–29).

The growth of chauvinistic nationalism in nineteenth-century Europe provided a catalyst for Jewish nationalism. Inspired by Giuseppe Mazzini's Rome and the rise of Italian nationalism, the *Rom und Jerusalem – Die letzte Nationalitätenfrage* (1862) of Moses Hess (1812–75) (Hertzberg 1959: 119–39) predicted the liberation of the Eternal City on Mount Moriah, after the fashion of the liberation of the Eternal City on the Tiber (Avineri 1981: 39–42). The earlier Hess considered Jews to have a future only if as individuals they broke from their group identity, and became citizens of the world. His 'New Jerusalem', based on nationalism rather than religion, would be built in the heart of Europe, not in Palestine. But now, in his judgement, Jews were a separate nation, a special race which should avoid assimilation, and reassert its uniqueness by reconstituting a national centre as a Jewish, model socialist commonwealth in Palestine. While Hess' views were unknown to either Pinsker or Herzl, their aspirations reappear in Jewish nationalist-socialist tendencies later.

While the Orthodox religious establishment retained its traditional approach to the notion of redemption through the Messiah, two rabbis suggested a more active role for Jews in bringing it forward. In his *Minhat Yehuda* (1845), Rabbi Judah Alkalai of Semlin (1788–1878) gave a territorial dimension to traditional Messianic redemption. While retaining traditional teleology, that final, supernatural redemption would be brought about by the Messiah, he argued that the physical return of the Jews to Zion must precede his advent. Alkalai supported his proposals with biblical and Talmudic texts, thereby deflecting the charge that he was 'forcing the End of Days'. He proposed the revival of *spoken* Hebrew, the establishment of a Perpetual Fund (*Keren Kayemet*), and a representative assembly of Jews (Avineri 1981: 50–51). In 1857 he called for the establishment of a Jewish state, and was, perhaps the first to do so. In old age he emigrated to Jerusalem. Herzl's paternal grandfather, Simon Loeb Herzl (1805–79), the son of a rabbi, and a pious, strictly Orthodox Jew, was a follower of Alkalai. Simon visited his family in Budapest annually, and, spoke enthusiastically of Alkalai's ideas, which, Wistrich suggests, may have been Theodor's first exposure to the notion of Palestinian Jewish resettlement (1995: 7). Moreover, Theodor Herzl's father, Jacob, had been a pupil of Alkalai. Later in Budapest, Jacob became a supporter of the Hungarian proto-Zionist rabbi, Joseph Natonek (1812–92). However, there is no trace of any influence of Alkalai's teleology in Theodor's Zionism.

As early as 1832, Rabbi Zwi Hirsch Kalischer of Posen (1795–1874) also declared that the redemption of Zion would have to begin with action on the part of the Jewish people, after which the Messianic miracle would follow. In the same year as Hess' pamphlet (1862), he published *Derishat Zion* (Seeking Zion), which had much in common with the views of Alkalai, but while reaching the same broad conclusions as Hess, had a very different ideological framework, that of the Bible, the Mishnah and the Talmud.

> The Redemption of Israel, for which we long, is not to be imagined as a sudden miracle. The Almighty, blessed be His Name, will not suddenly descend from on high and command His people to go forth. Neither will he send the Messiah in a twinkling of an eye, to sound the great trumpet for the scattered of Israel and gather them into Jerusalem.
>
> (Kalischer, in Hertzberg 1959: 110)

Settlement of Jews in the land of Israel would hasten redemption. It should take the form of self-supporting agricultural communities, which would make it possible to observe the religious commandments related to working the land: 'As we bring redemption to the land in this-worldly way, the ray of heavenly deliverance will gradually appear' (in Avineri 1981: 54).

Kalischer and Alkalai argued that it was possible to unite the nationalist and emancipationist spirit of the age with the traditions of rabbinic Judaism, subjecting the doctrine of passive Messianism to the influence of the vibrant aspirations for cultural and national identity of the age. The task of Jews was to take the first steps, and speed the coming of the Messiah's redemption. Although Alkalai and Kalischer were lone voices in the Orthodox rabbinate, they showed how it was possible to reinterpret Jewish identity and aspirations in a world which was changing drastically around them. Their stress on collective Jewish cultural and religious identity coincided with the aspirations of Zionists later in the century whose cultural roots were within the secularised, nationalist traditions of nineteenth-century Europe, more than within traditional religious ones.

Leo Pinsker (1821–91), a leading exponent of assimilation, had his confidence in the future of Jews in Russia dented by the Odessa riots of 1871, and destroyed by the pogroms of 1881. Unaware of the work of Hess, he published a pamphlet anonymously, arguing that antisemitism was an hereditary and incurable psychosis (1882).[12] Being at home nowhere, Jews were strangers *par excellence*. Just as sick people eschew food, Jews did not aspire to independent national existence. Russian Jews, to escape their parasitical condition, would have to emigrate and settle in a home of their own. The organised societies of Jews should convene a national congress with

---

12 *Autoemanzipation, ein Mahnruf an seine Stammesgenossen, von einem russischen Juden.* An English translation is in Hertzberg 1959: 181–98.

a view to purchasing a territory for the settlement of millions of Jews, for which the support of the Powers would be necessary. Since the Holy Land could not be the target, 'a land of our own' could be anywhere.

Several Jews openly canvassed the idea of settling in Palestine and reviving Hebrew as a living language. Already in 1877, the poet Yehuda Leib Gordon anonymously wrote a pamphlet proposing the establishment of a Jewish state in Palestine under British suzerainty.[13] Eliezer Perlman (*Ben Yehuda*) called for the revival of Hebrew as the spoken language, which could take place only in Palestine. Judging that Jews would always be aliens, Moshe Leib Lilienblum (1834–1910) declared, 'We need a corner of our own. We need Palestine', and from 1881 he advocated the purchase of land in Palestine.

However, although Herzl gives no evidence of having been influenced by his ideological predecessors, the surfacing of Zionist ideas in several places in the nineteenth century made the reception of his programme less forbidding. Moreover, the growth in acceptance of a 'Jewish Return' to Palestine was facilitated by Byron's *Hebrew Melodies* (1815), Disraeli's *Tancred* (1847), and George Eliot's portrayal of the idealist Zionist in *Daniel Deronda* (1876, which, on 7 June 1895, Herzl determined to read: I: 71). Indeed, Zangwill claimed it was Eliot who invented Zionism (1920: 78).

On the practical side, already in 1878–79, there had been an attempt by a group of Orthodox Jews from Jerusalem to establish an agricultural settlement, *Petah Tiqvah*, on 3,000 dunums, north-east of Jaffa. Although the attempt failed, the move inspired some from Russia, who turned out to be no more skilled in agriculture (Lehn 1988: 9). After the pogroms of 1881, Russian and Romanian Jewish immigration to Palestine increased, with the first settlement of fourteen families in August 1882 on 3,200 dunums south-east of Jaffa, at *Rishon le-Tsiyyon*. In the same year, about 200 Romanian emigrants established *Zikhron Ya'aqov* near the coast, south of Haifa, and fifty Romanian families established *Rosh Pinnah* east of Safed. An offshoot of *Chovevei Zion*,[14] the so-called *Biluim* (the plural of an acronym of the opening words of Isa 2.5, *bylw*, 'O house of Jacob, come, let us walk in the light of Yahweh!'), concluded that the only solution to the discrimination against Jews in Russia was national renaissance through the establishment of a Jewish state in Palestine. Although only fourteen *Biluim* immigrated in July 1882, and reached at most twenty by the end of 1884, they achieved an importance out of proportion to their numbers. Their programme involved the establishment of self-sustaining, exclusively Hebrew-speaking Jewish colonies, employing no non-Jewish worker.

---

13 *Die jüdische Frage in der orientalischen Frage.*

14 The Russian 'Lovers of Zion', while promoting small-scale settlement in Palestine, considered that the ultimate return to Zion would be brought about by the Messiah.

In all, by the end of 1884 there were eight new Jewish villages with a total population in 1890 of 2,415. The immigration to Palestine in the first aliyah of 1882–1903 represented only a tiny percentage of the emigration of Jews from Europe (Vital 1975: 93, 99–100), and it is estimated that while almost three million Jews emigrated from Russia between 1882 and 1914, only about one per cent went to Palestine (Avineri 1981: 5). Moreover, after the Balfour Declaration when entry of Jews into Palestine was unrestricted, only some 30,000 settled in the period 1917–21, while hundreds of thousands emigrated from east to west.

Conclusion

While a longing for Zion was present at virtually all periods of Jewish history a pious yearning for Jerusalem and its lamented Temple should not be confused with the desire to establish a nation state for Jews in Palestine. One must acknowledge the disjuncture between that perennial aspiration reflected in the Jewish texts and the determination even merely to take up residence in the land. And since aspiration is best measured by action, it is significant that at no period during the 1,800 years after the destruction of the Second Commonwealth prior to the nineteenth century, was there a concerted effort to resettle in *Eretz Yisrael*, not to speak of attempting to recover lost independence there. Jews settled massively in the Mediterranean basin throughout the period, and even strove to resettle in places from where they had been expelled.

Moreover, in a survey of Jewish thinking it would be easier to identify a host of 'anti-Zionist' champions, and to fashion a catena of proof-texts to support one's case. However, unless one can demonstrate a cause-and-effect relationship between the elements of each list, one may not legitimately regard an earlier statement as a development towards its inevitable consummation in a particular form of Jewish living. While there were forced expulsions of Jews, there has always been a widespread voluntary Jewish diaspora. Living in the diaspora had its advantages. Indeed, 'Zion' gradually became increasingly metaphysical, and, by virtue of a network of rabbinic institutions was 'portable': Palestine could live in Israel, if not Israel in Palestine (Zangwill 1937: 3–4).

The key question is whether the goals of political Zionism fulfilled the ideals of world-wide Jewry from the earliest times to today: that Jews throughout history felt themselves 'in exile' and longed to return 'home'. Generalisations based on extrapolating disparate comments from any number of Jewish thinkers are no substitute for examining the real circumstances of Jewish life in the diaspora. Betsy Halpern-Amaru has shown how a number of post-biblical Jewish authors adapted and rewrote the biblical paradigm of exile to reflect the changed political circumstances, historical contexts and contemporary interests of their own eras (1994). As we shall see (Chapter 7), in the Graeco-Roman period at least, diaspora Jews generally felt quite good about their situation, built permanent synagogues and interacted successfully with their Gentile neighbours: 'The diaspora was not Exile; in some sense it became a Holy Land, too' (Kraabel 1987: 58).[15]

The Zionist aspiration was prompted by a host of nationalist movements within the turbulent politics of post-French Revolution, nineteenth-century Europe, where about 90 per cent of the world's 2.5 million Jews lived at the beginning of that century. It was also a retort to the hope that civic emancipation would solve the Jewish problem. Although there were substantial differences between it and other European nationalist and imperialist movements, Zionism was a product of both of them. Several factors acted as catalysts for a tiny minority of emigrating Jews to promote the ideal of settlement in Palestine, after so many centuries of passivity: the lure of assimilation, the rise of antisemitism, the appearance of racist theories in Germany, the pogroms in Russia in 1881–82, etc. However, these alone do not account for the movement to Zion, since even in the face of persecution in different places, Jews had emigrated to other countries, but not to Palestine.

Although we have outlined aspects of both the political and religious motivation underlying the drive to establish a Jewish state, it is not at all clear how the two sources of inspiration impinged upon one another, nor is it easy to assess precisely the role which Jewish theology and appeal to the Bible played in the Zionist enterprise. In the following chapter we shall see how, rather late in the day, both Orthodox and Reform theology performed a *volte face*, and made common cause with secular, political Zionism. In this new context, appeal to the traditions of the Bible and their subsequent interpretation within Jewish theology afforded secular Zionism a theological support, which related colonialist settlement in the land with traditions much older than those of European nationalism and colonialism.

---

15 Against this view, Van Unnik (1993, posthumously) argues that diaspora Jews of the period considered their lives outside the land as a divine judgement, difficult to bear, for which the appropriate solution was return to the land. James M. Scott provides evidence to suggest that at least some diaspora Jews of the period understood themselves as living in an ongoing 'exile' which would be remedied by an eventual return to the land (1997: 185–218).

3 Zionism: from the secular to the sacred

The secular-sacred tension within Zionism, as well as in the State of Israel to this day, has deep ideological roots. Already the Herzlian dream of establishing a *Judenstaat* raised pressing questions. Would the state be the homeland of a mainly secular Jewish people, or would it be a 'Holy Land' in which the commandments of the Torah would be carried out? Was it legitimate to anticipate the divine initiative and use secular tools to establish a national homeland, against the prevailing trend within Jewish eschatology? Would not secular, political auto-redemption lead inevitably to total estrangement from the religious tradition?

From its very inception, Zionism was a secular ideology which was bitterly opposed by the religious establishment, since it was an extension into a nationalist mode of the Enlightenment spirit which threatened religious particularism. The cultural alienation of Jews was more pronounced for Herzl and his secular colleagues than it was for religious Jews, who had no identity problem, their *raison d'être* being to worship God. Since the diaspora was a condition ordained by God, who alone would bring it to an end, to describe it as a problem was to verge on the blasphemous. They cared little about the *goyim*'s assessment of them. For thoroughly secular Jews like Herzl, on the other hand, acceptance into secular society, and the aspiration for secular group identity were pressing exigencies. If secular European states could not integrate them into their polity, they might seek authentication through some form of Jewish nationalism. Paradoxically, today, religious nationalism has rekindled the fire of the jaded secular nationalism which brought the state into existence, a phenomenon recognised as the most important ideological development in the history of the state (E. Cohen 1995: 213).

I focus here on the religious component of a polyvalent discourse, recognising that each ingredient is interwoven into a complex of interactive determinants. Two recent dramatic events, above all others, highlighted the extent of the religious dimension within Israeli polity. On 25 February 1994, the feast of Purim, Dr Baruch Goldstein, a religious settler and a graduate of the most prestigious *yeshiva* (a Jewish seminary or Talmudic college) in the USA, massacred twenty-nine worshippers in the Ibrahimi Mosque in Hebron. Even advocates of the *Torah-from-Heaven* expressed shock at 'the unspeakably evil act of violence against those engaged in worship'. But what, one might ask, distinguishes Goldstein's behaviour from that presented as divinely mandated in some of the traditions of the Torah, and that which is a subject of rejoicing in the Book of Esther?

Goldstein was steeped in that book, whose legends are interwoven into the prayers for the feast:

> Blessed are you YHWH, our God, King of the universe, who takes up our grievance, judges our claim, avenges our wrong; who brings just retribution upon all enemies of our soul, and exacts vengeance for us from our foes. ... Accursed be Haman who sought to destroy me.

Moreover, clear allusions to the book occur in the stanzas of the *Krovetz* for Purim (Esther 2.17; 8.15). In the second, Saul is criticised for desecrating the word of God by allowing the Amalekite thorn to live, and thus his offspring, Haman to flourish. The twelfth stanza blesses God for the conquest of Haman. The fourteenth stanza rejoices that 'Haman's children trickled away to oblivion'. In the following stanza, we have 'The prayer of the slumbering [Patriarchs] went up from Machpelah, and through it Seir and his successors were cast down to destruction'. One wonders to what extent the Torah and the books of Joshua and Esther may have contributed to the world view of Dr Goldstein. His actions were supported by some Zionists who lean heavily on a literalist reading of the biblical text (see Prior 1994b).

Goldstein is revered as a hero-martyr within some sections of the religious-settler community, not least in his own settlement in Kiryat Arba, adjoining Hebron, which was founded by Rabbi Moshe Levinger. His burial-place in the settlement, called Kahane Park in memory of the late Rabbi Meir Kahane, has the character of both a garden of remembrance and a shrine, equipped for prayer services for pilgrims.[1] Admirers kiss his tomb, and pray over the grave of what the inscription describes as an upright martyr – a mourner explained to me that all those killed simply because they were Jews were martyrs. On the occasion of the *bar mitzvah* of Goldstein's son, Kiryat Arba's Chief Rabbi Dov Lior addressed him: 'Ya'akov Yair, follow in your father's footsteps. He was righteous and a great hero' (*Jerusalem Report* 12 December 1996, p. 10). Prime Minister Rabin reacted to the crisis only with a promise to install metal detectors to prevent arms being brought into mosques in future

By a sad irony, Rabin himself was gunned down at a Tel Aviv Peace Rally on 4 November 1995 by a religious Jew, who claimed to be acting in God's

---

1   Members of the Knesset were offered firearms for their protection after MK Ron Cohen's car was burned by right wing protesters who opposed his views, including his proposal to remove Goldstein's monument in Kiryat Arba (*Jewish Chronicle* 23 October 1998).

name, and to have derived his motivation from *halakhah*. Yigal Amir, the son of an Orthodox rabbi, was a student in the Institute for Advanced Torah Studies in Bar-Ilan University.[2] Among the books found in his room was one lauding Goldstein (*Jewish Chronicle*, 10 November 1995, p. 3). Already on the eve of Yom Kippur, just weeks before the assassination, a group of Jewish Kabbalists assembled before Rabin's house, lit black candles, blew the shofar, cursed him with the *pulsa denura* (lashes of fire), and intoned:

> And on him, Yitzhak, son of Rosa, known as Rabin, we have permission
> . . . to demand from the angels of destruction that they take a sword to
> this wicked man . . . to kill him . . . for handing over the Land of Israel
> to our enemies, the sons of Ishmael.[3]
>
> (*Jewish Chronicle*, 10 November 1995, p. 27)

Prior to Rabin's assassination, Likud leader Binyamin Netanyahu had sat on platforms at rallies at which Rabin was lampooned as a Hitler, and demonstrators had cried out *Rabin boged* ('Rabin is a traitor'). Besides, a number of American rabbis had stressed that not an inch of occupied land could be surrendered, and Rabbi Abraham Hecht of Brooklyn added that any Jewish leader doing so should be killed (Hertzberg 1996: 37). Shortly after the assassination, Hecht, President of the Rabbinical Alliance of America, an influential Orthodox group opposing the peace process, was banned from entering Israel (see *Jewish Chronicle* 3 April 1998, p. 7).

Although the activities of Goldstein and Amir evoked widespread revulsion in Israel and among Jews world-wide, there was considerable support for them within the most zealous and uncompromising wing of religious Zionism. The secular left laid the collective blame for Rabin's assassination at the feet of the religious nationalist camp.

The integration of Zionism with religion: from Orthodox to Political Messianism

Until the modern period, the predominant view among religious Jews was that the Jews were living in exile because of their sins. Eventually, in the New Age of his own making, God would restore them to their land through the Messiah, who would conquer the land, rebuild the Temple, and reconstitute a

2 Unusually, Amir was a product of both the Ultraorthodox and the national religious (Orthodox) educational systems. He attended an Ultraorthodox Agudat Yisrael-affiliated elementary school, a National Religious Party yeshiva secondary school, and the National Religious Party-affiliated Bar-Ilan University.

3 Avigdor Eskin was convicted in May 1997 of violating the Prevention of Terrorism Act by putting a curse on Rabin a month before he was assassinated.

Jewish society in *Eretz Yisrael* based on the Torah. God would grant glory to Israel, and all peoples would acknowledge his dominion, at which point there would be universal peace (see e.g. Tob 14.4–7). The predominantly secular Zionist movement was a rebellion against and a conscious repudiation of classical Judaism and its theological tenets. Nevertheless, political Zionists with some sensitivity to the religious element in Judaism could tap into the ancient symbols of the Promised Land and the Covenant, and give them a new significance, refracted through the modern conditions of the Jewish people (see Wistrich 1995: 2). Hence, Zionism could be endowed with particular religious significance, if not immediately, at least *post factum*.

The choice of the Hebrew name, Keren Kayemet L'Yisrael, for the Jewish National Fund, established at the Fifth Zionist Congress in Basle (1901), illustrates a secular manipulation of religious traditions. In the daily Morning Service of the *Siddur*, after preliminary prayers, the readings from Exodus 13.1–16 enliven the memory of the deliverance from Egypt, and invite readers and listeners to consider *themselves* to be on the journey from slavery to freedom. The Blessings for the study of the Torah and the Priestly Blessings (Num 6.24–26) follow. Then, in the second text from the Babylonian Talmud (*Shabbath 127a*), we read,

> These are the precepts whose fruits a person enjoys in This World but whose principal (fruit) remains intact for him (*ha-keren kayemet lô*) in the World to Come. They are the honour due to father and mother, acts of kindness, early attendance at the house of study morning and evening, hospitality to guests, visiting the sick, providing for a bride, escorting the dead, absorption in prayer, bringing peace between man and his fellow – and the study of Torah is equivalent to them all.

The Hebrew name for the Fund, then, evoked the foundational legend of deliverance from Egypt and entrance into the promised land. It appealed to the sacrificial spirit of Jews to make a generous offering as a gesture of thanksgiving, corresponding to the offering of 'the firstborn of *your* livestock'. While the liturgical offering was to Yahweh, the contemporary one would be to the Fund, an act of sacrifice on a par with those other commandments, which in addition to meriting returns in this life (through gathering interest), would be rewarded in the World to Come.

Nevertheless, classical religious, Messianic Zionism contrasted sharply with the political Zionism which ultimately fashioned the State of Israel. Moreover, the religious Jews who came to Palestine before the advent of Zionism did so without any political aspirations, considering all efforts to create a Jewish state to be 'sinful interference with the Messianic time-table of Almighty God' (Petuchowski 1966: 41). The pietists who made up the old Jewish settlements in Palestine were bitterly opposed to the secularists who systematically violated the Torah. The Latin Patriarch in Jerusalem, Monsignor Luigi Barlassina, reported to the Vatican in 1919 that 'atheism,

communism and immorality were rampant among recent Jewish immigrants' (in Rokach 1987: 13–14). The newcomer Zionists, for their part,
considered the pietists to be decadent parasites who were blind to the vision
of Jewish redemption. This state of affairs was to change.

Rabbi Avraham Yitzhak Kook (1865–1935)

The key figure in accommodating the ideology of secular Zionism to
classical Orthodoxy – putting the new wine of activist, secular and political
Zionism into the old bottles of Orthodox Judaism – was Rabbi Avraham
Yitzhak Kook (HaRav, or, simply Rav), the first Ashkenazi Chief Rabbi of
Palestine (1921–35). His task was formidable, since virtually the whole of
Orthodox (and Reform) Jewry was opposed to Zionism, and his tolerance of
the secularists who mocked at traditional sanctities brought abuse from
many noted rabbis (see Bokser in A.Y Kook 1979: 10). The Orthodox who
gradually supported Zionism did so after stripping it of any religious
significance, while the Ultraorthodox remained its and Rav Kook's sworn
enemies (Aran 1997: 297–98).

His teachings provided the first attempt to integrate traditional, passive
religious longing for the land with the modern, secular and aggressively
active praxis of Zionism, giving birth to a comprehensive religious-
nationalist Zionism.[4] He saw secular Zionism as an instrument of God to
further the Messianic redemption and restoration not only of Jews, but of all
humanity (A.Y. Kook 1979: 135, paragraph 3). All human history was
evolving towards divine perfection: even the secular had sparks of the sacred.
Such was the immediacy of God that everything had an outer crust with an
inner, divine essence.

On taking up his appointment as rabbi of Jaffa in 1904, much to the
annoyance of the non-Zionists of the old Yishuv, he ministered among the
mainly irreligious socialist pioneers of the second and third aliyahs. They
desecrated even the Sabbath and bade farewell to ghettoised Orthodox
Judaism. The Orthodox saw secular Zionism as so riveted to the soil that its
eyes missed the skies: 'They refuse to mention God' (in Yaron 1991: 216).
For Rav Kook, however, the divine plan depended on the totality of the
Jewish people, and not on the Orthodox alone. He was convinced that God
was leading Jews, whether secular or religious, to return to the Holy Land,
where ultimately the nation would return to its faith. The divine energy was
at its strongest in the creative pioneers of the secular Zionist revolution who,
unknowingly, were agents of God.

---

4 Many of the Rav's writings were published only after his death in 1935, and some remain
   unpublished. Bokser 1988 gives a selection in translation. See also Kook 1979: 390–92 for the list of
   publications up to that date.

In conformity with his unique Kabbalistic Messianic view – more is hidden from the eye than is seen – the 'Divinely inspired' Balfour Declaration 'mirrored the Dawn of Salvation' (Yaron 1991: 226).[5] Practical activities were inseparable from spiritual aspirations, and social activity had religious meaning: stirrings 'down below' were a necessary preamble to evoking Messianic grace 'from above' (Hertzberg 1996: 39). Whereas cultural Zionists stressed the spiritual dimension of the return, and secular Zionists the political, Rav Kook sought a synthesis, holding that the political and metaphysical dimensions would be united in a state.

His synthesis of Orthodoxy, nationalist Zionism, and the liberalism of the Enlightenment offered something for everyone. Orthodoxy had run dry, and nationalism alone would not satisfy the longings of the Jewish heart for long. Zionism was a means of realising the ancient ideal of settlement in the land, thus hastening divine redemption. Return to the real, terrestrial Jerusalem, was an immediate imperative for every Jew: *Eretz Yisrael* constituted the indispensable basis for the fulfilment of the Jewish People's Divine vocation, and no genuine Jewish life could prosper outside it. Israel's Divine genius will shine forth and illuminate the world once the entire Nation is physically and spiritually reunited with the land. Israel's re-establishment in its Homeland is a precondition of the consummation of corporate Jewish sanctity. The acquisition of land from Gentiles implemented the divinely ordained conquest of *Eretz Yisrael* (in Yaron 1991: 208–12).

While denying the ultimate coming of the Messiah, the activities of the self-professed atheistic proponents of secular Zionism speeded up his arrival. Without realising it, they were instruments in the divine plan. Religious Jewry should penetrate beyond the shell of secular atheistic nationalism into the divine spark at the core of Zionism. The spirit of God and the spirit of Israel (Jewish nationalism) were identical. The pioneers dedicated to the revival of the nation and the land, notwithstanding their desecration of the Torah, were 'righteous despite themselves' – an aphorism which continues to inspire Kook's followers in their radical behaviour (Aran 1997: 301). Such a fusion of secularism and Orthodoxy, a sacralization of the profane, evoked strong opposition. Some rabbis in Palestine ceremonially excommunicated the Zionist pioneers.

While Rav Kook's success was limited during his lifetime, his writings, and perhaps especially his founding of *Merkaz HaRav* (the Rabbi's Centre) in 1921 as a *yeshiva* for the entire Jewish People (Yaron 1991: 177–79) have been critical in the renaissance of religio-political Zionism. It was only after

---

5 He wrote to Lord Rothschild after the Balfour Declaration, and stated at a London rally after the Declaration: 'I have not come to thank the British but to congratulate them for being privileged to be the source of this Declaration to the People of Israel' (Yaron 1991: 318 note 12).

his death that the Rav was accorded glory, becoming somewhat of a cult hero and idolised spiritual guide in the 1970s after Gush Emunim claimed him as their forefather, and carried out his legacy, under the guidance of his son. Rabbi Zvi Yehuda Kook produced doctored versions of his father's writings, reducing them to collections of articles that distilled Judaism to Zionism by means of Messianism. One such collection, *Orot* (Lights) has become the 'red book' of the Gush Emunim cadres (Aran 1997: 305).

The available excerpts of Rav Kook's writings take little account of the indigenous Arab population of Palestine. In the light of developments which took place thirteen years after his death, one speculates whether Rav Kook would have been disturbed by the outrages attendant upon the partial realization of the secularist Zionist dream in 1948–49, and of the iniquities which have been perpetrated by his disciples up to the present. Perhaps, like Herzl, his death before the first beginnings of the Messianic era in 1948 saved his reputation as a mystic, a philosopher and a saint from being terminally tainted. His influence has penetrated into the core of the educational system in Israel (see Aran 1997: 325).

Despite the best efforts of Rav Kook, however, religious support for Zionism was not forthcoming. Agudat Israel, for example, formed in Germany in 1912 to preserve the strictest adherence to religious laws, was vehemently opposed to it because of its arrogating to itself the divine initiative of state-building. It has never swerved from its ideological non-Zionism, and even anti-Zionism, and with the exception of the first cabinet (which had its leader Rabbi Y.M. Levin as Minister of Social Welfare), it has never accepted cabinet office, even though it has been part of a coalition, since doing so would necessitate taking an oath of office to a secular state.

The integration of Zionism with religion: from the universalism of Reform Judaism to Jewish nationalism

If Orthodox Judaism could experience such a metamorphosis in its attitude to Zionism, the *volte face* of Reform Judaism is no less striking. Although Reform Judaism was established in Germany in the aftermath of the French Revolution and in the spirit of the Enlightenment, its intellectual leadership passed to the United States where it enjoyed spectacular success (see Plaut 1963; Plaut, ed. 1965). The movement rejected all forms of Jewish nationalism, and utterly repudiated Zionism. In highlighting the universalist values of the unity of the human family, and the ideals of liberty, equality and fraternity, it sought to wean Judaism away from its parochialist features, and insert it into the liberal spirit of the day. Whereas traditional Judaism viewed practices which required residency in Palestine (e.g. agricultural and Temple rituals) as merely in suspension, the Reform leaders regarded them as no longer valid.[6]

Viewing Jewish history as evolutionary and dynamic, and according no essential significance to any one period, Reform Judaism rejected the notion that Jews outside of Palestine were 'in exile', and insisted that Jews constituted a religious community, and not a nation. They had made their homes in and had become citizens of many states. As Gustav Pozanski put it in 1841, 'This country is our Palestine, this city our Jerusalem, this house of God, our Temple' (in Halperin 1961: 71). For the American Reformers, the majority of American Jewry in the 1880s, living among other peoples provided Jews with an opportunity of letting their light shine among the nations. American Jews were Americans of Mosaic persuasion (Greenstein 1981: 129). The establishment of a separate, Jewish state was unnecessary, and was a hindrance to Judaism's world-wide mission. The first prayerbook of the movement removed all references to Jews being in exile, and to the traditional hope that a Messiah would miraculously restore Jews to the homeland and rebuild the Temple in Jerusalem. It also eliminated all prayers for a return to Zion.

Reform Judaism's most unequivocal theological dissent from traditional Jewish eschatological soteriology was expressed in the eight-point credal proclamation by the nineteen rabbis who met in Pittsburgh, in November 1885 (the so-called Pittsburgh Platform). *Inter alia*, the Platform denied the notion of Jewish nationalism of any kind:

> We recognize in the era of universal culture of heart and intellect, the approaching realization of Israel's great Messianic hope for the establishment of the kingdom of truth, justice and peace among all men. We consider ourselves no longer a nation but a religious community. And therefore expect neither a return to Palestine, nor a sacrificial worship under the administration of the sons of Aaron, nor the restoration of any of the laws concerning the Jewish state.
>
> (paragraph 5).

The Pittsburgh Platform provided the most succinct, authoritative position of Reform Judaism. For these Jews, as for virtually all American non-synagogue-affiliated Jews, America was their nation state. Such Jews were to reject vehemently Herzl's insistence that antisemitism was endemic and incurable.

---

6 Conservative Judaism responded to the perceived excesses of both Orthodox and Reform Judaism, and opted for a middle position, in which the ancient teachings were accorded respect, while acknowledging the need for constant modification in the light of changing circumstances. It founded the Jewish Theological Seminary in the US in 1887, whose graduates became a significant base of support for Zionism (see Halperin 1961: 103).

Isaac Mayer Wise (1819–1900), the most prominent leader of the American Reform movement, strove, unsuccessfully, to unite all American Jews, traditional and reformed (see Mezvinsky 1989: 315–20). At his inspiration, delegates from thirty-four Reform congregations established the Union of American Hebrew Congregations in 1873, of which he became President. The following year, the Union established Hebrew Union College, the first Jewish seminary in the USA, and I.M. Wise became its President. He was also the President of a national organization for Reform rabbis, the Central Conference of American Rabbis, from its foundation in 1889 until he died. He wrote extensively in rejection of Jewish nationalism and in opposition to Zionism which he regarded as an anathema. He detested both its premise, that antisemitism was an absolute condition in every place wherein Jews were a minority, and its proposed solution, the establishment of a Jews-only nation state. Already in 1879, he wrote,

> The colonization of Palestine appears to us a romantic idea inspired by religious visions without foundation in reality. ... The idea of Jews returning to Palestine is not part of our creed. We rather believe it is well that the habitable become one holy land and the human family one chosen people.
>
> (*American Israelite*, 24 January 1879)

Later he argued that Israel's redemption could be achieved only by 'the final redemption of Gentiles', insisting that he strove for the equality and solidarity of all mankind (*American Israelite*, 19 March 1891, p. 4).

In response to Herzl's convening of the First Zionist Congress in 1897, the Central Conference of American Rabbis reaffirmed its earlier position, resolving that

> We totally disapprove of any attempt for the establishment of a Jewish state. Such attempts show a misunderstanding of Israel's mission which from the narrow political and national field has been expanded to the promotion among the whole human race of the broad and universalistic religion first proclaimed by the Jewish prophets. ... We affirm that the object of Judaism is not political nor national, but spiritual, and addresses itself to the continuous growth of peace, justice, and love in the human race, to a messianic time when all men will recognize that they form 'one great brotherhood' for the establishment of God's Kingdom on earth.
>
> (in Halperin 1961: 72)

In the late 1890s, I.M. Wise attacked what he called 'Ziomania', and suggested that the Herzl-Nordau scheme was as important to Judaism as 'Christian Science' was to medicine. Because that scheme was so fraught with the possibility of mischief, it was the duty of every true Jew to take an active part in efforts to destroy it (Editorial, *American Israelite*, 19 January 1899,

p. 4). He pronounced Zionism to be at best a romantic, misguided nostalgia that would brand Jews fossils and mummies:

> No normal man can believe that we Jews leave the great nations of culture, power and abundant prosperity in which we form an integral element, to form a ridiculous miniature state in dried-up Palestine. ... We can never identify ourselves with Zionism.
>
> (I.M. Wise 1899: 47)

A statement to the Peace Conference of 1919

On the wider front, the petition with 300 signatures of mostly Reform Jews, presented to President Wilson on 4 March 1919 (in Tekiner, Abed-Rabbo and Mezvinsky, eds, 1989: 341–49), for transmission to the Peace Conference at Paris, reflected the Reform position. It denounced Zionist efforts to segregate Jews as a political unit, in Palestine or elsewhere. It noted that Zionists in America constituted only some 150,000 of a Jewish population of some 3,500,000 (*American Jewish Year Book 1918*, Philadelphia). While supporting the efforts of Zionists to secure refuge in Palestine or elsewhere for Jews living in oppression, it protested against the demand for the reorganisation of the Jews as a national unit, to whom territorial sovereignty in Palestine shall be committed. This demand misinterpreted the history of the Jews, who ceased to be a nation 2,000 years ago. Zionism arose out of the conditions forced on the some six to ten million Jews in Russia and Romania, for whom the authentic solution was to secure full rights in those countries. Reform Judaism rejected any form of segregation as being 'necessarily reactionary in its tendency, undemocratic in spirit and totally contrary to the practices of free government' (in Tekiner, Abed-Rabbo and Mezvinsky, ed. 1989: 343–44). The remainder of the text consists of five objections to the segregation of Jews as a political unit (pp. 344–49).

The Peace Conference statement asserted that the overwhelming bulk of the Jews of America, England, France, Italy, Holland and Switzerland have no thought of surrendering their citizenship in order to resort to a 'Jewish homeland in Palestine' (Objection 1). Since most of the inhabitants of Palestine were non-Jews bitter and sanguinary conflicts would be inevitable, initiating a crime against the triumphs of Jewish history and the world-embracing vision of the prophets (Objection 3). The most advanced nations were composed of many races and religions. To unite Church and State as under the old Jewish hierarchy would be a leap backward of 2,000 years. Zionism's assurance of respect for the rights of other creeds and races is condescension and tolerance, rather than justice and equality. The multi-religious and multicultural nature of Palestine demands reorganisation of the country on the broadest possible basis (Objection 4).

Finally, it objected to political segregation because Jews are bound, not by national character, but by common religious beliefs, aspirations, traditions, customs, and experiences, largely of shared trials and sufferings. The emancipation of Jews is but part of a more general emancipation. Its steady progress in the West since the eighteenth century was checked by the reactionary tendencies which caused the expulsion of Poles from Eastern Prussia and the massacre of Armenians in Turkey. The solution lay in reinstituting reforms to ensure the full rights of citizenship of Jews in every land. It expressed the hope that Palestine would become a 'land of promise' for all races and creeds, safeguarded by the League of Nations, that it be constituted as a free and independent state, under a democratic government recognising no distinctions of creed or race or ethnic descent. It concluded, 'We do not wish to see Palestine, either now or at any time in the future, organised as a Jewish State' (Objection 5).

From the universalism of Reform Judaism to Jewish nationalism

Reform Judaism retained its opposition to Zionism up to the time of the Balfour Declaration and beyond. In his address at the opening session of Hebrew Union College on 14 October 1916, its President, Kaufmann Kohler – the principal author of the Pittsburgh Platform – charged that 'ignorance and irreligion are at the bottom of the whole movement of political Zionism' (*Hebrew Union College Monthly* 3 (1): 2). Although after 1917 there was an increase in the number of Hebrew Union College students who were more sympathetic to Zionism, the ethos of the college remained anti-Zionist. However, a shift towards Zionism was discernible in the 1920s, and in 1928 the College awarded an honorary degree of Doctor of Hebrew Letters to Chaim Weizmann, the then President of the World Zionist Organization. By the following year the editorial of the *Hebrew College Monthly* applauded the cultural and economic rehabilitation of Palestine, and lauded the efforts of the Jewish Agency (October 1929, 17: 4).

However, the Union of American Hebrew Congregations opposed the Zionist aim to achieve an independent Jewish state. Moreover, most members of the Central Conference of American Rabbis continued to be either non-Zionist or anti-Zionist into the 1930s. The inclusion in the *Union Hymnal* in 1930 of *Hatikvah*, the nationalist song, later to become the national anthem of the State of Israel, provoked a conflict. That the Conference voted to retain it the following year does not necessarily indicate a shift, since many saw the song as witnessing to a yearning for Zion, rather than for Zionism. However, there were signs of a gradual conversion to Zionist values, seen firstly in support for the efforts of the labour movement in Palestine.

The influx of eastern European Jews into the USA in the 1930s tilted the balance away from Reform Judaism's opposition to Zionism. The persecution of Jews under Hitler precipitated support for the Jewish Agency in rebuilding Palestine, and this was endorsed by the Union of American Hebrew Congregations. It had a corresponding effect within the Central Conference of American Rabbis. With Rabbis Stephen Wise (1874–1949) and Abba Hillel Silver (1893–1963) steadily building up support for Zionism within the Conference, there was growing agitation for a rethink on the Pittsburgh Platform.

The Central Conference of American Rabbis held a symposium (1935) to reconsider the Pittsburgh Platform. Silver launched a major assault on paragraph 5. The Conference approved a 'Neutrality Resolution', that acceptance or rejection of Zionism should be determined by individual members. However, the Conference would continue to support the economic, cultural and spiritual tasks of the Jewish community in Palestine (see Mezvinsky 1989: 324–25). Moreover, a committee of six, with David Philipson being the sole anti-Zionist, would draft a new set of 'Guiding Principles'. By the following year, a Zionist, Felix Levy was elected president, and it appeared that a number of rabbis might mobilise enough support to reverse the traditional anti-Zionist stand of the Conference. Moreover, by 1937 the student body of Hebrew Union College was sympathetic to Zionism (see Greenstein 1981: 127).

The committee presented its report at the gathering in Columbus, Ohio in 1937. It stressed that it was through its religion that the Jewish people had lived. With respect to Palestine,

> we behold the promise of renewed life for many of our brethren. We affirm the obligation of all Jewry to aid in its upbuilding as a Jewish homeland by endeavouring to make it not only a haven of refuge for the oppressed but also a centre of Jewish culture and spiritual life.

Nevertheless, the report reasserted Israel's mission to witness in the face of paganism and materialism, and Reform Judaism's commitment to universal brotherhood, justice, truth and peace on earth: 'This is our Messianic goal' (in Mezvinsky 1989: 328–29). Although the report was endorsed, with a majority of only one vote of those present, the Columbus Platform of 1937 was now replacing the Pittsburgh Platform of 1885. However, with such fragile approval of the rabbis, and widespread opposition from lay members, conflict raged for some six years, particularly spurred on by the endorsement by the Conference in 1942 of the formation of a Jewish army.

In that year, out of concern for the penetration of Zionism into Reform Judaism and most American Jewish institutions, a number of Reform rabbis, non- and anti-Zionist led by Rabbi Jouis Wolsey, founded the American Council for Judaism, the only US Jewish organisation ever formed to fight Zionism. On 23 November 1942, it elected Rabbi Elmer Berger as its Executive Director, who became the Council's brain, heart, spirit and central driving force (Kolsky 1990: 198). The following day, the USA State Department confirmed rumours of the Nazi mass extermination of Jews, which swelled support for Zionism.

The Council issued a statement on 30 August 1943, insisting that it cherished the same religious values of the dignity and equality of man, irrespective of his status, after the example of the Hebrew Prophets, who placed God and the moral law above land, race, nation, royal prerogatives and political arrangements. It abhorred the Nazi barbarism towards Jews, based on the false claim that there were racial barriers separating Jews from others. 'The Jew will rise or fall with the extension or contraction of the great liberal forces of civilization'. Strengthened in not being segregated and making exclusive demands, it wished to join with all lovers of freedom. While commending Jewish settlement in Palestine, it opposed the efforts to establish a National Jewish State in Palestine or anywhere else as a philosophy of defeatism, and one which does not offer a practical solution of the Jewish problem. It went on,

> We dissent from all those related doctrines that stress the racialism, the nationalism and the theoretical homelessness of Jews. ... Palestine is a part of Israel's heritage, as it is a part of the heritage of two other religions of the world. We look forward to the ultimate establishment of a democratic, autonomous government in Palestine, wherein Jews, Moslems and Christians shall be justly represented; every man enjoying equal rights and sharing equal responsibilities; a democratic government in which our fellow Jews shall be free Palestinians whose religion is Judaism, even as we are Americans whose religion is Judaism.
>
> (see Kolsky 1990: 203–5)

In 1943 also, the Beth Israel Congregation in Houston reinstated the anti-nationalist principles of the Pittsburgh Platform. Despite internal opposition which threatened to split it, after 1943 the Reform movement actively supported the Zionist drive to establish a Jewish state in Palestine. By the time of the biennial convention of 1946, there was a dramatic shift in numbers towards Zionism among lay and rabbinic leaders. The formation of the American Council for Judaism was the last stand of classical Reform Judaism against the rising tide of Zionism (Greenstein 1981: 128, 30).

Since the establishment of the state in 1948 the Reform movement has virtually purged Reform Judaism of its original anti-Zionism. Mezvinsky sketches the changed climate as illustrated by Julian Morgenstern, a staunch anti-Zionist, who even up to October 1943, in his opening day address as President of Hebrew Union College, declared that it would be foolish, sad and tragic for the Jewish people, which had proclaimed the message of world unity, to itself reject its message, faith and destiny and to seek for itself a salvation impossible of realization, an exploded theory of restored, racial statehood. Alumni were particularly upset by his dismissal of Jewish nationalism as being 'practically identical with Nazi and Fascist theory' (in Mezvinsky 1989: 331–32).

By 1946, however, Morgenstern had undergone a metamorphosis. While retaining his conviction that in America Jews could survive only as a religious community, he granted the validity of a section of the Jewish people becoming once again an independent and self-governing nation in the land of its fathers (in Mezvinsky 1989: 332). By 1947 he was sure that the formation of a Jewish state was inevitable and imminent, and that the vast majority of Jews supported it. The task ahead was to reach a level of harmonisation between universalism and particularism, with nationalism being the necessary expression of particularism at that time. But there were also conversions in the other direction, as instanced by Morris Lazaron, who from being a 'spiritual Zionist' became a leading anti-Zionist, and Judah Magnes who began as a Zionist, but rejected the programme to establish an exclusivist Jewish state in Palestine.

The stark differences between classical Reform Judaism and Zionism can be represented as follows:

Reform Judaism	Zionism
Jews will have equal rights in all lands, living according to universalist principles of justice and freedom	Antisemitism is an absolute human condition
Nationalism is the problem of Jewish suffering	Nationalism is the solution
Jews have a universal mission to preach the ideals of justice, brotherhood and peace	To survive, Jews must have a separate state
Ethnic differences are of little significance	Ethnic bonds unite all Jews

Clearly, Zionism was the antithesis of every principle that was sacred to the majority of early Reformers. The Pittsburgh Platform had anticipated a new world order in which Jews would enjoy equal rights and privileges, whereas Zionism insisted that Jews would be strangers everywhere 'until they could reclaim their homeland' (Greenstein 1981: 129).

The establishment of the State of Israel precipitated a major crisis for the American Council for Judaism. Despite calls for its disbandment, it determined to prevent Zionists dominating American Jewish life, and supported an impartial American foreign policy in the Middle East. It emphasised the spiritual, rather than the nationalist values of Judaism, and while it had considerable success in this matter, its philanthropic programme was no match for the United Jewish Appeal. It was unable to stop the Zionist 'juggernaut', and had to settle for being a protest group. Altogether, 'the ACJ became no more than a marginal, isolated, unpopular, and largely ignored gadfly, an irritating critic of Zionism of all shades and degrees' (Kolsky 1990: 194). Nevertheless, it persisted in its judgement that the establishment of the Jewish state was regressive, undemocratic and contrary to Jewish interests. It continued to regard Zionism as a philosophy of despair, destined to a future guided by ghetto-like self-segregation.

Ironically, despite its relegation to second-class status in Israel, the Reform movement world-wide, with notable exceptions, supports the state, even if in Orthodox eyes Reform Jews are despised. Its task now is to 'save the Jewish State from the ravages of an ultra-Orthodoxy that threatens both her democratic character and the nature of Judaism itself' (Boyden 1996: 203).

The State of Israel and far-right Zionism

The struggle between the secular and religious registered itself in the earliest days of statehood, and it did not take long for the religious parties to use their political power to obtain financial and other advantages. On 20 January 1949, the Cabinet voted that the Ministry for Religion jointly control the importation of meat, ensuring that non-kosher food not be imported. More recently (15 March 1990), the Labour alignment withdrew from the National Unity government after Shimon Peres was unable to win the support of the religious parties to form a Labour-led coalition. Instead the religious parties realigned with the right and Premier Shamir. However, religious values are not confined to the Israeli religious parties, and on some fundamental questions such as territoriality, agreement transcends party boundaries.

The extent to which the ideology of non-parliamentary groups can infiltrate the political discourse is a distinctive feature of the Israeli body politic. Its electoral system guarantees minority ideologies a greater influence than their numerical support would enjoy elsewhere. Any party or electoral list winning 1.5 per cent of the national vote gains representation in the Knesset in proportion to its vote. This has led to a proliferation of parties, most of which obtain only a few, but critical seats in the 120 member Knesset. In the May 1996 election there were twenty lists, of which eleven won seats, five winning no more than five seats. Moreover, since no political party has ever won an overall majority, all Prime Ministers have had to construct coalitions involving religious parties.[7] In May 1996 some 90 per cent of the supporters of the religious parties voted for Binyamin Netanyahu who was elected Prime Minister with the narrowest of

---

7   Parties rise and disappear quickly in the turbulent world of Israeli politics. For example, the Citizen Rights Movement, Ratz, founded in 1973 by Shulamit Aloni who broke away from Labour, joined forces with two other left-wing parties (Mapam and Shinui) in 1992 to form Meretz, which won 10 per cent of the national vote (and 12 seats in the Knesset) in 1992, and joined Labour in government. Aloni was removed from her post as education minister for her relentless opposition to the coercion of the religious parties, including Shas which also was a member of the coalition. The spiritual mentor of Shas, Rabbi Ovadiah Yosef, is reported to have said that there will be celebrations when Aloni dies.

margins. He was able to form a coalition involving the ten Members of the Knesset (MKs) of the Shas party (Shas being an acronym for Shomrei Torah Sephardim, Sephardi Guardians of the Torah), the nine of the National Religious Party (NRP), with the support of the four United Torah Judaism MKs. In the newly-formed 'rainbow coalition' of Russian professionals, Sephardi proletarians, anti-Zionist Haredim and ultra-Zionist (religious) settlers, Shas and NRP members took control of the ministries of education and culture, labour and interior, and increased their numbers on several Knesset committees.[8]

The synergy between the secular and religious authorities is particularly striking when a Likud-led coalition governs. On the Feast of Purim (24 March 1997) Premier Netanyahu paid a courtesy call to Rabbi Ovadia Yosef, the Shas spiritual mentor. Yosef presented Netanyahu with a copy of his latest book, *Meor Yisrael* (The Light of Israel), on which he inscribed a blessing, 'To my friend in soul, may he rule with a mighty hand and may all his enemies perish'. Later in the day, leading Kabbalist Rabbi Yitzhak Kadourie called on the Prime Minister, bearing gifts of a silver ornament and two inscribed parchment scrolls. He added a blessing, asking 'the Almighty to keep and protect the Prime Minister, may he live long and offer true and right leadership, defeat all his enemies and win the next elections' (*Jerusalem Post*, 25 March 1997, p. 2). In the survey which follows, I review some of the ways in which Torah values penetrate Israeli society.

The fusion of the far-right

The far right, or radical right in Israel refers to those groups which aspire to a Greater Israel, with borders extending beyond the Green Line of the 1949 armistice. While some far right groups confine their interests to the Occupied Territories, others aspire to the east bank of the Jordan, southern Lebanon and parts of Syria and Iraq also. Such groups include both religious and secular ultra-nationalist bodies, such as Gush Emunim, Tehiya, Tzomet, Morasha,

---

8   The 1996 election yielded thirty seats to Labour, thirty-two to the Likud/Gesher/Tzomet list (with twenty-three to Likud, five to Gesher and four to Tzomet), ten to Shas, nine to the NRP, nine to Meretz, seven to Israel ba-Aliya, five to the Democratic Front for Peace and Equality (DFPE), four each to United Torah Judaism, Third Way, United Arab List, and two to Moledet. The nine other parties/lists which contested the election won 3 per cent of the national vote between them, but no seats. In order to obtain a working parliamentary majority, Netanyahu formed a government with Shas and the NRP, and with Israel ba-Aliya, the Third Way, as well as with the Gesher and the militantly nationalist Tzomet factions of his own list, giving a total of sixty-two seats, and the additional four supporting votes of United Torah Judaism. The three religious parties increased their combined Knesset representation from sixteen to twenty-three. Labour, Meretz, DFPE and the United Arab List formed the main body of opposition. Israeli-Arab representation reached a new high of eleven (four DFPE, whose fifth MK is Jewish, four UAL, two Labour and one Meretz) – see Peretz and Doron 1996.

Moledet and the now illegal Kach, the most extreme in its advocacy of an overt, Torah-driven xenophobic policy of expulsion of all Arabs. Gush Emunim has been the most influential group. Expansion beyond the Green Line, of course, has been a policy of all Israeli administrations since 1967, whether Labour- or Likud-led. Nevertheless, in the world of Israeli politics, Labour's commitment to Jewish settlement in the Occupied Territories, albeit in violation of international law, does not disqualify it from its perceived left-centrist position in the political spectrum.

The ascendancy of the nationalist-religious right wing since the 1980s is one of the features of Israeli politics, with the result that what earlier were rejected as extreme nationalistic, ethnocentric, xenophobic and militaristic positions have become respectable, and, often, objects of admiration. Appeal to religion and the Torah feature prominently in such ideologies, which in many cases advocate violence and fascist activities to advance their politico-religious goal. Such groups constitute a fundamentalist belief system, with uncompromisable tenets and transcendental imperatives to political action (Lustick 1988: 6).

If the outline of a Jewish renaissance was laid down by the elder Rav Kook, it was left to his only son, Rabbi Zvi Yehuda Kook and his disciples in the *Merkaz HaRav* to carry it forward. While the elder Kook's view that the Messianic era had begun was not taken seriously in his own day, his son supported it later with a programme of Messianic political activism. Gush Emunim discovered first the son and later the father: 'The father is generally seen through the prism of the son, and the son, with the halo of the father' (Aran 1997: 295). The younger Kook emphasised the unique and holy nature of the Jewish people, and of every Jew, and saw in the rebirth of the Jewish state the first step towards the coming of the Messiah. All the institutions of the state were means to a Messianic end: the government and the army were holy, and God's agents: 'From the spiritual depths, from the most profound recesses of Torah ... comes the military aspect of the nation' (Z.Y. Kook 1991: 353, 171).

Already in the 1950s an embryonic form of what would develop into Gush Emunim had appeared when twelve students from a religious high school, rebelling against their parents and the religious establishment, determined to arrest the progressive abandonment of Orthodoxy and dedicate themselves to strict observance, and to build up the modern, independent state. Torah Judaism was to be the source of a pioneering Zionism. They called their semi-formal framework *Gahelet*, literally, 'glowing ember', but as an acronym it stood for 'core of pioneer Torah students'. In their dress, asceticism and devotion to their religious duties and studies they distinguished themselves from other Israeli youth. Their influence spread to other schools and branches of the youth organization, *B'nai Akiva*. A number of the youth met the younger Kook, and a fruitful partnership developed, with him becoming their mentor. It was through him also that the youth came to know of the Messianic mysticism of his father. As graduates of *Merkaz HaRav* in the early 1960s, these young men spread their tidings as rabbis and educators.

The 1967 War

The June War of 1967 provided the catalyst for a rejuvenated religious Zionism, and brought to public prominence a culture of eschatological Zionism which up to then had been confined to a number of *yeshivot*. It led to the founding of the Land of Israel Movement in August 1967, which proclaimed that the conquest of Arab territory was irreversible, and that Israel could embark on the absorption of more immigrants and settlement (see Sprinzak 1991: 38–43).

On the eve of Independence Day 1967, Rabbi Zvi Yehuda Kook addressed a gathering of the alumni of *Merkaz HaRav*, and bewailed the partition of historic *Eretz Yisrael*. The 1947 UN Partition Plan had cut *Eretz Yisrael*, 'the inheritance of our forefathers' into pieces, placing 'portions of our country in foreign hands', leaving him in 1947 devastated in his father's old room in Jerusalem, while Jews were dancing in the streets outside. Now in 1967, recalling that sad day, and reflecting on 'They have divided my land' (Joel 3.2), he bewailed,

> Where is our Hebron? Do we forget this? And where is our Shechem? Do we forget this? And where is our Jericho? Do we forget this too? And where is our other side of the Jordan? Where is ... each part and parcel, and four cubits of *Hashem's* land. Is it in our hands to relinquish any millimetre of this?

and answered, 'G-d forbid' (Z.Y. Kook 1991: 338–39).

When three weeks later Jerusalem, Hebron, Shechem and Jericho 'miraculously fell into our hands', and Israel was in control of a state three times the size of Israel, his disciples were sure that a genuine spirit of prophecy had come over their Rabbi on that day (Sprinzak 1985: 37–38).[9] The sermon, first published in *Hatzofeh*, the daily newspaper of the National Religious Party, some days after the end of the war, became a cornerstone of Gush Emunim.

The war signalled the revival of 'territorial maximalism', and, for those religiously inclined, a religious-national awakening. The occupation of east

---

9   Many religious Jews view the 1967 victory as a 'miracle', but are not agreed on the nature of the miracle. For some it refers to the salvation of the Jewish people, for others to the conquest of the territories. For others again, it was both. For the Lubavicher Rebbe, the late Menachem Mendel Schneerson, it was a miracle that he foresaw. The Satmar Hasidim, on the other hand, see the victory as the work of Satan. Their then Rebbe, Yoel Teitelbaum predicted that the conquest would cause the loss of much more life (Herb Keinon, 'A Miraculous Victory?', in *The Jerusalem Post*, 6 June 1997, p. 9).

Jerusalem, Hebron, Shechem and Jericho was proof that a process of divine redemption was underway, founded on the trinity of the Land, the People, and the Torah of Israel. The days of the Messiah were at hand, and his arrival could be speeded up by political action, including force. As one was to learn gradually, such views were shared by some of the most important Orthodox figures (Hertzberg 1996: 37). The ideology of the elder Rav Kook ('Kookism') provided a framework into which to integrate both the military victory and the determination to redeem the whole of *Eretz Yisrael*. The younger Rav Kook and his followers declared that there were no circumstances under which it was acceptable to sacrifice any part of the Holy Land (Aronoff 1985: 48–49). The 'liberation' of 'Judea and Samaria' ushered in the next stage of moral and spiritual redemption. Settling the newly-liberated land was a sacred duty for all Jews.

Rav Kook held that the Jews did not expel the Arabs in 1948–49. Rather, they ran away, 'whether from cowardice or exaggerated fear'. Moreover, Jewish claims to the land rest on parental inheritance, as witnessed in the Bible and history (Z.Y. Kook 1991: 196–98). Since the Holocaust symbolised the extent of the evil of the Gentiles and their deep hatred of Jews, it was all the more necessary for Jews to set up a state away from the Gentiles – thereby reinforcing some of the more xenophobic and ethnocentric traditions of the biblical narrative (e.g. Ezra 6.21; 9.1; 10.11; Neh 9.2; 10.28; 13.3).

No group was more prepared to build on what they believed God had handed them in the 1967 War than an alliance of rabbis who had come under the influence of the younger Kook in *Merkaz HaRav*. They included people who were to become household names over the next twenty years: Moshe Levinger, Haim Druckman, Eliezer Waldman, Ya'akov Ariel, Shlomo Aviner and Avraham Shapira. Most had been members of the *B'nai Akiva* youth movement, established in 1929 to promote the fusion of the pioneering ideals of secular Zionism with a commitment to Orthodox Judaism, and in the 1950s had studied in the newly established *yeshiva* high schools.

For the graduates of *Merkaz HaRav*, the biblical texts were no mere literary heritage, but constituted a living title deed. The army's conquest of Nablus evoked Yahweh's promise to Abraham (Gen 12.6–7), and every advance recalled the promise summarised in Deut 11.24, 'Every place on which you set foot shall be yours', waiting for some future time when 'Your territory shall extend from the wilderness to the Lebanon and from the River, the river Euphrates, to the Western Sea'. The capture of 'the Temple Mount' recalled Jeremiah's prophecy:

> Therefore, the days are surely coming, says Yahweh, when it shall no longer be said, 'As Yahweh lives who brought the people of Israel up out of the land of Egypt', but 'As Yahweh lives who brought out and led the offspring of the house of Israel out of the land of the north and out of all the lands where he had driven them.' Then they shall live in their own land.
>
> (Jer 23.7–8)

For Rav Kook and his disciples, the war was a turning point in the tortuous process of Messianic redemption. On its final day some of the rabbis carried their seventy-six-year-old mentor to the Western Wall, where he declared,

> We announce to all of Israel, and to all of the world that by a Divine command we have returned to our home, to our holy city. From this day forth, we shall never budge from here! We have come home!
>
> (Z.Y. Kook 1991: 375)

Since the dimensions of *Eretz Yisrael* were those of Genesis 15, rather than of pre-1967 Israel, Jews were obliged to fulfil the 'commandment of conquest', by settling in the whole land and defending Jewish sovereignty over it. Such settlement of Jews had redemptive and Messianic meaning, and would mark a Jewish renaissance. Those engaged in such a holy enterprise had souls equal to the most righteous Jew. The first settlements (Kfar Etzion, Kiryat Arba and Hebron) were founded by young rabbis from the *Merkaz HaRav*. Under their influence, the superficial nationalism that was secular Zionism was being displaced by a religious Zionism, issuing in the popular slogan, 'There is no Zionism without Judaism, and no Judaism without Zionism'.

Within a short time, this determination was to find expression in an ideology and organised strategy which shocked those Israelis who imagined that Zionism was consistent with Western liberal values. The most vociferous and aggressive advocate of the new brand of religious Zionism was the late Rabbi Meir Kahane, the son and grandson of rabbis, who was a veteran of civil disturbance in defence of Jews in the USA before he emigrated to Israel in 1971.

After the massacre of Israeli athletes in the 1972 Munich Olympic Games, Kahane announced on 21 September 1972, 'There is only one solution to Arab terror – Jewish counter-terror' (in Mergui and Simonnot 1987: 21). He founded Kach ('Thus it is') as a political party in 1972, and openly approved of the armed attacks on the West Bank Arab mayors in 1980. Kach approved of the killing of students at Hebron's Islamic University. Kahane was arrested more than a dozen times, but was never sentenced, due to lack of evidence. In 1980 he was given thirty days of administrative detention by Ezer Weizman, the then defence minister and current President of Israel. In 1984, Terror Against Terror was formed, which was suspected to be the armed wing of Kach.

For Kahane and his followers in Kach and Kahane Chai ('Kahane lives', its title after his assassination on 5 November 1990), God's Torah, rather than human democracy, is the basis of the state. Zionism and Western democracy are irreconcilable, and secular Judaism is but atheism wrapped in a prayer shawl. The Torah provides the only reason to live in the otherwise miserable and uninteresting land, which from a geographical as well as a material view-point, is an absolute disaster: God delivered the Jews from slavery in Egypt, gave them the Promised Land, and commanded Jews to live there. Jews should leave the diaspora and settle in the land, whose borders the Torah establishes: 'minimally, from El Arish, northern Sinai, including Yamit, part of the east bank of the Jordan, part of Lebanon and certain parts of Syria, and part of Iraq, to the Tigris river' (in Mergui and Simonnot 1987: 38–40, 54–55).

Kahane considered it to be God's desire that Jews live separately and have the least possible contact with what is foreign, in order to create a pure Jewish culture based on the Torah. In line with 'Kookism', he held that Zionism accelerated the coming of the Messiah, and that the creation of the state marked the beginning of the Messianic era. Such considerations overrode any concern for the indigenes. Arabs should be deported, with as little force as necessary. They have no right to be in Jerusalem, and Kahane would applaud anyone who blew up the two mosques on 'the Temple Mount' (Mergui and Simonnot 1987: 43–48, 85–86). Kahane claimed that all the rabbis supported the expulsion of the Arabs just as clearly, but only in private.

Throughout the 1970s until his assassination, Kahane was the most aggressive advocate of Jewish settlement of the land (see Friedman 1990; 1992; Sprinzak 1991). While his ideology was offensive to people who respect democracy, it was consistent with the divine mandate of the Torah, interpreted in a literalist fashion, which not only sanctions the expulsion of the indigenous population, but requires it as a commandment. He was elected to the Knesset in July 1984.

Rabbi Ben Yosef, formerly Baruch Greene who came on aliyah from New York in 1976, was the Kach candidate for mayor of Jerusalem in 1993. His Torah-observance demanded a totally Jewish Jerusalem, with no mosques or churches (idol worship), no *goyim* living there, and with borders constantly expanding, until Damascus (in Steve Leibowitz, *In Jerusalem, Jerusalem Post* 30 July 1993). Kahane's association of the State of Israel with the events of the Messianic end-time resonated sympathetically with the increasingly popular teleology of the religious-ultranationalist camp. His brazenly violent methods and offensive language confounded the political establishment. Kach was banned from the elections in 1988, and found its place on the 'lunatic' fringe of Israeli society. There were more subtle, and less embarrassing ways of arriving at a similar goal.

Gush Emunim

The Yom Kippur War of 1973 was even more decisive in the development of Jewish settlement. Seeing the war in terms of the Messianic process of redemption Rabbi Yehuda Amital emphasised the need to enlarge the Jewish presence in *Eretz Yisrael*, lest the gains of 1967 be frittered away. Early sporadic settlement was followed by the founding in February 1974 of Gush Emunim (Bloc of the Faithful) as an extra-parliamentary movement by former students of *Merkaz HaRav*. Already some three months after the war, the first steps had been taken to establish a settlement, Elon Moreh, near

Nablus. With the support of Rabbi Levinger, a group planted itself at a railroad depot, converting it into a makeshift *yeshiva*. In April 1975, Levinger led a march of 20,000 Jews into 'Samaria', and after protracted negotiations, the Labour-led government agreed to accommodate thirty of the settlers in a nearby army camp. The enterprise followed a pattern that was to be typical of the Gush's policy of *fait accompli*. Firstly, settlers established maximalist 'facts on the ground' illegally. Then they negotiated with the authorities, arriving at a compromise of a withdrawal from the maximalist position. Thus at a stroke, an 'illegal' settlement was legitimised, and afterwards received the government's blessing and financial support.

Frequently army outposts were established in the territories and later were transformed into civilian settlements with a zeal reminiscent of the pioneering days of the kibbutz movement. Settlement was facilitated by the arrangement (*hesder*) whereby religious Jews could continue their *yeshiva* studies while serving in the army. By the 1980s, many graduates of the *hesder yeshiva* system had joined the officer corps and the élite units of the army, and considered themselves to be the true heirs of Zionism (Heilman 1997: 336).

From the beginning, Gush Emunim was a professional, well-funded and influential organisation, whose membership came from the extreme right, the right and even the left. It was guided by the teachings of the late Rav Kook and those of his son, Rabbi Zvi Yehuda Kook, who became its major spiritual leader until his death in 1982. While it focused on settlement of Jews in the Occupied Territories the Gush saw itself as an agent for the general renewal of Zionism. After the establishment of the state Israeli Jews had settled for a materialistic society in which the individual's pleasure replaced the national goal and mission. The Gush determined to advance the process of national redemption as mandated by the Torah, and highlighted by 'Kookism'. Every Jew was obliged to play a part in the settlement of 'Judea and Samaria' which the Gush saw as a critical element in the process of Messianic redemption. According to Hanan Porat, its director of settlement activities, 'Working in a settlement is a spiritual uplift, an antidote to the materialism and permissiveness which have swept the country'. He added that the leadership of Israel had passed from the secular to the national-religious camp (Mergui and Simonnot 1987: 126–27).

The Gush injected a strong political and violent element into religious Zionism. From the beginning it was led by Rabbi Levinger, who having completed his army service in 1957 enrolled at *Merkaz HaRav*, then under the direction of Rabbi Zvi Yehuda Kook. At Passover in 1968, Levinger led a small group to the Park Hotel in Hebron for the celebration. They did not leave, despite the efforts of Prime Minister Levi Eshkol's Labour-led government. Two years later, Levinger, together with Rabbi Eliezer Waldman, was able to utilise splits within the government to establish a larger settlement in Kiryat Arba, adjoining Hebron, which housed over 5,000 people by 1972, and gained government listing as a rural settlement. It became a hotbed of colonising rabbis who spread their roots throughout the West Bank and the Golan Heights. Furthermore, at three o'clock on a March morning 1979, Levinger's wife, Miriam, led the occupation of *Beit Hadassah*, a property in the heart of Hebron, which became the nucleus of the some 400 Jews now living in fortress-like conditions among some 150,000 Palestinians.

In general, relations between the Gush and the different Israeli governments have been cordial. Indeed, a photograph at a celebration of the tenth anniversary of the settlement in Hebron shows Rabbi Kook flanked by Prime Minister Begin and Levinger, much admired by Begin (reproduced in Z.Y. Kook 1991: 376–77). However, when the Begin government was preparing to withdraw from Sinai in fulfilment of the Camp David Agreement, Kook wrote, 'All our generations protest … against the treachery of the present government' (1991: 357). To this day, Levinger and his followers pursue their goal, with distinctively knitted skull-caps, prayer books and machine-guns. Their appearance on television with guns ablaze in Hebron witnesses to a Torah-observance reminiscent of the Joshua narrative. Indeed, one armed religious settler assured me that his group were carrying on where Joshua left off. Levinger himself was jailed for ten weeks for the 'criminally negligent homicide' of a Hebron Palestinian in September 1988.

Because of its political independence, the Gush has influenced all governments. While the first settlements were set up by the Labour-led government, the rise to power of the Likud-led government of Menachem Begin in 1977 – an earthquake in Israeli politics, when the pariahs of Zionism had replaced the party that built the nation (Friedman 1992: 20) – gave the expansionist movement a legitimacy at the highest levels, and brought an end to the cautious settlement policy of the Labour-led administration (Sprinzak 1991: 71–105). The scene was set for a marriage of convenience between the proponents of secular, Jabotinsky-inspired expansionism and the militant, Messianic settler crusaders of Gush Emunim. While the Labour-led administration had built sparingly in the Occupied Territories, Likud was determined to absorb the Territories into Israel.

For Levinger settling 'Judea and Samaria', which prepared the way for the Messiah, was as sacred a duty as observing the Sabbath. The dozens of Torah communities which began to appear on the hills of 'Judea and Samaria' grew out of his insistence that the settlement was a straightforward commandant of the Torah. The members of the 'neo-orthodox' settlement investigated by Nevo in 1983 lived by their religiosity, their purpose deriving from their belief system of which the settlement was part fulfilment. Religiosity affected all aspects of life. The Bible 'provides the only serious justification for all their acts as a community, most specifically those biblical quotations which are seen as constituting their "title deeds" to the site' (Nevo 1985: 222, 240). But not all settlements were the fruit of religious motivation.

The Gush determined to settle a million Jews in the West Bank before the turn of the millennium, making territorial compromise impossible, and ensuring the eventual annexation of the territories. Having failed to get much support initially for aliyah from abroad, it encouraged Israeli Jews to settle in the Golan, the West Bank and Gaza, with full government approval. In Levinger's estimation, the Camp David Accords infected Zionism with 'the virus of peace', but despite his rearguard action in 1982, Yamit became the first Jewish settlement voluntarily dismantled by the Israeli government (Heilman 1997: 341). Rabbi Yvi Yehuda Kook died the same year, and being childless, left no obvious heir to the charismatic dynasty. However, yet more of his spiritual children occupied prominent positions in the settlement community.

While the ideological exhortation to settle in the West Bank might fall on the deaf ears of many Jews, the financial inducements were such as to make refusal to do so border on lunacy. A family buying a home in the West Bank in 1991 could take out a mortgage of US $71,000, of which all but $17,500 was interest-free, with interest of only 4.5 per cent on the $17,500. Moreover, after five years, $10,000 of the mortgage became a gift. In addition, the government provided free sewage, water and electrical lines, estimated to be worth a further $15,000, and from November 1990, Housing Minister Ariel Sharon gave free housing plots to Jewish settlers, who previously had to buy them from the Land and Development Authority which was responsible for the land confiscated from Palestinians. Between January 1988 and June 1991, more than 504,120 dunums had been confiscated on the West Bank (Friedman 1992: 79). It is estimated that in excess of 50 per cent of the settlers are secular, and in some settlements the percentage is much more (for example, some 85 per cent in Ariel). While the 'economic' settlers do not match the zeal of the eschatology-driven religious settlers who see themselves as doing God's work, nor that of the chauvinistic nationalistic secular settlers, the financial imperatives infusing them give them a real stake in the settlement enterprise. However, in the event of a Palestinian state being established, only 15 per cent of the settlers said they would stay under Palestinian sovereignty.[10]

Considering the land to belong to the Jews by Divine command the Gush cares little about the indigenous population, whose human rights are no match for the divine imperative: national self-determination for the Palestinians is meaningless since the universal principle of self-determination does not hold in the case of *Eretz Yisrael*. The Palestinians are illegitimate tenants and a threat to the redemptive process. They have three choices: to acknowledge the legitimacy of the Gush's version of Zionism and receive full civil rights; or, to obey the laws of the state without formal

10 The result of a survey of settlers in the West Bank, undertaken jointly by the Nablus-based Centre for Palestine Research and Studies and Bar-Ilan University's Begin-Sadat Centre for Strategic Studies, was published in January 1996, and is discussed in Isabel Kershner's, 'The Settlers Can Stay', in *The Jerusalem Report*, 7 March 1996, pp. 24–26.

recognition of Zionism, and be granted the full rights of resident aliens; or, to be granted incentives to emigrate to other Arab countries. In many instances, the inducements include force (see Friedman 1992: 81–86). Armed with the inerrant certainty of the Torah, which not only justifies violence, but gives the divine mandate for it, and driven on by the glorious example of Joshua, the Gush pursues its policy of settling. After the Arabs have learned that the land is Jewish, friendly relations may obtain. Rabbi Kook believed that conflict with the Arabs, a pure, monotheistic people, unlike the idolatrous Christians, was temporary. In any case, the Israeli army was strong enough to conquer 'Judaism's foes' (in Friedman 1992: 119).

The ideology of the Gush is only the tip of an iceberg of a broader religious subculture, which started its meteoric development in the 1950s (Sprinzak 1985: 27). It redefined in religious terms some of the pioneering values of secular Zionism at a time when it had lost much of its vision. Settlement was a natural complement to Torah, and each new settlement was a witness to God's choice of the People of Israel, to the truth of Torah, and to the word of God and his prophets: "This land that was desolate has become like the garden of Eden; and the waste and desolate and ruined towns are now inhabited and fortified", all the work of God (Ezek 36.34–36; see Z.Y. Kook 1991: 351–52).

Sacred and secular

The sacralization of Zionism by the Gush was matched on the secular side by a new pioneering spirit with which it was able to make common cause. Professor Yuval Neeman and Geula Cohen founded the Tehiya ('Renaissance') party in 1979, following Begin's 'treason' at Camp David. Tehiya's policy required the annexation of the Occupied Territories, to be made irreversible by increasing the number of Jewish settlements: the Arabs would forget 'Judea and Samaria', as they had forgotten Galilee.

Members of Gush and of the Land of Israel Movement joined, and Rav Kook gave his blessing. Although an atheist, Neeman defends the spiritual heritage of the Jewish people, and is in constant dialogue with the ultranationalist religious groupings. Tehiya saw itself as a bridge in the 'Kookist' spirit between religious and secular Jews, reflected in the participation of both Raphael Eitan, Israeli army Chief-of-Staff (1978–83) and *Merkaz HaRav* graduate, Rabbi Eliezer Waldman. Eitan joined Tehiya with his Tzomet ('Crossroads') group and announced his platform to annexe the territories, and deal firmly with recalcitrant Arabs. 'It is not for us to solve the Palestinian problem. There are 100 million Arabs; the Saudis have a $130 billion surplus; let them solve it' (quoted in Mergui and Simonnot 1987: 113). Eitan was elected to the Knesset in July 1984.

During this period an underground movement of Jewish radicals, the Machteret, surfaced. This loose federation of religious and ultranationalist secular activists considered war against their enemies as obligatory. They attacked the Islamic College in Hebron, blew up the cars of mayors in the

Occupied Territories, held that the Haram el-Sharif ('the Temple Mount' for Jews) must be wrested from the Muslims, that the Arabs must be expelled and democracy abandoned: 'The Holy One, blessed be He, expects us to act, that we bring the Redemption with our own hands' (in Heilman 1997: 343).

The orthodox purity and learned interpretation of the Scriptures of the religious element of this underground group, and the support they gained from prominent rabbis (e.g. Dov Lior, Eliezer Waldman) gave them considerable weight among the Israeli right (see Sprinzak 1991: 252–88). Rabbi Levinger is reported to have said that he would not have tried to prevent the Machteret from blowing up the Haram el-Sharif, and wished he had the honour of killing an Arab (Heilman 1997: 345). Its home-grown advocacy of Jewish terrorism shocked the Israeli establishment which, overlooking its own noble tradition of terrorism in pre-state days and the many examples of state-sponsored terrorism since, had come to denounce it as a peculiarly Arab barbarism. Within twelve years, the movement which began with Torah-driven, but illegal settlement in 'Judea and Samaria' promoted even indiscriminate terrorism. However offensive to Western liberalism, such a transformation was in line with fidelity to a particular reading of the biblical land traditions, and consistent with the culture of Zionist terrorism which preceded the establishment of the state.

Within the sphere of more conventional Israeli politics, Rabbi Eliezer Waldman, a disciple of Rabbi Zvi Yehuda Kook in *Merkaz HaRav*, was re-elected to the Knesset in July 1984, and became the religious figurehead of Tehiya. Fearing a polarization in Israeli society between religious and secular groupings, he justified belonging to the profane Tehiya by insisting on its Zionist ideals and pioneer spirit (in Mergui and Simonnot 1987: 115). Not an inch of the Promised Land should be ceded. 'In 1967, God gave us a unique opportunity. But the Israelis did not seize it. They did not colonise the newly conquered land' (in Mergui and Simonnot 1987: 114). Eitan split from Tehiya in 1987 and re-established Tzomet which won two seats in the 1988 election, and four seats in the 1996 election, after which Eitan was rewarded for his alignment with Likud by being made Minister of Agriculture and Environment Quality in the Netanyahu government.

Another indication of the movement to the right in the religious camp is provided by Rabbi Haim Druckman. As a senior Gush activist and a disciple of Rabbi Yehuda Kook, he was elevated to number two on the NRP list for the 1977 elections, and was elected to the Knesset. He became disillusioned with the party's attitudes towards Greater Israel, and in 1981 was re-elected under the banner of his own party, Matzad. Before the 1984 elections Matzad joined with Poalei Agudat Israel (a religious, working-class party) to form Morasha (Tradition), which won two seats in the Knesset. For Druckman Zionism is as integral a part of the Torah as is the Sabbath (in Mergui and Simonnot 1987: 167). He subsequently dissolved Morasha and rejoined the NRP, having ensured that it would allow Gush Emunim people into all echelons of the party.

In 1978, Rabbi Shlomo Aviner, also a graduate of *Merkaz HaRav*, helped to set up a *yeshiva* in the Muslim quarter of the Old City of Jerusalem, called Ateret Cohanim ('Crown of Priests'), devoted to preparing the way for the rebuilding of the Third Temple, and the advent of the Messiah. Matityahu Dan, also a disciple of Rav Kook, set up the *yeshiva*, believing that the Gush Emunim holy settlement crusade should be carried into East Jerusalem also. Kook encouraged Dan to devote himself to matters of how the Third Temple should function.[11] In 1982, some of the *yeshiva* students began to tunnel under the Haram in search of the gold vessels King Solomon is thought to have hidden there. A riot ensued, and the tunnel was closed.

Anticipating the arrival of the Messiah by making plans for the rebuilding of the Temple is a feature of the 'Temple Mount and *Eretz Yisrael* Faithful Movement' also. It sees a one-to-one correspondence between biblical prophecy and today's situation: 'Take care not to make a covenant with the inhabitants of the land to which you are going, or it will become a snare among you' (Exod 34.12), 'for the uncircumcised and the unclean shall enter you, O Jerusalem, the holy city, no more' (Isa 52.1) is sufficient to rule out any 'anti-godly' agreements with non-Jews, whether concerning the Golan or Jerusalem. Such agreements will precipitate the end-time war of Gog and Magog (*The Voice of the Temple Mount*, a pamphlet/newsletter, Autumn 1995, pp. 1–2). A separate movement, The Movement for the Preparation of the Temple, also, is active in promoting the restoration of its worship ('Visionaries Prepare for Third Temple', *Jewish Chronicle* 31 July 1998, p. 21).

Embarking on a scheme to replace the Arab population of East Jerusalem with Jews, Ateret obtained support from the highest sources of state and synagogue. In 1984, the Ashkenazi Chief Rabbi of Israel, Avraham Chana Shapira, appealed for funds for Ateret to assist it in its 'sacred burden … and restore the light of the Torah to within the Old City of Jerusalem' (in Friedman 1992: 99). It purchased a property in East Jerusalem in 1987 into which Ariel Sharon (currently Foreign Minister) moved, and over which he had erected a huge menorah, and from which draped the Israeli flag. In 1990, Ateret placed some of its students in St John's Hospice which it had

---

11 Soon after 1967, Gershon Solomon founded the 'Temple Mount Faithful' to remove all semblance of Muslim presence on the Haram, and rebuild the Temple. Virtually every year, at Sukkoth, its members clash with the Israeli authorities in their attempt to establish a Jewish presence on the Haram. They hope to do this in stages: firstly, by gaining the right to pray there; then, by building a synagogue; then by having the Muslim shrines demolished; and, finally, erecting the Third Temple. They were refused police permission in 1989 to raise a three-ton cornerstone to the Haram, to become the cornerstone of the Third Temple, and were largely responsible for the disturbances which precipitated the massacre of seventeen Palestinians on the Haram on 8 October 1990. The 'Temple Mount Faithful' enjoys the support of fundamentalist Evangelical Christians in the USA. For a discussion of *Ateret Cohanim* and 'Temple Mount Faithful' see Carmesund 1992.

taken over, and renamed it *Neot David* ('Oasis of David'), and the following year attempted to settle more of its students in Arab houses in Silwan, the site of David's city.[12] Aviner became chairman of the rabbinical council in the Occupied Territories and rabbi of the Bet-El settlement, as well as continuing to head Ateret Cohanim. By June 1998 Ateret's properties in the Muslim and Christian Quarters of the Old City had exceeded fifty, into which it had moved more than sixty-five Jewish families. It proposes also to build a block of flats and a school in the Muslim Quarter, where it erected seven tin sheds in May 1998, which were later demolished by the Israeli authorities. The organisation is partly funded by Irving Moskowitz, the American Jewish bingo magnate.

Since 1985 Rehavam Ze'evi, a retired major general, proposed the negotiated 'transfer' of all the Arabs in the Occupied Territories to the neighbouring Arab countries, and founded Moledet ('Homeland') with 'transfer' the sole plank of its platform. Together with Professor Yair Sprinzak he was elected to the Knesset in the 1988 election. Ze'evi's slogan, 'We are here, they are there, and peace for Israel!' enjoyed tremendous appeal. His literature demonstrates the central role of 'transfer' in Zionist ideology and praxis, and berates the hypocrisy of the centre-left establishment which, from the high moral ground of their kibbutzim founded on former Arab soil, accused him of racism and Kahanism. Moledet retained its two seats in the 1996 elections.

Throughout the period of the expansion of settlements, the rabbis of the Gush, in seeking to discover the will of God, looked to Rav Kook above all to provide *da'at Torah*, the wisdom to determine God's will on matters on which the Torah appeared to be silent. Their major concern were God's intentions for the territories of 'Judea', 'Samaria' and Gaza (*Yesha*, in its Hebrew acronym, a term also translated as 'salvation').[13] Kook issued the

---

12 The property of the Greek Orthodox Church, the St John's Hospice had been leased since 1932 to an Armenian, Martyros Matossian, who, on 28 June 1989 sublet it to a Panamian company, SBC Ltd, for $3.5 million. The company turned it over to Jewish settlers and, having waited ten months, some 150 armed settlers affiliated with the Ateret moved into its seventy rooms during Holy Week 1990, over which they erected a Star of David. The move provoked widespread protest, including the voluntary closure of the Holy Sepulchre. Prime Minister Shamir denied any governmental complicity, but David Levy, the then Housing Minister confirmed that $1.8 million had been channelled covertly by his ministry to a subsidiary of the Jewish National Fund which made the payment to SBC Ltd. Indeed, the ministry had helped *Ateret* in its purchases since 1986 at least. An Israeli court upheld the Church's charge that the subleasing was illegal, but allowed twenty 'security and maintenance employees' to remain in the building, pending litigation. The 'employees' are *Ateret* settlers, who are living in the hospice with their families. The American Friends of *Ateret Cohanim* was established as a charitable, tax-exempt foundation in New York State. Binyamin Netanyahu, the then Israeli ambassador to the UN was the keynote speaker at its inaugural annual dinner at the Hilton Hotel in Manhattan in 1987 and again in 1988. The keynote speaker at its 1989 fund-raising dinner, which raised some $2.25 million, was Ariel Sharon.

13 'Yesha is Here' became a bumper slogan used by the settlers later. In addition to proclaiming the Occupied Territories to be integral to Israel, it declared that (messianic) salvation was at hand through the activity of settlement.

da'at Torah which had the character of a doctrinal statement which guided all subsequent settlement activity:

> All this land is assuredly ours, everyone of us, and it is not permissible to give it to others. ... Therefore, once and for all let it be clear and resolved that there is no question here of any Arab territories or Arab lands, but lands of Israel, the eternal settlements of our forefathers ... and we shall never leave them or be cut off from them.
>
> (in Heilman 1997: 340)

Orthodox Rabbis

Nearly all the religious parties, and the overwhelming majority of Orthodox rabbis in Israel, have denounced the 'peace process'. In the midst of the prolonged *halakhic* debates on whether one may or may not cede Jewish land (i.e. land taken from the Arabs) to non-Jews, consideration of the human rights of non-Jews is seldom invoked. Some of the most vociferous and extreme opponents of 'territorial compromise' come from the Orthodox religious camp.

Fearing that the new, Labour-led government of Yitzhak Rabin (1992) might compromise with the PLO, and disengage from parts of the Occupied Territories, the rabbis of the religious settler community formed 'The Union of Rabbis for the People and Land of Israel', with a presidium which included rabbis Aviner, Druckman, Melamed, Levinger, Lior and Waldman. The Union issued the following rabbinic judgement:

> According to Torah law, it is a positive commandment to move to the Land of Israel, to settle there, to conquer it and to take possession of it. ... Any directive to cancel out Jewish settlements in the land of Israel is both a sin and bad counsel, and this is the Rabbinic opinion, of Rabbis in the Land of Israel and in the United States, against the Oslo accords.
>
> (in Heilman 1997: 347)

Ironically, Orthodox Jewry had earlier designated Zionism 'bad counsel'.

The Union presented its opposition to the Oslo Accords as a *pikuach nefesh* ('threat to life'), a principle of Jewish law which abrogated many others. In a 1994 address to the Union, former Ashkenazi Chief Rabbi Avraham Shapira argued that it was sinful to relinquish land given by God to Jews. The successor of Rabbi Zvi Yehuda Kook as head of the *Merkaz HaRav*, Shapira deviated fundamentally from the Kooks who had insisted that the secular leaders of Zionism were acting on behalf of God. The secular leaders, now, were 'bad counsellors', 'traitors', etc. He went on,

> There are Jews that agree to the goyim's claim that we are thieves. ... Unfortunately, many of these Jews are part of the government. ... They

don't believe in the Tenach and claim that the book of Joshua which describes how Joshua conquered Eretz Yisrael, should be expunged from the Tenach that is taught in the schools ... [In contrast we are] observant God fearing Jews that keep the whole Torah, oral and written, from beginning to end. We are willing to sacrifice our lives for every single Jewish custom. Thus we cannot agree to forgo even one square inch of our holy land.

(in Heilman 1997: 349)

At its meeting of 11 November 1993, a couple of months after the Oslo Declaration of Principles, the Union of Rabbis issued a binding rabbinic judgement based on *halakhah*, that,

According to the laws of the Torah, it is forbidden to relinquish the political rights of sovereignty and national ownership over any part of historic Eretz Yisrael to another authority or people. All of historic Eretz Yisrael which is now in our possession belongs to the entire Jewish people past, present and future, and therefore no one in any generation can give away that to which he does not have title. Therefore any agreement to do so is null and void, obligates no one, has no legal or moral force whatsoever.

(in Heilman 1997: 350–51)

The Union supported the continuation of protests, demonstrations and strikes within the framework of the law, to educate the masses about the falseness of this 'peace', and prevent the government from carrying out damaging policies (in Heilman 1997: 351). The Rabin government saw in the statement a clarion-call to insurrection.

Rabbi Schlomo Goren (1917–94), Rabbi Shapira's predecessor as Ashkenazi Chief Rabbi (1973–83) also typified the fusion of Orthodoxy and politics, calling on soldiers to disobey any orders they might receive to dismantle Jewish settlements. Already in 1967, Chief army chaplain Goren wrote to General Uzi Narkiss, requesting permission to use the heat of battle as a screen to blow up the Dome of the Rock and the Al-Aqsa mosque on the 'Temple Mount', on which he later promised to build a synagogue (Friedman 1992: 125–26). He had leaflets distributed to synagogues throughout the Occupied Territories on 18 December 1993 reiterating that Jews had a God-given right to the biblical land of Israel. Denying that he was inciting rebellion, he justified his action:

Any other orders contradictory to the orders of Moses [are] a rebellion against Moses, against the Torah, against Judaism. There does not exist any kind of rebellion if the refusal is based on obeying the laws of Moses.

(Derek Brown, *Guardian*, 20 December 1993)

He wrote that Yasser Arafat deserved death (from David Landau's Obituary of Rabbi Goren, *Guardian* 22 November 1994).

The Union of Rabbis contended in May 1994 that the government–PLO agreements were creating an atmosphere of civil war, and called for protests against 'the criminal act of signing this agreement'. In July 1995, the most definitive rabbinic ruling, handed down by Rabbi Shapira and fourteen of his associates on the executive, decreed that 'there was a prohibition from the Torah to evacuate [army] camps and transfer the location into the authority of Gentiles'. This call to soldiers to disobey the orders of the state brought an immediate response from President Weizman, who said that the ruling could invalidate the foundations of the state. Clearly these rabbis had gone beyond the 'Kookist' doctrine that the army and the government were holy instruments of God's will.

Debate raged in religious settler circles, including Ramat Gan's Bar Ilan University, as to whether Rabin was a *rodef* (one who puts the life of a Jew in danger, and who may legitimately be killed), or a *moyser* (one who hands Jews over to their enemies, and must be punished). Ya'akov Ariel, chief rabbi of Ramat Gan, concluded that Rabin was an 'indirect *rodef*', whom it was permissible to hurt, if doing so prevented danger. However, he judged that it would not (*Hatzofeh*, 31 December 1993). Rabin's killer, Yigal Amir, former student at the *hesder yeshiva* in Kerem Beyavneh, army veteran, and student at Bar Ilan, professed that the law permitted him to kill the Prime Minister. He sat through his trial with an eerie calm self-confidence, and a self-satisfied grin that perplexed most television viewers. Amir's action was doubly reprehensible in that it involved a Jew killing another Jew: 'It was so abhorrent, so unbelievable, so much against our ethos, our tradition and our values. ... ' (Raviv 1998: 257). However, there were precedents for Jew slaying Jew, in the late biblical period,[14] the pre-state period,[15] and after the foundation of the state.[16]

---

14 Matthatias slaughtered a Jew offering sacrifice on the altar in Modein (1 Macc 2.23–24).

15 After the Sixth Zionist Congress (1903) voted in favour of accepting the offer of Uganda, a Russian Jewish student fired two pistol shots at Max Nordau, exclaiming, 'Death to Nordau, the East African' (Gilbert 1998: 22). Other murders of Jews by Jews followed. On 24 June 1924, the Haganah murdered Israel de Haan, the ultra-Orthodox leader, who was about to persuade the British government that the Orthodox Jewish community in Palestine should not be under the authority of the secular Jewish institutions of the Jewish National Council. Moreover, Chaim Arlosoroff, the Mapai leader in Palestine, whose proposed deal with the Nazis led the Revisionists to portray him as a collaborator, was murdered on 16 June 1933 – three Revisionist suspects were acquitted of the assassination. Again, during the underground struggle against the British, the Irgun and Stern Gang killed suspected Jewish informers. Also, on 25 November 1940, the Haganah sank the *Patria* off Haifa, as it was preparing to receive the transfer of illegal immigrants, drowning more than 250 Jewish refugees.

16 On 20 June 1948, Ben-Gurion ordered the confiscation of an assignment of weapons destined for the Irgun, from the ship *Altalena*. In the ensuing exchange of fire two Israeli soldiers and six Irgunists

Speculation was rife that, despite his statement to the contrary, the assassin had not acted alone. There was 'moral complicity' in the murder, or, as Rabin's widow claims, at least an 'intellectual conspiracy' (L. Rabin 1997).[17] Moreover, people wondered which rabbi had given Amir the green light: a headline in *Yediot Aharonot* (17 November 1995) read, 'Provide for yourself a rabbi and acquire for yourself a gun,' satirising a well-known Talmudic adage (in Heilman 1997: 355). Moreover, Muli Peleg argues that there was a direct connection between the ideology and practices of Gush Emunim and the murder of the Premier (Peleg 1997), while Michael Karpin contends that there was a formal connection between the leadership of the right wing in the Knesset, the *Yesha* council of settlers, and an alliance of extremists who explicitly preached hatred, anti-Arab racism and violence.[18]

In December 1995, The Union of Rabbis issued another reminder that withdrawal from the Occupied Territories was a sin, and placed the Jewish people in mortal danger (*pikuach nefesh*). Opposition between the rabbis and the state grew, to a point where just before his death in December 1995,

continued: were killed. The boat sailed southward towards Tel Aviv, where Menachem Begin boarded it the following morning, broadcasting from the ship that army snipers had been given orders to assassinate him. Ben-Gurion demanded that the arms be turned over to the officials of the state. The Irgunists on board opened fire on the troops on the beach, who returned it, setting the ship ablaze. Most of those on board swam ashore, but among the forty Irgunists killed was one who had been charged with the murder of Arlosoroff (Gilbert 1998: 211–12). There was a real prospect of an inter-Jewish war between the State and the Irgunists before the Irgun capitulated on 20 September 1948. In 1957, three right-wing Israelis murdered government official Rudolph Kastner, accused of collaboration with the Nazis in war-time Hungary – the first assassination of a Jew by a Jew in the history of the state – and in 1982, Yohan Avrushmi threw a grenade into a Peace Now rally, killing Emil Grunweig.

17 Margalit Har-Shefi, a Bar-Ilan student and friend of Amir, was convicted in June 1998 of failing to inform the police of Amir's murderous intentions. He had boasted to her that he would murder Rabin to stop the 'peace process' and the 'handing over' of land to the Palestinians. She was acquitted of a second charge of aiding and abetting him to obtain arms illegally.

18 Karpin presented his case in a 60-minute film ('The Road to Rabin Square') on Israeli Channel 2's *Fact* programme on 13 May 1997. It included footage of demonstrators chanting 'Rabin is a traitor, a murderer', with Netanyahu, Sharon and others rousing the crowd, and portrayals of Rabin in the uniform of an SS officer and as a dog, and footage of demonstrators leaping up and down shouting, 'Death to Rabin', and burning posters reading 'The Traitor', with a bullseye over his face. Netanyahu is shown pausing in his speech at one Jerusalem rally, while the chant, 'Rabin is a traitor' grew louder. Karpin submits that the current Israeli Justice Minister, Tzahi Hanegbi was the Likud's operations officer against Rabin, who made links with religious and other extremists. He submits that Netanyahu and MKs Michael Eitan of Likud and Hanan Porat of the NRP – both of whom express regret and accept a share of responsibility for not ousting extremists from the protest camp – sat on the Knesset's right-wing political directorate. After his visit to Yigal Amir's parents, Karpin shows his mother saying that 'Gali was just the messenger' of God's will, and using *gematria* to argue that a passage in the book of Job foretells the advent of Hamas, Islamic Jihad, and the leftist parties of Labour, Meretz and Rabin himself. The passage, she claims, shows that Rabin 'will die, like this is his destiny'. A fifteen-minute segment of Karpin's work, focusing on the incitement of American Jewish extremists was not shown in Israel.

Rabbi Moshe Zvi Neria, the former head of the *K'far Haroeh yeshiva* high-school, who had received the Israel Prize in 1990, urged a change in the standard prayer for the State of Israel recited in synagogues world-wide: instead of praying for the protection *of* its leaders, the text should invite Jews to pray for protection *from* its leaders (in Heilman 1997: 352).

Moderate Israeli public opinion was shocked by a report on Channel 1 of Israel television (9 August 1996) showing three high-school girls who admired Yigal Amir, Rabin's assassin. Although the Education Minister described them as only 'weeds', Dr Nilly Keren's research illustrates that such a judgement is not altogether inconsistent with the world view and extremist ideas of children in the Israeli educational system, particularly in the religious sector. Moreover, a few months before the assassination of Premier Rabin, an Israeli army radio station broadcast a report by a teacher that some students in their examination papers had added slogans like, 'Death to Rabin', and 'Death to Peres' (Josef Algazy, *Ha'aretz* 15 August 1996).

As for their successor, posters began to appear in Jerusalem in June 1998, presenting Premier Netanyahu wearing a kefiyyeh, under the heading 'The Liar'. *Ma'ariv* newspaper warned Shin Bet of the potential for another assassination should Netanyahu sanction withdrawal from any portion of the West Bank (*Jewish Chronicle*, 12 June 1998, p. 3). After the Wye Accords in October, Netanyahu was pictured leaving his offices in the Knesset surrounded by a striking array of bodyguards. Meanwhile, it appears that the Israeli far right was then working to have Ariel Sharon stand against Netanyahu for the premiership in 2000 (*Jewish Chronicle*, 31 July 1998, p. 3).

Conclusion

We have seen how Zionism, an essentially secular, and mostly anti-religious enterprise, was endowed with particular religious significance, at least after the establishment of the state. Although vehemently opposed to its programme from the beginning, no body now is more supportive of its achievement than the religious establishment. The secular movement of Zionism, whose tenets diverged fundamentally from rabbinic eschatology has been transposed into an ideology which the majority of religious Jews regard as of divine origin. We are witnessing a process of resacralisation, whereby irreligious, secular, nationalist salvation has been endowed with the mythology of traditional Jewish soteriology.

Much of this transformation is due to Rabbi Zvi Yehuda Kook, who mediated particular teachings of his father, Rabbi Avraham Yitzhak Kook. He metamorphosed his father's interest in the universal, converting it into the narrow particularism of Jewish religious nationalism. While the elder Kook sanctified literature, science and the arts, the son's vision was circumscribed by Jewish nationalism. Only Jewish secular nationalism was charged with the sacred, and thus constituted the whole world (Aran 1997: 307). This led to the strange coupling of a strict Orthodoxy marked by Torah observance, and a

Messianic nationalism. The son wrested Messianic nationalism from the place it occupied side by side with the mystical in his father's thought, and focused on the political aspects of the state. The grand designs of cosmic redemption in his father's mystical-Messianic vision were reduced to the practical components of the land of Israel: its economy, army, police force and especially its conquest of territory. For the younger Kook, a sovereign Jewish state *is* redemption, as reflected in the title of one of his most important articles, 'The State as Realization of the Vision of Redemption'. This led to his elevation of militarism and war to a high point of political and religious values, and to his view that the army was sacred. Soldiers are as righteous as Torah scholars, and weapons, even those manufactured by gentiles, are as sacred as a prayer shawl and phylacteries. In his later years, the younger Kook identified redemptive Israeli politics with a particular brand of nationalism: he vehemently opposed withdrawal from conquered territories, and equated settlement and annexation of the Occupied Territories with truth, justice and religious fulfilment (see Aran 1997: 306–12).

Despite the opposition of such parties as Neturei Karta and the Satmar Hasidim, which we shall consider in Chapter 8, *Eretz Yisrael* features prominently in modern Jewish religious thought, and, in many religious circles the creation of the state is accorded Messianic and redemptive significance. The characteristics of the four main religious attitudes to the state can be charted as follows (adapted from Rosenak 1987):

Negation	Symbiosis	Theology of Torah	Theology of historical redemption
Ultra-Orthodox communities in Israel and elsewhere, and radical Reform movements hold that,	(Some) Israeli and diaspora Jews espouse the view that,	For many religious Jews in Israel and elsewhere,	For many religious Jews in Israel and elsewhere,
The State of Israel is an act of rebellion against God, because the initiative must be God's. It militates against Judaism.	Israel is significant as a vital feature of Judaism, but is not normative, but rather restores a constituent element of the whole of Judaism.	*Eretz Yisrael* is the normative context for the observance of the Torah. The land, therefore, has fundamental *halakhic* significance.	God is taking his people out of the house of bondage, and with fire and cloud, is leading them to the promised land.

Negation	Symbiosis	Theology of Torah	Theology of historical redemption
Zionists are heretics who espouse a false Messiah. Zionism has flouted the oath 'not to scale the walls', i.e. not to attempt to conquer the land, and not to rebel against gentile domination (BT Ket. 111a). According to Neturei Karta and the Satmar hasidic sect, Zionism is the most pernicious movement in Jewish history.	While Israelis who hold this view tend to disparage the diaspora, diaspora Jews insist that their way of life complements the other, providing an opening to wider international culture, and the challenge to maintain the Jewish faith and culture among the nations.	Not only are certain laws (e.g. the sabbatical year and the tithes) applicable only in *Eretz Yisrael*, but the entire Torah is designed for the people in *Eretz Yisrael*. Observing *halakhah* in the *galut* is only preparing one to do so in *Eretz Yisrael* (Nahmanides, Commentary on Lev 18.25).	*Aliyah* and the determination to build a just society are ideals. The *Shoah* itself can be interpreted within this matrix as promoting the redemption: it constitutes 'the birth pangs of the Messiah'.
The *miraculous* event of 1967 is merely the temptation of the righteous to be lured away from proper salvation.			The War of Independence and the 1967 war are moments of salvation: acts of God's intervention.

The degree to which the mixed marriage between irreligious political Zionism and religious Judaism has been consummated can be seen in Rosenak's assertion that for most modern Jews 'the emergence of the State of Israel is the central positive event in two millennia of Jewish history' (Rosenak 1987: 910). In the more modest estimation of Jonathan Sacks, Chief Rabbi of Britain, the State of Israel for many religious Jews is 'the most powerful collective expression' of Jewry, and 'the most significant development in Jewish life since the Holocaust' (*Daily Telegraph*, 31

December, 1993: 21).[19] Moreover, the religious wing is at the forefront of the opposition to political 'compromise' with the Palestinians, with very few Orthodox rabbis supporting it, and many at the vanguard of its destruction. That secular Zionism, largely agnostic and even atheistic was able to engage the support of religious Jews, both Orthodox and Reform, who bitterly opposed its programme for most of the period prior to the creation of the state, is one of the most remarkable ideological coalitions of the twentieth century.

19 Rabbi Sacks' proper title is, Chief Rabbi of the United Hebrew Congregations of the Commonwealth. Although his authority does not extend beyond the United Hebrew Congregations of Jews, he is commonly looked to as representing the religious voice of all Jews in Britain.

4 Zionism and the Churches

There are distinctive tendencies in the attitudes of Christian Churches to the existence of the State of Israel. While the indigenous Christian community in Palestine, which has lived there since the early Christian centuries under a variety of political rulers, sees no special importance in the state, and is prominent in the opposition to Israeli occupation and oppression, some ninety million Christian Zionists world-wide see Zionism as the instrument of God promoting the gathering of Jews into Israel. In some such circles, anyone who opposes Zionism opposes God himself. The mainline Christian Churches in the West take an intermediate position, distinguishing between the return of the Jews and the creation of a state.

The historical context of Church involvement

Before reviewing some of the perspectives of the Christian Churches on Zionism and the State of Israel, it is instructive to survey the attachment of Christians to the Holy Land, particularly to Jerusalem, recognising that this attachment reflected changing political interests. Jerusalem and the surrounding area were the scenes of the historical origins of their faith, and the location of the expected Second Coming of Christ. After Emperor Hadrian (AD 117–38) refounded the city as the Roman colony of *Aelia Capitolina*, statues of the new Roman gods were erected in the place of the ruined Herodian Temple. Emperor Constantine determined to relieve the Holy Place of the Cross and Resurrection of its pagan idol: the Temple of Venus was destroyed and the site excavated, in the course of which one rock tomb was identified as the Holy Sepulchre. Constantine ordered Bishop Macarius to build an appropriate surrounding for the Holy Sepulchre, which was dedicated in September 335 (see Hunt 1984: 25–26). Soon, the sacred cave at Bethlehem and that on the Mount of Olives also were adorned with churches, built under the supervision of Constantine's mother, Helena. Constantine also ordered Macarius to erect a basilica at the shrine of Abraham at Mamre near Hebron.

The news that the Holy Sepulchre had been discovered and that the site had been converted into a Christian basilica increased the number of pilgrims (see further Prior 1997b: 118–21). The position of Jerusalem in the sixth century mosaic in the church in Madaba (the *Madaba Map*) confirms the importance of the city for the Christian faithful. Whereas Jews had focused on the Temple, Christians could now focus on the Hill of Golgotha. The much later *Mappa Mundi* of Hereford Cathedral places Jerusalem and the Crucifixion at the very centre of the world.

By the time of the first Muslim conquest in 638 by Omar, the second caliph (634–44), a number of Church communities had come into being. There was still, however, only one Patriarch of Jerusalem, Sophronius, who negotiated with the Muslims on behalf of all the Christians of the area. Between that date and the establishment of the Crusader Kingdoms there was harmony among the various Christian communities in Jerusalem, in spite of the growing estrangement between Rome and Constantinople.

The capture of Jerusalem by the Seljuk Turks in 1071 was answered in the West by Pope Urban II's call in 1095 for a crusade to liberate the Holy Places. On the night of 13–14 July 1099, the Crusaders murdered all whom they met, men, women and children, emptying Jerusalem of all its Muslim and Jewish inhabitants. With none left to kill, the Crusaders went to the Church of the Holy Sepulchre to give thanks (Runciman 1951: 287–88). Saladin's decisive victory over the Crusaders at the Horns of Hattin on 4 July 1187 was followed by the capture of Jerusalem on 2 October. The hegemony of the Latin Church in the Holy Places, under a Latin Patriarch, followed.

The conquest of Constantinople by the Ottoman Turks in 1453 and their capture of Jerusalem in 1516 brought about fundamental change in the Middle East, introducing international politics into the controversies surrounding Jerusalem and the Holy Places. After King Francis I of France had signed the Capitulation Treaty with Sultan Suleiman the Magnificent (1535), the Western Church asked France to represent its interests in the region. France claimed the right to protect all Ottoman subjects who were members of the Latin or Eastern Catholic communions. Subsequently, following the Treaty of Kuchuk Kainarja in 1774, the Russians claimed a similar position in respect of Ottoman subjects with Orthodox beliefs. As the Empire weakened, the interests of the Great Powers increased. The Treaty of Berlin (1878) recognised France's rights, and stipulated that there be no alterations in the status quo in the Holy Places. The status quo of the Sultan's final *firman* (decree) of 1852 has been adhered to scrupulously up to the present.

Britain's interest in the Middle East increased in the late eighteenth century as a result of her acquisition of territories in India, with which it was necessary to secure safe and speedy overland passage. Moreover, Britain wished to protect her trade with the Persian Gulf region. She was anxious also to limit the power of Mohammed 'Ali of Egypt, who wished to set up an independent Arab state embracing Egypt, Greater Syria and the Arab Peninsula. Britain stationed the first European Consulate in the city in 1838, and in 1841 established the Protestant (Anglican) Bishopric in Jerusalem (El-Assal 1994: 131–32; the Right Reverend Riah El-Assal, enthroned in

1998, is the thirteenth Anglican Bishop of Jerusalem).

Throughout the second half of the nineteenth century Church institutions in the Holy Land expanded greatly. That period also witnessed an unprecedented increase in the number of Christian visitors to the Holy Land, especially from England and Russia (see Hummel and Hummel 1995), and the USA, including Scripture scholars, archaeologists, Protestant missionaries and pilgrims who were major formers of opinion in America (see Handy 1981).

The current variety of thirteen Churches of the Mother Church of Jerusalem (the Oriental Orthodox, Byzantine Orthodox, Catholic, Evangelical and Episcopal families) reflects developments which brought to the Jerusalem Church divisions which had occurred outside. Currently the Churches exhibit an unprecedented unity. The leadership has issued common statements, including that of 14 November 1994, *The Significance of Jerusalem for Christians*, which lays out the significance of the city for the indigenous Christian community.[1]

The Catholic Church, Zionism and the State of Israel

Relations between the Catholic Church and the representatives of Zionism prior to the establishment of the State of Israel in 1948, and with Israel itself since then reflect changing political circumstances, as well as warmer relations between Christians and Jews. The discussion which follows is restricted to an examination of the Catholic Church's attitude towards Zionism as a political movement and the State of Israel; other aspects of the dialogue are reviewed elsewhere (e.g. in Fisher, Rudin and Tanenbaum 1986; Widoger 1988; see relevant documents in Croner 1977 and 1985).

During the Ottoman period the primary interest of the Holy See was in the Christian Holy Places, and the voluminous Vatican files dealing with Palestine during the last years of Pope Leo XIII's pontificate (1896–1903) do not mention Zionism, nor the growing presence of Jews there (Kreutz 1990: 51 note 20).[2] Theodor Herzl's tactics for advancing the Zionist cause included intensive diplomatic lobbying (11 May 1896, Herzl 1983–96, II: 340–41), and with that end in view he requested Baron Gleichen-Russwurm on 9 May 1901 to secure an audience with the Pope: 'I am convinced that they [the Pope and Cardinal Rampolla] would bestow their favour on the

---

1   The three Patriarchs (Greek Orthodox, Armenian and Latin) meet bi-monthly under the presidency of the Greek Patriarch to discuss matters of common concern. The completion of the repair and decoration of the dome of the Holy Sepulchre (2 January 1997), whose ownership reflects the complexity of the histories of the Churches, marked a welcome level of co-operation.

2   The Holy See, being the juridical personification of more than 1,000 million Catholics who are in communion with Rome, enjoys the rights to make international agreements and receive and dispatch representatives.

cause if they had detailed information' (Herzl 1960, 3: 1096–97). Two years later he would try to get an introduction to the Pope (19 October 1903, Herzl 1960, 4: 1566–67), and had written already to the President of the Italian Zionist Federation, in the hope that his proposal would be accepted by the Pope: 'We want only the profane earth in Palestine. ... The Holy Places shall be ex-territorialised for ever. *Res sacrae extra commercium*, as a right of nations' (September 1903, Kreutz 1990: 32).

With failing health, Herzl visited Rome on 23 January 1904 and met Pope Pius X, who refused to support the Zionist intentions: 'We cannot prevent the Jews from going to Jerusalem – but we could never sanction it. The soil of Jerusalem, if it was not always sacred, has been sanctified by the life of Jesus Christ' (Herzl 1960, 4: 1602–3). According to Herzl's account, the Pope also said:

> It is not pleasant to see the Turks in possession of the Holy Places but we have to put up with it; but we could not possibly support the Jews in the acquisition of the Holy Places. If you come to Palestine and settle with your people there, we shall have churches and priests ready to baptise all of you
> (Herzl 1960, 4: 1601–2)

Prior to the Balfour Declaration the major concern of the Holy See focused on the likely fate of the Holy Places 'in the custody of the synagogue'. Fearful of the declaration and Britain's conquest of Palestine in 1917, the Secretary of State, Pietro Cardinal Gasparri, remarked: 'It is hard to take back that part of our heart which has been given over to the Turks in order to give it to the Zionists' (Minerbi 1990: xiii). On 6 March 1922, Gasparri severely criticised the draft British Mandate for Palestine of 7 December 1920 as being incompatible with the Covenant of the League of Nations. The British plan would establish 'an absolute economic, administrative and political preponderance of Jews', and would act as 'the instrument for subordinating native populations' (in Kreutz 1992: 115). One detects here the emergence of a concern for the rights of the Palestinians in the land, whose Christians were among the staunchest Arab opponents of Zionism, and supporters of nascent Arab nationalism.

It is equally clear, however, that the Holy See had little enthusiasm for an Arab government in the area. As late as January 1948, Monsignor Montini (the future Paul VI, then the Under Secretary for Ordinary Affairs) informed the British Minister to the Vatican that the Holy See preferred that 'a third power, neither Jew nor Arab ... have control of the Holy Land' (Perowne in Rome to Burrows, 19 January 1948 – FO 371/68500, in Kreutz 1992: 116). However, such was the international support for Zionism in the wake of the virtual annihilation of mainland European Jewry that it was virtually impossible for the Holy See to challenge it publicly.

While the Zionist expulsion of more than 700,000 Palestinian Arabs, including some 50,000 Christians – 35 per cent of all Christians who lived in Palestine prior to 15 May 1948 – was acknowledged to be a disaster, it did not induce the Holy See to make any diplomatic representations. In his Encyclical Letter *In Multiplicibus* of October 1948, Pope Pius XII expressed only his anguish at the general conditions of refugees, and in *Redemptoris Nostri* six months later he was no more specific. However, the Holy See's envoy insisted that the return of the Christian exiles was 'basic to an Israeli-Church rapprochement' (Kreutz 1992: 117). Nevertheless, the Palestinian issue was not mentioned publicly for the next twenty years.

'Through the Second Vatican Ecumenical Council (1962–65) the Church, in Pope John XXIII's words, opened a window to the world, abandoning its citadel character. The Council's Declaration on the Relationship of the Church to Non-Christian Religions (*Nostra Aetate*, 28 October 1965) reflected the new climate of respect for and better relations with other religions, including, of course, Judaism. The American Jewish Committee played a prominent role both before and during the Council's deliberations, providing Vatican officials with documentation tracing the 2,000 years of 'the Catholic teaching of contempt towards Jews and Judaism' (Rudin 1986: 14). Nevertheless, despite the warm tone of its acknowledgement of Christianity's roots within Judaism, this *Magna Carta* of the Jewish-Christian dialogue made no mention of the State of Israel. During that period also, there was a growing sense in the Church of the relationship between the Gospel and issues of justice and peace, reflected in a range of papal encyclicals (*Mater et Magistra* and *Pacem in Terris* of John XXIII, *Populorum Progressio* and *Evangelii Nuntiandi* of Paul VI, and later *Redemptoris Hominis* and *Laborem Exercens* of John Paul II). Translated to the Middle East, two conflicting tendencies were developing: a greater respect for the Jews, and a growing sympathy for the plight of the Palestinians.

A number of significant factors influenced future developments. The victory of Israel in 1967 imposed a new sense of the power of the Jewish state. Contacts between Jews and Catholics increased. Pope Paul VI, who had already visited the Holy Land in 1964, concerned at the decrease in the numbers of Christians there, lamented that if their presence were to cease, 'the Holy Land would become like a museum' ('Concerning the Increased Needs of the Church in the Holy Land', 1974). In addressing Israeli Jews on 22 December 1975, the Pope acknowledged the rights and legitimate aspirations of the Jews to a sovereign and independent state of its own, and appealed that the Jews 'recognise the rights and legitimate aspirations of another people, which have also suffered for a long time, the Palestinian people' (*Acta Apostolicae Sedis*, January–March 1976, p. 134).

At the level of documents also there was progress. In 1975, the Holy See's Commission for Religious Relations with the Jews issued its 'Guidelines and Suggestions for implementing the Conciliar Declaration *Nostra Aetate*'. The Guidelines suggested ways in which the ideals of *Nostra Aetate* could be implemented. Again, while stressing the place of the 'mystery of Israel' within the mystery of the Church, it was silent on the role of the State of Israel. The International Jewish Committee for Interreligious Consultations expressed its regret at the omission (Higgins 1986: 31).

By 1983 Monsignor W. Murphy, Under-Secretary of the Pontifical Commission for Justice and Peace, acknowledged that the Holy See recognised the factual existence of Israel, its right to exist within secure borders, and other rights that a sovereign nation possesses. Pope John Paul II welcomed Shimon Peres, the Israeli Prime Minister, to the Vatican on 19 February 1985, after which the Vatican spokesman referred to divergencies on essential problems, which included the status of Jerusalem, the sovereignty of Lebanon, and the lot of the Palestinian people. The Pope's visit to a Roman synagogue on 25 June 1986 marked another stage in the growing cordiality between the two bodies. According to Fr Giovanni Caprile the remaining problems concerned: a just solution to the Palestinian problem, and the establishment of a Palestinian homeland; an internationally guaranteed special status for Jerusalem, with access to, and equality for Christians, Jews and Muslims, making Jerusalem a real centre of spiritual and fraternal development; and an improvement in the legal rights and social situations of the Christian communities living under Israeli control (in *La Civilta Cattolica*, 16 February 1991: 357–58).

The appeal for recognition of the rights of both peoples has been a constant call of John Paul II, whose statements about the State of Israel must be seen against the wider background of his treatment of the relations between Christians and Jews (see Fisher and Klenicki 1995). The most comprehensive expression of the Pope's concern is contained in his communiqué after the visit of Yasser Arafat on 15 September 1982 (*La Documentation Catholique* 73, 17 October: 921, 947). In his Apostolic Letter, *Redemptionis Anno* of Good Friday 1984, he expressed the desire to feel the same joy and emotion of heart which Paul VI had experienced on his visit to the Holy Land in 1964. Moving beyond expressions of personal piety, he added,

> The Palestinian people who find their historical roots in that land and who for decades have been dispersed, have the natural right in justice to find once more a homeland and to be able to live in peace and tranquillity with the other peoples of the area.
>
> (*Secretariatus pro non-Christianis*, Bulletin 57 (1984), XIX(3), p. 254)

In his audience with American Jewish Committee leaders on 15 February 1985 to commemorate the twentieth anniversary of *Nostra Aetate*, the Pope reviewed progress in Jewish–Christian relations since its promulgation, and expressed the hope that 'The Lord give to the land, and to all the peoples and nations in that part of the world, the blessings contained in the word *shalom*' and 'that the sons and daughters of Abraham – Jews, Christians and Muslims – may live and prosper in peace' (in Tanenbaum 1986: 58–59).

The wide-ranging document of the Holy See's Commission for Religious

Relations with the Jews ('Notes on the Correct Way to present Jews and Judaism in Preaching and Catechesis in the Roman Catholic Church' 1985) affirms the religious attachment between the Jewish people and the land of Israel, with its roots in the biblical tradition and as an essential aspect of Jewish covenantal fidelity to the one God. However, it adds that 'the existence of the State of Israel and its political options should be envisaged not in a perspective which is in itself religious, but in their reference to the common principles of international law. The permanence of Israel ... is an historical fact and a sign to be interpreted within God's design' (paragraph 25). Although this marks the first statement concerning the State of Israel in an official Vatican document, one wonders with Widoger (1988: 119) what possible sense preachers and others could make of such a contorted formulation.

During his visit to Austria in June 1988, the Pope called again for equality for Israeli Jews and Palestinians, and pointed out that full diplomatic relations between the Holy See and Israel are 'dependent on a solution to the Palestinian Question and the international status of Jerusalem'. The Palestinians have a right to a homeland, 'like every other nation, according to international law'. In his Easter Message of 1991, he pleaded, 'Lend an ear ... to the long ignored aspirations of oppressed peoples such as the Palestinians, the Lebanese, the Kurds, who claim the right to exist with dignity, justice and freedom'. In his 1994 Encyclical, *Tertio Millennio Adveniente*, the Pope reiterated his desire to visit Lebanon, Jerusalem and the Holy Land in the year 2000, and visit the places associated with Abraham, Moses (Egypt and Mount Sinai), as well as Damascus, the city which witnessed the conversion of Saint Paul (paragraph 24). He achieved part of that ambition by visiting Lebanon in May 1997.

The Holy See–Israel Fundamental Agreement

The Fundamental Agreement between the Holy See and Israel, signed on 30 December 1993, marked the culmination of the work of a bilateral commission set up in 1992. The fifteen articles deal, *inter alia*, with freedom of religion (art. 1), antisemitism and the Holocaust (art. 2), respect for the status quo in the Christian Holy Places (art. 4), Christian pilgrimage to the Holy Land (art. 5), as well as matters of organisation of the Church in Israel (schools, art. 6, media, art. 8, charitable functions, art. 9, property rights, art. 10). While 'both parties declare their respective commitment to the promotion of the peaceful resolution of conflicts among States and nations', the Holy See committed itself solemnly 'to remaining a stranger to all merely temporal conflicts, which principle applies specifically to disputed territories and unsettled borders' (art. 11). The major significance of the Agreement is the establishment of full diplomatic relations between the two parties immediately on the implementation of the Agreement (art. 14).

According to the Archbishop Monezemolo, the then Apostolic Delegate of the Holy See and one of the architects of the Agreement, on the occasion of the third anniversary of its signing (30 December 1996, Notre Dame Centre, Jerusalem) there were three interconnected processes behind the Agreement: the peace process, the process of reconciliation between Catholicism and Judaism, and a process of normalisation between the two international entities. Montezemolo's own role was significant. In 1991 when Israel's President Chaim Herzog was due to visit Montevideo, Montezemolo was asked if he wished to have somebody substitute for him – he was Dean of the Diplomatic Corps – in meeting Herzog. Without consulting his superiors Montezemolo decided to meet Herzog as Dean. When Montezemolo came to the Holy Land later in 1991 he explored the possibilities of normalisation. With permission from the Holy See he obtained a private audience with Herzog in Jerusalem. By 1992 a working party was constituted which met confidentially.

According to Britain's Chief Rabbi, the agreement 'counts as one of the great interfaith achievements of the century' (*Daily Telegraph*, 31 December 1993, p. 21). *Nostra Aetate*, for all its significance in Jewish–Christian relations, had failed to mention the State of Israel, whose creation was 'the most significant development in Jewish life since the Holocaust'. The Chief Rabbi hints that the Holy See had withheld diplomatic recognition up to then mainly because of traces of ancient theological prejudices. There is an abundance of evidence pointing to quite different reasons: the lack of fulfilment of the other half of UN Resolution 181 (29 November 1947), which urged a two-state solution, with Jerusalem as a *corpus separatum*; the failure of Israel to comply with UN Resolution 242, requiring withdrawal from territory occupied in the 1967 War; the absence of a solution to the problem of Palestinian refugees, etc.

For the Holy See to enter into full diplomatic relations with what Rabbi Sacks calls 'the most powerful collective expression of Jewry, its state', is a less than sanguine enterprise. An innocent people had paid, and was continuing to pay a heavy price. One might expect of the Chief Rabbi signs of some moral perturbation concerning the circumstances under which the state was established, and is maintained. To grant diplomatic recognition to the State of Israel might be considered to accord ethical, and even religious legitimacy to the destruction of the Palestinians. Indeed, many, including numerous Jews, see in the emergence of the Zionist movement a retrogression of Jewry into that part of its past, which is marked by its most elementary and primitive forms of the concept of God. The biblical inspiration for the establishment of the state has been drawn from those portions of the Hebrew Scriptures that betray a narrow and exclusive concept of a tribal, xenophobic and militaristic god, rather than from those which highlight the universalist outlook which is characteristic of a more progressive, ethical Judaism.

Meanwhile, there was widespread disaffection within the indigenous Arab Christian Churches with the Holy See's initiative, but before signing, Montezemolo assured the Notre Dame Centre audience that he had met each Jerusalem Church leader to explain that the Holy See was not acting on behalf of other Christians, nor did it seek to gain any special privilege.

In addressing the diplomatic corps accredited to the Holy See on the subject of Jerusalem (14 January 1996), Pope John Paul II began by welcoming His Excellency Afif Safieh, the recently appointed Director of the Office of Representation of the PLO to the Holy See.[3] The Pope expressed the fear that the hope for peace in the region 'could prove ephemeral if a just and adequate solution is not also found to the particular problem of Jerusalem'. He reiterated the Church's position on the religious and universal dimension of the Holy City, which 'demands a commitment on the part of the whole international community in order to ensure that the City preserves its uniqueness and retains its living character':

> The Holy Places ... would lose much of their significance if they were not permanently surrounded by active communities of Jews, Christians and Muslims, enjoying true freedom of conscience and religion, and developing their own religious, educational and social activities.

Trusting that 1996 would see the beginning of negotiations on the definitive status of the territories under the administration of the National Palestinian Authority, and on the sensitive issue of the City of Jerusalem, the Pope hoped that the international community would offer the juridical and diplomatic instruments capable of ensuring that Jerusalem may truly be a 'crossroads of peace' (in PASSIA 1996: 32–33).

On 27–28 October 1998, at the invitation of the Latin Patriarchate of Jerusalem, the Presidents or Delegates from several Roman Catholic Bishops' conferences in Europe, the Americas, Africa and Asia, together with the members of the Assembly of Catholic Ordinaries of the Holy Land, assembled in Jerusalem, to reflect on the question of Jerusalem. Archbishop Jean-Louis Tauran, Secretary for the Holy See's Relations with States, presented a paper outlining the Holy See's position on Jerusalem. Metropolitan Timotheos read a paper outlining the Greek Orthodox position, and Latin Patriarch Michel Sabbah presented the 1994 Memorandum.[4]

Archbishop Tauran reiterated the Holy See's insistence on the intimacy between the Holy Places and social realities:

> It is obvious that the Holy Places derive their meaning and their cultic and cultural uses from their intimate connection with the surrounding environment, to be understood not merely in terms of geography but

---

3   Afif Safieh is a Jerusalemite Christian, who, because he was studying in Europe in 1967 when Israel occupied Jerusalem, has been refused residency with his family in his native city.

4   Archbishop Tauran's paper, and the Final Communiqué are published in *Bulletin Associated Christian Press* 403 (November–December 1998): 2–8, Jerusalem: Christian Information Centre.

also and most especially in its urban, architectural and above all human community and institutional dimensions.

The current situation in Jerusalem, he insisted, was brought about and is maintained by force, and the 1967 military occupation and subsequent annexation of East Jerusalem are illegal. Unilateral action, or any arrangement imposed by force cannot be a solution. The Holy See rejects every exclusive claim to Jerusalem, since the city is sacred to Jews, Christians and Muslims, and is the cultural heritage of everybody, including those who visit it.

> Jerusalem is an unparalleled reality: it is part of the patrimony of the whole world. ... The Holy See continues to ask that it be protected by 'a special internationally guaranteed Statute'. The historical and material characteristics of the City must be preserved; there must be equality of rights and treatment for those belonging to the communities of the three religions found in the City; and the rights of access to the Holy Places must be safeguarded.

He added that 'The sacred character involves Jerusalem in its entirety, its holy places and its communities with their schools, hospitals, cultural, social and economic activities'. Any proposed solution must have the support of the three religions, both at the local and international level. In addition to the presence of the contending parties (the Israelis, Palestinians and the sponsors of the Peace Process), there must be wider representation to guarantee that no aspect of the problem is overlooked – a bid, perhaps, for the Holy See's own participation in the discussions.

The Final Communiqué reiterated the unique value of the City for the three religions, the region and the whole world, expressing the hope that Jerusalem would be a universal symbol of fraternity and peace. It should be a place of encounter and reconciliation among religions and peoples. While down the centuries Jerusalem has been viewed as 'the Mother Church' for Christians, it is a city of three religions and two peoples, for whom it embodies 'the heartland of their respective national aspirations'. In working towards a final solution political leaders ought to take account of the concerns and hopes of believers. In a context of the ongoing closure of the city to Palestinians who live outside, it reiterated that 'Free access to Jerusalem should be guaranteed to all, local people and pilgrims, friends and opponents'. Finally, there should be a special statute for Jerusalem's most sacred parts, and that statute should be supported by international guarantee.

The Protestant Churches, Zionism and the State of Israel

Because of the diversity of its membership and the more complex patterns of its leadership it is more difficult to gain a representative picture of the attitudes of the Churches of the Reformation to Zionism and the State of

Israel than was the case with respect to the Catholic Church. The divisions within, and the complicated structure of the World Council of Churches (WCC) militate against the emergence of a unified perspective.

Protestant attitudes to Zionism pre-1948

There was little support for Zionism and the establishment of the state in the USA (see Drinan 1977: 55–67). The non-denominational main-line weekly, the *Christian Century* was consistently unsympathetic to Zionism. After the Balfour Declaration, a 'mischievous and ambiguous promise', it disavowed any connection between the Old Testament anticipation of the restoration of Israel and the Jewish people in the modern period. Even with the persecution of Jews beginning in Germany in 1933, it displayed hostility to Jewish nationalism, and approved of the British government's White Paper of 1939. While it supported the creation of a cultural and spiritual centre for world Jewry it repudiated the ambition to create a Jewish state.

While the Federal Council of Churches of Christ (the forerunner of the National Council of Churches) expressed concern at the Nazi policy of extermination of European Jewry it did not mention Palestine as a possible place of refuge for Jews (Drinan 1977: 56–59). Of course, individual Protestants, e.g. Reinhold Niebuhr, did favour Zionism. However, other American Protestant leaders founded the Committee for Justice and Peace in the Holy Land in February 1948, to induce the UN to reconsider its partition proposal of 1947, but it disbanded in February 1950.

The World Council of Churches

During its meeting in West Germany in February 1986 the WCC's Consultation on the Church and the Jewish People resolved to bring before a wider public the fruits of Jewish–Christian dialogue, and named a task force to examine statements on the Jewish people made by member Churches and the WCC since its foundation in 1948. In 1988, the WCC published a collection of twenty documents, gathered from earlier publications, with a commentary by Allan Brockway, Paul van Buren, Rolf Rendtorff and Simon Schoon, which is the main source of my references to the documents (rendered WCC 1988). In line with my emphasis, however, I confine my comments to only one aspect of the Jewish–Christian relations, that concerning Zionism and the State of Israel.

Five of the six Assemblies of the WCC up to 1988 had passed formal resolutions on Jewish–Christian relations. The Founding Assembly in Amsterdam (1948) received the report of a committee, 'The Christian Approach to the Jews'. In dealing with the emergence of Israel as a state, it called for attention to the moral and spiritual aspects of the question, especially concerning the need to provide a refuge for 'Displaced Persons' far more generously than had yet been done (WCC 1988: 8). The Assembly called for more detailed study of 'the many and varied problems created by establishment of a State of Israel in Palestine' (WCC 1988: 9).

The Second Assembly (Evanston, Illinois 1954) voted to remove from its statement on 'Christ our Hope' a section on the sub-theme, 'The Hope of Israel', but published a minority statement by twenty-four theologians (WCC 1988: 10 – see Brockway's discussion, pp. 133–34). The 'Resolution on Anti-Semitism' at the New Delhi Assembly in 1961 reiterated the First Assembly's stand against antisemitism, and urged its members to resist every form of it.

It was the June War of 1967 that elevated the State of Israel to being an issue of debate within the WCC. The general assemblies dealt almost exclusively with the political dimensions of the matter, while some member Churches, especially those geographically closest to the scene of the Nazi terror accord the state theological significance. The Commission on Faith and Order, meeting in Bristol a short time after the 1967 War drew attention to the annihilation of six million Jews. It recognised the tremendous importance of the State of Israel for the great majority of Jews, but also the suffering and injustice it had brought to Arab people, but found itself unable to adjudicate on the matter (WCC 1988: 17).

The Fourth Assembly (Uppsala 1968) acknowledging that the menace of the situation in the Middle East showed no signs of abating, passed a 'Statement on the Middle East', affirming the independence, territorial integrity and security of all nations in the area, rejecting annexation of territory by force, and calling for a solution to the problem of displaced persons (WCC 1988: 29). This marked a shift of emphasis from viewing the Jewish people in purely theological terms to considering their political identity in a nation state.

The Fifth Assembly (Nairobi 1975) adopted two resolutions related to the State of Israel, calling for the withdrawal of Israel from territories occupied in 1967, the right of all states to live in peace within secure borders, and the implementation of the rights of the Palestinians to self-determination. It also affirmed the centrality of Jerusalem for the three religions, and expressed concern for the Christian Holy Places, which should not become 'mere monuments of visitation' (WCC 1988: 31–33).

The Executive Committee of the WCC (Geneva 1982) received and commended to the Churches for study and action the document, 'Ecumenical Considerations on Jewish-Christian Dialogue', with the assurance that corresponding considerations would be produced later for specific dialogue with Muslims, Buddhists, Hindus, Marxists and others. The Considerations begin with the affirmation that dialogue in general allows participants to describe and witness to their faith in their own terms. In its survey of Jewish history it notes that there were times and places in which Jews were allowed to thrive and make a distinct contribution to the wider culture. 'There were even times when Jewish thinkers came to "make a virtue out of necessity" and considered diaspora living to be the distinct genius of Jewish existence' (paragraph 2.14). It adds

2.15: Yet, there was no time in which the memory of the Land of Israel and of Zion, the city of Jerusalem, was not central in the worship and hope of the Jewish people. 'Next year in Jerusalem' was always part of Jewish worship in the diaspora. And the continued presence of Jews in the Land and in Jerusalem was always more than just one place of residence among all the others.

2.16: Jews differ in their interpretation of the State of Israel, as to its religious and secular meaning. It constitutes for them part of the long search for that survival which has always been central to Judaism through the ages. Now the quest for statehood by Palestinians – Christian and Muslim – as part of their search for survival as a people in the Land, also calls for full attention.

2.17: Jews, Christians and Muslims have all maintained a presence in the Land from their beginnings. While 'the Holy Land' is primarily a Christian designation, the Land is holy to all three. Although they may understand its holiness in different ways, it cannot be said to be 'more holy' to one than to another.

2.18: The need for dialogue is the more urgent when under strain the dialogue is tested. Is it mere debate and negotiation or is it grounded in faith that God's will for the world is secure peace with justice and compassion?

(WCC 1988: 39–40)

The Sixth Assembly of the WCC (Vancouver 1983) passed a 'Statement on the Middle East', including treatment of 'the Israeli–Palestinian conflict', 'Lebanon' and 'Jerusalem'. It considered the Israeli settlement policy on the West Bank to have resulted in a *de facto* annexation, flagrantly violating the basic rights of the Palestinian people, whose relocation and expulsion are feared. It referred to the detention of a large number of Palestinians in prisons and camps. It called for a peaceful settlement along the lines of UN Security Council Resolution 242 and other UN resolutions, and for 'the withdrawal of Israeli troops from all territories occupied in 1967', 'the right of all states, including Israel and Arab states, to live in peace with secure and recognised boundaries', and 'the implementation of the rights of the Palestinians to self-determination, including the right of establishing a sovereign Palestinian state'. It affirmed that the Middle East conflict cannot be resolved by force, and called for negotiations towards a comprehensive peace involving Israel, the PLO and neighbouring Arab states. The interests of the world would be best served by the UN, with the USA and the USSR having special responsibility. Churches should become more aware of the urgency and justice of the Palestinian cause, encourage dialogue between Palestinians and Israelis, and 'remind Christians in the Western world to recognise that their guilt over the fate of Jews in their countries may have influenced their views of the conflict in the Middle East and has often led to uncritical support of the policies of the State of Israel, thereby ignoring the plight of the Palestinian people and their rights', and 'to support movements within Israel, which are working for peace and reconciliation' (WCC 1988: 43–45).

The Assembly called for the withdrawal of all foreign forces from Lebanon. On the question of Jerusalem, it reaffirmed the Nairobi 1975 declaration that 'Jerusalem is a Holy City for three monotheistic religions', and that the tendency to minimise its importance for any one religion should be avoided, and also the WCC Central Committee's 1980 call that dialogue be initiated with Jews and Muslims with a view to sharing the city, a project to which the Churches should give priority, while continuing efforts to secure a general settlement of the wider Middle East conflicts. It called the attention of the Churches to the need for 'actions which will ensure a continuing indigenous Christian presence and witness in Jerusalem', and 'wider ecumenical awareness of the plight of the indigenous Muslim and Christian communities suffering from the repressive action of the occupying power in East Jerusalem and other occupied territories'. It called upon all Churches to express their concern at the serious difficulties that often prevent Arab Muslims and Christians from visiting the Holy City (WCC 1988: 46).

The Eighth Assembly of the WCC, meeting in Harare (3–14 December 1998) issued a comprehensive statement on the status of Jerusalem. It *reaffirms* earlier positions of the WCC, and *reiterates* the significance and importance of the Christian communities in the city, condemning once again the violations of the fundamental rights of Palestinians in Jerusalem, which oblige many to leave.[5] It *considers* that negotiations concerning the future status of the city should take place without delay, and should be a product of a comprehensive settlement for the region, which should take account of a number of factors.[6] It *recalls* the framework established in international law related to the status of Jerusalem.[7]

5 Jerusalem is a holy city for three religions; the legitimate rights of all three must be respected; the *status quo* arrangements concerning the Christian communities must be safeguarded; 'the settlement of any problems with regard to the holy places should take place through dialogue and under an international aegis and guarantees'; the holy places should serve as living places of worship for the indigenous Christians and for visitors; Jerusalem should be seen as part of a general settlement of the wider Middle East conflict.

6 These factors would include developments in negotiations on the Israel–Palestinian conflict since 1991; the implications of the conflict for international peace and security; the legitimate concerns of all for justice, peace, security, equal rights and full participation in decisions; the rights and welfare of the Churches; the mutual recognition of the PLO and Israel; and the rights of the Palestinian people to self-determination and statehood.

7 This framework comprises the British Mandate confirmed by the League of Nations in 1922 concerning the Holy Places and religious communities; the 1947 UN General Assembly designation

The statement *notes* that the United Nations, as the embodiment of the international community retains authority and responsibility for Jerusalem, and that 'no unilateral action nor final legal status agreed by the parties can have the force of law until such consent is given'. It *welcomes especially* the Joint Memorandum of the Heads of Christian Communities in Jerusalem on the Significance of Jerusalem for Christians (14 November 1994), which calls on all parties, 'to go beyond exclusivist visions or actions, and without discrimination, to consider the religious and national aspirations of others, in order to give back to Jerusalem its true universal character and to make of the city a holy place of reconciliation for humankind'. The statement *recognises* that the solution to the question of Jerusalem is in the first place the responsibility of the parties directly involved, but that the three religious communities have a central role to play in the negotiations.

The Assembly adopted the following principles which must be taken into account in any final agreement:

8.1 The peaceful settlement of the territorial claims of Palestinians and Israelis should respect the holiness and wholeness of the city.

8.2 Access to the Holy Places, religious buildings and sites should be free, and freedom of worship must be secured for people of all faiths.

8.3 The rights of all communities of Jerusalem to carry out their own religious, educational and social activities must be guaranteed.

8.4 Free access to Jerusalem must be assured and protected for the Palestinian people.

8.5 Jerusalem must remain an open and inclusive city.

8.6 Jerusalem must be a shared city in terms of sovereignty and citizenship.

8.7 The provisions of the IV. Geneva Convention must be honoured with respect to the rights of Palestinians to property, building and residency; the prohibition of effecting changes in population in occupied territories; and the prohibition of changes in geographical boundaries, annexation of territory, or settlement which would change the religious, cultural or historical character of Jerusalem without the agreement of the parties concerned and the approval of the international community.

of the city as a *corpus separatum*; UN General Assembly Resolution 194 (December 1948) specifying the special status of Jerusalem and the right of return of Palestinian refugees; the applicability of the Fourth Geneva Convention (1949) regarding parts of Palestine as 'occupied territory'; UN General Assembly Resolution 303 (9 December 1948), restating the General Assembly's intention 'that Jerusalem should be placed under a permanent international regime' and 'be established as a *corpus separatum* under a special international regime ... administered by the United Nations'; and UN Security Council Resolutions 242(1967) and 338(1973) 'demanding Israeli withdrawal from all occupied territories including Jerusalem'.

Regional councils of Churches

In addition to pronouncement of the world body, regional assemblies of Churches produced statements on the matter, which reflect two main issues, antisemitism and the *Shoah*, and Christian mission to the Jews. The Synod of the Evangelical Church in Germany in 1950 passed a 'Statement on the Jewish Question', also referred to as 'Statement of Guilt Regarding Israel'. The Netherlands Reformed Church in 1950 included in its constitution a special section on the dialogue with Israel. Neither document mentions the State of Israel.

The General Synod of the Netherlands Reformed Church in 1970 adopted an extensive study document on 'Israel: People, Land and State. Suggestions for the Theological Evaluation' – English translation of the whole document is in Croner (1977: 91–107). Surveying the Old Testament witness to the Jewish people, it drew attention to its being chosen freely by God, being given a land, noting that 'chosen people' and 'promised land' belong together. The land forms an essential part of the election, and living outside it is always something abnormal. However, living in the land does not require political independence, but merely the opportunity to live in quiet and peace, according to the order willed by God (paragraphs 13–14). The fifth section, 'the State of Israel' attached special significance to the influx of Jews into Palestine 'in our time'. Since it is a sign of God's will to be on earth together with man, 'we rejoice in this reunion of people and land', 'which is a confirmation of God's lasting purpose with his people' (paragraphs 41–42, WCC 1988: 55). It laments that hundreds of thousands of Palestinian refugees live miserably around the borders of Israel, and professes that 'it belongs to Israel's vocation that it should know itself to be responsible for them' (paragraph 49, in Croner 1977: 105; WCC 1988: 58).

The return, however, is to be distinguished from the establishment of the state. Jews have lived in the land before without a state, and that may be the situation at some point in the future. Since neither a bi-national state, nor a confederation is viable, 'As matters are at the moment, we see a free state as the only possibility which safeguards the existence of the people and which offers them the chance to be truly themselves.' Respecting the distinction between the return and the state, it accepts as a temporary measure the separate nature of the Jewish state, and seems to prefer that at a future date Israeli Jews can fulfil their vocation better if they are part of a larger whole. 'We are convinced that everyone who accepts the reunion of the Jewish people and the land for reasons of faith, has also to accept that in the given circumstances the people should have a state of their own' (paragraph 43, WCC 1988: 56). The document excuses the violent means of the establishment of the state in 1948 by reference to that which accompanied the entry of Joshua and the return under Nehemiah (paragraph 44, WCC 1988: 56). Whoever accepts a role for the Jewish people among the nations must accept their right to a state of their own. But the state must comport itself in an exemplary fashion. In particular, it must acknowledge its responsibility for the creation of the Palestinian refugee problem, and do all it can to put right the injustice done to them. Moreover, Israel must accord its not-Jewish fellow citizens full freedom and dignity (paragraphs 49–50, WCC 1988: 58).

The General Conference of the United Methodist Church in the USA adopted a 'Statement on Inter-religious Dialogue: Jews and Christians' in 1972, which recognised the problem for the dialogue posed by the turbulence in the Middle East. The Seventh General Convention of the American Lutheran Church adopted a statement on 'The American Lutheran Church and the Jewish Community' in 1974. It recognises the conflicting claims of the legitimacy of the Jewish state and the rights of the Palestinians, on which subject there exists a diversity of views among the Lutherans (WCC 1988: 72–73).

The Study by the Council of the Evangelical Church in Germany in 1975 ('Christians and Jews') affirmed that the task of the State of Israel is

> to guarantee the existence of [the Jewish] people in the country of their forefathers. This implication has meaning for Christians as well. … Christians are obliged to recognise and support the internationally valid United Nations Resolution of 1948 (sic!) which is intended to enable Jews to live a secure life in a state of their own. … Neither should the Palestinians Arabs alone have to bear the consequences of the conflict, nor should only Israel be held responsible for the situation.
> (in Croner 1977: 144–45; also WCC 1988: 81–82)

The Synod of the Evangelical Church in the Rheinland in 1975 also distinguished between the Jewish People and the State of Israel, but affirmed, 'The continuing existence of the Jewish people, its return to the Land of Palestine, and also the creation of the State of Israel, are signs of the faithfulness of God toward His people' (in Croner 1985: 207).

The Central Board of the Swiss Protestant Church Federation published 'Reflections on the Problem "Church–Israel" ' in 1977. It begins section VI on 'Zionism – State of Israel' with the statement that 'Zionism is a movement rooted in biblical as well as post-biblical traditions'. Having traced the realisation of Herzl's dream it adds,

> As often happens in world history, in this political growth of the new state the good fortune of some has become the misfortune of others. Together with the anxiety for the Jewish people we feel painfully concerned for the Palestinian Arabs who live inside and outside Israel.
> (VI,4)

It binds in duty the Christian Churches and all Christians 'to stand by Israel in her growing isolation' (VI,6), and to intervene so that the right to live and the conditions of life of Palestinian Arabs be appreciated. In this connection we regard it as an urgent task to work out a clarification of the concept 'Palestinian' and to examine their possibility of self-determination.

(VI,7) (WCC 1988: 87–89)

The (Lutheran) Norwegian Bishops' Conference passed a statement on 'Our Attitude Towards the People and the State of Israel' in 1977, rejecting antisemitism, and affirming Israel's 'right to survive as a state of its own, within safe and guaranteed borders, and that the Arab inhabitants in the area be granted full rights to develop their distinctive character and traditions'. It adds that to characterise 'Zionistic ideology' which stands behind the state as 'racism' reveals both a lack of historical and religious understanding, and intolerance. It ends by calling on the people of Norway 'to show a clear and fearless attitude over against any form of anti-Semitism, including the aggressive anti-Zionism' (WCC 1988: 90–91).

The Synod of the Evangelical Church in the Rheinland adopted a statement 'Towards Renovation of the Relationship of Christians and Jews' in 1980. The Church was brought to the historical necessity of attaining a new relationship of the Church to the Jewish people by four factors: 1) 'the recognition of Christian co-responsibility and guilt for the Holocaust'; 2) new biblical insights concerning the continuing significance of the Jewish people within the history of God; 3) 'the insight that the continuing existence of the Jewish people, its return to the Land of Promise, and also the foundation of the State of Israel, are signs of the faithfulness of God towards his people'; 4) the readiness of Jews, in spite of the Holocaust, to engage in encounter, common study and co-operation. The Synod confessed 'with dismay the co-responsibility and guilt of German Christendom for the Holocaust' (4,1), and affirmed the permanency of God's election of the Jewish people. The Christian use of 'new' in biblical exegesis (new covenant; new People of God), by way of replacement of the old people of God condemned the Jewish people to non-existence. 'Thereby we have made ourselves guilty also of the physical elimination of the Jewish people' (4, 7) (WCC 1988: 92–93). The document does not refer to the indigenous Arab population of Palestine.

The League of Reformed Churches in 1982, in its document, 'Wir und die Juden – Israel und die Kirche' ('We and the Jews – Israel and the Church') also praised the faithfulness of God, who had chosen his people, leading to the creation of the State of Israel.[8] In 1982 also, the Texas Conference of

---

8   Reproduced in *Handreichung Nr. 39 der Evangelischen Kirche im Rheinland*. Düsseldorf, 2nd edn 1985: 128–33.

Churches adopted a statement on 'Dialogue: a Contemporary Alternative to Proselytisation', in the new spirit of inter-faith dialogue, and against the background of the Holocaust. It does not refer to the State of Israel.

Other Evangelical Churches issued statements after the initiative of the Evangelical Church in the Rheinland. The Synod of the Evangelical Church in Berlin (West) in 1984 adopted its 'Points for Orientation on "Christians and Jews" ', very much in the shadow of guilt for the Holocaust. It unites its affirmative stand towards the existence of the State of Israel with its concern for a peaceful solution in the Near East which also includes the rights of the Palestinian Arabs and the Christians among them (WCC 1988: 100–4). In 1984, the General Assembly of the Church of Scotland issued a 'Common Statement on the Relations between Jews and Christians', which affirm that Zion is seen as an expression of the fulfilment of biblical prophecy, a home for the dispersed, and a spiritual centre.

The Presbyterian Church (USA), in its General Assembly of 1987 commended to the Church for study and reflection a wide-ranging document, 'A Theological Understanding of the Relationship between Christians and Jews', at the core of which are seven theological affirmations and explications. The document is particularly sensitive to the double context of its likely reception, firstly in the USA wherein Christians and Jews live side by side, and also in the Middle East. It reaffirms the previous year's General Assembly's acceptance of the right of statehood in Palestine for Palestinians, and the right of the State of Israel to exist within secure borders established by the UN General Assembly resolutions (WCC 1988: 106). It begins its explication of the sixth affirmation, 'We affirm the continuity of God's promise of land along with the obligations of that promise to the people Israel', with the acknowledgement that it was 'entering a minefield of complexities across which is strung a barbed-wire entanglement of issues, theological, political and humanitarian'.

The affirmation deals with the Genesis narrative of promise of land to Abraham as if its genre were history, in the sense of recording what happened in the past. It acknowledges that while some Jews see the State of Israel as fulfilling God's promise, and others regard it as an unauthorised attempt to flee divinely imposed exile, other Jews interpret it in exclusively secular terms. Recognising the diversity of views among Christians also, it affirms that 'The State of Israel is a geopolitical entity and is not to be evaluated theologically'. It recognises that 'we' who affirm the divine promise of land must also uphold the divine right of the dispossessed, and goes on to confess:

We have indeed been agents of the dispossession of others. We confess our complicity in the loss of land by Palestinians, and we join with those of our Jewish sisters and brothers who stand in solidarity with Palestinians as they cry for justice as the dispossessed.

Rejecting any teaching that peace can be secured without justice, the

Presbyterian Church (USA) looks with dismay at the violence and injustice in the Middle East. While acknowledging that the covenant promise of land is an essential element of the self-understanding of the Jewish people, it considers the reduction of it to a specific geographical entity on the eastern shore of the Mediterranean as inadequate. If affirms that 'land' is understood as more than place or property: ' "land" is a biblical metaphor for sustainable life, prosperity, peace and security', and affirms the rights of these essentials for the Jewish people, and for all other peoples. It disavows the views of some dispensationalists and some Christian Zionists who see the formation of the State of Israel as a signal of the end-time, which will bring the Last Judgement, and a conflagration which only Christians will survive, since such views contradict the words of Jesus against seeking to set the time or place of the consummation of world history. Lastly, the Church calls on all people of faith to engage in the work of reconciliation and peace-making (WCC 1988: 116–18).

As Paul van Buren remarks, nothing in the Church's tradition had prepared it for dealing with the State of Israel. Moreover, the major WCC documents do not analyse the relationship between the Jewish people and the land, perhaps for fear of awakening eschatological fervour, out of aversion for the sacralisation of any territory, or out of concern for the predicament of the Palestinians, or of Christians in Arab or Islamic lands (WCC 1988: 170). However, a number of regional member Churches have moved in that direction, beginning with the Netherlands Reformed Church in 1970, although in several cases there is a clear lack of consensus. Van Buren suggests that a minimum consensus might be developed around the following points:

> 1. Because the State of Israel is in part the product of the ancient and living hope of the Jewish people and is of deep concern to almost all Jews, disregard for its safety and welfare is incompatible with concern for the Jewish people. 2. No degree of support for or theological validation of the State of Israel should imply, or be taken by others to imply, that all specific policies and actions of the Israeli government are beyond criticism. ... 3. Christian concern for the safety and survival of the State of Israel can in no way exclude Christian concern for the Palestinian people, and especially for Palestinian Christians of Israel and of the West Bank and Gaza. They, too, have a claim on the attention and concern of the church as to their situation, rights, and hopes. Christian concern for the legitimate rights of the Palestinians, however, may not annul Christian concern for Israel's legitimate right to live in safety. 4. Because God's covenant with the Jewish people has from its beginning been evidence of God's incarnate concern for the whole, concrete creation, the Jewish state is at the least a reminder of 'the earthly, historical dimension of God's promises'.

> (in WCC 1988: 173)

The Palestinian *intifada* led to a growing awareness of the situation of the Palestinians in the Churches in the West. The British Council of Churches sent a delegation to Israel and the Occupied Territories and published its report, *Impressions of Intifada* (British Council of Churches 1989). On the reality of life under the occupation an Arab Christian priest says, 'Occupation is always a corrupting situation both for occupier and occupied. A wooden cage or a golden cage is still a cage' (p. 20).

The 1998 Lambeth Conference passed Resolution V.20, expressing its deep ongoing concern about the tragic situation in the Holy Land. It calls for Jerusalem to be the capital of two sovereign states, Israel and Palestine, and criticises the continued building and expansion of Jewish Settlements within East Jerusalem and the Occupied Territories. It urges political leaders world-wide to encourage the Israeli Government and the Palestinian Authority to work urgently for a just and lasting peace settlement, respecting the right of return for Palestinians dispossessed. Although more strident than many Church documents, the Resolution offers no critique of the fundamental injustice done to the indigenous population of Palestine by the incursion on their land of Zionists from abroad, nor of the clearly discriminatory nature of the Jewish state.

Zionism and the Jewish–Christian dialogue

Having surveyed some of the developments in the Churches' attitudes to Zionism and the State of Israel it is instructive to reflect also on the inter-religious dialogue. The dialogue takes place at different levels, and at different paces in the various regions, sometimes at a representative level. In several countries there is a national Council of Christians and Jews which enjoys the support of the national leadership of Church and Synagogue, and, in Britain, of the Crown. There is also the International Council of Christians and Jews, as well as local councils. Moreover, the Churches themselves designate bodies to further inter-religious dialogue, e.g. the Roman Curia's Pontifical Council for Inter-Religious Dialogue.

The dialogue between Christians and Jews deals with a wide range of topics. Since it accepts the principle that the two parties recognised each other's self-definition the status of the State of Israel assumes great importance, since it is at the heart of the self-understanding of most Jews. In the discussion which follows, attention will be confined to attitudes to Zionism and the State of Israel. Let us begin with a survey of the dialogue between Roman Catholics and Jews in the twenty years since *Nostra Aetate*. We shall then comment on a popular programme for promoting the dialogue in the USA devised in the 1990s by a Jewish and a Christian scholar, and, finally, discuss guidelines for the Churches of Britain and Ireland on the subject.

Twenty years of Jewish–Christian relations

Fisher, Rudin and Tanenbaum have edited a collection of essays by participants in the Jewish-Christian dialogue in the USA: six rabbis, six priests and a Jewish laywoman (1986). Typically the dialogue proceeds with a level of mutual admiration unusual in even academic circles.[9] In acknowledging that 'today Israel is at the centre of every serious Christian–Jewish encounter', Rabbi A. James Rudin affirms that, 'a free Jewish State with Jerusalem as its capital represents the core of Jewish existence and aspirations' (1986: 17). For Monsignor John Oesterreicher, who played a decisive role in drafting Vatican II's *Nostra Aetate*, the living reality of the State of Israel should evoke the respect and admiration of the Christian theologian. He cannot see 'how the renewal of the land could be anything to the theologian but a wonder of love and vitality, how the reborn State could be anything but a sign of God's concern for his people' (in Higgins 1986: 35).[10]

For Father Edward Flannery, the State of Israel is essential to Judaism itself, considered both historically and theologically: 'What is sacred to virtually all Jews must be accorded the full acceptance and understanding that it merits, not only for the sake of good relations but in the interest of truth and justice' (1986: 73). Christians should 'rejoice in the return of the Jewish people to a small sliver of their ancient homeland – if not from compassion and a sense of justice at least from a sense of guilt and repentance' (p. 76). Flannery invests Zionism with a sacred character that would embarrass many Jews, on whose lips, he claims, it is 'a sacred word' with an 'honourable history'. Zionism is above reproach since it is an essentially religious phenomenon and an integral part of Jewish self-definition. Hence support for it is a *sine qua non* of the dialogue ('the Jewish–Christian embrace', p. 79) (Flannery 1986: 76–77). He will set the historical record straight, especially about the allegations that Zionism damaged the Palestinians.

Father Flannery's passion for truth and justice leads him to criticise even Pope John Paul II, who, in a homily in 1980 had noted that 'a sad condition

---

9   In this volume, Rabbi Rubin describes Father Flannery as 'truly a legend in his time', and a fellow editor as 'the extremely gifted' Dr Fisher (Rudin 1986: 15). Monsignor Higgins speaks of Rabbi Marc Tanenbaum, the third editor of the volume, as 'a good friend and highly esteemed collaborator' (Higgins 1986: 33). Elsewhere Robert Drinan refers to 'the brilliant Professor A. Roy Eckardt ... one of the most prolific and profound writers about contemporary Judaism and Zionism' (Drinan 1977: 63), while Elie Wiesel in the foreword ('A Word of Gratitude') to Father Drinan's study, describes him as a 'friend and defender of Israel ... [who] will occupy a special place in Jewish history. ... His name is signed to every petition in behalf of the persecuted' (Wiesel in Drinan 1977: xi).

10 Monsignor Oesterreicher, a convert from Judaism, affirmed in 1971 that Israel's success was due to the 'outstretched arm' of the Lord of Exod 6.6, rather than to the cunning of her statesmen, the superior strategy of her generals, the bravery of her soldiers, and the steadfastness of her citizens (in Drinan 1977: 88).

was created for the Palestinian people who were excluded from their homeland'. Like some other Christians who see the establishment of the State of Israel as a serious injustice inflicted upon the Palestinian Arab population the Pope had fallen victim to the effectiveness of Arab propaganda. Flannery sets about the task of dispelling the misinformation, resting the foundation of the State of Israel 'on solid juridical and moral grounds' (Flannery 1986: 79). The Balfour Declaration of 1916 (sic), was followed by the 1947 UN Partition Plan, which gave the Jews those portions of the land where they constituted a majority – 'an important but little known fact', he claims.

Having thus established the solid juridical grounds, Father Flannery moves on to the moral question. That an alien people expelled the indigenous Arabs – 'a ubiquitous myth circulated by Arab and pro-Arab propaganda' – is contradicted by Joan Peters' exhaustive work of research (with 1,800 annotations), which 'puts definitively to rest the popular myths touching the conflict' (Flannery 1986: 86, 80). Putting his trust in Peters' thoroughly discredited and fraudulent propaganda, Father Flannery tells us that much of the population of Palestine was nomadic, and a large portion of its population was of recent immigration, much of which was the result of the prosperity engendered by Jews. Since Peters's work has long been known to be a 'sheer forgery', and was dismissed in Israel itself almost universally as 'sheer rubbish, except maybe as a propaganda weapon' (Yehoshua Porath, in Finkelstein 1995: 46–47) it is distressing that a prominent educator should be taken in by the fraud, and that his excesses were not picked up by such distinguished editors.

The Palestinian refugees, we learn, left voluntarily, often with the urging of their leaders, in the hope of returning when Israel was permanently crushed. As we shall see (Chapter 7) this piece of propaganda was thoroughly discredited as long ago as 1961. Nevertheless, twenty five years on, Flannery can conclude: 'In no sense can it be said that the Jewish people expelled the Arab Palestinians from their homeland to make room for themselves' (1986: 81). Alas, many non-Arab Christians accept such myths of anti-Israeli propaganda. Flannery fails to mention the destruction of the Arab villages, to ensure that no Arab would return home. It is a matter of concern that sensitive issues of inter-communal dialogue are undertaken on behalf of a national hierarchy by a person of such scholastic ineptitude, ignorance of history, and political naiveté. Such an unbecoming state of affairs, alas, is not confined to the USA.

For Father Flannery, any criticism of Israel is likely to result from 'a species of unconscious theological hangover' related to 'a residue of the deicidal myth'. Anti-Zionism is not necessarily, but is almost always a symptom of 'the antisemitic virus' (1986: 82). He appeals for a Christian theology of Israel as a land, and points to Rom 9.4–5 to show Judaism's continuing election. That text, however, which acknowledges that 'the adoption, the glory, the covenants, the giving of the law, the worship, and the promises, the patriarchs' belong to the Israelites, makes no reference to land, and certainly not to a national state. Moreover, it asserts that from them, according to the flesh, comes the Messiah, a Pauline claim Flannery does not pursue. In his zeal to accord Messianic significance to the State of Israel, Flannery is sympathetic to the view that the modern state fulfils some of the prophecies of the First Covenant which the Christian dispensation did not fulfil. He exhorts his Christian readers to repent for the contribution Christianity has made to the Jewish-Christian rift over the centuries and for the impasse in the Middle East (Flannery 1986: 84–85).

The adulation of Zionism is no less striking in Father Robert F. Drinan, Dean of Boston College Law School. With language that would have surprised the Zionist visionary, Drinan describes Herzl as having pursued his 'Messianic pilgrimage' with a zeal 'infused with a compelling humanitarianism combined with traces of Jewish mysticism' (Drinan 1977: 32). The 'mystery' and 'majesty' of Zionism appears in its glory from Herzl's tomb (p. 39). Now that the state is established, Christians should support it 'in reparation or restitution for the genocide of Jews carried out in a nation whose population was overwhelmingly Christian' (p. 1).

Father Drinan's reputation for always raising his voice 'for the victims who are forgotten, cheated, or betrayed' (Wiesel in Drinan 1977: xi) is not evidenced in the case of the Palestinians. Moreover, his grasp of the facts leaves something to be desired. Writing of 'The Miracle of Israel's Rebirth' he informs us that Jews 'had constituted a majority [in Palestine] for more than a century', and that destruction stared Israel in the face in 1948–49 (1977: 85–86). Moreover, the Zionists never intended any disadvantage to the Palestinians: the public utterances of Ben-Gurion guaranteeing respect for Arab rights, and Chaim Weizmann's assurance that 'not a hair of their head shall be touched', point to 'the clear and unmistakable intention of the Jewish founders of Israel' (p. 91).

Despite such reliable assurances, however, as many as 590,000 (sic) Arabs 'emigrated' from Israel in 1947 and 1948, despite 'the objective evidence that Israelis in many instances urged Arab residents to remain', proved by the radio broadcasts (already demonstrated to be bogus some sixteen years prior to Drinan's book – see Chapter 7), as well as Israel's Proclamation of Independence calling upon the Arab inhabitants of Israel 'to return to the ways of peace'. Even the destruction of the Arab villages – not mentioned in his study also – is not sufficient to convince Father Drinan that 'the vast migration of Arabs' bore witness to Israel's real desires for the indigenous people. While he recounts Count Bernadotte's report to the UN that elemental justice demanded the right of the innocent victims of the conflict to return, he accepts Ben-Gurion's excuse that to do so would be to admit a 'fifth column' (pp. 91–95). In a somewhat novel interpretation of natural justice, Father Drinan affirms that

> The Palestinians, who claim that they have a right to return to land which thirty years ago their ancestors may have owned or occupied, can hardly be deemed to have a moral right to that of some 800,000 Jews

who were quite literally driven out of Arab lands after the establishment of Israel in 1948.

(1977: 119)

Jews and Christians: a troubled family

The widely read book of Professor Walter Harrelson and Rabbi Randall M. Falk (1990), a product of a graduate seminar of the Divinity School of Vanderbilt University (launched in 1986), also illustrates how the State of Israel features in the Jewish–Christian dialogue. The intention is to provide basic knowledge in the most crucial areas of Jewish and Christian traditions and beliefs, and to present enough background information to make these understandable (Harrelson and Falk 1990: 11).

After a co-authored Introduction, there are eight chapters in which Rabbi Falk gives a Jewish outlook, followed by a Christian outlook from Professor Harrelson, followed by a conclusion by the two.[11] The book reflects the urbane, eirenic spirit, in which the two participants, long-time friends and associates, independently express their views on areas of common interest (1990: 193). Despite the new atmosphere in the post-Vatican II Roman Catholic Church and in the mainline Protestant Churches old stereotypes remain (Falk 1990: 13). The fundamental disposition suffusing the discussion is that both faiths lead to the same pinnacle on the mountain, albeit by different paths (Harrelson and Falk 1990: 10). Some will be unhappy with it, since it places all forms of Judaism and Christianity on an equal footing: Rabbinic Judaism, Orthodox Judaism, Reform Judaism, revivalist nationalist Judaism (e.g. Gush Emunim), the anti-Zionist Judaism of Neturei Karta, and the no less distinctive brands of Christianity. Harrelson is timid on the question of those qualities of Christianity which go beyond the world views of Rabbinic Judaism.

While one would dispute several of the perspectives of both Falk and Harrison, it is to their presentation of the State of Israel that one takes most exception. Falk's treatment of the birth of Zionism and the State of Israel contradicts both the theory of Zionism and its implementation in 1948. Reflecting a totally benevolent interpretation of events, it distorts facts of history, omits core elements of the discourse, and makes claims that lack substance. Having defined Zionism as a political movement, Falk immediately invokes van Buren's assessment that for many Jews, Messianism

---

11 The chapters are titled 'How We View Each Other'; 'Historical Perspectives on the Relationships of Jews and Non-Jews'; 'Understanding Our Scriptures'; 'Understanding Our God Concepts'; 'Understanding Our Relationship to Jesus'; 'Understanding Anti-Semitism and the Holocaust'; 'Understanding the State of Israel'; 'Understanding Election, Covenant, and Mission'.

was the primary element in Zionism, and that the formation of the state was a step in the direction of the fulfilment of biblical promises. The fact that from the beginning Zionism was rejected as a sin by the Orthodox establishment, and as a reversion to irredentism by Reform Jewry is metamorphosed into a statement that 'some extreme orthodox Jews' do not accept the existence of Israel (Falk 1990: 153).

Discussion of the treatment of the indigenous population of Palestine is naïve, if not cynical. For Falk, Israel bears no responsibility for their exodus. He describes their expulsion as a (voluntary) flight. The Jewish defeat of 'the heavily armed Arabs' who greatly outnumbered the Jews is one of the miracles of the twentieth century. On three more occasions, Israel was forced to defend its borders (1956, 1967, 1973). We learn that in 1967 Israel was threatened 'by a new attempt at genocide by seven Arab states' (Falk 1990: 39), and that, while on the verge of extinction, she miraculously routed her enemies. The Christian Churches and Christian nations remained harshly silent on that life-threatening occasion (Falk 1990: 149–51). Despite his partiality to life-threatening conditions, Falk's summary of Israel's history makes no mention of the several invasions of Lebanon (1978, 1982, 1994, 1996). On several occasions he laments the lack of support of Christians for Israel, and charges that 'the anti-Israel stance of many Christian leaders and their followers is really anti-Semitism by another name' (Falk 1990: 153; see also 39–40).

Falk concedes that Israel would not allow the Palestinians to return to their homes, but pays no respect to its obligations in international law. Instead he shifts the blame to the surrounding Arab states: 'None of the Arab nations that forced them to leave Israel would accept these refugees within their borders' (Falk 1990: 146). He implies that the numbers of refugees were swollen by the exile of Palestinians from Jordan, Syria and Lebanon. He criticises Christian concern for Palestinian refugees, in the absence of concern for Israel's refugees who had to flee from Europe's nightmare and Arab persecution. He makes no mention of the fact that driving out the Palestinians was a necessary condition for creating a Jewish state, nor of the wilful destruction of Arab villages, nor of Israel's persistent violations of International Law and refusals to abide by numerous Resolutions of the UN since 1967. The major problem resulting from the Six Day War was what to do with the predominantly Arab populations (Falk 1990: 150). Withdrawing and leaving them alone, in accordance with the requirements of law and UN Resolutions, is not entertained.

Falk's treatment of the biblical basis for a Promised Land is facile. He does not pay sufficient attention to the literary forms and purposes of the biblical documents. In general, he appeals to the legends of the Patriarchal and Pentateuchal Narratives as though they were reliable witnesses to the history of the periods they purport to narrate. He does not allude to the biblical mandate to wipe out the peoples who inhabited the land, and moves on immediately to the background of modern Zionism, which he situates within a framework of continuity with allegedly perennial Jewish aspirations. He claims that there was an independent Jewish state for some one third of the 4,000 years of Jewish presence in the land (Falk 1990: 147).

The customary asymmetries within the Jewish–Christian dialogue are restated. On the one hand, individual Christians today, even those in the USA, are required to say, 'I am sorry for what my Christian forebears and contemporaries have done to Jews. And I am sorry for my own part in it'. Collectively, the Church should observe the Days of Remembrance of the *Shoah*, and the world-wide Christian community should erect a memorial to the victims of the *Shoah* (Harrelson and Falk 1990: 195–97). Christians, then, are required to protect Israel, deny the Palestinian catastrophe, and acknowledge the sole legitimacy of the Zionist historiography of Judaism.

There is no question of a collective of Jews acknowledging Zionist responsibility for the catastrophe perpetrated on the Palestinian Arabs precisely in order to establish a Jewish state. There is no requirement to say 'I am sorry' for what Zionism has enforced on the indigenous population within the lifetime of many Israelis, and no suggestion that a monument might be erected in Israel itself to provide a memorial to the plunder. In the absence of the acknowledgement of any responsibility by Jews, the moral imperative is swung again to the Christians who together with Jews must seek and find a common ground on which to build firm support for the State of Israel, and at the same time join in the quest for securing basic human rights for the Palestinians (Falk 1990: 155–56). The contradiction between the two aspirations does not appear to have struck Rabbi Falk.

In his summary of the biblical witness to land, Harrelson's invocation of Exod 3.8 includes the land's description as 'flowing with milk and honey', but evades the moral problem by disregarding the second half of that verse ('to the country of the Canaanites, the Hittites, the Amorites, the Perizzites, the Hivites, and the Jebusites'). Instead we are brought to the idealised picture of Ezek 47.1–12; Zech 14.8; and Psalm 104. This marvellous hymn in praise of God and land leads to his question, 'Who can possibly live without land?' – to which one might reasonably reply, 'the Palestinians'. Harrelson, forgetting much of the Pentateuch and all of Joshua, sees the biblical gift of land as sheer grace to 'all living beings', and not to Israel alone. He evades the narrative's mandate to destroy utterly the indigenous population, and finds recourse in the usual exhortations about showing concern for the rights and needs of others (1990: 159–60). His treatment of 'land' in New Testament perspectives is sparse. There is nothing of the missionary spirit of Luke–Acts or Matt 28.16–20. Christians, while not entirely sharing their view of the land, should understand very well its distinct place for Jews, which leads Harrelson on to dealing with Zionism and the State of Israel. But his task has been rendered easier: 'Rabbi Falk has laid out the story clearly and well above' (Harrelson 1990: 164).

Harrelson considers that Western Christians have been more sympathetic towards the Arabs than Jews, and applauds the solid and dependable affirmation of Israel's right to exist among evangelicals (1990: 165) – even though their hopes are for the ultimate demise of Judaism. Without indicating why, he supports the self-determination of the Palestinians. Nevertheless, he is in admiration of the remarkable achievement of Israel, in being 'a champion of public justice and of the rights of its individual citizens' and a democratic state. He acknowledges that this achievement has been at considerable cost to Palestinians, and adds that injustices continue to be perpetrated, on both sides (p. 166) – thereby following the convention unique to this case of according the occupier and the occupied equal standing before justice.

By way of summary, the book is an example of a courteous and respectful exposition of many common and distinctive elements of Judaism and Christianity. While it retains those qualities in its treatment of Zionism and the State of Israel, it offends against historical truth and perennial justice. It accords with the major terms of the Zionist fabrication of Jewish historiography. It bears witness to the emasculation of even liberal, mainstream, Judaism by the Zionist ideology, and, no less seriously, illustrates how Christianity might suffer a like fate.

Christians and Jews. A new way of thinking

Christians and Jews. A New Way of Thinking. Guidelines for the Churches, published in 1994 by the Council of Churches for Britain and Ireland's Commission for Inter-Faith Relations inevitably deals with 'The importance of Israel' (p. 14). The comment is noteworthy both in what it states, and in what it leaves unstated.

The trilogy that 'Israel is important to nearly all Jews as a vital focus of Jewish faith, as a culmination of an age-old Jewish longing and as a place of security after centuries of persecution' reflects a partial reading of history, and ignores vital ingredients of the discourse. There is no evidence to show that the establishment of a Jewish state would be considered to be 'a culmination of an age-old Jewish longing' before the advent of political Zionism. Political Zionism arose in a context of European nationalism in the nineteenth century, and the realisation of its goal, partial up to the present time, owes much to the interests of the imperialist powers, from the beginning to the present day. To equiparate the State of Israel with the highest ideals of Judaism is to regard political Zionism as the most authentic expression of the Jewish spirit.

The claim that 'Israel is a place of security after centuries of persecution' is contestable as a matter of fact, as the wars of 1948, 1956, 1967, 1973 and 1982 suggest. To accept that the establishment of a nation state was the appropriate response to 'centuries of persecution' is no less contestable. To state as an ideal the gathering of all the Jews of the world into the region of Jewish origins is to accept the impossibility of Jews living authentically among the *goyim*.

The document adds that many Churches recognise the State of Israel as the 'imperative reality of contemporary Jewish life', and suggest that 'disregard for Israel's safety and welfare is incompatible with the Church's necessary concern for the Jewish people'. It is not clear whether the alleged rights of Jews constitute an absolute imperative, irrespective of the conflicting rights of others. Are Christians required to accord absolute authority to the alleged rights of Jews only? However, 'Christians also have to balance this with acute concern for justice for the Palestinian people'. It is not clear what 'acute concern for justice' requires. Does it include the acknowledgement that what Zionists did to the Palestinians in 1948 and since is wrong, for which atonement and compensation should follow, as in a normal moral discourse? Is it not clear that the demands of justice for Palestinians conflict fundamentally with the desire of Zionists to establish a state for Jews at their expense? On what basis, then, does one require support for the Zionist state, and something less for Palestinians?

Conclusion

In the course of this century the attitude of the Holy See to the Holy Land has changed profoundly, in line with the momentous changes which have taken place in the Middle East and in its own perception of its role in the world. Several factors have influenced its approach to the region: a greater awareness of its mission to be 'the Church of the Poor', with liberation from social and political oppression becoming increasingly an integral part of its programme, and a growing involvement in dialogue with Islam.

The Holy See's reasons for establishing diplomatic relations with regimes of various complexions owe as much to the pragmatism of *Realpolitik* as to the moral vision of Jesus. The Fundamental Agreement with Israel is primarily one by which the two bodies look to their own interests. It would be a scandal if it were construed to accord approval to the plunder associated with the expulsion of up to a million Palestinians, Israel's persistent violation of international laws and conventions and failure to deal justly with the Palestinians. If the Holy See chooses to take advantage of this new relationship to use its good offices to promote peace and justice in the region so much the better.[12] If the Catholic Church considers that it has much to do

---

12 The results so far are not impressive. In an intervention which Archbishop Montezemolo invited after his Notre Dame Centre lecture, I informed him that I had expected that the Fundamental Agreement would have given the Holy See some leverage in putting pressure on Israel *vis-à-vis* the Palestinians, if only on the matter of entry into Jerusalem for worship, which was severely restricted since March 1993, in violation of one of the most fundamental human rights, one guaranteed also in the Agreement. The observation appeared to ruffle some of the audience of exclusively Israeli Jews and expatriate Christians, with no Palestinian Christian in sight. The Apostolic Delegate asked rhetorically if I did not think that the Holy See was doing all it could. At the reception afterwards, another architect of the Agreement berated me in a stridently rude and aggressive manner for my intervention. I had violated the grand silence.

to atone for its brutality towards Jews in the past, let it be done graciously, and at its own expense. Present-day Palestinians, as the innocent third party, should not have to pay the price for the sins of others.

Several features of the debate within the Churches of the Reformation suggest that one is dealing with an unique discourse. The guilt of Western Churches in the face of the persecution of Jews in the past, and most immediately during the period of the Third Reich casts a long shadow. The documents of these Churches – and it is only the Western Churches which have felt the need to define their religious identity in relation to Judaism – betray a certain 'Orientalist' approach to the indigenous population of Palestine, displaying little awareness of the core element of Zionism which required its expulsion. They underplay the extent of the catastrophe which befell the indigenous Arab population of Palestine in 1948–49, 1967, and since. Nor is there adequate engagement with Israel's discriminatory policies towards non-Jews within the state, and of the ongoing oppression in the Occupied Territories.

No reference is made to the fact that political Zionism came on the scene as a conscious abrogation of, and rebellion against religious Judaism, and of the general opposition to its programme until the mid-1930s. Moreover, there is no significant alignment with the requirements of international law and conventions on human rights. While according something of a national character to Jews, there is hesitation to do so to the Palestinian Arabs. The balance of sympathy leans heavily in favour of the Jewish people, with little evidence of a critique of the actions of the Zionists that one might expect in our post-colonial culture. The 'bottom line' is that the Jewish people needed a state, and where there is acknowledgement that somebody would have to pay for its creation, critically it is someone else who pays, ironically a people with no record of persecution of Jews.

Western Christian support for the State of Israel has been facilitated by the Jewish-Christian dialogue, in which one detects a virtually unconditional support for the State of Israel. This is noticeable also in the publications and statements emanating from organisations committed to the dialogue, which frequently embarrass people of goodwill. Whatever its intentions its *modus operandi* reflects an asymmetric ecumenical pact whereby Christians are required to condemn *sine die* the outrages committed against Jews over 2,000 years, while denying, or maintaining silence on the injustices done the Palestinians in our own day: 'for the first hundred years, Christians must be silent in their contact with Jews, and just listen and learn' (in Higgins 1986: 33–34).

Outsiders to the Christian–Jewish discussions may not detect such a marked diversity of views as one expects to find in dialogue between two parties holding contrasting or contrary views. Indeed, one is struck by the coalition of perspectives, particularly those reflecting enthusiastic support for the State of Israel, irrespective of the challenges to international legality, justice and human rights its behaviour offers. Those who engage in the dialogue demonstrate an exceptional unanimity of purpose wherever they are to be found, and appear to see their mission as not only to be uncritical supporters of the policies of the State of Israel, but to be a highly organised, if somewhat naïve pressure group determined to stifle public criticism of Israel's behaviour. The discourse might more appropriately be described as a monologue in two voices, which would not in itself be fatal, if it were not also dependent upon a distortion of truth and a denial of natural justice and international legality. The American Jewish theologian Marc Ellis advocates that it is time to bury 'the ecumenical bargain' of Christian guilt and silence on the Palestinian catastrophe, and engage in a new dialogue, guided by honesty, in which the interests of truth, justice and peace would be determinative. The critical question on which the integrity and credibility of the dialogue depends is its attitude in the face of the threat to survival of the Palestinian people (*The Tablet* 20 January 1988).

Although the behaviour of the State of Israel towards the Palestinians has been met by widespread international criticism, and is a cause of great distress among many people, including many Jews, mostly secular, the response of the Churches as reflected in the documents we have addressed reflect little of the tradition of dissent and the prophetic tradition protesting against the exploitation of people. Instead we detect a distinctive mode of discourse, in which the perceived needs of Jews at one, rather eccentric period of their history becomes a moral imperative that does not have to contend with the needs or rights of any other community. Zionism defines its own moral terms and provides what it is pleased to regard as its own moral justification. However, recourse to moral discourse cannot rest easily on Zionist shoulders. The establishment of the State of Israel was possible only on the basis of land-theft and massive expulsion. No amount of legal gymnastics could ever justify such acts against the indigenous population. From that point on, the consolidation of the foundational immorality became the only possible form of the exercise of legal power. Hence the corruption of the normal discourse of jurisprudence, which instead of being an instrument of morality would compound the original crime. For religious bodies to accord legitimacy to such activity is highly problematic, even in consideration of good relations between two religious traditions.

5 Zionism within Christian theology

It is clear from the writings of theologians and the views and activities of different groups that the State of Israel has enjoyed widespread support in many Western Christian circles, at least until recently. There is a Christian Zionism which encompasses a wide range of organisations and individuals. This Christian support is virtually unconditional and uncritical, and derives from theoretical considerations which override any evaluation of the actual conditions under which the state was established and behaves. It is rare that such support is accompanied by a concern for the Palestinian people. Some Christian groups financially support Jewish settlement in the Occupied Territories. While mainstream Christian support stems from a desire to atone for the ill-treatment of Jews in the past, especially in the wake of the *Shoah*, some evangelical Christians view the state as a manifestation of God's salvific purposes, seeing its establishment as constituting a partial fulfilment of the prophecies of the Hebrew Scriptures. We shall assess each of these movements in turn.

Mainstream Christian Zionism

The role of the *Shoah* in Western Christian thought has been critical. Jewish–Christian dialogue has been dominated by Holocaust theology, with its emphasis on suffering and empowerment, frequently making Christians silent partners to Israeli policy. Christian theological support of Zionist theology is reflected in Reinhold Niebuhr, who celebrated the birth of Israel as a triumph of justice and liberation (Fox 1987: 209–10), and continues in the work of Franklin Littell, Paul van Buren, Alice and Roy Eckardt, Robert McAfee Brown, John Pawlikowski, and others. Reflecting Western Orientalist attitudes, Niebuhr was disdainful of Arab culture and saw 'Jewish Palestine and Christian Lebanon as islands of Western civilization confronted by the hopeless picture of an Arab-Moslem Middle East' (in Ellis 1990: 134–36).

For Alice and Roy Eckardt, Christian faith is yoked spiritually to *Eretz Yisrael* (1970: 262–63). They assert that if Jesus were living today he could be identified only as an Israeli Jew, without speculating on what part of the spectrum from Gush Emunim to Neturei Karta he would fall – perhaps he would be among the Rabbis for Human Rights. They criticise Western Christians for having done almost nothing to educate Christian Arabs as the rightful claims of the Jews in Israel (1970: 259). Paul van Buren sees in Zionism the fulfilment of the diaspora longing for a return to *Eretz Yisrael*. The land, 'desolate and untended' needed its people to care for it. Resistance to Zionism should give way to gratitude and thanksgiving, for God's fidelity. Instead of resisting Israel, the peoples of the First and Third Worlds should emulate her (van Buren 1980).

Robert McAfee Brown appeals to the *Shoah* to justify the charge that, while he had been a champion of human rights he had not criticised the behaviour of Israel: 'A high degree of Christian complicity in the murder of six million Jews ... has cast a heavy shadow over my view of the world, my understanding of God, my estimate of human nature and my theology of the church'. While he acknowledges that this approach failed to take with equal moral seriousness the displacement of the Palestinians, criticism of Israel would be interpreted as a continuation of the almost two thousand years of Christian anti-Jewishness. He would want neither to alienate his Jewish friends and expend the 'capital' he had accumulated through years of dialogue, nor face the opprobrium of being called antisemitic. Moreover, Christians did not wish to aid 'the enemies of Israel, who are antisemitic, terroristic, chauvinistic, unreasoning, or all of the above'. But with the *intifada* it was impossible to remain silent. Israel should not be given 'a blank moral cheque', for, 'What shall it profit the State of Israel to gain the whole of the Middle East and lose its own soul?' (R.M. Brown 1990b: 139–42). McAfee Brown's comments reflect his assumption that the Zionist venture was valid from the beginning, and went astray only later. He views Israel effectively only from the perspective of Israeli Jews, and Jews almost exclusively from the perspective of the *Shoah* (1990b: 145). He also posits the Palestinian–Israeli problematic as though the contending parties enjoyed equal rights, although it is clear that he considers Israel's rights to be 'more equal'. His position appears to be that the dilemma of Jews must be solved at whatever cost to others.

John Pawlikowski, too, is a self-confessed partisan for Israel. He embraces the 'rediscovery of the cardinal role that the "land tradition" plays in the Jewish Scriptures', authenticated by W.D. Davies and W. Brueggemann. He assumes Israel's right to exist as axiomatic even in a place already inhabited by another people. While he postulates the 'equal claim' to sovereignty of Palestinians and Israelis he pays little attention to the sufferings of the Palestinian population. He repeats the claim that Arab institutions and commanders ordered Arabs to abandon their territory in 1948, and suggests that evidence (which he does not provide) shows that a fair number of the families now living on the West Bank/Gaza do not have long-time Palestinian roots, but came in as Jews began to improve the living conditions to a level unparalleled in the Middle East. This Professor of Social Ethics accepts that displacement of people from their ancestral homes is justified, since their allegiance was to villages or cities, rather than to a larger national identity. And, in any case, 'we cannot forget that some six hundred thousand Jewish refugees were also forced from Arab countries where most often they too suffered serious human rights deprivations'. The existence of Israel as a solution for such people 'adds basic moral weight to Israel's right to exist as a cardinal value in the current Middle East picture' (Pawlikowski 1990: 160–63). His exigency to defend Israel draws him away from the foundations of universal moral discourse, and propels him into equating what is not equal, ignoring central facts of history, accepting propagandistic distortions of truth, and, above all, according legitimacy to an enterprise which could achieve its goal only at the expense of another people. Such views diverge from a fundamental Christian perception that all humankind, being created in the image and likeness of God, consists of people who are one in their origin and destiny, rather than being divided according to less fundamental and noble categories.

'Evangelical Christians' and Zionism

We have seen that mainstream Christian theological commentary on Israel–Palestine is driven by guilt feelings concerning the treatment of Jews in the past, and is characterised by a detachment from the international political context of Zionism, by naïvety or misinformation concerning the realities of its conquest of and rule over Palestine, and by a certain paralysis of conscience regarding the unjust treatment of the indigenous population. The evangelical fundamentalist wing adds its own distinctive theological perspective.

Christian Zionism is a central plank of the evangelical 'right', which includes the International Christian Embassy of Jerusalem, Christians' Israel Public Action Campaign, Friends of Jerusalem, Bridges of Peace, the American Messianic Fellowship, The Messianic Jewish Alliance of America, Jews for Jesus, the Churches Mission Among the Jews, the Christian Friends of Israel, the Evangelical Sisterhood of Mary and, although it is not restricted to fundamentalist Christian perspectives, the Council of Christians and Jews (see Sizer 1994: 32). To the surprise of many in Europe where it is only at the fringes of Church life, the evangelical fundamentalist wing is particularly influential in the USA.[1]

While allowing for variations in location and among groups, characteristically Christian Zionism takes its cue from a particular reading of certain passages of the Bible, leading to a peculiar theological interpretation of the State of Israel. It is insensitive to the human rights of the Palestinians, demonises Islam, and assists in the immigration of Jews to Israel. It supports Israeli governments indiscriminately, as a step in the direction of the coming of the millennium, while having little respect for Judaism as such.

---

1   For Christian Zionism in Britain see Sizer 1999, and in Scandinavia see Gunner 1999.

The International Christian Embassy, which is quartered in the former family home in Jerusalem of Edward Said, is the most overtly political supporter of Israel, and has been exploited by all Israeli Prime Ministers since its foundation in 1980. It proclaims that the ingathering of the Jewish People and the rebirth of the nation of Israel are in fulfilment of biblical prophecies. Since God gave the land to the Jewish people as an everlasting possession, they have absolute rights over all of it, including Judea, Samaria, Gaza and the Golan. God will bless, or curse nations in accordance with their treatment of the Chosen People of Israel.[2] Similarly, Basilea Schlink of the Evangelical Sisterhood of Mary warns,

> Anyone who disputes Israel's right to the land of Canaan is actually opposing God and his holy covenant with the Patriarchs. He is striving against sacred, inviolable words and promises of God, which He has sworn to keep.
>
> (Schlink 1991: 22)

In such circles, biblical attitudes of justice, mercy, love of one's enemies, etc., are either ignored or reinterpreted when applied to Israel.

Fundamentalist Evangelical Christian Zionism

In evangelical Christian theology there is a strong emphasis on a literalist fulfilment of biblical prophecy, on eschatology and, in some circles, on millenarianism, that brand of eschatology which affirms that the Second Coming of Christ will be followed by a thousand year reign of blessedness.[3] With regard to the State of Israel, there are two major strands: fulfilment of

---

2   From International Christian Zionist Proclamation (25–29 February 1996). A united Jerusalem is to be the capital of Israel only; no nation should recognise a Palestinian in any part of the land, etc. In April 1990, the leader of the Knesset presented the embassy with the Quality of Life Award for its positive role in Israeli life. In August 1994, I conducted an interview with its founder and current leader, Jan Willem van der Hoeven, whose perspective excluded all consideration of human rights' issues, against the background of the overriding, allegedly divine authorisation of the affairs of the state of Israel. He has been its major ideologue since its foundation.

3   The broad term 'evangelical' refers to the pietistic strands of Christianity which stress a literal interpretation of Scripture as the framework for the 'born again' conversion experience. It includes left, centre and right perspectives over a range of issues. Current estimates in the USA number some fifty-five to sixty million, chiefly from the mainline Protestant Churches, and some twenty million from the African-American Evangelical Churches. On the right, Jerry Falwell, W.A. Criswell and Pat Robertson lead some sixteen million enthusiastically pro-Israel, and anti-Islam supporters. The evangelical centre covers some forty million, representing the forty-six Protestant denominations in the National Association of Evangelicals, the evangelical alternative to the National Council of Churches. It publishes *Christianity Today* and has Billy Graham as its best known spokesman. Exposure to the plight of the Palestinians has brought about some changes in this traditionally pro-Israel constituency. The left wing (some 10 per cent) is an influential minority which espouses issues of social concern (Wagner 1992: 3).

biblical prophecy, and the association of the state with a theology of the end-time. Regina Sharif argues that the basis for such an association can be traced to the religious changes that accompanied the Protestant Reformation in Europe (1983).

The Protestant Reformation unleashed a new interest in the Old Testament with its stress on the notions of Chosen People and of Yahweh's covenant with it, an emphasis which helped to consolidate the notion of the essential separateness of Jews and their biblically-based link with Palestine. The Christian doctrine of the Second Coming of Christ, moreover, had associated with it the eventual return of diaspora Jews. Thus, the biblical paradigm of Chosen People and Promised Land could be deployed later in favour of political Zionism, and, for those seeking theological motivation, constitute its inner logic. This is not to suggest that the new biblical exegesis provided the catalyst for the emergence of the *Zeitgeist* which produced Herzl's programme, but only that the reawakened interest in a 'literalist', as opposed to an allegorical reading of the Scriptures contributed to the renewal of interest in a collective, 'national' identity of the Jewish 'people' who were desirous of a return to the homeland, and produced, virtually for the first time in Western Christianity, a certain Judaeophilia.

The Protestant Reformation also had the effect of resurrecting particular elements of eschatological thought, such as Messianism and Millenarianism, concerning the (second) coming of the Messiah and his reign on earth. Whereas earlier Christian Theology interpreted the Old Testament mainly in a teleological sense of the inexorable fulfilment of its promises, with the goal already achieved in the coming of Jesus the Messiah, Reformation Theology facilitated the identification of contemporary Jews with the ancient Hebrews, and many Protestants began to associate their ingathering with the Second Coming of Christ. The Bible was understood now in a straightforward, literalist mode. Although this brought one closer to the world of the Old Testament narrative, and rescued it from being a mere prefigurement of Christian fulfilment, the stress on the clear sense of the text did not encourage one to distinguish between narratives depicting the real past from legends fabricated centuries after the alleged events they narrate. Protestant Europe was much more aware of the traditions of the migration of Abraham than of any other migration, and of the kingdom of David than of other kingdoms. Thus the Old Testament nourished popular piety and learning, and provided Europe's only insight into the history of the Middle East, one refracted through the particularising lens of the biblical authors. With the controlling voice exercised by them the wider history of the region was effectively silenced.

The Protestant Reformation, then, was the vehicle through which a whole matrix of belief patterns and values favourable to subsequent Zionism infused Western Protestant thought in the sixteenth century, found multiple expression in several parts of Europe in the seventeenth century, and continued to find expression in Protestant millenarian circles ever since. The Old Testament continued to influence Western culture, and in the eighteenth century was a major source of inspiration in the arts both in England and in mainland Europe. Even in the so-called Age of Reason, the notion of Jewish restoration featured in the writings of prominent European philosophers and scientists: Locke, Newton, Hartley, Kant, Fichte, Rousseau, Herder and others (see Sharif 1983: 36–38).

John Nelson Darby (1800–82), perhaps more than anyone else, laid the foundations for the development of Fundamentalist Evangelical Christian Zionism, whose influence in the USA today is so powerful and utilised by the Israeli establishment to further its interests. A minister of the Church of Ireland, Darby renounced the visible Church (1962, Vol. 20: 456), and organised a group of 'Brethren', whose distinctive theology was devised for the final days of history. While the division of history into a number of periods (dispensations) antedated his theological speculations, Darby divided it into seven epochs, beginning with Creation, and ending with the millennial Kingdom of Jesus, following the Battle of Armageddon, views he claims to have derived from his exegesis of Scripture and from personal proddings of the Holy Spirit (Darby 1962, Vol. II: 6–7, 108).

Rather than subscribing to the view that the Church had replaced Israel, Darby claimed that Israel would replace the Church, which was a mere parenthesis to God's continuing covenantal relationship with Israel. Those portions of biblical prophecy and apocalyptic which had not been fulfilled already would be completed in the future. He invoked the apocalyptic language of Col 3.4 and 1 Thess 4.15 to postulate a two-stage Second Coming of Christ. The first 'invisible appearing' would involve the 'rapture of the saints': the faithful remnant of the Church, especially his own followers, would go up to meet Christ in the air, before his appearing on earth (Darby 1962, Vol. II: 153–55). The raptured saints, having joined the Lord in the air, would return to earth with him after seven years, as indicated in 1 Thessalonians (Darby n.d. Vol. V: 91). The seven-year long rapture in the air would be marked on earth by the 'Great Tribulation' of natural disasters, wars and civil unrest. After the rapture, a faithful Jewish remnant would observe the Law, and rule on earth for a millennium (Darby 1962, Vol. I: 94).

B.W. Newton, his chief assistant in Plymouth, considered Darby's insistence on two dispensations, one for the Church, and the second for Israel, as a departure from biblical orthodoxy, and proposed a variant: the Jews would be restored only after the return of Christ, who would bring them to faith in the Messiah, making them into a kingdom of priests and a holy nation (1838: 306). With his authority waning in Britain, Darby concentrated on North America, where he influenced such evangelical leaders as Dwight L. Moody, William E. Blackstone and C.I. Schofield and the emerging Bible and Prophecy Conference movement which set the tone for the evangelical and fundamentalist movements in North America between 1875 and 1920 (Wagner 1995: 89). Typically, Dispensationalism predicates that the present age is the penultimate one: biblical prophecy finds its fulfilment in the birth of the State of Israel, and soon Christ will come in glory to bring matters to a cataclysmic triumph over the forces of evil at Armageddon.

Fundamentalist Evangelical Christian Zionism in the USA

There has been strong support for the establishment of a Jewish commonwealth among American evangelicals for well over a century, due in no small measure to Darby and those whom he influenced (Bass 1960: 17, 63). For William E. Blackstone Zionism was 'the fulfilment of prophecy'. He visited Palestine in 1889 and was impressed by the agricultural settlements and other developments in the first aliyah, all 'signs of the times', indicating that the end-time would come very soon (1908: 210–13, 236–41). In 1891, he organised a national campaign to urge President Harrison to support the establishment of a Jewish state in Palestine, with the morally superior USA like a modern Cyrus speeding the return of the Jews. Hearing that Herzl was considering Uganda or Argentina, Blackstone sent him a Bible, marking every passage which referred to Palestine, with instructions that it alone was to be the site of the Jewish state (see Wagner 1992: 4). In 1916 he presented a second petition to the President of the USA, this time co-ordinating with American Zionist leaders, Louis Brandeis, Steven Wise and Jacob de Haas (Ariel 1992: 439). The Zionist leaders passed over Blackstone's real hopes for the Jews and his disparagement of the Jewish Law as an agent of salvation as the price for his support for the Zionist venture.

The evangelical constituency was critical of the British policy of limiting the numbers of Jewish immigrants, and was disdainful of Arab opposition: they would pay dearly for their rebellion against God (see Ariel 1992: 441–42). Christian support was taken up by the Pro-Palestine Federation, and the Christian Council on Palestine, founded in 1932 and 1942, respectively, which included in their membership Reinhold Niebuhr and Paul Tillich.

A coalition between Christian evangelicals and secular Zionists had enough advantage for each party to co-operate on the one issue of the establishment of a Jewish state. Their example has been followed by all Israeli Prime Ministers since Begin in 1977. Up to the 1970s, the evangelicals did not have significant influence over American policy, but have exerted considerable since. When it came to power in 1977, the Likud Party in Israel began to use religious language to advance its Revisionist Zionist agenda, which was popular with some branches of American Christianity, and efforts were made to forge bonds between evangelical Christians and pro-Israel lobbies. The evangelical Christian constituency was a major factor in the election of Jimmy Carter to the Presidency in 1976, and of Ronald Reagan in the 1980 election. Reagan was open to a particular reading of the Old Testament:

You know, I turn back to your ancient prophets in the Old Testament and signs foretelling Armageddon, and I find myself wondering if – if we're the generation that's going to come about. I don't know if you've noted any of those prophecies lately, but believe me, they certainly describe the times we're going through.[4]

The President's statement reflected an attitude to biblical prophecy which is prevalent in fundamentalist evangelical Christianity: Armageddon is the goal of history (Rev 16.16), and the futurist and eschatological thinking in the Old Testament is presumed to relate to the events of human history. The stage was set for promoting a cynical alliance between the conversionist goals of evangelical Christianity and the political aspirations of revisionist Zionism.

The establishment of the State of Israel is an important element in such a world view. The Jews have returned to their ancient homeland and allow themselves to be ruled by a Jewish impostor of the Messiah. But the return of Jesus, the true Messiah, will end the anti-Christ's rule and establish the millennial kingdom. Those Jews who survive will welcome Jesus as their Saviour. During the 1,000 year reign, Jesus would establish his capital in Jerusalem, the centre of world government, and the Jewish people, now living within the boundaries of the ancient kingdom of David, would assist him in his administration. The evangelical world viewed the birth of Israel as the first clear sign of the fulfilment of biblical prophecy and the final countdown to Armageddon. Israel's amazing victory over Arab armies in June 1967 confirmed the prophetic scenario. Immediately after the war L. Nelson Bell, editor of the mouthpiece of conservative evangelicalism, wrote, 'That for the first time in more than 2,000 years Jerusalem is now completely in the hands of the Jews gives the student of the Bible a thrill and a renewed faith in the accuracy and validity of the Bible' (*Christianity Today*, 21 July 1967, in O'Neill and Wagner 1993: 80–81).

Hal Lindsey's *The Late, Great Planet Earth* (1970), of which some twenty-five million copies have been bought, reflects a mixture of biblical literalism and political analysis, which is typical of a brand of evangelicals, with biblical predictions fulfilled almost to the letter: the establishment of Israel (Ezek 30–40); Jewish control over all Jerusalem (Zech 12–14); the alignment of Arab and Black African states against Israel (Ezek 30.4–5); the conversion of Africa to Communism (Dan 11.35–45); the Soviet threat in the north (Ezek 38–39), and the Chinese one in the east (Rev 9); the rise of the Common Market as the new Roman Empire (Dan 7.17), etc. In

4   From President Reagan's intimate phone conversation with Tom Dine, the Executive Director of the American Israel Political Affairs Committee (AIPAC), Israel's powerful US lobby (see Wagner 1992: 1).

Lindsey's interpretation of the sign of the fig tree (Matt 24.32), the most important sign for Matthew was to be the restoration of the Jews to the land in the rebirth of Israel: when the Jewish people, after nearly 2,000 years of exile became a nation again on 14 May 1948, the 'fig tree' put forth its first leaves. But the restoration was only a stage in Lindsey's eschatology. Under attack from godless Communism and militant Islam the State of Israel would fight an apocalyptic battle at the mount of Megiddo (Har Megiddo = Armageddon), in which Jesus Christ would come to the rescue, be proclaimed King of the Jews, and rule over the nations from the rebuilt temple in Jerusalem, at which point, 'Jerusalem will be the spiritual centre of the entire world. ... All people of the earth will come annually to worship Jesus who will rule there' (Lindsey 1983: 165).

The October War of 1973 gave further fuel to Armageddon theology. When President Carter shocked the fundamentalists with his concern for human rights, and used the words, 'Palestinian homeland' in a speech in March 1977 full-page newspaper advertisements appeared throughout the country, proclaiming, 'The time has come for evangelicals to affirm their belief in biblical prophecy and Israel's divine right to the Holy Land'. Reflecting its concern that Carter's advocacy of Palestinian rights might conflict with their interests, the text went on, 'We affirm as evangelicals our belief in the promised land to the Jewish people. ... We would view with grave concern any effort to carve out of the Jewish homeland another nation or political entity' ('Evangelicals' Concern for Israel', *Christian Science Monitor*, 3 November 1977, in O'Neill and Wagner 1993: 82). The swing of the evangelical 'right' from Carter to Reagan in the 1980 election was a major factor in the former's defeat.

Jerry Falwell's 'Friendship Tour to Israel' in 1983 included meetings with top Israeli government and military officials, a tour of Israeli battlefields and defence installations (Wagner 1992: 3). Falwell's 'Prophecy Trips' to Jerusalem heralded the immigration of Jews into Israel as *the* sign of the imminent Second Coming of Christ (Mahoney 1992: 2). Jesus would rapture true Christians into the air, while the rest of humankind would be slaughtered below. Then 144,000 Jews would bow down before Jesus and be saved, but the remainder would perish in the mother of all *Shoah*s. This could happen even while the evangelical pilgrims were in Jerusalem, thus giving them a ringside seat, as it were, at the Battle of Armageddon. In such a literalist reading, biblical prophecy is striving to bring about its fulfilment in the Middle East today: Saddam Hussein was reconstructing Babylon to the same specifications of splendour as in the days of Nebuchadnezzar, and the city would ignite the events of the end-times (Dyer 1993: 128–29, back cover).

The views summarised here are at the core of the normal creed of evangelicals, the result also of a carefully orchestrated and heavily financed campaign, co-ordinated by Jerry Strober, a former American-Jewish Committee employee, who recognised the value of the evangelicals to the Israelis. As the Committee's national interreligious affairs director, Rabbi

Marc Tannenbaum, attested later, the pro-Israeli lobby, feeling abandoned by the mainstream Protestant Churches, which, together with the National Council of Churches, were sympathetic to Third World countries, and supported the Palestinians, targeted the evangelicals, who had fifty-to-sixty million Americans, and a lot of money (*Washington Post*, 23 March 1981). Prime Minister Begin presented Jerry Falwell with the Jabotinsky Award from the Government of Israel in appreciation of his support. Pat Robertson charted the Israeli invasion of Lebanon in 1982 with daily reports on CBN, interpreting the events according to the end-time fulfilment of biblical prophecy. Israel's attack was a modern Joshua event. He urged American viewers to phone President Reagan immediately, offering encouragement to Israel's war against the Palestinians (O'Neill and Wagner 1993: 82–84).

Together with the power of the Jewish lobby, the influence of the North American evangelical right wing is a major factor preventing the USA from exercising even-handedness in the Middle East (see Wagner 1999). For example, on 27 January 1992 a full-page advertisement in the *Washington Times* claimed, 'Seventy Million Christians Urge President Bush to Approve Loan Guarantees for Israel' (Pikkert 1992: 19), and Hal Lindsey became a consultant on Middle East affairs to both the Pentagon and the Israeli government (Wagner 1992: 4). However, Pikkert argues that the media coverage of the Palestinian *intifada* has contributed to changing attitudes among even the evangelicals.

In a poll in *Christianity Today*, 88 per cent held that Israel should be bound by the same standards of justice and human rights as any other nation. Only 24 per cent said that the biblical mandate for Christians is to support the State of Israel, and 20 per cent said Israel has no legitimate claims on the territories won in 1967. Nevertheless, the evangelical 'right' was responsible for the pro-Israel advertisement in the *New York Times* on 10 April 1997, 'Christians Call for a United Jerusalem', supporting the uncompromising Likud position on Jewish sovereignty over the entire city. Moreover, some evangelical bodies have compensated for the fall-off of some USA Reform and Conservative Jewish support for the Jewish National Fund by providing substantial financial donations (see Wagner 1999), and by adopting settlements (see Sarah Honig, 'Adopt-a-Settlement Program', in *Jerusalem Post* 2 October 1995).

In Jerusalem itself, the leader of the International Christian Embassy continues to insist that Israel be faithful to its role within God's cosmic plans (van der Hoeven 1993). Israel should listen to God, rather than to the US Secretary of State, and not give up territory. In van der Hoeven's apocalyptic reading of human history Islam is satanic, and the mosques on the Temple Mount must be destroyed to prepare the way for the coming of the Lord, and the rebuilding of the temple (in Ariel 1997: 379–84). Indeed, no event in everyday Israeli political life is above the possibility of being interpreted as a fulfilment of a biblical prophecy.[5] In the USA Pastor John Hagee established himself 'as not just a prophetic voice on the end-times but "a prophet for our generation" '. Even the assassination of Rabin was in fulfilment of biblical prophecies, auguring the imminent arrival of Armageddon and the end of days. The peace process will result in the most devastating war Israel has ever known, after which the Messiah will come (Hagee 1996).

For their part, successive Israeli governments have entered into a marriage of convenience with the International Christian Embassy, happy to use it as a means of gaining support for Israel from some groups of Christians, while ignoring its eschatological expectations. Premier Netanyahu addressed its annual conference at the Jewish Feast of Tabernacles again in 1998. Ehud Olmert, the Mayor of Jerusalem, assured the gathering, 'I'm going to tell the Prime Minister, the Defence Minister, the Chief of Staff you are part of our army, of our power, of our defence'. The audience contained representatives of Christian Friends of Israeli Communities, an organisation that twins Churches in the USA with Israeli settlements (Sara Presant-Collins, *The Tablet*, 24 October 1998, p. 1387).

Critique of fundamentalist Evangelical Christian Zionism

Since the issues involved are of such significance for our interpretation of contemporary events, it is necessary to consider them in some detail. The theory of Millenarianism, on which Christian Zionism leans heavily, appeared early in the history of the Church, arising from discussions about the Second Coming of Christ. Chapter 20 of the Book of Revelation is the classical text of the thousand year reign:

> Then I saw an angel coming down from heaven, holding in his hand the key to the bottomless pit and a great chain. He seized the dragon, that ancient serpent, who is the Devil and Satan, and bound him for a thousand years, and threw him into the pit, and locked and sealed it over him, so that he would deceive the nations no more, until the thousand years were ended. After that he must be let out for a little while. Then I saw thrones, and those seated on them were given authority to judge.

---

5   Norma Archbold's work (1993) relates the return of the Jews to Palestine and the settlement in the West Bank to the Bible, especially chapters 35 and 36 of Ezekiel (1993). Before the return of Jews, the land was without inhabitants, except for a remnant of Jews (p. 25). Bedouins moved freely, unhindered by borders, and Islamic Arabs came into Palestine only after Jewish improvement of the land (pp. 26–30). Christians of Arabic descent should not have a problem with the State of Israel, since they believe in the Bible, serve in the Israeli army and defend their country (p. 52). Those seeking a Palestinian state oppose God (p. 57). In addition to the Bible, Archbold's other source of enlightenment is the discredited book of Joan Peters (1984). Israel shoulders none of the blame for the Palestinian refugees (p. 96).

I also saw the souls of those who had been beheaded for their testimony to Jesus and for the word of God. They had not worshipped the beast or its image and had not received its mark on their foreheads or their hands. They came to life and reigned with Christ a thousand years.

(Rev 20.1–5)

Proponents held that after his Second Coming, Christ would reign from Jerusalem for a thousand years. Others, basing their prediction on Rev 19.11–16, held that the millennium would precede the Second Coming of Christ. In espousing these positions, Christians took over the two-age structure of the dream in Dan 7, this age and the age to come which fall on either side of the coming of the son of man (verse 18). To fill out the details, recourse was had to other biblical texts, e.g. 'A thousand years in your sight are like yesterday when it is past' (Psalm 90.4), and 'With the Lord one day is like a thousand years. … ' (2 Pet 3.8), and, in the Old Testament, Ezek 38–39, as well as to a host of non-biblical Jewish apocalyptic writings (e.g. *1 Enoch, 2 Enoch, 4 Ezra, 2 Baruch, 3 Baruch*, the *Apocalypse of Abraham*, etc.).

In the second century BC, apocalyptic speculation was widespread, and the hope for a better future began to move in the direction of a dramatic divine intervention, expressed in a range of metaphors. The victory of Yahweh over the forces of evil takes place beyond this world, in the heavenly world unknown to mortals (e.g. Dan 7). In the Dead Sea Scrolls, the final battle between the Sons of Light and the Sons of Darkness is predicted (1QM). Eschatology was becoming primarily other-worldly, with the future holding out a fundamental transformation of the present, described through various metaphors.

While Millenarianism was espoused in some circles in the early Church (e.g. Gnostics, Montanists) it was hardly heard of again until the thirteenth century. At the Reformation, the Anabaptists and the Bohemian and Moravian Brethren were Millenarians, while Calvin rejected it as too childish a notion to merit refutation. The Pietist Movement in Germany in the seventeenth and eighteenth centuries supported it. By the eighteenth century, novel forms of millennial eschatology were emerging in England also, rooted in the piety and literal hermeneutics of English Puritanism, a fascination with the 'new Israel', and a biblical hermeneutics that viewed the prophetic texts as having a literal, future fulfilment (see Wagner 1999). In the nineteenth century new advocates grew up in the USA and Great Britain (Irvingites, Plymouth Brethren and Adventists), and, as we have seen, apocalyptic speculation is a vibrant part of much evangelical Christianity today. Many evangelicals postulate that the thousand year reign would be preceded by portentous events, including the creation of a Jewish homeland. Hence, the Balfour Declaration, the creation of the State of Israel, the conquest of Jerusalem in 1967, and the rebuilding of the temple, etc. were given theological significance, and were construed as fulfilling biblical prophecy, and speeding up the Second Coming of Christ.

While twentieth century Christian theology has reinstated eschatology to the heart of Christian theology (see Moltmann 1967: 16), it is altogether different from the fundamentalist evangelical kinds, which employ modes of biblical interpretation virtually untouched by the findings of modern biblical research and other sciences. The literalist interpretations of biblical texts fail to take account of their literary form, which had purposes quite different from predicting the details of the future. It is essential to distinguish between prophetic and apocalyptic literature. Prophetic eschatology relates to the future, but allows for divine intervention *within* history: one thinks immediately of the future restoration outlined in the Hebrew prophets (e.g. Isa 40–55; 56–66). Apocalyptic eschatology, on the other hand, goes *beyond* what can be realised in history, and focuses on the heavenly world and a new creation. The Book of Revelation and the Jewish apocalyptic writings of the period 200 BC–AD 100 reveal aspects of the transcendent sphere beyond history and the known cosmos.[6]

Christian eschatology proclaims a better future for a humanity which knows itself to be fundamentally incomplete, relying on the achievement of God in creation, and of Jesus Christ in his redeeming life and death. Its purpose is to generate hope, and unleash humanity's energies towards the completion of what is radically incomplete. It affirms the mystery of God as the absolute future of humanity's dreams and hopes. The person of Jesus is the norm and foundation of Christian eschatology, which brings his teaching to bear on our understanding of life, its present meaning and its ultimate destination. The Christian future is an extrapolation of what has already been achieved in Christ, whose crucifixion and resurrection is the hope of the future of the world.

Christian eschatology goes beyond what has been created and what we have experienced as redemption. The New Order at the heart of its hope is qualitatively different, being no mere linear development of the life we know, which ends in death. In Christian hope, the known of the past and present will yield to the unknown of God's promise. What God has in store for the universe is more than our puny imaginations can envisage, and more eloquent than our mutterings can describe. The metaphors and myths of eschatological discourse, which are derived from extrapolations of what our imaginations can conjure up, cannot match what the God of creation has in mind. In Paul's words, the life to come in Christ will be, 'What no eye has seen, nor ear heard, nor the human heart conceived, what God has prepared for those who love him' (1 Cor 2: 9).

No language is adequate to describe the extent of this Christian hope, since human language cannot exhaust the mystery of God. Humans are no

---

6   The Book of Daniel, and the non-canonical *1 Enoch, 2 Enoch, 4 Ezra, 2 Baruch, 3 Baruch*, the *Apocalypse of Abraham*, etc.

better equipped to describe with accuracy the disposition of the end-time than children in the womb are to inform about the world outside it. Biblical-literalist Christians do a disservice to the wonder of eschatological hope by considering its symbolic and metaphorical language to be precise predictions of future events. Christians would do better to enquire into the Passion, Death and Resurrection of Jesus as a stimulus to future hope, than to search for a one-for-one conformity between the metaphorical language of the predictions of an earlier age and contemporary life.

Mainstream Christianity is suspicious of the genre of apocalyptic, mainly because of its obscure imagery and its use in fundamentalist circles. Millenarianism runs counter to the insights of a more enlightened understanding of the literary genres of biblical prophecy and Christian eschatology. Biblical studies and mainstream Christian theology view the apocalyptic material as works of literary imagination – poetry rather than dogma – which ought not to be construed as providing factual information about either the past or future. The first task of biblical scholarship is to identify the literary form of texts. In the case of apocalyptic texts the language is distinctively metaphorical, and their content is directed towards the renewal of life on earth. Although the futurist 'Day of the Lord' would bring upheaval and destruction, it would be followed by renewal and return to God's ways. The struggle between Good and Evil was expressed characteristically in myth and metaphor, such as in the strife between God and the Monster from the deep (Isa 27.1). It should be clear that eschatological statements, expressed in the characteristic language of symbol, myth and metaphor, do not convey information about the details of the future, whether about serpents and sea dragons or nuclear warfare. In the Christian understanding, they are statements about the potential of human experience, graced by the reality of the Christ-Event and Pentecost. In postulating an order different from the present one they promote hope and endurance, especially among those heavily burdened or persecuted. Christian eschatology, then, is more than a lesson in the politics or cosmology of the end-time.

Christian critics of Zionism

For an increasing number of Christians from abroad knowledge of the consequences of Zionism for the Palestinians has led to criticism of the State of Israel. Before she saw things for herself Rosemary Ruether was a staunch supporters of the Jewish cause. Contact with the Palestinians exposed the injustices inherent in the ideology and practice of Zionism, to such an extent as to make it impossible to be in solidarity with both Jews and Palestinians.

Ruether visited Israel-Palestine in 1987, and with her husband, Herman, described the intransigence and violence of the Israeli government (1989). They judged that the chief impediment to peace, historically and today, is the expansionism and violence of the State of Israel. While a Jewish homeland is a powerful part of contemporary Jewish identity, it does not give Jews a political right to found a state, and much less to displace the Palestinian people in the process. One must counter three myths: Jews have an *a priori* right to the whole of Palestine; the Palestinians as a national community have no parallel claim on the land; and Israel must be oriented towards Europe rather than be part of the Middle East. These three Zionist myths have walled Israel into a segregated, hostile and violent relationship to their neighbouring communities (Ruether and Ruether 1989: 244).

They note that Christian thinking about Jews swings between two unrealistic polarities: Jews as superior to Christians, paragons of wisdom, and Jews as inferior to Christians, incapable of a moral and spiritual life. The solution is to see Jews as distinctive, and, at the same time, as like us. Rosemary Ruether holds that the reality of the Jews in Israel is that of a dominating, conquering power, displacing another people, and attempting to make them disappear (see R. Ruether 1990). The *sabra* (Israeli born Jew) redeemed from diaspora weakness, with a gun in one hand and a plough in the other, has become a military-political-industrial ruling élite, which no longer works the land or does manual labour, 'Arab work' unbefitting a Jew. The Israeli urban managerial élite rules over their inferiors who do the manual work. The dream of redemption through working the land has evaporated in the reality of a colonialist, capitalist organisation of the economy. The relegation of Palestinians to third-class citizens or stateless subjects of military rule destroys the Messianic myth of Israel as a model social democracy, a 'light to the nations' (Ruether and Ruether 1989: 237).

For the Ruethers Zionism is false Messianism which evokes a dream of redeemed life, whether expressed in romantic, liberal, socialist, or religious terms. The dream is used to cover up contrary realities, conceal the contradiction between symbol and ethical substance. False Messianism demands deception, since those who predicate their activities as redemptive must lie about contradictory realities. This deception also must be covered up, and those who expose it must be vilified. The Israeli state propaganda covers up the deception, and vilifies those who seek the truth, as in other modern forms of failed Messianism, such as state communism, fascism, and even the American self-perception of 'making the world safe for democracy' (Ruether and Ruether 1989: 238). David Biale's review of their work, published under the heading, 'The Philo-Semitic Face of Anti-Semitism' (*Tikkun* 4, May–June 1989: 101), fulfils the Ruethers' expectations. Biale sees the 'polemic' as an anti-Zionist diatribe cloaked in the sweet light of Christian universalism, which stands as a singular warning of how Christian critique of Israel can slide unwittingly into the swamp of antisemitism.

Writing somewhat later, against the background of the brutal repression of the *intifada*, Rosemary Ruether questions to what extent a separate Jewish ethnic state is desirable, in either theological or pragmatic terms, and adds,

I believe that the Zionist concept of a Jewish state is a remnant of a racist concept of nationalism that arose in Europe in the nineteenth century and has caused havoc around the world wherever it has been exported and taken over by anti-colonialist movements.

(R. Ruether 1990: 196)

Her ideal for the future is a temporary Jewish state for Jews who have been traumatised by the *Shoah*, and a temporary Palestinian state, which eventually can grow together beyond ethnic-religious nationalisms towards an umbrella entity which will encompass the stories, histories and cultures of all the inhabitants.[7] This is the goal to which Christian faith should dispose one. Belief in a God who loves all peoples and bids them live together in mutual respect can never elevate particular political identities into ultimates, but only penultimates. Distinctive national or ethnic identities belong to historical particularities, and not to the divine will and purpose. Mutual affirmation of multi-particularities must form the basis for co-existence (R. Ruether 1990: 197).

Most recently, Rosemary Ruether, contrasts the relative success achieved in post-apartheid South Africa with what is called 'the peace process' in Israel-Palestine. The policy of the State of Israel, whether through its Labour- or Likud-led governments, is designed to consolidate Israel's interests, while leaving the Palestinians with only a series of bantustan-like enclaves which bear no resemblance to an independent state. She inculpates the Christians of Europe and the USA in the genocide of the Palestinians insofar as they legitimise the foundational injustice done to the Palestinians by regarding the prize of Zionism as due to the Jews, in virtue both of the biblical land claims and as compensation for the *Shoah*. Moreover, Western Christians, as a way of salving their bad consciences regarding the past genocide of European Jews, collaborate in creating a wall of silence around the injustice to the Palestinians (1999).

Palestinian liberation theology

Palestinian Christians have a particular perspective on Zionism. World-wide they number 400,000, constituting some 7 per cent of six million Palestinians. There are 114,000 Palestinian Christians in Israel, and 50,352 in the Occupied Territories, giving a total of 165,000 Christians in Israel-Palestine, or 41.3 per cent of all Palestinian Christians world-wide (see Sabella 1994 and Geraisy 1994). For the Christians of the Holy Land, who refer to themselves as the 'Living Stones', Jerusalem is a spiritual centre, and

---

7   One notes that the trenchant criticism of the Ruethers accords rights to Jews in virtue of the trauma of the *Shoah*. However, the programme to establish a Jewish state was underway fifty years before the *Shoah*.

for those who live in Jerusalem itself, it is their home.[8] However, the very survival of these Christians is under threat.

In addition to the devastation of the 1948 Nakba, the Israeli occupation has resulted in massive emigration of Christians from the region, to the extent that the Christian population of Jerusalem has fallen from some 40,000 in the 1940s to some 10,000 today. Emigration surveys show that Palestinian Christians leave both the Occupied Territories and Israel for identifiable economic and social reasons, reflecting the dire political situation: they lack the opportunity of earning their living, and ensuring some stability and future for their children. The claim that the growth of Islamic fundamentalism has added to Christian emigration is not supported by the findings of any of the emigration surveys (see Sabella 1994 and Geraisy 1994). The survival of Christians in the Land of Jesus is contingent upon the establishment of tolerable political and social conditions.

The *intifada* politicised the Christian Churches in the Holy Land, and brought about a new awareness of their situation in the Churches in the West (see British Council of Churches 1989). The Middle East Council of Churches sent a delegation to Britain in November–December 1989, which left British Christians in no doubt that Palestinian Christians aspired to a Palestinian state. Parallel to the mass movement of opposition to the Israeli occupation, an indigenous liberation theology was developing, which continues to influence opinion within the Churches abroad. These intellectual movements have resulted in the founding of organisations promoting justice for the Palestinians, the production of significant studies,[9] and the convening of international conferences, both at home[10] and abroad[11] which have exposed the human cost of the Zionist venture to the Palestinian community.

8   A new type of pilgrimage has developed in recent years. *Living Stones'* pilgrims set out to meet the people, and become aware of the social context in which their pilgrimage takes place. For them sharp moral issues are not submerged in archaeology or tourism. They discover for themselves that for present-day Arab Christians in the Holy Land Golgotha is not a sad memory of a distant past, but is part of the everyday indignity and oppression which they share with all other disadvantaged peoples of the world. Their *Via Dolorosa* is no mere ritualistic procession through the narrow streets of the Old City, but the fate of being subjugated and humiliated in their own land. See Hilliard and Bailey 1999.

9   For example, Chacour 1985, 1992; Ateek 1989; Rantisi 1990; Ruether and Ellis 1990; Ateek, Ellis, and Ruether 1992; Cragg 1992, 1997; O'Mahony, Gunner and Hintlian 1995; Raheb 1995 and Prior 1997a, 1998b.

10 The most significant are those convened by the Palestinian Liberation Centre, *Sabeel*, which in addition to publishing the proceedings (e.g. Ateek, Duaybis and Schrader 1997; Ateek and Prior 1999) produces its own newsletter, *Cornerstone*, which gives a running theological commentary on the changing events in the region and is distributed world-wide.

11 In Britain alone, in addition to the Cumberland Lodge Conference (see Prior and Taylor 1994), there have been conferences on Christians in the Holy Land in London University (1991 and 1993), Cambridge University (1992), and in Warwick University (1993 – see the special edition of *The Month* 26, December 1993 for some of the papers).

Since the *intifada*, the leadership of the Churches in Jerusalem has issued common statements, including *The Significance of Jerusalem for Christians* (14 November 1994), which addresses the political climate in which the indigenous Christians lived. It appeals for reconciliation and harmony, repeating the lesson of history that Jerusalem cannot belong exclusively to one people or one religion, but should be 'the capital of humankind'. For these local Christian community Jerusalem is not only a Holy City, but their native city, in which their rights must be respected fully (in PASSIA 1996: 22–55).

For Palestinian Christians biblical hermeneutics and the relation between the Testaments are not mere matters of rhetorical debate.[12] Their theologians are themselves victims of Zionist conquest. Naim Ateek's story is typical. He recalls how his town, Beisan (Beth Shean), was occupied on 12 May 1948, two days before the declaration of the State of Israel. On 26 May the military governor informed the leading men that Beisan must be evacuated by all its inhabitants. His father's pleading was met with, 'If you do not leave, we will have to kill you'. The whole population of 6,000 Arabs was expelled, the Muslims being sent across the Jordan, and the Christians to Nazareth which had not yet been occupied by the Zionists.[13] On the declaration of the State of Israel he found himself condemned to second-class citizenship. On his first visit back to Beisan in 1958 he saw that the Anglican church had become a storehouse, the Roman Catholic one had become a school, and the Orthodox one had been left to rot. His family was not allowed even to look at their own house (Ateek 1989: 8–13). Audeh Rantisi's personal history also encapsulates the Palestinian problem.[14]

Ateek sharply focuses the problem of how the Old Testament can be the Word of God, and how a Palestinian Christian can read it in the light of its use to support Zionism (1991: 283; see also 1989: 77–78). Whereas one

---

12 In his Pastoral Letter, written just after the Rabin–Arafat handshake at the White House in 1993, Latin Patriarch of Jerusalem, Monsignor Michel Sabbah, himself a victim of Zionist colonialism, tackles head-on some of the most difficult aspects of the Bible for a Christian for whom the text appears to warrant her or his oppression. He searches for a hermeneutic of the Bible that will be valid both biblically and theologically, and finds it in the person of Jesus Christ (1993: 25–31). He asks what influence the promises, the gift of land, the election and covenant have for relations between Palestinians and Israelis, and whether it is possible for a just and merciful God to impose injustice or oppression on another people to favour his chosen people (paragraph 8).

13 Nevertheless, in a manner typical of Zionist fabrication of the state's origins, the *Encyclopaedia Judaica* (1974) states, 'Beth-Shean capitulated on May 12, 1948, to Jewish forces, who found it deserted by its former inhabitants' (4: 762, 765). At least, this statement was better than that of the official at the Museum who assured our group in 1981 that no one lived in the town prior to 1948.

14 On Sunday, 11 July 1948, when he was eleven, he and his family were driven from Lydda, never to return again. His second upheaval occurred in the 1967 War, when Ramallah was occupied. Although Rantisi has suffered under the occupation – his life has been threatened, his car burnt, and he has been interrogated by the military authorities many times – he is a man of peace and reconciliation (1990).

looks to it for liberation, the Bible offers Palestinians little more than slavery, injustice, and death to their national and political life. Since the establishment of the State of Israel, which was a seismic tremor that shook the very foundation of their beliefs, the Old Testament has generally fallen into disuse among both clergy and laity, because of its direct application to the twentieth-century events in Palestine.

Ateek judges that the Zionist movement is a retrogression of Jewry into its most primitive forms of the concept of God. Zionism, fuelled by those portions of the Old Testament that betray a concept of a tribal god, has reanimated the nationalist tradition within Judaism. The finely worded Declaration of Independence of the state, pledging that the principles of liberty, justice and peace as conceived by the Prophets of Israel will uphold the full social and political equality of all its citizens, without distinction of religion, race or sex, is a mask behind which its retrogressive values hide. Ethical, universalist Judaism has been swamped by the resurgence of a racially exclusive concept of a people and their god (Ateek 1989: 101–2).

Fifty years after the establishment of the state, Ateek's spirit has not been devoured by hatred or despair. He accepts the existence of Israel in his Palestine, not as of right, but as of need, 'since the elimination of Israel would mean greater injustice to millions of innocent people who know no home except Israel' (1989: 164). Any genuine solution, he insists, must pass the test of two sayings of Jesus: 'So whatever you wish that men should do to you, do so to them; for this is the law and the prophets' (Matt 7.12), and, 'You shall love your neighbour as yourself' (Mark 12.31).

His solution moves out from the major premise: 'Palestine is a country for both the Jews and the Palestinians'. Ideally Jews, Muslims and Christians should live together in one united democratic state. Since the Jews insist on a Jewish state, the best solution is to have two states, relating to one another in peace. The minor premise, and the first of four stages of progress towards a final settlement, then, is the creation of a Palestinian state in the West Bank and Gaza, in which all inhabitants would live as first-class citizens, alongside the State of Israel. With the two states living side by side, the way would be open to fostering the patient work of reconciliation. His dream of peace goes beyond the federation of the states of Israel and Palestine, and includes Lebanon and Jordan in a Federated States of the Holy Land. A united Jerusalem, shared by both peoples, would be holy to Judaism, Islam and Christianity, and should become the federal capital of a United States of the Holy Land, with Beirut being Lebanon's capital, Amman being Jordan's, a West Bank town being Palestine's, and Tel Aviv being Israel's. Micah's apocalyptic vision for Jerusalem (Mic 4.1–4) completes the picture. His proposal has the quality of magnanimity and simplicity, and offers a better future than is likely to emerge from the exclusivist policies of Israel. Israel will never be secure until it makes peace with its 150 million Arab neighbours, and a generous peace with the Palestinians should be its immediate strategy.

The leadership of the Church in Jerusalem has been particularly active in responding to the ongoing oppression of the Palestinians. It issued a statement on 29 September 1996, a few days after the bloody events in the Holy Land, insisting that there could be no peace which is not founded on justice. Peace could never be imposed by the power of arms: 'Justice must come first, and then peace will follow; a peace that will lead to security'. The leadership judges Israel's formula for peace, 'security first and then peace', to be false. It called on Israel to end all discriminatory policies, to abstain from the confiscation of land, and to return already confiscated land to its rightful owners, to stop the demolition of houses, and to respect all signed agreements. It called on the Israeli government to close the tunnel in the Old City of Jerusalem – whose opening 'was only the straw that broke the camel's back' – and to desist from offence to their Muslim brothers and sisters. They warned that a peace imposed by the strong on the weak would be temporary. The Palestinians would never submit to exclusive Israeli sovereignty over the city. They call for an open Jerusalem, the capital of two states, a model for peaceful co-existence between the Israelis and the Palestinians, and between the three faiths (in PASSIA 1996: 33–34).

The Latin Patriarch issued a statement on the same day, also condemning the opening of the tunnel, and listing the accumulated injustices and sufferings imposed upon the Palestinians: the repeated closures, the confiscation of land, and of the identity cards of Jerusalem residents who are living outside the city, the demolition of houses, the holding of Palestinian prisoners, and the daily humiliations and harassments which reduce the lives of the Palestinians 'to a miserable level'. He appealed to the Israeli authorities to attend to the demands of justice as a pre-requisite for peace. He announced that there would be a prayer service on Sunday 29 September in St Anne Basilica, which I was pleased to attend. The Patriarch appealed for a resumption of the peace process with new determination, inviting the parties to 'go out of the tunnel of fears and hesitation, to build a new civilisation founded on peace, justice and love, in the Holy City and throughout the region' (in PASSIA 1996: 34–35).

Conclusion

When it comes to approval of the State of Israel there is a certain alignment in some religious and theological circles between the attitudes of religious extremists and those of academic and ecclesiastical commentators. Although the more 'liberal wing' of Western Christianity reacts to the State of Israel through the lens of the *Shoah*, many others see in the establishment of the state the fulfilment of God's promises as outlined in some of the traditions of the Torah and the prophets, and some, interpreting the apocalyptic texts in a literalist fashion, see it as a stage preliminary to the Messiah's End-Time Kingdom. In such circles, opposition to the oppressive policies of the state inhibits the fulfilment of God's plans.

Fundamentalist Christians who embrace the State of Israel as the forerunner of apocalyptic Messianism betray an insensitivity to the genre of apocalyptic imagery. Despite the onslaught from academic biblical studies of some two hundred years such literalism survives, mainly because of the perceived need to protect the absolute authority, inerrancy and inspiration of the Bible. Fundamentalist Christian Zionism promotes an aberrant expression of the Christian faith through an erroneous, literalist interpretation of the Bible, which fails to distinguish between the metaphorical language of eschatological discourse and the ultimate destination of the cosmos.[15] In its espousal of political Zionism it distorts Christian faith, ignoring the cries of the poor, and legitimises their oppression in the name of the Gospel. It displaces the universal appeal of the Gospel, with its emphasis on the equality and dignity of all, substituting for it a moral recklessness that posits the Christian God as an avenger worse than any the world has seen.

There is clear evidence that encounter with the reality of the sufferings of the Palestinians has induced a considerable change in attitude to the State of Israel among many Christians, including evangelicals. The LaGrange Declaration of 1979, signed by over 5,000 US Christians, stated,

> Forthrightly, we declare our conviction that in the process of establishing the state of Israel, a deep injustice was done to the Palestinian people, confiscating their land and driving many into exile and even death. ... We confess our silence, our indifference, our hardheartedness and our cowardice, all too often, in the face of these dehumanising realities.
>
> (*Sojourners Magazine*, July 1979, p. 24)

Contact with the realities on the ground, especially during the Israeli invasion of Lebanon in 1982, marked a turning point in evangelical Christian views of Israel. A series of fact-finding visits by prominent evangelical leaders, on average two per year between 1983 and 1991, exposed them to the underside of the fulfilment of biblical prophecy. Ongoing contact with the indigenous Christian in the Holy Land has also played its part in changing attitudes, to the extent that 88 per cent of evangelicals believe that,

---

15 The Pontifical Biblical Commission produced a wide-ranging discussion of the interpretation of the Bible in the Church (1993). Topics relevant to biblical interpretation, including 'hermeneutics', 'apocalyptic', 'millenarianism', 'the Book of Daniel', etc., are discussed in Brown, Fitzmyer and Murphy 1989, and in Coggins and Houlden 1990. The relationship between the biblical text, the Church and the world is discussed in Watson 1994, while Thiselton 1992 discusses fundamental theoretical concerns as well as practical questions relating to modern interpretation of the Bible. See also Childs (1976), Exum and Clines (1993), and Morgan with Barton (1989).

Christians should hold the State of Israel to the same standards of justice and human rights in its international and internal affairs as any other state.

('For the Love of Zion', in *Christianity Today*, 9 March 1992: 46–49)

Christian evangelicals have had to contend with the collision between the conflicting claims of biblical social justice and millennialist interpretation of biblical prophecy. There is evidence that the straightforward reading of the State of Israel as the fulfilment of biblical prophecy is under severe strain. John Stott for one, after much study, concluded that Zionism, and especially Christian Zionism are biblically untenable (in Wagner 1992: 7). A substantial amount of the change of attitude one discerns in many Christian circles is due to greater engagement of Western Christians with Palestinians. The Palestinian Liberation Theology Centre, *Sabeel*, has played no small part in facilitating such engagement.

Since for many Christians the Bible provides the major ideological support legitimating the Zionist conquest of Palestine, overriding any rights of the indigenous population, it is instructive next to interrogate those very texts.

Part III

The biblical justification for Zionism

6 The Bible and the Land

The link between the Zionist conquest and the Bible is reflected widely, whether in the propagandistic claim of Ben-Gurion that the Bible is the 'Jews' sacrosanct title-deed to Palestine ... with a genealogy of 3,500 years' (1954: 100), in the mainstream theology of the Jewish religious establishment, or in much Christian ecclesial and theological opinion. That the Bible provides the title-deed for the establishment of the State of Israel is so pervasive, not only in Christian Zionist and Jewish Zionist circles but even within mainstream Christian Theology and university biblical studies, that the very attempt to raise the issue is sure to elicit opposition.

The widespread Western support for the Zionist enterprise is particularly striking from a moral perspective. Whereas elsewhere the perpetrators of colonial plunder are objects of opprobrium, the Zionist conquest is widely judged to be a just and appropriate accomplishment, with even unique religious significance. Much of the rationale for this derives from literalist interpretations of particular traditions of the Bible: the Zionist prize is no more than what the Jewish people deserves in virtue of God's promises.

The Bible narrates God's promise of Canaan to Abraham and his posterity, and to Moses and his fellow escapees from Egypt. The conquest and settlement of the land are recounted in the Books of Joshua and Judges. These traditions have implications for our understanding of God, and his relation to the people of Israel, to non-Israelites such as the Canaanites and, by extension, to all other peoples. Before considering the implications, however, let us review the biblical record, firstly that of the promise and preparation (from Genesis to Deuteronomy), and then that of the conquest-settlement (in Joshua and Judges). The moral problem posed by these texts when read at face value will be seen in its starkness.

The land traditions of the Bible

The land traditions from Genesis to Deuteronomy

In the biblical narrative Yahweh promised the land of Canaan to Abram and his descendants (Gen 12.6–7). With divine approval, Abram came to dwell at Hebron, and Yahweh made a covenant with him, reiterating the promise of land, from the river of Egypt to the Euphrates, the land of the Kenites, the Kenizzites, the Kadmonites, the Hittites, the Perizzites, the Rephaim, the Amorites, the Canaanites, the Girgashites and the Jebusites (Gen 15.18–21). Subsequently, the promise is made to Isaac also (Gen 26.3–4), and Isaac prayed that the promise would be fulfilled in Jacob (Gen 28.4; see also 28.13–15; 35.12). Finally, Joseph dying in Egypt said to his brothers, 'God will ... bring you up out of this land to the land that he swore to Abraham, to Isaac, and to Jacob' (Gen 50.24).

The Exodus theme symbolises God's deliverance of those in bondage:

> I have come down to deliver them from the Egyptians, and to bring them up out of that land to a good and broad land, a land flowing with milk and honey, to the country of the Canaanites, the Hittites, the Amorites, the Perizzites, the Hivites, and the Jebusites.
>
> (Exod 3.8; see also 6.6–8)

Moses' Song of Victory after the crossing of the Red Sea included reference to the consternation which the destruction of the Egyptians brought on the inhabitants of Philistia, the chiefs of Edom, the leaders of Moab, and all the inhabitants of Canaan (Exod 15.1–16). Already the Israelites are virtually settled (Exod 15.17–19). Between the exodus from Egypt and the settlement in Canaan Yahweh encounters Moses on Mount Sinai (Exod 19.1–40.38), and gives all that an ancient people in transition requires, a leader, an identity and a promise of a future resting place. Yahweh confirms Moses as the leader and speeds the people on their way to possess the land of Canaan. Chapters 21–23 detail the ordinances, including those befitting a settled people, including,

> When my angel goes in front of you, and brings you to the Amorites, the Hittites, the Perizzites, the Canaanites, the Hivites, and the Jebusites, and I blot them out, you shall not bow down to their gods, or worship them, or follow their practices, but you shall utterly demolish them and break their pillars in pieces.
>
> (Exod 23.23–24)

The warrior god surely would drive out 'all your enemies' (Exod 23.27–33; 33.1–3). Nevertheless, despite the widespread slaughter of the indigenes, we find the command not to oppress a resident alien (Exod 22.21; 23.9). Yahweh promised to perform marvels for the people, and demanded uncompromising loyalty, and separation from the indigenous groups (Exod 34.11–15; see also 34.24).

The gift of the land of Canaan is reiterated in the Book of Leviticus (Lev 14.34). Adherence to the laws of purity and Yahweh's statutes ensures residence in the land (Lev 18) – the inhabitants of Canaan would be vomited out because of their abuses (Lev 18.24–30; see also 20.22–27). Chapter 26 outlines the blessings which will befall the people if they carry out what Yahweh requires: fertility of the soil, peace, victory over enemies, abundant offspring, and the assurance of Yahweh's presence (26.3–13). Disobedience will be rewarded by sevenfold punishment (Lev 26.11–39), dispersion and exile (Lev 26.32–39). But even in exile, Yahweh will not break his covenant (Lev 26.44–46).

The Book of Numbers is constructed around the organisation of the community before its departure from Sinai (Num 1.1–10.10), the march through the desert from Sinai to the Plains of Moab (Num 10.11–21.35), and the preparation for entry into the Promised Land from there (Num 22.1–36.13). No less than 603,550 males (Num 1.45–46), and 8,580 Levites would set out (Num 4.48), marching through the desert from Sinai, as in a liturgical procession, punctuated by moanings of nostalgia for Egypt (Num 10.11–12.16), on to the threshold of the Promised Land (Num 13.1–15.41). The scouts reported that the indigenous people were strong, and had very large, fortified towns (Num 13.27–29). Nevertheless, Israel made a vow to Yahweh that they would utterly destroy the towns (Num 21.1–3). After King Sihon of the Amorites refused free passage, Israel put his troops to the sword, and took his land (Num 21.21–24). King Og of Bashan met a similar fate (Num 21.34–35).

Yahweh appointed Joshua to succeed Moses (Num 27). Chapter 31 brings us back to the war against the Midianites, the killing of every male and of the five kings of Midian. The Israelites captured the women of Midian and their little ones, took all their cattle, burned all their towns and encampments, retaining all the booty, both people and animals. Moses was particularly aggrieved that they allowed the women to live (Num 31.8–16). He ordered the killing of every male child, and every woman who had slept with a man – the young girls who had not done so were to be kept alive for themselves (Num 31.18). Then they were to return to the more serious matters of purifying themselves and their garments (Num 31.19–20). The booty was divided, and due offerings were made to Yahweh. In the plains of Moab by the Jordan at Jericho, Yahweh directed Moses to speak to the Israelites, saying,

> When you cross over the Jordan into the land of Canaan, you shall drive out all the inhabitants of the land from before you, destroy all their figured stones, destroy all their cast images, and demolish all their high places. You shall take possession of the land and settle in it, for I have given you the land to possess. . . . But if you do not drive out the inhabitants of the land from before you, then those whom you let remain shall be as barbs in your eyes and thorns in your sides; they shall trouble you in the land where you are settling. And I will do to you as I thought to do to them.
>
> (Num 33.50–56)

One of the distinctive emphases of Deuteronomy is the connection between the people and the land. The book reiterates the promise of the land to

Abraham and his descendants (Deut 1.6–8). The people were not to be intimidated by the fortified cities, because Yahweh promised to fight for them (Deut 1.30–31). After the Amorite King Sihon refused passage Yahweh gave him over to the Israelites, who utterly destroyed all the cities, killing all the men, women, and children (Deut 2.33–34). The fate of Og, King of Bashan was no better (Deut 3.3). The centrality of observing the Law is repeated, and after the *Shema* we read,

> And when the Lord your God brings you into the land which he swore to your fathers ... to give you, with great and goodly cities, which you did not build, and houses full of all good things, which you did not fill, and cisterns hewn out, which you did not hew, and vineyards and olive trees, which you did not plant, and when you eat and are full, then take heed lest you forget the Lord. ... You shall fear the Lord your God ... lest the anger of the Lord your God be kindled against you, and he destroy you from off the face of the earth
>
> (Deut 6.10–15; see also 6.18–19).

Yahweh's role in the conquest is reassuring:

> When Yahweh your God brings you into the land that you are about to enter and occupy, and he clears away many nations before you – the Hittites, the Girgashites, the Amorites, the Canaanites, the Perizzites, the Hivites ... and when Yahweh your God gives them over to you ... you must utterly destroy them. ... Show them no mercy. ... For you are a people holy to Yahweh your God; Yahweh your God has chosen you out of all the peoples on earth to be his people, his treasured possession.
>
> (Deut 7.1–11; see also 9.1–5; 11.8–9, 23, 31–32)

The territory shall extend from the wilderness to the Lebanon, and from the Euphrates to the Western Sea (Deut 11.24).

In the rules for the conduct of war (Deut 20.1–21.14), if a besieged town does not surrender, the Israelites shall kill all its males, and take as booty the women, the children, livestock, and everything else in the town (Deut 20.11–14). The narrative, then, presents 'ethnic cleansing' as not only legitimate, but as required by the divinity:

> But as for the towns of these peoples that Yahweh your God is giving you as an inheritance, you must not let anything that breathes remain alive. You shall annihilate them – the Hittites and the Amorites, the Canaanites and the Perizzites, the Hivites and the Jebusites – just as Yahweh your God has commanded, so that they may not teach you to do all the abhorrent things that they do for their gods, and you thus sin against Yahweh your God.
>
> (Deut 20.16–18)

Mercifully, in a gesture of ecological indulgence, the fruit-bearing trees are to be spared, as is a captive 'beautiful woman whom you desire and want to marry' (Deut 21.11).

The two ways are put clearly before the people: if they obey the commandments of Yahweh they shall thrive in the land; if not, they shall not live long in the land (Deut 30.15–20; 32.46–47). The book ends with Moses' sight of the promised land before he dies (Deut 34.1–3). Moses left a worthy successor, Joshua, who, after he had lain hands on him, was full of the spirit of wisdom (Deut 34.4–12). So much for the preparation for entry into the Promised Land.

The land in the Books of Joshua and Judges

Joshua is presented as the divinely-chosen, worthy successor of Moses, who is destined to complete his work (Josh 1). The first part (2.1–12.24) describes in epic style the conquest of the land, concentrating on the capture of a few key cities, and their treatment in accordance with the laws of the Holy War. Then we have the division of the land (13.1–21.45), followed by an appendix (22.1–24.33).

The crossing of the Jordan (Josh 3.1–5.1) is followed by the ceremonies at Gilgal (Josh 5.2–12), and the destruction of Jericho (Josh 5.13–6.27). The city and all that was in it would be devoted to Yahweh for destruction (Josh 6.17). The ban (*herem*) required that the enemy be utterly destroyed as a sacrifice to the deity who had made the victory possible. The slaughter of all the men and women, oxen, sheep and donkeys, and the burning of the city followed, sparing only the silver and gold, etc. for the treasury of the house of Yahweh, as well as Rahab's family. Joshua pronounced a curse on anyone who would try to rebuild Jericho (Josh 6.21–27).

The marauding party moved on to Ai at Yahweh's command, to do to it what was done to Jericho: not one of the twelve thousand inhabitants survived or escaped, and Joshua made it forever a heap of ruins (Josh 8.2, 19–29). The liturgical *Te Deum* and reading of the Law followed in style, with one choir on Mount Gerizim and the other on Mount Ebal (Josh 8.30–35). The ravaging troops encountered a concerted defence of the Hittites, the Amorites, the Canaanites, the Perizzites, the Hivites, and the Jebusites (Josh 9.1–2). The inhabitants of Gibeon, spared the conditions of the *herem*, were destined to become 'hewers of wood and drawers of water for all the congregation' (Josh 9.21, 23, 7). The elders complained at this lapse in fidelity to the mandate to destroy all the inhabitants of the land (Josh 9.24).

The next two chapters give details of the shift in the theatre of marauding, with chapter 10 describing the campaign in the south, and chapter 11 that in the north, in each case, assuring the rigorous enforcement of the *herem*. Joshua took Makkedah, utterly destroying every person in it (10.28). A similar fate befell other cities (10.29–39): everything that breathed was destroyed, as Yahweh commanded (10.40–43). The northern campaign also left no one surviving: Joshua utterly destroyed the inhabitants (11.1–23). Yahweh gave to Israel all the land that he swore to their ancestors he would give them (21.43–45).

The picture in the Book of Judges is considerably different from that recorded in the Book of Joshua. Whereas Joshua gives details of the conquest in a series of 'punctiliar', efficient military activities, Judges sees it as a more complex and gradual phenomenon, punctuated by partial success and failure.

The land in other Books of the Bible

The theme of land recurs in several traditions within the Bible. While Psalm 65.9–13 lauds Yahweh for his benevolence towards the land in general, Psalm 78.54–55 does so for his specific care of the Israelites: He brought them to the holy hill his right hand had won. He drove out nations before them and settled the tribes of Israel in their tents. This theme is reiterated in other psalms: 'You brought a vine out of Egypt; you drove out the nations and planted it' (Psalm 80.8; see also Psalm 105.43–44). However, the details of the conquest are inconsiderable. Psalm 114 does refer to the stopping of the flow of the Jordan, and Psalms 78.54–66 and 81.11–12 refer to the disobedience of Israel.

However, the evidence that the stories of the conquest were in circulation before the period of the Babylonian exile (586–538 BC) is meagre. In the eighth-century Judean prophets, Isaiah and Micah, we read only of the Midian story (Isa 10.26). In the northern kingdom, we have a reference to the Amorites in Amos 2.10, and a possible reference to the outrage at Gibeah in Hosea 9.9. Similarly, with respect to the celebration of the occupation of the land within the cultic life of the community there is little that one would have to put earlier than the exile. There is no reason to insist that these compositions pre-date the exile, or that they were not derived from the books of Joshua and Judges.

There is a notable lack of evidence, therefore, for the popularity of the conquest and settlement traditions prior to the exile. In that period, they assume an importance in both Jeremiah and Ezekiel. However, neither in Jeremiah nor Ezekiel is there specific reference to the land having been conquered by Joshua and the Judges. Moreover, there are no clear allusions to the conquest and settlement traditions in Isa 40–55 or in the post-exilic prophets. It is remarkable that, with the exception of their importance from Exodus to Judges, the conquest and settlement traditions occupy such an insignificant place within the Bible. Yet, however late the traditions, the narratives pose moral problems.

The moral problem of the biblical land traditions

By modern standards of international law and human rights, the land narratives from Exodus to Joshua mandate 'war-crimes' and 'crimes against humanity'. Readers might seek refuge in the claim that the problem lies with the predispositions of the modern reader, rather than with the text itself. One cannot escape so easily. One must acknowledge that much of the Torah, and Deuteronomy in particular, contains menacing ideologies and racist, xenophobic and militaristic tendencies.

Yet biblical scholars retain a high esteem for the book, assessing it to be a theological book *par excellence*, and the focal point of the religious history of the Old Testament. Indeed, in the 1995 Lattey Lecture in Cambridge University, Norbert Lohfink argued that Deuteronomy provides a model of a utopian society in which there would be no poor (Lohfink 1996). In my role as the formal proposer of a vote of thanks, I invited him to consider whether, in the light of that book's insistence on a mandate to commit genocide, the utopian society would be possible only after the invading Israelites had wiped out the indigenous inhabitants. The protocol of the Lattey Lecture left the last word with me, and subsequently I was given a second word, being invited to deliver the 1997 Lattey Lecture, for which I chose the title, *A Land flowing with Milk, Honey, and People* (1997b). However highly one esteems the theological thrust of Deuteronomy, the narrative does require the genocide of the indigenous population.

The implications of the existence of dubious moral dispositions, presented as mandated by the divinity, within a book which is canonised as Sacred Scripture invites the most serious investigation. Moreover, not only do these traditions have the capacity to infuse exploitative tendencies in their readers, but they have in practice fuelled virtually every form of militant colonialism emanating from Europe, resulting in the sufferings of millions of people, and loss of respect for the Bible.[1] And yet, as we shall see, until recently the theme of land has been neglected in biblical scholarship.

Manifestly, the biblical narrative poses a moral problem for anyone who takes it only at face value. The Hebrew slaves who left Egypt invaded a land already occupied, and engaged in systematic pillage and killing. What distinguishes the biblical account, whether through the *Blitzkrieg* mode represented in the Book of Joshua, or the more gradual one reflected in the Book of Judges, is that it is presented as having not only divine approval, but as being mandated by the divinity. In the Book of Joshua, in particular,

---

1 In *The Bible and Colonialism: A Moral Critique* (1997a) I focus on three different regions and periods, in which each colonialist enterprise gained the support of a distinctive religious ideology: the invasion of Latin America in the fifteenth century, the Dutch incursion into the Cape Colony of southern Africa in 1652, and its sequel in the nineteenth and twentieth centuries, and Zionist settler-colonialism of Palestine in this century. Earlier, while the Crusader Templars ate their meals in silence they enjoyed public readings from the Bible, with special emphasis on the Books of Joshua and Maccabees. All found inspiration in the ferocious exploits of Judas, his brothers and their war-bands in reconquering the Holy Land from cruel infidels (Seward 1995: 32).

the Israelites killed in conformity with the directives of God. This presentation of God as requiring the destruction of others poses problems for anyone who presumes that the conduct of an ethical God will not fall lower than decent, secular behaviour. The moral problematic is exacerbated by the fact that the traditions belong within a literature which enjoys unique authority within both Synagogue and Church. In the estimation of Jews, the Torah emanates from heaven, and a punctilious observance of its laws is the supreme religious duty (Schürer 1979: 314). The Torah, in such an interpretation, must be accepted in all its parts. The Bible enjoys a corresponding authority in the Church as the Word of God.

The commandment that, 'You shall devour all the peoples that Yahweh your God is giving over to you, showing them no pity' (Deut 7.16) is seen in a new light, when one recalls how such texts were used in support of colonialism in several regions and periods, in which the native peoples were the counterparts of the Hittites, the Girgashites, etc. Were it not for their religious provenance, such biblical sentiments would be regarded as incitements to racial hatred. *Prima facie*, judged by the standards of ethics and human rights to which our society has become accustomed, the first six books of the Hebrew Bible reflect some ethnocentric, racist and xenophobic sentiments, which appear to receive the highest possible legitimacy in the form of divine approval. On moral grounds, one is forced to question whether the Torah provides divine legitimacy for the occupation of other people's land, and the virtual annihilation of the indigenes.

G.E.M. de Ste. Croix, the greatest authority on the history of class politics in the ancient world, notes the unprecedented character of the biblical traditions of divinely mandated ferocity:

> I can say that I know of only one people which felt able to assert that it actually had a divine command to exterminate whole populations among those it conquered; namely, Israel. Nowadays Christians, as well as Jews, seldom care to dwell on the merciless ferocity of Yahweh, as revealed not by hostile sources but by the very literature they themselves regard as sacred. Indeed, they continue as a rule to forget the very existence of this incriminating material. ... There is little in pagan literature quite as morally revolting as the stories of the massacres allegedly carried out at Jericho, Ai, and Hazor, and of the Amorites and Amalekites, all not merely countenanced by Yahweh but strictly ordained by him. ... The Greek and Roman gods could be cruel enough, in the traditions preserved by their worshippers, but at least their devotees did not seek to represent them as prescribing genocide.
>
> (De Ste. Croix 1981: 331–32)

Suspicious of the possible impact of the biblical narratives on the formation of conscience, the Israeli socio-psychologist, Georges Tamarin, surveyed the presence of prejudices in the ideology of Israeli youth. He was anxious to evaluate the degree to which an uncritical teaching of notions of the 'chosen people', the superiority of monotheistic religion, and the study of acts of genocide carried out by biblical heroes contributed to the development of prejudice. He chose the Book of Joshua, in particular the genocides at Jericho and Makkedah, because of that book's special position in the Israeli educational system, both as national history and as one of the cornerstones of Israel's national mythology. He asked two questions: 1. Do you think Joshua and the Israelites acted rightly or not? 2. Suppose that the Israeli Army conquers an Arab village in battle. Do you think it would be good or bad to act towards the inhabitants as Joshua did towards the people of Jericho and Makkedah? Only 20 per cent of the respondents disapproved of Joshua's behaviour, while 62 per cent would disapprove of genocide carried out by the Israeli Army. The figures were quite different when Tamarin substituted a fabricated 'Chinese version' of the Book of Joshua, with 'General Lin' committing a god-inspired genocide. Seventy-five per cent of the respondents totally disapproved of General Lin's genocide. Tamarin concluded that,

> The uncritical teaching of the Bible – to students too young – even if not taught explicitly as a sacred text, but as national history or in a quasi-neutral atmosphere concerning the real or mythological character of its content, no doubt profoundly affects the genesis of prejudices ... even among non-religious students, in accentuating the negative-hostile character of the strangers.
>
> (Tamarin 1973: 189)

His findings were a severe indictment of the Israeli educational system. His research brought him unsought and unexpected notoriety and led to his losing his professorship in Tel Aviv University. In a letter to the senate he wrote that while embarking on his scholarly investigation he had never dreamt that he would become the last victim of Joshua's conquest of Jericho (Tamarin 1973: 190).

Understandably, the symbiotic relationship between the political and religious discourses is most focused in the case of Zionism and Palestine. If other peoples can apply the biblical paradigm of conquest and plunder by recourse to claims to analogous 'rights', the rights of Jews are accorded canonical and unique status and are warmly supported in the West. The religious-political link was illustrated dramatically on 13 September 1993, when President Clinton introduced the Prime Minister Rabin and President Arafat on the White House lawn. He announced to the world that both people pledged themselves to a shared future, 'shaped by the values of the Torah, the Koran, and the Bible'. According to a report in the *Washington Post* (14 September, A1), the President woke at 3.00 a.m., and resumed work on his speech, drafted by National Security Council aide, Jeremy Rosner. According to senior officials Clinton reread the Book of Joshua (Prior 1994b:

20). His mode of address later was a mixture of Bible-based exhortation in the Baptist tradition, and shrewd political manœuvring. The late Premier Rabin's speech also referred to the Bible. However, in the light of the history of reception of these texts one must question whether 'the values of the Torah, the Koran, and the Bible' can be relied upon to promote justice and peace, and underpin the imperatives of human rights.

Baruch Goldstein's massacre of twenty-nine worshippers in the Ibrahimi Mosque in Hebron in 1994 on the feast of Purim, and the assassination of Prime Minister Rabin a year later by Yigal Amir, who claimed to have derived his motivation from *halakhah* focused attention on serious religious questions. British Chief Rabbi Sacks invited the Orthodox rabbinate to question whether they were really teaching Jewish values: the Torah was given, 'not to wreak vengeance, but to create kindness, compassion and peace'. He stressed that it is 'people of religious conviction, who must most forcibly defend the democratic process. We must absolutely – as a matter of Jewish principle – reject utterly the language of hate' (*Jewish Chronicle*, 10 November 1995, p. 56). Neither Moses, Joshua nor modern colonisers would concur with the Chief Rabbi's benevolent hermeneutics, which, perhaps, owes more to the ideals of Enlightenment philosophy than to those traditions which read the biblical text in a literalist way.

With respect to biblical hermeneutics, Goldstein and Amir are merely the tip of the iceberg of literalism, which justifies outrages on the basis of an alleged divine mandate. Constant exposure to a literalist interpretation of the Torah, whether in the curriculum of Israeli schools, or through some of the many schools of biblical and Talmudic learning avoids with difficulty descent into attitudes of racism, xenophobia and militarism. Dr Nilly Keren's research shows that, while knowing a great deal about antisemitism and the *Shoah*, Israeli children, especially those in the religious sector, have little appreciation of other forms of racism. While some 30 per cent of children in state schools considered the Arabs of Israel to be enemies of the state, no less than 70 per cent of those in the religious sector did so. The research suggests that the deeper the religious factor in education, the more likely ideological extremism (Josef Algazy, *Ha'aretz* 15 August 1996). Moreover, there is abundant evidence, both in traditions of imperialist colonialism emanating from 'Christian' countries, as well as in the practice of Israeli religious settlers today, for appeal to sacred writings to justify inhumane behaviour.

Indigenous colonised peoples recognise the link between religion and oppression, and reserve particular criticism for the Bible (Prior 1997a: 260–61). Andean and American Indians left Pope John Paul II in no doubt about their assessment of the role of the Bible in the destruction of their civilization. They asked him to take back the Bible and give it to their oppressors. A popular saying sums up an appraisal of the Bible in the oppression of black South Africans:

When the white man came to our country he had the Bible and we had the land. The white man said to us, 'Let us pray'. After the prayer, the white man had the land and we had the Bible.

Not everyone agrees with Archbishop Tutu that the Blacks got the better deal. The problem of the Bible has been noted in the colonisation of Palestine (Ateek 1989: 75–78) and of Asia also (Kwok 1995: 1–2).[2]

The land in modern biblical scholarship

Even though the biblical paradigm has been used to sanction the British conquest of North America, Ireland and Australia, the Dutch conquest of southern Africa, and the Zionist conquest of Palestine, discussion among biblical scholars on the Israelite settlement in Canaan is distinguished by its indifference to the indigenous inhabitants of the region.

Biblical commentators are unperturbed that the behaviour of the God of the land traditions of the biblical narrative does not conform to even the minimum conditions for waging war as laid down by the Fourth Geneva Convention.[3] Indeed, only a decade after the full horrors of the Nazi 'ethnic cleansing' had been revealed, William Foxwell Albright, the doyen of biblical archaeologists this century, had no qualms about the plunder attendant upon Joshua's enterprise, which he understood in a largely historically reliable way:

> From the impartial standpoint of a philosopher of history, it often seems necessary that a people of markedly inferior type should vanish before a people of superior potentialities, since there is a point beyond which racial mixture cannot go without disaster. ... Thus the Canaanites, with their orgiastic nature worship, their cult of fertility in the form of serpent symbols and sensuous nudity, and their gross mythology, were replaced by Israel, with its pastoral simplicity and purity of life, its lofty monotheism, and its severe code of ethics.
>
> (Albright 1957: 280–81).

Prior to Keith Whitelam's critique (1996a: 88) no commentator had drawn attention to Albright's undisguised racist attitudes, which were typical of virtually every Western colonial enterprise which predicated that the

---

2   Nevertheless, liberation theologians world-wide have appropriated the Exodus story in their struggle against colonialism, imperialism and dictatorship, being impressed by the story's deliverance of the oppressed. One's perspective takes on a different complexion, however, when the biblical narrative is read 'with the eyes of the Canaanites', that is, of any of several cultures which have been victims of a colonialism justified in religious terms.

3   Even Gerd Lüdemann's strident denunciation of Deuteronomy's 'utopia of violence' is diluted by virtually restricting its evil effects to Ezra and Nehemiah's prohibition of miscegenation (1997: 73–75).

'superior' peoples of the West had the right to exploit, and in some cases exterminate the 'natives'. Reflecting these conventional values, Albright also judged that through Zionism Jews would bring to the Near East all the benefits of European civilisation (1942: 12–13). In a similar vein, George E. Wright, another distinguished American biblical scholar, justified the genocide of the narrative of Joshua in terms of the inferiority of the indigenous culture (1960: 109).

Yet, given its alleged centrality in Old Testament covenant theology, it is surprising that 'the land', which occurs some 1,705 times in the English Bible, has attracted so little scholastic attention. Even though Gerhard von Rad lamented in his 1943 pioneering essay (1966: 79) that, despite the importance of the theme in the Hexateuch, no thorough investigation had been made, in fact no serious study of the topic was undertaken for another thirty years. The timing of the studies of W.D. Davies and Walter Brueggemann was no coincidence.

In the Preface to his 1982 study W.D. Davies informs his readers that his seminal *The Gospel and the Land* (1974) was written at the request of friends in Jerusalem, who just before the war in 1967 urged his support for the cause of Israel (p. xiii). Moreover, he wrote *The Territorial Dimensions of Judaism* (1982) under the direct impact of that war, and its updated version because of the mounting need to understand the theme in the light of events in the Middle East, culminating in the Gulf War (1991). One is intrigued by the frankness with which Davies publicised his hermeneutical key: 'Here I have concentrated on what in my judgement must be the beginning for an understanding of this [Israeli–Palestinian] conflict: the sympathetic attempt to comprehend the Jewish tradition' (1982: xiii-xiv). While Davies considers 'the land' from virtually every conceivable perspective, little attention is given to broadly moral and human rights' issues.[4]

Walter Brueggemann's *The Land* (1977) treats 'the land' as a central, if not 'the central theme' of biblical faith. The significant moment before entry into the Promised Land is an occasion for a profound pause: the gift of the land is *sola gratia* (p. 48). He bypasses the treatment to be meted out to the indigenous inhabitants, affirming, 'What is asked is not courage to destroy enemies, but courage to keep Torah' (p. 60), avoiding the fact that 'keeping Torah' demands accepting its xenophobic and destructive militarism. He acknowledges that the land of promise is never an eagerly waiting vacuum anticipating Israel, but is always filled with Canaanites – but that is how the

---

4   Consistent with virtually all biblical scholarship, Alfaro's survey (1978) also does not deal with the fate of the indigenous population. Orlinsky bemoans the neglect of 'the land' in studies on the covenant (1985), and treats the biblical text as though it were a record of what actually happened, also paying no attention to the indigenous inhabitants. While his study attends to questions of Hebrew syntax questions of morality and ethics are not raised.

promise comes (p. 68). For Brueggemann Judaism's attachment to the land could find expression only in the formation of a modern nation state, of whatever complexion. While he concedes 'Arab' rights in theory, he shows no appetite for addressing them. He offer no critique of the moral character of the values implied in the biblical account.

For Davies, what Jews believe to have happened constitutes a historical datum of undeniable historical and theological significance (1991: 97). The legend of the promise of land, so reinterpreted from age to age that it became a living power in the life of the people, acquired its own reality (1991: 5–6). Whether or not the land was ever promised by God in fact, the narrative makes it real. Davies argues for an unseverable connection between Israel, the land, and its God from the early Israelite period to the modern, while acknowledging that it was the pressure of Zionism that made discussion of the land theme possible. He insists that neat dichotomies between the religious and political factions in Zionism are falsifications of their rich and mutually accommodating diversity (W. Davies 1991: 76).

Davies defends the Jewish claim to territory, because without such territory, there is a loss of security, stimulation, identity, and political self-determination (1991: 90). He has not been swayed by the view that the way of Torah, in the emerging rabbinic movement, enabled each individual to bring holiness into daily life without the Temple. He bemoans the spiritualisation of the notion of land in both Christianity and Judaism, and lauds the sense of rootedness which the materiality of the concept keeps alive. Davies excluded from his concern, 'What happens when the understanding of the Promised Land in Judaism conflicts with the claims of the traditions and occupancy of its other peoples?'. He excuses himself by saying that to engage that issue would demand another volume (1991: xv), without indicating his intention to embark upon such an enterprise. Similarly, at the end of his 1981 article (p. 96), he claimed that it was impossible to discuss that issue.

Davies' 1991 work includes a symposium in which Krister Stendahl sees Zionism as a liberation movement, and the State of Israel as the fulfilment of biblical promise (in W. Davies 1991: 111–12). Arthur Herzberg insists that Judaism cannot survive in its full stature in the diaspora, since the bulk of the 613 commandments can be observed only in Israel, which religious insight, he claims, is the prime source of Zionism (in W. Davies 1991: 106). R.J. Zwi Werblowsky also is not perturbed by the implications of the Torah-driven piety implied in Zionism. David Noel Freedman hints at Davies' omission of the moral dimension, drawing attention to the longed-for guidance for serious people disturbed by the consequences of the doctrine of the Land in the Near East today – almost a re-enactment of the first Exodus, conquest, and settlement. However, to deal with such questions is too much to ask (Freedman, in W. Davies 1991: 104). But not for Kenneth Cragg who points to the perpetual crisis which arises when the granting of covenanted territory to a covenanted people through a covenanted story conflicts with the identity of other inhabitants (in W. Davies 1991: 101).

For Jacob Neusner, the obsession with the land in some biblical traditions is explained by the fact that they reached their final form outside the land. But, according to the Babylonian Talmud, one can practise the Torah anywhere, anytime. Neusner notes that the Babylonian Talmud ignores virtually the whole of the Mishnah's repertoire of laws on cultic cleanness, as well as the first division of the Mishnah on agriculture. The great sages of Babylonia made the Mishnah relevant to the diaspora. Neusner adds that American Jews today react to the claim that normality is to live in the land and abnormality is to live abroad, by doing what they want, amiably professing feelings of remorse and guilt (in W. Davies 1991: 109). J.S. Whale brings the moral question to the fore. His criticism of Davies' indifference to the fate of the indigenous people in antiquity and today is as devastating as it is polite: Davies 'must know that conquest is always cruel, even when perpetrated by God's Elect; and that empire is always huge robbery, whether Roman or British, Muslim or Christian' (in W. Davies 1991: 116).

Davies added further reflections in response to the symposium. He justifies the State of Israel in terms of the Holocaust. While he acknowledges that the value of the land may be tempered by appeal to the primacy of the sanctity of life within Judaism he does not elaborate. He settles for an accommodation of the two people as an utter necessity: land can be traded for peace (W. Davies 1991: 120, 130). However, one wonders where the logic of his biblical thesis would have led had the Holocaust not occurred, and how his earlier logic can tolerate such a derogation from the divine mandate as a land-for-peace deal requires.

Reflecting a somewhat elastic moral sense, Davies, although perturbed by the aftermath of the 1967 conquest, takes the establishment of the State of Israel in his stride. The colonial plunder of 1947–49 appears to enjoy the same allegedly divinely sanctioned legitimacy and mandate as the Joshua-led encroachment on the land. One wonders whether Davies would be equally sanguine had white Anglo-Saxon Protestants, or even white Catholics of European provenance been among the displaced people who paid the price for the prize of Zionism. He shows no concern for the fundamental injustice done to the Palestinian Arabs by the encroachment on their land by Zionists, and for the compensation that justice and morality demands. Despite the foundational injustice done in the Nakba of 1948, Davies writes later as if there were a moral equivalence between the dispossessed Palestinians and the dispossessor Zionists. The rights of the rapist and the victim are finely balanced.

Davies moves seamlessly from the religious motivation to live the fullness of the Torah in the land to the conclusion of the legitimacy of establishing a state, at whatever cost to others. Nor does the behaviour of Israel towards the Palestinian Arabs, in Israel itself, in the Occupied Territories, and towards those expelled mute his sense of bible-based propriety. Apparently whatever is apportioned to the people of Israel in their foundation documents constitutes an absolute right.

While Davies concedes that the Zionists superseded the intentions of the

'Lovers of Zion', who were indifferent to whoever would exercise political power, the clear evidence of colonial Zionism does not shake his fundamental satisfaction with his major thesis, thereby playing down the disjuncture between his romanticised biblicism and the reality of the upheaval that always attends 'ethnic cleansing'. While Davies is forced into confrontation with some of the realities of the implications of his theology of land today his sensitivity to issues of Human Rights and International Law is not impressive. His somewhat confused moral position may be summed up as follows: the State of Israel is justified in terms of the Holocaust; the dislocation of 1948 is above reproach – only the post-1967 occupation is a problem; yet, compromise is a necessity to accommodate the two people; and loyalty to the Torah is more precious than even the blessing of living in the land.

While its most distinctive aspect is the virtual absence of any sensitivity to the moral questions involved in one people dispossessing others, the modern scholastic discourse on the land suffers from other serious limitations. Typically, even scholars settle for a synchronic reading of the biblical text, ignoring its provenance and literary evolution. Secondly, and out of harmony with scholarship in all other areas of the discipline, they treat the texts of the origins of Israel as though their literary genre were history. Thirdly, they do not differentiate between the different periods in the life of 'the people of Israel', e.g. before occupation of Canaan, during and after exile, and today. Fourthly, they assume that the people of Israel is homogeneous, ethnically, culturally and religiously one at all periods, and that modern Jews are their unique descendants. Fifthly, they make no value judgement on the biblical attitudes towards the land. Finally, they assume that the attitudes to land portrayed at one (biblical) period have an automatic currency at all times, and achieve a natural flowering in political Zionism.

The absence in biblical scholarship of concern for 'the natives' reflects the deeply ingrained Eurocentric, colonialist prejudice which characterises virtually all historiography, as well as that discipline itself (see Whitelam 1996a, 1998 and Prior 1997a, 1998a). An exegesis that is not sensitive to the dispossessed people is an accomplice by omission in the act of dispossession. In the light of the biblical exegesis discussed above, one speculates as to the relationship between epistemology and the moral character of the exegete. Clearly an academic discourse and religious faith nourished on the Bible as understood by the prevailing biblical scholarship as described above conflicts with universally agreed perspectives on human dignity and rights. Any authentic discussion of the Bible must include a moral critique which respects the discourse of human rights and international law. It must also respect the provenance and literary genre of the narratives as well as other evidence, archaeological, literary, etc.

Moral exegesis

It is undeniable that terrible injustices have been committed through colonialist enterprises which have been fuelled by biblical and theological discourse. Yet, in the discipline of biblical studies there is no serious consideration for the victims of such activity. Even scholars accepts blandly that the Canaanites did not have the right to continue to occupy a region which they had profaned with their idolatry and abominations (Deut 9.5; see also Deut 18.9–14; Lev 18.24–25; 20.22–24), and hence deserved the violence against them. The existence of such texts of unsurpassed violence within Sacred Scripture is an affront to moral sensitivities. The Holy War traditions, and especially that of the *herem*, pose an especially difficult moral problem (Niditch 1993: 28–77; see also Lind 1980; Hobbs 1989 and Barr 1993: 207–20). They portray God as one who cherishes the sacrifice of the crown of his creation. Moreover, the killer is not only acquitted of moral responsibility for his destruction, but acts under a religious obligation. Thus, the *herem* both reduces the nature of the crime and exonerates the culprit. It is little consolation to the victims of unsolicited slaughter that their murder is an act of piety which redounds to the glory of God and advances the sanctity of the perpetrator. For many modern readers, clothing such activity in the garment of religion and piety adds to the problematic.

'Ancient Israel' did not invent such perspectives, nor were they left unchallenged within Israelite moral reflection, as the variety of war traditions within the biblical text itself makes clear.[5] The *herem* tradition is appealed to in support of the deuteronomistic ethic, which emphasises the priestly values of separating the good from the bad, etc. These authors, of course, had no intention of applying the letter of their war traditions to their own context, nor were they in any position to do so. Their real interests lay in promoting the ideal that the 'Israelites' should separate themselves from the impurity of others, a relatively innocuous, if not particularly attractive

---

5   In the priestly ideology of war recounted in Num 31 there is a variant of the *herem* paradigm, with perspectives on justifying killing, or not killing in war. In the symbolic world of the priests everything is weighed in terms of the duality of clean (us) and unclean (them), with special attention to sexual status. Even though the cause of war be holy, and its execution of the order of a ritual, nevertheless, killing defiles, from which one must be purified (see Niditch 1993: 78–89). This ideology tries to have it both ways: killing the 'Other' is a divine mandate, but at the same time is a defiling activity. Niditch discusses also the bardic tradition of war, in which heroes and fair play feature prominently (pp. 90–105). 'The chivalric texts of the Hebrew Bible impose a patina of noble order on the chaos that is real war' (p. 103). She examines the ideology of tricksterism in war, in which the weak justify their indiscriminate fighting on the grounds of the justness of their cause (pp. 106–22). The ideology of expediency applies to those war situations in which the powerful consider themselves to be justified in exercising extreme brutality with God's blessing (pp. 123–33). Finally, Niditch examines the ideology of non-participation, by which the powerless leave the fighting to be done by way of a miraculous divine intervention (pp. 134–49).

disposition. Had these authors used a less morally problematic metaphor than the *herem*, colonised peoples up to the present time might have been saved some of the racist outrages inflicted upon them, fuelled by a simplistic reading of these traditions. It is small consolation that some passages in the biblical land narrative reveal a sense of guilt and remorse at the occupation of what belonged to others (see e.g. Josh 24.13; 1 Macc 15.33–34). Nevertheless, in the legend, whatever rights the Canaanites had in terms of the prevailing international order evaporate in the pens of some of the biblical theologians, for whom religion defined the terms of discrimination, leaving believers with all the rights and unbelievers with none.

There are major errors involved in a naïve interpretation of the Bible, and every effort must be made to rescue it from being a blunt instrument in the oppression of one people by another. A major problem with some of the traditions of the Old Testament, especially those concerned with the promise of land, is its portrayal of God as, what many modern people would regard as a racist, militaristic xenophobe, whose views would not be tolerated in any modern democracy. People with moral sensitivities and concern for the dignity of other peoples, will question the kind of biblicism which sees the core of biblical revelation to be frozen in the concepts of Chosen People and Promised Land, when the application of such views can have such morally questionable outcomes as discussed here. If a naïve interpretation of the Bible leads to such unacceptable conclusions, what kind of exegesis can rescue it?

The problem is not new. As a way of eliminating the scandal caused by particular texts of the Bible, the Fathers of the Church had recourse to the allegorical method. For example, Pseudo-Barnabas saw Moses' prayer with extended hands, interceding for the victory of Joshua over the Amalekites as a 'typos' (foreshadowing, or prefigurement) of the Cross and the Crucified (12.2–3), and considered Joshua to be a figure of Christ (12.8–10). For Justin, Joshua was a type of Christ: just as he led the people into the land of Canaan, so Christ leads Christians into the true promised land (*Dial* 113). Cyril of Alexandria also interpreted the Pentateuch in a christological way, from Cain and Abel to Joshua. Hilary attached christological significance to Joshua (see Simonetti 1994: 14, 20, 33 note 14, 79, 89). In his Homilies of the Book of Joshua, Origen saw Joshua's crossing of the Jordan as a 'type' of Christians passing through its waters in Baptism. The destruction of Jericho symbolised the collapse of this world, predicted by the prophets. Rahab, once a harlot, is joined to Christ. How? In virtue of the scarlet rope given her by the Israelite spies, which symbolised the saving blood of Christ, etc.

Although the allegorical method is out of vogue today, it represented one way of confronting texts which were scandalous. Another mode of dealing with such texts is to assert that the Bible reflects a moral development, which finds its completion in the New Testament: the writings of the Old Testament contain certain 'imperfect and provisional' elements (*Dei Verbum* 15), which the divine pedagogy could not eliminate right away (Pontifical

Biblical Commission 1993: 113–14). The Church supplies yet another means of dealing with scandalous biblical texts: censoring them out of public use (see Prior 1997a: 273–78). While such attempts to deal with texts one considers unacceptable on moral grounds have something to commend them, there is another method which is more amenable to modern sensibilities, one which takes seriously the literary forms of the materials, the circumstances of their composition and relevant non-literary evidence.

History and narrative

In the wake of the seminal works of Thompson (1974) and Van Seters (1975) it is now part of the scholarly consensus that the patriarchal narratives of Genesis do not record events of an alleged patriarchal period, but are retrojections into a past about which the writers knew little, reflecting the author's intentions at the later period of composition, perhaps that of the attempt to reconstitute national and religious identity in the wake of the Babylonian exile (see further Prior 1997a: 216–23). Therefore, it is naïve to cleave to the view that God made the promise of progeny and land to Abraham after the fashion indicated in Gen 15. Nevertheless, despite their legendary character, both Church and Synagogue continue to treat the patriarchal narratives as though they were a record of what actually happened. The scholarly community for its part evades the problem by confining itself to the literary power of the narrative, rather than enquiring into the events which it purports to describe (e.g. Brettler 1995: 1–2; Neusner 1990: 247).

Much of the scholastic reaction against viewing the Abraham narrative as late and largely legendary is motivated by 'confessional' considerations: 'Without Abraham, a major block in the foundations of both Judaism and Christianity is lost; a fictional Abraham ... could supply no rational evidence for faith' (Millard 1992: I.40). One is reminded of the earlier debates about the historicity of the creation accounts, in which any deviation from 'historical' truth was judged to be a derogation from religious truth, on the presumption that history ('what really happened') was the only genre capable of communicating religious truth.[6] However, an authentic biblical faith must respect the variety of literary forms of the biblical narrative, and acknowledge that the narrative of the folkloric and legendary 'events' of the past functions as an honourable medium for the communication of truth. To abandon one's attachment to the historicity of the events of the narrative in the light of compelling contrary evidence is not to forsake belief.

---

6   E.g. 'Si la foi historique d'Israel n'est pas fondée dans l'histoire, cette foi est erronée, et la notre aussi' (de Vaux 1965: 7).

I have argued elsewhere that the narratives from Genesis to Deuteronomy are best understood as common traditions of Judah sometime after 600 BC, and should not be used as historiographical sources for the period before 1000 BC, and should be used only very cautiously for the period of the monarchy itself (Prior 1997a: 223–28). While ancient Israelite historiographers may not have been much different from the later Jewish rabbis, for whom 'there was no question more meaningless or boring than the purpose and usefulness of an exact description of what actually transpired' (Moshe David Herr, in Brettler 1995: 2), the questions concerning whether God's promise of land to an Abraham and his descendants, and the mandate to commit genocide actually happened are of some importance, especially if the narrative has significant social consequences.

The narrative of Deuteronomy is disdainful of the indigenous population. Moreover, at a practical, moral level, the history of reception of the text shows how it has been used as an ideological support for the mistreatment of indigenous peoples (see Prior 1997a). A literalist reading of parts of the text predicates a god who is an exclusivist, ethnicist and xenophobic militarist. In the light of the fact that modern biblical scholarship is unanimous that the narrative of the Pentateuch does not correspond to what actually happened (Whybray 1995: 141) one trusts that modern readers, especially in the context of formal worship, would be inspired by these texts rather less energetically than were earlier theologians justifying the conquest of other peoples' lands.

A historiography of Israelite origins based solely, or primarily on the biblical narratives is an artificial construct influenced by certain religious motivations obtaining at a time long post-dating any verifiable evidence of events. The way forward is to write a comprehensive, independent history of the Near East into which the Israelite history of origins should be fitted. While there is nothing like a scholarly consensus in the array of recent studies on Israel's origins there is virtual unanimity that the model of tribal conquest as narrated in Josh 1–12 is unsustainable (see e.g. Thompson 1987: 11–40).[7] Leaving aside the witness of the Bible, we have no evidence that there was an Israelite conquest. Moreover, there is a virtual scholarly consensus that the biblical narratives which describe the conquest-settlement

---

7   Soggin (1984) and Miller and Hayes (1986) question our ability to say anything sure about Israel's origins, and concur in the judgement that little can be learned from the Bible on the subject, judging the traditions of Genesis–2 Kings to be of limited use for that purpose. At the level of reception, the societal contexts of modern historians of Israelite origins are reflected in their work. One detects in German historiography of 'ancient Israel' a preoccupation with the nation state after the model of Bismarck's unification of Germany. In American scholarship, the recent history of the 'pilgrim fathers' stressed the model of a chosen people in search of a promised land. In the case of Israeli historiographers, these emphases find an echo in terms of the origins of the modern state of Israel (see Coote and Whitelam 1987: 173–77).

period come from authors writing many centuries later than the 'events' described, who had no verifiable information about that distant past (see the discussion in Prior 1997a: 228–47).

The Exodus–Settlement accounts reflect a particular genre, the goal of which was to inculcate religious values, rather than merely present empirical facts of history. The modern historian must distinguish between the actual history of the peoples and the history of their self-understanding. The archaeology of Palestine must be a primary source for tracing the origins of Israel, and it shows a picture quite different from that of the religiously motivated writings (Ahlström 1993: 28–29). The evidence from archaeology, extra-biblical literature, supplemented by insights from the independent methodologies of geography, sociology, anthropology, historical linguistics, Egyptology, Assyriology, etc., points in an altogether different direction from that propounded by Josh 1–12. It suggests a sequence of periods marked by a gradual and peaceful coalescence of disparate peoples into a group of highland dwellers whose achievement of a new sense of unity culminated only with the entry of the Assyrian administration. The Iron I Age settlements on the central hills of Palestine, from which the later kingdom of Israel developed, reflect continuity with Canaanite culture, and repudiate any ethnic distinction between 'Canaanites' and 'Israelites'.

Israel's origins were within Canaan, not outside it. There was neither invasion from outside, nor revolution within. Moreover, the 'Israel' of the period of the biblical narrative represented a multiplicity of 'ethnic' identities, reflecting the variety of provenances in the Late Bronze–Iron Age transition, and that brought about by three waves of systematic, imperial population transfer and admixture (Assyrian, Babylonian and Persian). The predication of Israelite ('ethnic') distinctiveness prior to the Persian period is illusory, and the unity of the biblical 'children of Israel' is a predilection of the biblical authors, rather than the reality reflecting a commonality of ethnic identity or communal experience (Prior 1997a: 228–47).

It is essential to differentiate between story/legend and history in the sense of informing about the past. In dealing with the past scholars must respect the new evidence and attempt to reconstruct it accordingly, however inadequate and imperfect the reconstruction. Authentic and moral scholarship prefers the imprecision of a reconstruction of the past to the security of embracing fictitious and unsustainable fabrications of it. The old paradigm of the unity of Bible and history is not sustainable (Thompson 1995: 697–98), and we shall have to learn to live with ambiguity (Redford 1992: 311). Any reconstruction of the Israelite past must distinguish between 'historical Israel' and 'biblical Israel', respect the archaeological evidence, and give due weight to the nature of the biblical narrative, recognising the ideological intentions of its authors (see P. Davies 1995). However, the task is far from being a straightforward one, since, as widely conceded, Israelite historiography is in a state of crisis.

On the literary side, there needs to be some level of resolution on the highly disputed question of the value of the biblical narratives for describing some of the reality of the periods with which they purport to deal. Do they portray some of the past, or are their descriptions of it critically compromised by the ideological stance of their much later redactors, who in fact are more authors than mere compilers? The 'revisionist school' of Israelite historiography (including Ahlström, P. Davies, Garbini, Thompson and Whitelam) agree that the texts of the Hebrew Bible are late post-exilic, and even Hellenistic, not only in their present edited form but with respect to their content as well, and hence are of no value as witnesses to the periods before the Judges, and of very limited value for that of the monarchy. The invective one detects in the debate about 'ancient Israel' makes one suspicious that more is at stake than customary objective scholarship in search of an elusive past. The real academic crime is that of trespassing on a carefully protected discourse which has implications for the legitimacy of developments in Palestine in our own time.[8]

Although no great admirer of the new tendency,[9] a somewhat more eirenic William G. Dever now acknowledges that the new historiographers have raised the relevant historiographical issues sharply (1997: 298), and confesses that, 'No responsible scholar today doubts the late date of the final redaction of the [biblical] tradition' (1997: 301). He points out, however, that the finished biblical product may contain genuinely historical material, some of it possibly contemporary with the events the narrative purports to describe. He concedes that there is need for a fresh approach to 'ancient Israel', one that is truly critical, comparative, generative, synthetic and ecumenical (1997: 305).

With respect to material culture, issues connected with the Bible have long set the agenda for the archaeological investigation of the land of Israel, and currently there is a very lively debate on the relative value of (the biblical) text and artefacts in attempting to construct the past. Moreover, the biblical stratification of (ethnic) groups is under strain with recent studies on

8   See for instance the 'friendly critique', 'in the hope of fostering a truly interdisciplinary dialogue between specialists', which William G. Dever offered to Whitelam's survey of the 'state-of-the-art' on the literature of Israelite origins (Dever 1996). Dever complains that none of the 'revisionist' historians has any significant credentials in archaeology (p. 5). To Dever's charge of incompetence, H. Shanks elsewhere adds that because 'Whitelam is no kook' his scholarship is insidious, even if it is 'woefully unbalanced and mean-spirited', as well as full of 'considerable cunning'. Whitelam's spirited (and amusing) rejoinder defends his attempt and that of others to challenge the dominant discourse of biblical studies for over a century (Whitelam 1996b; for Shanks' views see note 3). Whitelam will not be intimidated into silence. Indeed, it is clear that much of the emphasis of the 'revisionist school' is now centre stage in the discipline of biblical studies. See also Thompson 1995.

9   Concerning the search for Israelite origins Dever judges Philip Davies' *In Search of 'Ancient Israel'* (1995) to be 'curious' and 'certainly not persuasive', and to lead to ultimate absurdity. Moreover, the attempts of Thompson (1992) and Ahlström (1993) to write a history of ancient Israel confirm the exhaustion of the philological method (1997: 293–94).

group identity stressing the fluidity of the concept of ethnicity and the subjective element in its alleged classification. In particular, they caution against identifying specific material cultures with precise ethnic groups (Canaanites, Israelites, etc.), since elements of material culture may indicate only common cultural and trade interests rather than group or ethnic cohesion (see e.g. I. Finkelstein 1997, Hesse and Wapnish 1997, Small 1997, and Thompson 1998).

Nevertheless, there is reluctance to abandon the conventional confidence in the biblical writers as genuine historians. Even though Marc Brettler acknowledges that the Deuteronomist modified and diverged from his sources radically, and 'fabricated' history, he is excused, because he honestly believed his ideology, and can be regarded to be 'writing history like all other historians' (1995: 78). *Pace* Brettler's rather strained attempts, it is not acceptable to retain the term 'historiography' for much of the biblical narrative (pp. 10–12), on the basis that its importance lies in what can be learned from the narrative, rather than in the integrity of its witness to what actually happened in the past. If such narratives are to be read in terms of the meaning which they convey, rather than as a record of past events (p. 41), it must be clear that their meaning reflects the period and preoccupations of the authors rather than those of an unrecoverable past.

No amount of special pleading is sufficient to justify the classification 'history' for the biblical narrative of Israelite origins, and the period of the alleged conquest. Biblical scholarship can include the narratives from Genesis to 2 Kings within the genre of historiography only by a tortuous expansion of the definition. Such a designation confuses the world of historiography which deals with the real past with that of fictional literature which reflects the conceptual world of the author. The material from Genesis to 2 Kings, which preserves fragmentary sources emanating from many authors reflecting diverse ideologies and retaining disharmonious tale variations, does not merit the genre of self-conscious historiography as understood in antiquity or today. The one responsible for transmitting these traditions appears to have been driven by an antiquarian's desire to preserve the diversity of what was old, while giving it a loosely chronological catalogue of a sequence of great periods. The genre is not simple history, but the authors' fabrication of the past, reflecting their own religious and political ideologies. A 'didactic history' which 'patterned the past after the present', or even fabricated the past for allegedly honest paraenetic motives should not be confused with the discipline of history whose criteria are accuracy and adequacy of portrayal of the past, independently confirmed where possible. History proper must be distinguished from a series of ideologically motivated assertions about the past (see Thompson 1992: 373–78, 404–405).

Conclusion

As we have seen, the biblical claim of the divine promise of land is integrally linked with the claim of divine approval for the extermination of the indigenous people. It is assumed widely that its literary genre is history, even though this view runs in the face of all serious scholarly comment. The biblical narratives which deal with the promise and gift of land are potentially corrupting in themselves, and have in fact contributed to war crimes and crimes against humanity in virtually every colonised region, by providing allegedly divine legitimation for Western colonisers in their zeal to implant 'outposts of progress' in 'the heart of darkness'. While colonialist and imperialist enterprises derive from a matrix of interactive determinants, all too frequently their ideological underpinning is related to the biblical paradigms of 'ethnic cleansing' and 'belligerent settler colonialism', the legitimisation of which has the authority of Sacred Scripture. These land traditions, which have been deployed in support of barbaric behaviour, pose fundamental moral questions, relating to one's understanding of God, of His dealings with humankind, and of human behaviour. The communities which have promulgated them must shoulder some of the responsibility for what has been done in alleged conformity with the values contained within them. The ongoing identification in subsequent history with the warring scenes of the Hebrew Bible is a burden the biblical tradition must bear. The fact that its particular violence has served as a model for persecution, subjugation and extermination for millennia makes investigation of these traditions a critical task (see Niditch 1993: 4).

Nevertheless, the ethnocentric, xenophobic and militaristic character of the biblical narratives of Israelite origins is treated in conventional biblical scholarship as if it were above any questioning on moral grounds, even by criteria derived from other parts of the Bible. Most commentators are uninfluenced by considerations of human rights, when these conflict with a naïve reading of the sacred text, and appear to be unperturbed by the text's advocacy of plunder, murder and the exploitation of indigenous peoples, all under the guise of fidelity to the eternal validity of the covenant of Sinai.

Many theologians sensitive to issues of human rights, especially those whose traditions depend heavily on the Bible face a dilemma. While they revere the sacred text, they see how it has been used as an instrument of oppression, and seek refuge in the view that it is the mis-use of the Bible, rather than the text of the Bible itself which is the problem. The blame is shifted from the non-problematic biblical text to the perverse predispositions of the interpreter. This 'solution' evades the problem. Examples from the past and the present indicate the pervasiveness, the persistence and the moral seriousness of the question. Several traditions within the Bible lend themselves to oppressive interpretations and applications, precisely because of their inherently oppressive nature.

The neglect of the moral question in biblical scholarship is not unrelated to the fact that conventionally the history of ancient Palestine has been merely a backdrop to the history of Israel, Judah and Second Temple Judaism, with the Bible centre stage, and all other evidence in its service

(Coote and Whitelam 1987: 13). The driving force within biblical studies has been the search for ancient Israel as the taproot of Western civilisation, and the antecedent of Christianity, and more recently, has been reinforced by the foundation of the State of Israel, with Israeli scholars searching for their own national identity in the past (Whitelam 1996a: 2–3, 119). The wider history of the region has been written out – there is urgent need to construct a 'secular history' of the region or a 'history without the Bible' (Dever 1997: 305). Moreover, the recent interest in the theme of the land among both Jewish and Christian scholars of the Bible is not unrelated to events in Palestine in this century. While young nations invariably attempt to reconstruct their past to suit the newly discovered national identity, Israeli archaeology has to contend with the fact that the nation displaced a culture which had been in place for millennia (see Elon 1997 and Shavit 1997).

The contemporary needs of the final redactors of the biblical narrative influenced their ideological stance, and issued in an ideal model for the future which they justified on the basis of its retrojection into the past of Israelite origins, the details of which only the surviving conflicting folkloric traditions provided. If we excuse the biblical writers for their misrepresentation of the past to promote their own religious or political interests, we ought not to be equally indulgent with theologians and Church and Synagogue members for whom the evidence of what happened in the past is more reliable. The legendary account of Josh 1–12 offers no legitimising paradigm for land plunder in the name of God, or by anyone arrogating to himself His authority. Indeed, the extra-biblical evidence promotes a respect for the evolution of human culture, rather than for a process that can deal with adjustment to changed circumstances only by way of violent destruction.

While generations of religious people have derived both profit and pleasure from the retelling of the biblical stories, victims of colonialist plunder are less sanguine in their attitude to the texts, and would welcome any attempt to distinguish between the apparent ethnocentricity of the God represented from Genesis to 2 Kings, and the paranaetic and political intentions of authors writing much later. A major epistemological question arises. Do texts which we recognise to belong to the genre of folkloric epic or legend, rather than of history, legitimise the 'Israelite' possession of the land and subsequent colonialist enterprises, when their original legitimacy depended on the presumption that the biblical narrative was factual history? Does a judgement which was based on the premise that the genre of the justifying text was history not dissolve when it is realised that the text belongs to the genre of 'myths of origin', which are deployed in virtually every society in the service of particular ideologies?

Biblical scholarship must set its own house in order by articulating ethical criteria by which dispositions unworthy of a civilised person may not be accorded a privileged place as part of a sacred text. When the sacred pages are manipulated by forces of oppression, biblical scholars cannot continue to seek refuge by expending virtually all their intellectual energies on an unrecoverable past, thereby releasing themselves from the obligation of engaging in contemporary discourse. Nor are they justified in maintaining an academic detachment from significant engagement in contemporary issues. It is high time that biblical scholars, Church people, and Western intellectuals read the biblical narratives we have discussed 'with the eyes of the Canaanites' (see Said 1988 and Warrior 1991). While it may be conceded by some that 'social and political action is not the direct task of the exegete' (Pontifical Biblical Commission 1993: 68), I can think of no circumstance in which such activity is not incumbent on a Christian exegete, *qua* Christian.

While religious and theological comment on contemporary developments in Palestine is substantial, that reflecting a moral sensitivity to the disruption of the indigenous Arab population is modest. Biblically and theologically based discussion is singularly deficient in its interest in those issues with which human rights and humanitarian bodies concern themselves. This is not only surprising but alarming, since biblical scholars and theologians in virtually every other arena inform their discussions with a sensitivity to the victims of oppression. A major factor in the benevolent attitude in the West to the developments in Palestine in this century is the success of the promulgation of the State of Israel's self-portrayal, both with respect to the intentions of Zionism and the behaviour of the state. Having traced the history of Zionism and discussed the attitudes of religious bodies to its flowering in the State of Israel, and having interrogated the biblical narratives with a sensitivity to indigenous people, it is time now to examine these claims.

Part IV

The mythological justification for Zionism

7 The foundational myths of the State of Israel

The West's benevolent assessment of Zionism and the State of Israel is due in no small measure to the success with which the ideologues of Zionism and the historiographers of the state hid from the public the real intentions of the Zionist enterprise and the realities surrounding the establishment of the state and its behaviour since. Despite the catastrophic consequences for the people of the region, Israeli propaganda, thanks to one of the most successful disinformation campaigns in modern times, has succeeded in masking the fact that the creation of the state resulted in the planned dispossession and dispersion of another people, and in claiming that this was forced upon it by circumstances. The fabricated Zionist history claims that Zionism's birth was an inevitable result of Gentile pressures and persecution in Europe, that the Zionists intended no ill to the Arabs of Palestine, and that their intentions did not necessitate a clash or displacement; that, nevertheless, Israel was born into an uncharitable, predatory environment; that Zionist efforts at compromise and conciliation were rejected by the Arabs, who, though far stronger politically and militarily nonetheless lost the 1947–49 war; that, in the course of the war, the Palestinian leadership ordered their people to quit their homes, thus laying the Jewish state open to charges of expulsion (see Morris 1990a: 4–5).

The fabricated history also claims that 'the land was empty' and neglected; that it was redeemed by Jewish labour, which made the desert bloom; that Zionism never damaged, and indeed benefited the natives, who nevertheless remain ungrateful; that the Zionists acted without the assistance of interested imperial powers; that the few unsavoury actions in 1947–49 were the result of the stresses of war; and that all its wars and invasions, and its actions against the Palestinians were purely defensive, and so forth. That fabricated history, consistently taught to Israeli children, has shaped the minds of Israeli and diaspora Jews, and has moulded the perceptions of governments and much of the international community. Even in the face of overwhelming evidence to the contrary, the cant is repeated, not least, as we have seen, in religious and theological circles. Indeed, it appears that Nakba denial is a necessary tenet of Jewish–Christian dialogue.

Zionist colonialism

Although in our post-colonial culture Zionists are embarrassed by the association of Zionism with colonialism, its initiators had no such scruples, as the names of some of their associations illustrate: the Jewish Colonisation Association, the Society for the Colonisation of the Land of Israel, the Palestine Jewish Colonisation Association, the Jewish Colonial Trust, etc. Moreover, Herzl looked to the support of Bismarck, 'the greatest living empire builder' (1960: 120), and of Cecil Rhodes, a role model in matters colonial (1960: 1193–94). Moreover, the Twelfth Zionist Congress set up a 'Colonisation Department'. Likewise, Weizmann compared the Zionist movement with the French colonisation of Tunisia (1949: 191). As will become clear, Zionism deployed the full battery of colonialist attitudes, not least a disdain for the indigenous population.

While there is no one unified ideology and practice across the broad spectrum of colonial enterprises, one detects recurring attitudes towards the indigenous populations: invariably the incoming society established itself through a foundational injustice to them. The original inhabitants were included, more or less, in the enterprise, or, in the case of Zionism, altogether excluded. While several motivations combined to exclude indigenes, for those influenced by religious considerations the biblical paradigm provided a ready justification for it. The exclusivist tendencies in North America and South Africa, for example, have been ascribed to the influence of the Old Testament in the Puritan faith in the case of the former, and in the Dutch Reformed Church in the latter.

The following chart illustrates the self-perception of the colonising peoples and their attitudes to the indigenous population, in the Old Testament paradigm and in three colonising enterprises (see Prior 1997a: 175–84):

	Old Testament	Latin America	South Africa	Palestine
chosen or privileged people	yes	yes	yes	yes
racially superior	yes	yes	yes	yes
frontiers of inclusion	no	yes	no	no
extermination of indigenes	yes	limited	limited	limited
displacement of indigenes	yes	limited	limited	yes
corralling of indigenes	no	yes	yes	yes
enslavement of indigenes	yes	yes	yes	yes
miscegenation and intermarriage	no	yes	no	no
religious motivation	yes	yes	yes	yes
attempt at conversion of indigenes	no	yes	limited	no
compunction	no	yes	yes	no

Without pretending that 'parallels' indicate equivalence, there is a similarity in underlying attitudes, and in specific techniques of colonisation. One detects a uniformity in the mythology of conquest. A core element in the rhetoric is that adventurous Europeans pioneered in a savage wilderness and brought civilisation to it. The stereotypical myth of colonialism postulates that the land was in a virgin state, or, that habitation was irregular; the people (to be) conquered were of an inferior status; and that the enterprise was one of civilising (or even evangelising) the natives. Although some colonising enterprises pretended to altruistic motives, invariably the colonisers benefited through wreaking havoc on the indigenous populations. Europe's glory was gained at the expense of the tragedy of the indigenous populations. Frequently, in rationalising the subjugation of the indigenes, moral scruples are stifled and embarrassing facts are suppressed.

Although Zionism has much in common with other forms of settler colonialism some aspects give it an unique position in the discourse. Even though nationalist colonialism is long out of vogue with liberal Western intellectuals, and is an object of disdain among Christian theologians, support for Zionism is widespread. The existence of a Jewish state is justified by appeal to some combination of the following factors: the need for a haven; the biblical mandate; the unique historical claim; persistent diaspora longing; unbroken Jewish residence in the land; the decision of the United Nations; the reality of military conquest, etc. Since the relative value attached to each element of legitimation has varied at different stages, and among different groups, it is naïve to construct a composite legitimisation by blending them all together, reducing them to a form in which their unique identity is subsumed, and their relative importance is undifferentiated. However, the array of justificatory arguments is unparalleled in subtlety and imagination (Gee 1998: 15).

Many Jews allege an unique derivative link between the biblical paradigm of conquest and Zionist settler colonialism today. If other forms of colonisation could appeal to the alleged legitimisation provided by the biblical mandate, the Jewish claim was unrivalled. Uniquely in the case of colonialism, Zionism appeals to an historical link between the settler population and the land to be settled: all Jews have an historical right to the land, in virtue of unbroken habitation there by Israelites/Jews, even when at times the Jewish population was very small.

The early realisation by its ideologues that the Zionist dream would require an Arab nightmare was carefully kept from the wider public. Moreover, after the establishment of the state in 1948, the history of events was scrupulously fabricated into foundation myths, involving 'the voluntary emigration of Arabs', 'making the desert bloom', and being 'the only democracy in the Middle East', etc. Israelis began systematically to rewrite Palestinian history, legitimising Jewish and repudiating Arab claims to the land: it had been virtually vacant for the 1,800 years since the expulsion of the Jews;[1] Arabs had lost any right to it in virtue of having allowed it to become a wasteland; the new Jewish settlers had now redeemed it,[2] etc. Ben-Gurion claimed that on the eve of Zionist colonisation, Palestine was in 'a virtual state of anarchy ... primitive, neglected and derelict'. Jewish settlement 'revitalised' the land, and the indigenous Arab population became merely the 'Arab problem' (Ben-Gurion 1971–2: xx, 25, 47). Let us review the nationalist mythology.

Attitudes to the indigenous population

Since it is an established part of Israel's propaganda, and widely believed in the West, that the Zionists never intended any harm to the indigenous Arab population, but desired to live in harmony with it, it is instructive to examine the matter in some detail. Although at that time, the population of Palestine was 95 per cent Arab, and 99 per cent of the land was Arab-owned (W. Khalidi 1992: 17), the First Zionist Congress (1897) made no mention of the indigenous population. Even by 1906 there were only 55,000 Jews, of whom only 550 were Zionists, among the some 700,000 inhabitants of Palestine (Teveth 1985: 9–10). In line with the mood of the period, however, the intentions of the colonisers overrode every other consideration. Herzl's *Der Judenstaat* also had ignored the needs and rights of the indigenous people, and much of the Zionist public discourse proceeded as if Palestine were a *terra nullius*, or a land at the free disposal of the imperial powers. In Balfour's ignominious phrase, the 670,000 indigenous Arab population became the 'non-Jewish communities in Palestine', that is, they were defined in terms of the 60,000 Jews living there. As we shall see, nullification by nomenclature would soon be followed by physical annihilation.

Population transfer

Privately, Herzl and the majority of Zionists after him were in no doubt that the realisation of the Jewish dream would require a nightmare for the indigenous population. Despite public protestations to the contrary, Zionist leaders from the beginning were aware of the demographic reality in Palestine, and as early as November 1882 the use of arms was envisioned by

---

1   Despite clear evidence to the contrary, there was no shortage of such claims, as reflected in the slogan, 'A land without a people for a people without a land'. There is 'a profusion of evidence' that Palestine was 'uninhabited' on the eve of the modern Zionist colonisation (Peters 1984: 170). Prime Minister Levi Eshkol, Prime Minister Golda Meir and Shimon Peres are on record along the same lines.

2   'There is no Arab people living in intimate fusion with the country, utilising its resources and stamping it with a characteristic impress: there is at best an Arab encampment' (Zangwill 1920: 104); 'A wild landscape devoid of trade and shade ... where the inhabitants were strange and alien, wild like the land itself', and 'desolate under Arab rule' (Shapira 1992: 53, 214).

some: 'The Jews, if necessary with arms in their hands, will publicly proclaim themselves masters of their own, ancient fatherland' (see Lehn 1988: 10). Moreover, in Moshe Smilansky's dialogue between two Zionist pioneers (1891), the revolutionaries would expel the Arabs to Transjordan, and later further. Nahman Syrkin, the ideological founder of Socialist Zionism, too, insisted in 1898 that Palestine must be evacuated for the Jews (in Masalha 1992: 9–11). Herzl was no exception. His diary entry of 12 June 1895, 'We shall endeavour to expel the poor population across the border unnoticed ... ', confirms his real intentions, despite his public protestations of furthering the interests of the native population. This kind of duplicity was a characteristic of Zionist discourse, producing 'a not-undeserved reputation in the world for chronic mendacity' (Sykes 1965: 26), both with respect to true Zionist intentions and the distortion of what was done in their execution.

Although Israel Zangwill had seen the situation for himself in Palestine in 1897, and had acknowledged the reality publicly, he spoke of 'a land without a people for a people without a land'. Chaim Weizmann spoke of the necessity of fitting the gem (the Jewish people without a country) into the ring (the country without a people). It is clear from other comments of Zangwill and Weizmann that 'without a people' meant 'without a people worth considering': 'a kind of civilisational barrenness' (see Masalha 1992: 5–6; 1997: 62). Zangwill added that,

> If we wish to give a country to a people without a country, it is utter foolishness to allow it to be the country of two peoples. This can only cause trouble. The Jews will suffer and so will their neighbours. One of the two: a different place must be found either for the Jews or for their neighbours.
>
> (Zangwill, in Masalha 1992: 10)

Although mainstream political Zionists were determined to displace the indigenous population, others were critical of such an enterprise. As we shall see (Chapter 8) the Ukrainian cultural Zionist, Ahad Ha'am (1856–1927) foresaw the obstacles to large-scale Jewish colonisation, and protested against the ethnocentric behaviour of the Jewish 'pioneers'. Yitzhak Epstein, who arrived in Palestine from Russia in 1886, also drew attention in 1907 to the moral and political problem of Jewish settlers. The most weighty question was that of 'our relations with the Arabs'. Concern for the Arabs merited almost no mention in the literature of Zionism. Epstein criticised those who purchased land from absentee Arab landlords requiring the Arab tenants to leave. Such activities were bound to cause political confrontation later (in Masalha 1992: 8). But such opposition counted for little against the Zionist determination that Palestine belong exclusively to Jews: superiority rather than 'Semitic symbiosis' was the characteristic attitude towards Arabs (D. Goldberg 1996: 163).

Whereas before the Balfour Declaration the expulsion of the Arabs was a private aspiration, such hopes took on a more pragmatic form with British support for a Jewish homeland. At the Paris Peace Conference (1919), Weizmann pressed the Zionist case for a British Mandate over a Palestine extending north to the Litani River (in Lebanon), and to the Hijaz rail line well east of the Jordan River, and called for a Palestine which would be as Jewish as England is English. Although he did not declare it openly, his conversation with fellow delegate Aaron Aaronsohn shows that he regarded the expulsion of the Arabs as a prerequisite (see Masalha 1992: 12–13). Weizmann described the native population as the rocks of Judea, obstacles that had to be cleared on a difficult path (see Flapan 1979: 56, and Ingrams 1972: 31–32).

After the Declaration, Zangwill began to campaign openly for transfer, declaring that an 'Arab exodus', based on 'race redistribution', or a 'trek like that of the Boers from Cape Colony' was 'literally the only "way out" of the difficulty of creating a Jewish State in Palestine' (Zangwill 1920: 103). The grand design of Zionism would harbour no opposition:

> We cannot allow the Arabs to block so valuable a piece of historic reconstruction. … And therefore we must gently persuade them to 'trek'. … There is no particular reason for the Arabs to cling to these few kilometres. 'To fold their tents' and 'silently steal away' is their proverbial habit: let them exemplify it now.
>
> (Zangwill 1920: 93)

The Zionist determination to establish a Jewish state, and to promote unrestricted Jewish immigration and the purchase of Arab land precipitated a serious level of disharmony. The British feared that the solution to the 'Arab problem' would not be plain sailing. However, diplomatic duplicity would help. When addressing Arabs in Palestine (March 1921), Winston Churchill assured them that the Zionist project was 'a great event in the world's destiny', taking place without injury to anyone; transforming waste places into fertile, to the great benefit of all (PRO.CO.733/2, in Ingrams 1972: 119–20). Earlier (25 October 1919) he had written of 'the Jews, whom we are pledged to introduce into Palestine, and who take it for granted that the local population will be cleared out to suit their convenience' (Gilbert 1975: 484). And why not, given his racial preference:

> I do not agree that the dog in a manger has the final right to the manger, even though he may have lain there for a very long time. I do not admit … that a great wrong has been done to the Red Indians of America. … I do not admit that a wrong has been done to these people by the fact that a stronger race, a higher grade race, or at any rate, a more world-wise race … has come in and taken their place.
>
> (Churchill in Ponting 1994: 254)

While Ben-Gurion acknowledged after the riots of 1929 that the Palestinian Arabs constituted a national movement, and that they understood ongoing Jewish immigration to presage the loss of their homeland, other Zionist leaders were less complimentary. In 1936 Yitzhak Tabenkin spoke of the Palestinian national movement as a 'Nazi' movement, and Berl Katznelson described it as 'Nazism'. He referred to 'typical Arab bloodlust', and in January 1937 spoke of 'Arab fascism and imperialism and Arab Hitlerism' (cited in Masalha 1992: 19). Acknowledgement of Palestinian identity, forged by centuries of living in their homeland, was further eroded by the Zionists who placed them within an indiscriminate Arab nation, whose real homeland was in Syria, Iraq or in the Arabian peninsula. Henceforth, Palestinians could be driven out of Palestine to any Arab land, without undue prejudice.

On 31 August 1934, Ben-Gurion proposed to the Palestinian Arab leader, Musa al-Alami, that Palestine and Transjordan be reconstituted as a single Jewish state, confederated with Arab states, and that the displaced Palestinian population would be helped to settle in other Arab countries, who could count on more Jewish help. Ben-Gurion insisted that the Zionist enterprise would not replicate the situation in South Africa, where the white owners lorded it over the black workers (Masalha 1992: 22–23). No such problem would present itself if the Arabs could be encouraged to leave Palestine.

From the beginning the Zionist enterprise entailed *redemption of the Land*, and *Hebrew-only* labour. Although couched in biblical language, this meant ideally an *Arab-rein* Palestine – a state cleansed of Arabs. Ben-Gurion made the aspiration quite explicit at a meeting of the Yishuv's National Council on 5 May 1936: 'if we want Hebrew redemption 100 per cent, then we must have a 100 per cent Hebrew settlement, a 100 per cent Hebrew farm, and a 100 per cent Hebrew port' (Ben-Gurion 1971–2: 163).

The build-up of the Yishuv's military capacity in the 1930s reflected its growing perception that the solution to the demographic problem lay in arms, rather than in diplomacy. By the summer of 1937 the Haganah had prepared the Avner Plan, a military strategy to conquer Palestine in three stages, without, of course, publicising its intentions. Somewhat more modestly, the Yishuv temporarily favoured a legislative council, based on 'parity' between Arabs and Jews (while the Jews constituted only some 17 per cent of the population, and owned some 5 per cent of the land). However, with the growing strength of the Yishuv, the parity option was abandoned by Ben-Gurion as being incongruous with Zionist aims.

While it is true that the Yishuv contained a number of factions that advocated bi-national options (e.g. *Brit Shalom*, whose members included Judah Magnes, Martin Buber and Hans Kohn), these never gained wide popularity, and had little impact on the policies of the Yishuv (see Segev 1993: 61). The main division within the Yishuv was between the Revisionists – founded by Jabotinsky in 1925, advocating a 'revision' of the Mandate to include Transjordan – who were maximalist and uncompromising, and the more pragmatic, gradualist Labour Zionism. Jabotinsky's policy towards the Arabs derived from his judgement that Zionist colonisation could only be carried out in defiance of the will of the native population by force. 'To formulate it any other way would be hypocrisy'. Confrontation with the Arabs was inevitable. Already in 1925 he had written, 'Zionism is a colonising adventure and, therefore, it stands or falls on the question of armed forces'. Moreover, the Arabs must make room for the Jews in *Eretz Yisrael*, and he proposed driving them to Iraq and Saudi Arabia. 'We Jews, thank God, have nothing to do with the East. ... The Islamic soul must be broomed out of Eretz-Yisrael' (in Masalha 1992: 28, 45 note 71, 29).

Already by 1930, there were high-level discussions between the Yishuv and the British government on the transfer of Palestinian Arabs to Transjordan. On 4 March 1930, Weizmann met Dr Drummond Shiels, the parliamentary Under-Secretary for the colonies, who, according to Weizmann's notes, advocated that the Arabs be told frankly that Palestine was to be a national home for the Jews, and that they should go to Transjordan and Mesopotamia. Lord Passfield, the Colonial Secretary, also favoured Transjordan as a refuge for the Palestinian Arabs who would be evicted. Weizmann suggested the creation of a Development Company which would acquire a million dunums of land in Transjordan to serve as a reserve for Arab resettlement, the details of which plan he committed to Pinhas Rutenberg, Chairman of the Yishuv's National Council (Masalha 1992: 33). However, the plan was rejected by Lord Passfield and by Ramsay MacDonald's government, who ruled out any large-scale Palestinian resettlement in Transjordan, because of its prohibitive cost, and because of Arab opposition. Instead, Lord Passfield's White Paper of October 1930 recommended that restrictions be placed on Jewish immigration, because of the effect it had on the Palestinian peasants.

Weizmann countered this temporary setback by insisting that the Arabs of Palestine and Transjordan were one in race, language and culture, and that movement from one to the other involved little more than the crossing of a narrow stream. On 4 December 1930, he proposed to the Prime Minister that a Round Table Conference be convened with the Arabs to discuss the problem of the congested area in Cisjordan which could be solved by the migration of Arabs to Transjordania. Already on 17 June 1930 the Directorate of the JNF had discussed the proposal of transferring Arabs from Palestine to Transjordan, and it came up again on 29 April 1931. Also in 1931 the Jewish Agency proposed the transfer of displaced Arab peasants to Transjordan. In the following year, the representative of the Zionist Organisation at the League of Nations suggested in a secret memorandum the partition of Palestine, provided that 120,000 Arabs be removed from the Jewish area (Masalha 1992: 36–37).

While these negotiations were carried out in secret, one of the leading figures of the Yishuv publicly called for the transfer of Palestinian Arabs to other parts of the Middle East: 'We have a greater and nobler ideal than preserving several hundred thousands of Arab fellahin' (Menahem Ussishkin in Masalha 1992: 37). Such public statements would stiffen Arab opposition, upset the prospects of ongoing Jewish immigration, and alienate public opinion in the West. Therefore, two days later (30 April 1930), the Jewish Agency Executive condemned it, even though it proposed a transfer plan the following year. The cornerstone of subsequent argumentation was that there was nothing 'immoral' about transfer – the transfer of the Greek and Turkish populations provided a precedent – and that the transfer of the Palestinians to any part of the Arab world was merely a relocation from one Arab district to another.

Before 1937, discussion of transfer proposals was conducted only in private negotiations with British officials – the project could not be carried out without British approval and support. By that time, Jewish immigration to Palestine had increased from 30,000 in 1933, to 42,000 in 1934, to 61,000 in 1935, thereby increasing the Jewish percentage of the population of Palestine from 17.8 to 29.5 (W. Khalidi 1991: 82). On 30 March 1936, Weizmann's 1930 proposal to transfer the Palestinians to Transjordan was discussed at a meeting of the Political Committee of Mapai, the dominant party within the Yishuv and headed by Ben-Gurion, which later was transformed into the Israeli Labour Party. On 19–20 May 1936 the transfer issue was raised again at meetings of the Jewish Agency Executive. Realising that 'the Arabs' would not agree to transfer to Iraq, Ussishkin proposed that Transjordan be included within the Land of Israel, either for settlement of Jews, or for the resettlement of Palestinian Arabs, since 'this country belongs to us and not to them' (in Masalha 1992: 51).

At the October 1936 meetings of the Jewish Agency Executive, Yitzhak Ben-Zvi, the president of the Yishuv's National Council who later became the second President of the State of Israel, argued for removing dispossessed Arab peasants to neighbouring countries, including Transjordan, a proposal supported by Moshe Shertok, the head of the Political Department of the Jewish Agency. The majority of the Executive, including Ben-Gurion, Weizmann, Ben-Zvi, Kaplan and Shertok favoured a transfer policy to be promoted discretely in talks with the Peel Commission. In summarising the debate, Ben-Gurion expressed his sympathy for mass transfer to Transjordan – 'there is nothing morally wrong in the idea' – but judged it to be impracticable, since, 'We are not a state and Britain will not do it for us'. In the final vote on 29 October, only two of the twenty-one member Executive opposed the 'voluntary' transfer of displaced Arab farmers to Transjordan. One of them, David Werner Senator, protested that 'We cannot say that we want to live with the Arabs and at the same time transfer them to Transjordan' (in Masalha 1992: 53–54).

The Yishuv made every effort to influence the Royal (Peel) Commission, and, after its departure, sent Shertok, Weizmann (in February), and Ben-

Gurion (in May 1937) as emissaries to London, to lobby cabinet ministers, MPs, and senior officials at the Foreign and Colonial Office. Population transfer was promoted in conjunction with the proposal of partition. Reginald Coupland, who ultimately formulated the Peel Commission's report, proposed partition in a private meeting with Weizmann, indicating British support for Jewish sovereignty, albeit over only part of Palestine. It appears that the transfer proposal that was ultimately made by the Peel Commission originated from Jewish Agency leaders, including Ben-Gurion, Shertok and Weizmann (see Masalha 1992: 55–57).

While the Yishuv was negotiating with Emir Abdallah of Transjordan a proposal to raise money to resettle displaced Palestinians in Transjordan, and settle Jews east of the Jordan, Shertok left the Mapai Central Committee (5 February 1937) and the Zionist Actions Committee (22 April 1937) in no doubt about the difficulties of inducing the Palestinian Arabs to leave. Britain would not have the courage to transfer the 300,000 Arabs who would fall under Jewish rule, and he acknowledged that the Arabs would lose everything, including the richest part of Palestine. Such a project, resulting in rivers of blood, would not be realistic for the next ten years (in Masalha 1992: 58–59).

The Peel Commission report on 8 July 1937 gave His Majesty's government's approval for the partition of Palestine into an Arab state, including Transjordan and the Arab part of Palestine, and a Jewish state which would comprise some one-third of the country. While Jews owned only 5.6 per cent of the land of Palestine, the Jewish state would embrace the most fertile parts, including the plain of Esdraelon, most of the coastal plain, and the wholly Arab-owned Galilee. The British would maintain enclaves at Haifa, Jerusalem, Bethlehem, Tiberias, Nazareth, Acre and a corridor from Jaffa to Jerusalem. The Arab state would consist of the remainder of Palestine, including the Negev. The British propensity for balance would be retained in its proposal for an 'exchange' of populations: some 225,000 Arabs would leave the proposed Jewish territory, and some 1,250 Jews would leave the Arab one. In the last resort, the Commission insisted, the exchange could be compulsory.

Not surprisingly, the Peel recommendations were rejected by all shades of Palestinian opinion, but were accepted privately by Ben-Gurion and the Yishuv leadership as a temporary expedient.[3] Indeed, while the Commission had been deliberating, Weizmann had said to the British High Commissioner, 'We shall expand in the whole country in the course of time. . . . This

3　Ben-Gurion had outlined already in 1918 the dimensions of a future Jewish state: the Litani river to the north; the Wadi 'Owja, twenty miles south of Damascus to the north east; the Syrian desert, including the furthest edge of Transjordan to the east; and the southern border stretching at least up to Wadi al-'Arish in the Sinai (Teveth 1985: 34–35).

is only an arrangement for the next 25 to 30 years' (in Masalha 1992: 62). Moreover, Weizmann insisted privately to William Ormsby-Gore, the Colonial Secretary, that the British government, rather than the Jews, should carry out the transfer of the Arab population, while pretending publicly that the transfer would occur voluntarily.

Accepting the Peel partition proposal, Ben-Gurion wrote in his diary: 'The compulsory transfer of the Arabs from the valleys of the proposed Jewish state could give us something which we never had, even when we stood on our own feet during the days of the First and Second Temple' (12 July 1937), giving a Galilee free of Arabs; he emphasised his determination to have it carried out. On 27 July he wrote somewhat disingenuously to his sixteen-year-old son, Amos:

> We have never wanted to dispossess the Arabs [but] because Britain is giving them part of the country which had been promised to us, it is only fair that the Arabs in our state be transferred to the Arab portion
>
> (Ben-Gurion 1971–2: 297–99, 330–33)

By 5 October he reverted to 'adult-speak':

> We must expel Arabs and take their places ... and if we have to use force – not to dispossess the Arabs of the Negev and Transjordan, but to guarantee our own right to settle in those places – then we have force at our disposal.
>
> (Teveth 1985: 189)[4]

It is clear that for Ben-Gurion as for Weizmann and Shertok, the evacuation of the Palestinian Arabs was a prerequisite for accepting the Peel partition plan. Without such an evacuation, demography alone would have made the proposed Jewish state, already with half its population Arab, nonviable.

Within a month of its publication the Twentieth Zionist Congress (3–21 August 1937) debated the Peel Commission's proposals. Ben-Gurion spoke enthusiastically about the viability and acceptability of transfer, carefully preferring the rhetoric of 'transfer and settlement' to that of 'dispossession and transfer'. Others enshrouded the human suffering of the operation by suggesting that transfer would benefit those expelled, while others again

---

4   Efraim Karsh's attempt to portray Ben-Gurion as aspiring in the 1930s and 1940s to create a 'Jewish–Arab semitic alliance', and a 'true partnership among equal citizens' (1997: 68) is strained and unsuccessful. Whatever is said about the lines which were crossed out of the original MS from which the Teveth quotation is taken, the fact remains that Ben-Gurion is nowhere on record as being against the concept of transfer. On the contrary, his words in several different situations betray his real intentions, and, more significantly, his actions in 1948 demonstrate his commitment to the transfer project. See Morris' critique of Karsh's work (1998).

(e.g. Golda Meir) had no qualms about its morality, but only about its feasibility. Eliahu Hacarmeli, however, proposed that forcible transfer was a just, logical, moral and human programme in all senses (see Masalha 1992: 69–73). The Congress adopted a resolution rejecting partition, but empowering the Zionist Executive and the Jewish Agency Executive to negotiate with the British government to clarify specific terms of the British proposal to establish a Jewish state in Palestine. Rabbi Meir (Bar Ilan) Berlin, head of the Mizrachi World Movement and a member of the executive of the Jewish National Fund summarised his views: 'The basis of Zionism is that the land of Israel is ours and not the land of the Arabs, and not because they have large territories, and we have but little. We demand Palestine because it is our country' (in Gorny 1987: 274).

The First Population Transfer Committee

Immediately after the Congress, Dr Selig Eugen Soskin, formerly Director of the Land Settlement Department of the JNF, wrote to the Political Commission of the Twentieth Zionist Congress, advocating the compulsory transfer of Arabs with the greatest speed possible, since a Jewish state would be unthinkable without it (in Masalha 1992: 81–82). The Zionist Executive lost no time in forming the Population Transfer Committee in November 1937. At its second meeting (21 November), Josef Weitz outlined his plan for the transfer proposal, based on two principles: in addition to diminishing the Arab population, the transfer would release Arab land for the Jewish inhabitants. However, since Britain was not likely to agree to carry out the transfer it could take place in stages by a combination of international agreements between the parties and inducements to the Arabs, for which he gave precise proposals. Shertok, Ben-Gurion and Weizmann were kept fully informed of the Transfer Committee's deliberations (see Masalha 1992: 94–99).

During the following year other prominent leaders joined sub-committees of the Transfer Committee. Early in 1938, the Mandatory authority agreed to the request of the Transfer Committee to copy all its material on Arab agriculture and land ownership in Palestine. However, the British government's rejection of the Peel Commission's plan for the compulsory transfer of Arabs (January 1938) precipitated some panic in the Transfer Committee which met on 27 May to give a response to Sir John Woodhead's invitation to produce five memoranda, including one on transfer. Discussion centred around plans for transfer to Syria and Iraq. One of the Committee's members, Alfred Bonné, proposed a new transfer plan, which advocated a complete and forcible evacuation of Arabs from the proposed Jewish state, and sent it in a confidential memorandum to Ben-Gurion on 27 July 1938. Ben-Gurion himself had already informed the Jewish Agency Executive Committee meeting on 7 June 1938 that

[I am not] satisfied with part of the country, but on the basis of the assumption that after we build up a strong force following the establishment of the state – we will abolish the partition of the country and we will expand to the whole land of Israel.

In response to a question as to whether population dislocation would be achieved by force, Ben-Gurion replied:

This is only a stage in the realisation of Zionism and it should prepare the ground for our expansion throughout the whole country through Jewish–Arab agreement ... The State, however, must enforce order and security and it will do this not by moralising and preaching 'sermons on the mount' but by machine-guns, which we will need.

(in Masalha 1992: 108)

While Ben-Gurion, Weitz and other Zionist leaders advocated 'transfer', they usually expressed their views only in closed Zionist circles. For Ussishkin a combination of force and money would be necessary to transfer the Arab population to Transjordan: Britain should provide the force and world Jewry the money. Ruppin favoured a 'voluntary' transfer. Mapai Remez, however, declared that since the British would never put the transfer into effect, the task would be left to the Yishuv. Berl Katznelson, too, insisted on the principle of compulsory, and speedy transfer, including the compulsory confiscation of Arab land, but added, 'There are delicate things that it is not easy to talk about'. Ben-Zvi reduced the whole discussion concerning the creation of a Hebrew state to two principles: the necessity of promoting Jewish immigration and settlement, and promoting Arab transfer and resettlement. Eliahu Berligne, the leader of the Zionist religious party, Knesset Yisrael, declared that the Yishuv should insist on compulsory transfer. While Eliezer Kaplan thought that some transfer might be arranged with the help of financial inducements, he supported Ben-Gurion's emphasis on forced removal, which he made very explicit at that meeting of the Jewish Agency Executive (12 June 1938, in Masalha 1992: 112–17):

I support compulsory transfer. I do not see anything immoral in it. But compulsory transfer could only be carried out by England. ... There are two issues here: 1) sovereignty and 2) the removal of a certain number of Arabs, and we must insist on both of them.

(Ben-Gurion, in Masalha 1992: 117).

Ben-Gurion went on to explain that it would be more tactful in public discourse to replace the formula for compulsory transfer with less unacceptable ones ('citizenship control', 'state agricultural development policy', etc.). Moreover, Ben-Gurion deleted such references in published protocols:

Ben-Gurion ... preached behind the closed doors of the Zionist Congress in 1937 the virtues of transferring Palestine's Arabs ... but in the printed text of his speech solemnly expatiates on creating 'one law for the foreigner and the citizen in a just regime based on brotherly love and true equality ... that will be a shining example for the world in treating minorities'.

(see Morris 1995)

Shabtai Teveth, Ben-Gurion's biographer, acknowledges the disjuncture between Ben-Gurion's public protestations and his private aspirations:

A careful comparison of Ben-Gurion's public and private positions leads inexorably to the conclusion that this twenty-year denial of the conflict was a calculated tactic, born of pragmatism rather than profundity of conviction. The idea that Jews and Arabs could reconcile their differences ... was a delaying tactic. Once the Yishuv had gained strength, Ben-Gurion abandoned it. This belief in a compromise solution ... was also a tactic, designed to win continued British support for Zionism.

(Teveth 1985: 198–99)

The debates of the Jewish Agency Executive meeting of June 1938, then, marked the culmination of discussions which had been underway in Zionist circles for a number of years, and, as we have seen, were consistent with a core requirement of population transfer for the establishment of a Jewish state in an area with Arab inhabitants. There was a clear consensus on the moral acceptability of population transfer. The need to rid the land of Arabs was an integral part of the programme of the Jewish National Fund from its inception, despite its contrary claims (see Lehn 1988: 55–57). Furthermore, according to the testimony of Moshe Menuhin, the future Zionist leaders, schooled in the Herzlia Gymnasia in Palestine, had it drummed into their young hearts that 'the fatherland must become ours, *"goyim rein"* (clear of Gentiles–Arabs)' (Menuhin 1969: 52).

However, the Woodhead Commission reported in October 1938 that the partition plan of the Peel Commission was unworkable, mainly because of the large numbers of Arabs within the area assigned to a Jewish state. It concluded that the prospects of voluntary Arab transfer, if they existed at all, were extremely slight. The White Paper of 1939, prohibiting the transfer of Arab land to the Yishuv in most of Palestine, and restricting Jewish immigration to 15,000 per year, marked the British abandonment of the Peel plan. Its advocacy of a unitary Palestinian state after ten years severely diluted Britain's earlier support for a Jewish state. In a climate in which public discussion of transfer enterprises would be counter-productive, and in which Britain was reneging on its support of Zionism, the Yishuv began to seek out an alternative sponsor for their project, and turned their attention to the USA. Despite the onset of the First World War, population transfer and statehood remained at the core of Zionist aspirations.

Ben-Gurion wrote a memorandum to the Zionist Actions Committee meeting of 17 December 1938, urging that the Zionist delegation to the Arab–Palestinian–Zionist conference on Palestine (the St James Conference of February–March 1939) should be united under a single programme: the Arabs had already been given more than enough in Iraq, Syria and Saudi Arabia, and that Iraq should be paid Palestinian £10 million to settle 100,000 Palestinian Arab families there.

On 17 October 1939, Weizmann assured Clement Attlee, the leader of Britain's Labour Party, that Palestinian Arabs would experience dislocation, like millions of others in the wake of the Second World War, and that he intended discussing with President Roosevelt a plan for a Jewish state with boundaries wider than those in the Peel proposal. The Palestinian Arabs would be evacuated to make way for 3–4 million Jewish immigrants. In May 1941, he told a conference of American Jewish delegates of the Zionist search for large tracts of land in Transjordan and Iraq for the transferred Palestinian Arabs, carefully laying the responsibility of carrying out the transfer on the British. In his 'Lines for Zionist Policy' of 15 October 1941, he acknowledged that a general evacuation of Palestinian Arabs would be impossible without brutal compulsion, and looked to the War as providing a context in which it would be viewed as the most secure means to solve the dangerous problem of minorities. He repeated that it would be politically and tactically imprudent for the Zionists to advocate and campaign publicly for the transfer. In a departure from the privacy with which transfer plans were discussed, Weizmann in an article, 'Palestine's Role in the Solution of the Jewish Problem', in the American quarterly, *Foreign Affairs* 20 (1942): 337–38, called on the Western powers to support the creation of a Jewish 'commonwealth' in Palestine, and to pressure the Arabs to accept a population transfer. Moreover, Roosevelt's personal envoy, General Patrick Hurley was assured during his visit to Palestine in 1943, that the Yishuv leadership was determined to establish a Jewish state in the whole of Palestine and Transjordan, and was intent on forcing the eventual transfer of the Arab population to Iraq. Nevertheless, the Zionist leadership was reluctant to raise the transfer plans in public (see Masalha 1992: 128–30).

While the Zionist leadership realised that transfer would have to await the end of the Second World War, Yosef Weitz's unedited, as distinct from his sanitised, edited diary reflects the thinking during the War years.[5]

---

5   The unedited diary, which Weitz began in 1932 and continued until his death in 1970, is in the Central Zionist Archives in Jerusalem, and is the source of the quotations and references which I have extracted from Masalha 1992: 130–41. Weitz edited five volumes which were published in 1965: *Yomani Veigrotai Lebanim* (My Diary and Letters to the Children) (Tel Aviv: Massada). For a discussion of disjunctures between the original handwritten diary and the sanitised version of it that was published see Morris 1995.

The entry for 20 December 1940 indicates his overall assessment of the situation:

> Amongst ourselves it must be clear that there is no room for both peoples in this country ... After the Arabs are transferred, the country will be wide open for us; with the Arabs staying the country will remain narrow and restricted. When the war is over, and the English have emerged victorious ... our people should bring their petitions and claims before them; ... the only solution is the Land of Israel, or at least the Western Land of Israel, without Arabs. There is no room for compromise on this point. ... The only way is to transfer the Arabs from here to neighbouring countries, all of them, except perhaps Bethlehem, Nazareth, and Old Jerusalem. Not a single village or a single tribe must be left. And the transfer must be done through their absorption in Iraq and Syria and even in Transjordan. ... Only then will the country be able to absorb millions of Jews and a solution will be found to the Jewish question. There is no other solution.
>
> (Weitz, in Masalha 1992: 131–32)

Weitz's work for the JNF, involving frequent visits up and down Palestine, convinced him more and more that the complete transfer of the Arab population was the only solution (see his entries for 18 and 20 March, 4 May, 26 June and 17 July 1941) – the purchase of land would never achieve the necessary result.[6] Because the Arabs were too many and too rooted in the country, the only way was to cut and eradicate them from the roots, and replace them with Jewish redeemers planted on the land (26 June 1941). If the Arabs could be removed to northern Syria and Iraq, and the frontiers of the Jewish state were to stretch north to the Litani River, and to the east to include the Golan Heights Palestine would not be small at all. From then on, all Yishuv activities should be directed towards working out a secret plan based on the removal of the Arabs, a plan which the Yishuv should inculcate into American political circles, and he added, 'We will not live here with the Arabs' (22 June 1941).

The Second Population Transfer Committee

On 10 July 1941, Weitz proposed to Shertok and Kaplan that the Jewish Agency should appoint a three to five member committee to investigate

---

6   Indeed as late as 1937, despite its relentless efforts, the JNF, which owned more than one half of the land of the Yishuv, had managed to purchase only 3.5 per cent of Palestine.

ways of implementing the evacuation of the Palestinian Arabs to Syria, Iraq and Transjordan. They agreed, and Weitz proposed himself, Zalman Lifschitz and Yosef Nahmani for membership of the second Transfer Committee. Berl Katznelson approved of Weitz's plans (28 August), and confided that he had been of like mind for years that transfer was the only solution, and would be possible at the end of the war. Katznelson, the ideologist and 'conscience' of Jewish nationalist socialism, was a firm advocate of transfer right up to his death in 1944. Both Katznelson and Ben-Gurion saw transfer as the continuation of a natural process that had begun when Zionist settlers displaced Arab farmers (see Masalha 1992: 136).

In August 1941 Weitz was given the go-ahead to survey 'very cautiously' al-Jazirah in north-eastern Syria, a region which featured in earlier transfer proposals, with a view to establishing it as a destination for the Palestinian Arabs. After visiting the region Weitz concluded that Syrian and Iraqi Jazirah could absorb up to two million Palestinian Arabs (18 September 1941). He recommended to Kaplan (4 October) that he report on his visit to a meeting with Shertok, Katznelson, Bernard Joseph and others, to decide general lines of action. Kaplan suggested that Joseph prepare material for implementation in the post-war period. Joseph set off on a secret mission to Syria later in October, and by 25 November, Kaplan, Weitz, Joseph and others were discussing further the Syrian and Transjordan options for the transfer.

Meetings continued throughout 1942. On 31 May, Weitz discussed the plan of transfer with Avraham Granovsky, the new chairman of the JNF. Granovsky informed Weitz that a committee of himself, Kaplan, Shertok and Joseph had been set up to work out a plan for transfer activities, but warned that such planning should be carried out very cautiously. Weitz agreed to prepare an outline of the investigation work for population transfer (7 September 1941), and on the following day informed Kaplan of the need to formulate a detailed plan to evacuate the Hula region of its Arab inhabitants at the end of the war. Weitz's activities in preparing the ground for transfer were fundamental during the war. Of course, he was not alone, other proposals being made with varying success: e.g. Edward A. Norman, H. St John Philby, and Eliahu Ben-Horin (see Masalha 1992: 141–55, 155–57, 161–65).

All the while, the Irgun and *Lohamei Herut Yisrael* (Fighters for the Freedom of Israel, LEHI, called the 'Stern Gang', after its founder, Avraham Stern, which broke from the Irgun in 1940) – disciples of Jabotinsky – advocated transfer. Stern promoted the transfer of not only Palestinians, but of Lebanese, Transjordanians and Syrians who lived in what would become the land of Israel. He made contact with fascist Italy in the hope that if Mussolini conquered the Middle East he would allow a Jewish state in Palestine. When Mussolini's troops were defeated in North Africa, Stern tried to make contact with Hitler to ensure the same end after Germany had defeated Britain (Gilbert 1998: 111). In its memorandum to the United

Nations Special Commission on Palestine in 1947, and in its political programme of July–August 1948 in preparation for the first Knesset elections, LEHI called for the compulsory evacuation of the entire Arab population of Palestine, preferably to Iraq, and proposed a population exchange between Palestinian Arabs and Jews from Arab countries as the best solution to the relations between the two peoples (Masalha 1992: 30).

The position taken by the British Labour Party Conference in December 1944 pleased the Zionists to the point of embarrassment. The resolution to 'Let the Arabs be encouraged to move out, as the Jews move in', and the commitment to 're-examine the possibility of extending the present Palestinian boundaries, by agreement with Egypt, Syria or Transjordan' (Annual General Conference Report, p. 9, in Mayhew 1975: 34, in Adams and Mayhew 1975) was drafted by Hugh Dalton, who had once called for the establishment of a Jewish state on both sides of the Jordan and in Sinai.[7] An earlier draft (November 1943) had its wording changed in consultation with Weizmann, and the revised draft was discussed by the Jewish Agency Executive (7 May 1944), and was received by Ben-Gurion with great satisfaction, although he was uneasy at its wording, fearing that the public might balk at the link between Arab transfer and Jewish immigration. Although the Labour Conference passed the resolution, it did not become part of the party's platform when it came to power in 1945. Although not as significant as those emanating from Ben-Gurion, Weizmann, Shertok, Kaplan, Golda Meir and Weitz, the transfer proposals of individual Jews, and the intentions of the British Labour Party helped to create a climate which made the expulsion of 1948 less unpalatable.

The myth of 'no expulsions'

The disjuncture between what actually happened to the indigenous Arab population of Palestine in 1947–49 and the official Israeli version is striking. The Israeli government pamphlet on the refugee question, first published in 1953, proclaimed that the Palestinian Arabs were induced or incited to leave temporarily by express instructions broadcast by the president of the Arab Higher Executive (the Mufti, Haj Amin Husseini) and surrounding Arab states, to afford the Arab forces the opportunity to defeat the Zionist invaders without Palestinian losses. The charge is a component of the standard Israeli myth of origins, notwithstanding the absence of corroborating evidence, and the presence of abundant proof to expose it as false.

7   In recognition of his work in support of Zionism, and in particular for that done in drafting the Labour Party Convention resolution in 1944, the State of Israel honoured Dalton in 1950 by giving his name to a newly established moshav on the site of an evacuated Arab village in eastern upper Galilee.

Even the report of the intelligence branch of the Israel Defence Force ('Emigration of the Arabs of Palestine in the Period 1.12.1947–1.6.1948') ascribes the flight of 72 per cent of the Palestinian refugees (some 391,000 people during that critical period) to Israeli military force. It stresses that the exodus was *contrary* to the desires of the Arab Higher Committee and the neighbouring Arab states. In fact, Arab broadcasts encouraged the population to stay put, to the extent of issuing threats to stave off the exodus (see Hitchens 1988: 75). The myth is still repeated, despite the fact that already in 1961 Erskine Childers revealed that as a guest of the Israeli Foreign Office in 1958 he requested to see the primary evidence for the charge that the Palestinians had been urged to flee by the Arab leadership. Despite claims of 'a mountain of evidence' and a 'wealth of evidence', no evidence, though promised, was produced then, or since (London's *Spectator* 12 May 1961).

The evidence customarily offered is a recourse of desperation. The allegation of an 'announcement made over the air' by the Arab Higher Committee to account for the flight of Arabs in the Deir Yassin 'incident' appears to have emanated from a Cyprus-based correspondent, who depended on an uncorroborated Israeli source. The second plank, the contention that the Greek-Catholic Archbishop of Galilee had urged his flock to leave has been denied categorically by the Archbishop himself. In an effort to clear up the matter, Childers examined both the BBC records which had monitored all Middle East broadcasts throughout 1948, and a corroborating American monitoring unit, and found that,

> There was not a single order, or appeal, or suggestion about evacuation from Palestine from any Arab radio station, inside or outside Palestine, in 1948. There is repeated monitored record of Arab appeals, even flat orders, to the civilians of Palestine *to stay put*.
>
> (in Hitchens 1988: 77)

Moreover, there is abundant evidence for systematic 'horror recordings' and a 'psychological blitz' on the part of the Yishuv to clear the area of Arabs (see Childers 1987: 183–202).

Yitzhak Rabin, who presided over some of the most ruthless expulsions of the 1948 war, sought to perpetuate the myth that the expulsion of the Palestinians was brought about by the Mufti's alleged call to the Arabs to leave (N. Finkelstein 1995: 195 note 55). On 12 July 1948, after the slaughter of more than 250 Arabs in Lydda – they were caught in cross-fire according to Gilbert (1998: 218) – Head of Operations Rabin ordered: 'The inhabitants of Lydda must be expelled quickly without attention to age. . . . Yiftah (Brigade HQ) must determine the method'. A participant in the 'death march' from Lydda recalls, 'I cannot forget three horror-filled days in July of 1948. The pain sears my memory, and I cannot rid myself of it no matter how hard I try' (Rantisi 1990: 23). Although a similar order was issued for the expulsion of the inhabitants of neighbouring Ramle Israeli historians during the 1950s, 1960s and 1970s insisted that the inhabitants had violated the terms of surrender, and 'were happy at the possibility given them of evacuating' (Morris 1990a: 2–3). Rabin's admission that what happened in Lydda and Ramle had been 'expulsions' was excised from his text by Israeli government censors, but to his embarrassment the *New York Times* later published the offending passage (23 October 1979 – see Kidron 1988: 90–94).

Anita Shapira justifies the 'population transfer', to which she devotes less than two pages, in terms of the 'positive experience' between Turkey and Greece, etc. (1992: 285–86). Even Benny Morris confesses that, if pressed to evaluate morally the Yishuv's policies and behaviour in 1948, he would be loath to condemn, and opines that 'any sane, pragmatic leader' would have done the same (Morris 1990b: 20–21). However, a 'sane, pragmatic leader' is not necessarily a moral one (N. Finkelstein 1995: 187 note 8).

Israel's real, but publicly undeclared intentions are confirmed by its ongoing insistence up to the present day on not allowing the Palestinians to return: 'Israelis like to argue whether the Arabs escaped voluntarily or were expelled by us. As if this made any difference. We could always have let them return after the war' ('The 1948 Refugees are the Original Sin of Israeli Society', *Ha'aretz* 5 December 1993). Whether they left 'under orders, or pressure' or not, justice and international law demand that their right to return on the cessation of hostilities be honoured.

That Ben-Gurion's ultimate intention was to evacuate as many Arabs as possible from the Jewish state can be deduced from the range of methods he employed: an economic war aimed at destroying Arab transport, commerce and the supply of foods and raw materials to the urban population; psychological warfare, ranging from 'friendly warnings' to intimidation and exploitation of panic caused by underground terrorism; and the destruction of whole villages and the eviction of their inhabitants by the army (Flapan 1987: 92). Israeli attempts to expel more and more Arabs between 1949–96, especially in the wake of the 1967 War, are discussed in Masalha 1997. After the 1967 War, IDF troops routinely shot men, women and children trying to slip back home (see McDowall 1989: 302 note 109).

The myth of 'self-defence'

In typical fashion, Shapira argues that the Zionist movement never intended to resort to force, but was only driven to it by an accumulation of circumstances. In making no ethical distinction between the Zionist aim to transform Palestine into a Jewish state, and the indigenous Palestinians' determination to resist it (Shapira 1992: 107–25) she reduces the conflict to a clash of rights, more or less equal – a perspective which dilutes somewhat the assumption that the Zionist claim is stronger, if not absolute. 'Self-defence' can be applied only in an Orwellian sense to the conquest of

1947–49, the aggression against Egypt in 1956, the invasion of Lebanon in 1977 and 1982, and the frequent bombardments of Lebanon since. The applicability to even the 1967 War is dubious. Three pretexts are offered for its initiation of the war: Syrian bombardments of northern Israel and its support of Syrian-based terrorism, Egyptian concentration of troops in Sinai, and the Egyptian blockade of the Straits of Tiran. It is helpful to examine the validity of these claims.

There were two sources for the hostilities on the Syrian-Israeli border, one the result of Israeli incursions into the demilitarised zones separating the two nations, and the other of Syrian-based Palestinian guerrilla activities. Motivated by greed for good agricultural land Israel had consistently encroached on the zones, evicted the Arab villagers and demolished their houses, and refused to conform to the UN Security Council's call to allow the villagers to return. Syria's shelling from the Golan Heights to deter Israeli encroachments was regularly countered by punishing retaliatory strikes, in violation of the armistice agreements. In the period between 1949 and 1967 no Security Council resolution condemned Syria, while four condemned Israel's aggression. UN observers in the field, and UN votes confirm that the principal responsibility for hostilities along the Syrian-Israeli border lay with Israel.

While the Syrian-based Palestinian guerrilla incursions, legitimate or otherwise, clearly aggravated the situation, they cannot be considered to have posed a threat to Israel's existence. Had the combination of Syrian bombardments and Palestinian guerrilla incursions posed such a threat Israel would scarcely have delayed some days before opening up the northern front during the June War, and to have done so only on the initiative of Moshe Dayan after Syrian planes had attacked Israel (Dayan 1977: 357). UN Secretary General U Thant informed the UN Security Council on 19 May that Israel was increasing tensions in Syria and other Arab capitals with its bellicose statements and threats of military action.

Against the background of Israel's threat to the Syrian regime, and its earlier incursion into the West Bank town of Samu (13 November 1966) – methodically destroying 125 homes, a clinic, a school and killing eighteen people, including fifteen Jordanian soldiers – and taunts from both Syria and Jordan to act in conformity with Egypt's military pact with Syria, Egyptian President Nasser moved Egyptian troops into Sinai. Although his original intention was to require a redeployment of UN forces, rather than a total withdrawal, Nasser was left with an 'all-out or none-out' ultimatum from U. Thant. Accordingly, on 17 May, Nasser ordered the UN Emergency Force out of Sinai. Israel refused U Thant's request that the UN force be repositioned on the Israeli side of the border – the original General Assembly resolution of February 1957 mandated that the force be placed on both sides of the armistice line. Israel also rejected a late May proposal to reactivate the UN force on both sides of the Egyptian-Israeli border. Both U Thant and Odd Bull, the Chief of Staff of UN forces in the Middle East considered later that the war would have been averted had Israel agreed to the Secretary General's request (N. Finkelstein 1995: 128).

Egypt's decision on 22 May to close the Straits of Tiran to Israeli shipping is the third pretext for Israel's attack on Egypt, and, in the Israeli version of events, constituted the first act of war. Nasser's blockade was not tantamount to armed attack, and therefore, according to international law, did not warrant Israeli hostilities against Egypt. The Israeli Cabinet resisted the temptation to initiate its pre-emptive strike against Egypt as early as 25, 26 and 28 May in order to retain as much international political support as possible, recalling how Israel's attack against Egypt in 1956 had left it so isolated. Israel was aware of the Egyptian Vice President's preparedness to go to Washington on Wednesday 7 June to engage in talks that might have resolved the issue without recourse to war.[8]

It is widely conceded that Nasser's actions were merely face-saving, having failed to act after Israeli raids against Syria, and that, despite Nasser's belligerent rhetoric, Israel was under no significant threat, let alone in mortal danger. Israeli Foreign Minister Abba Eban, Chief of Staff Rabin, Cabinet Minister Menachem Begin, and others conceded later that Egypt did not intend to launch an attack against Israel, and that if it did, it would have been rebuffed easily. The CIA and British intelligence estimated in late May that Israel would win a war against all the Arab states in between a week and ten days, and a speedy Israeli victory was assumed by a host of military and political experts, including USA President Johnson and Defence Secretary Robert McNamara (see N. Finkelstein 1995: 134–35), as well as by Israel's Minister of Defence, Moshe Dayan, who predicted that the Sinai campaign would last from three to five days (1977: 339). And as it turned out, the war was virtually won on the first day, during which Israel destroyed more than 400 Egyptian, Syrian and Jordanian aircraft, many while still on the ground, giving it mastery of the air from Sinai to the Golan Heights. In all, Israel's self-presentation as employing purely defensive measures is merely a public relations device, which has no substantial evidence to support it.

The myth of 'purity of arms'

The myth of Israel's self-perception as morally superior in its 'purity of arms' – the slogan of the Haganah in early 1948 – also has had to be abandoned in

---

8 The Israeli claim that its access to the Port of Eilat in the Gulf of Aqaba was vital for its survival is not borne out by the facts. A mere 5 per cent of Israel's trade passed through that port, and in the previous two and a half years not a single Israeli-flagged ship had used the port (see N. Finkelstein 1995: 132–40 for details). In Moshe Dayan's view, the importance of reopening the Straits to Israeli shipping lay in disproving Nasser's thesis that Israel could not stand up to the Arabs, which, were it the case, would lead to a steady deterioration of Israel's position (1977: 322).

the face of the evidence. That Jews, too, were capable of committing atrocities has been comprehensively unmasked. The 'socialism' embraced by the Yishuv Labour leadership, being that of Stalinist Russia, legitimated the use of terror, the killing of the aged, women and children, the execution of suspected Jewish collaborators, the extortion of funds and acts of robbery, etc., during the Arab Revolt of 1936–39 (Shapira 1992: 247–49, 350) – the socialist end justified the means. Moreover, Israeli sources confirm that in almost every Arab village occupied by Jews during the War of Independence war crimes, such as murders, massacres and rapes were committed (see N. Finkelstein 1995: 110–12).

Israeli war crimes did not end with the war of 1948–49. Rokach's *Israel's Sacred Terrorism* records the state terrorism against its neighbours, including civilian targets, during the 1950s. On the night of 28–29 August 1953 an attack was launched on a house in the Bureij refugee camp in Gaza, in the course of which twenty Palestinian refugees, including seven women and five children were killed. In a further act of reprisal, sixty-six civilian men, women and children were deliberately killed by Israeli troops in the West Bank village of Qibua on 14 October 1953, when their homes were demolished over their heads. While both attacks against innocent civilians were officially denied by the Israeli Government at the time, they were the work of Unit 101, a special forces battalion of the regular IDF, under the command of Ariel Sharon, subsequently Israel's Defence Minister, and, in the Likud-led government of 1996, Minister of Infrastructure, and currently Foreign Minister. Moreover, between 1949 and 1956 some 3,000 to 5,000 unarmed civilians were killed by the IDF without compunction (McDowall 1994: 35).

Benny Morris suggested that the IDF's behaviour at least down to 1953 reflected a pervasive attitude that Arab life was cheap and that only Jewish life was sacred. Killing, torturing, beating and raping Arab infiltrators was not particularly reprehensible and might well go unpunished (Morris 1993: 166). McDowall notes that, while sadistic racism exists in all armies, the real issue is how vigorously senior commanders enforce discipline and punish offenders (McDowell 1994: 36). The IDF committed several atrocities, which were covered up and denied: forty-nine civilians in Kafr Qasim (October 1956); over 500 men in Khan Yunis and Rafah some days later; eighteen in Samu (West Bank) in 1966; air attacks on Irbid (Jordan, 1968), killing thirty civilians, on the Abu Za'abel factory (Egypt, 1970) killing seventy civilians, Bahr al Baqr (Egypt) killing forty-six civilians, and Beirut (1981) killing over 200 civilians (McDowall 1989: 204, 302 note 106 – see further Rokach 1980).

The Israeli daily *Ma'ariv* (2 August 1995) exposed the killing of some 140 Egyptian prisoners of war, including forty-nine Egyptian workers in 1956 by the élite paratroop unit 890, on the orders of Rafael Eitan, who later became the IDF Chief-of-Staff, subsequently founded the Tzomet party and now serves as Minister of Agriculture and Environment Quality in the

Netanyahu government. Israel's 'purity of arms' culture was further rocked by the revelation of former Labour MK, Michael Ben-Zohar, that he had witnessed the fatal stabbing of three Egyptian PoWs by two Israeli chefs during the 1967 June War. Military historian and also former MK, Meir Pa'il knew of many instances in which soldiers had killed PoWs or Arab civilians. In response to these revelations Prime Minister Rabin regretted that 'things have been said so far. I won't add anything to this' (*Jewish Chronicle*, 18 August 1995, p. 1).

More recently, the racism inherent in Zionism reached unacceptable levels in the slogan, 'Death to the Arabs' which appeared on Hebrew graffiti, e.g. on the wall of the Fifth Station on the *Via Dolorosa* for a number of years. Moreover, soldiers exposed to the history of the *Shoah* were planning ways to exterminate Arabs: 'Too many soldiers were deducing that the Holocaust justifies every kind of disgraceful action' (IDF education-corps officer, Col. Ehud Praver, in Segev 1993: 407). Both within Israel and outside comparisons were made between the Israeli army and the Nazis. Yeshayahu Leibowitz introduced the term *Judeo-Nazis* in protest against the Israeli attack on Lebanon, and in some circles the term *Asken-Nazis* was being hurled as a sign of ethnic tension. Moledet, the Israeli party publicly espousing Arab 'transfer', was described as *neo-Nazi*. After a Tel Aviv judge sentenced a Jewish citizen to six months of public service for killing an Arab boy, Professor Zeev Sternhell, a Hebrew University expert on the history of fascism stated, 'The end came to German democracy not on the day the Nazi militias killed their first leftist demonstrator but when a Nazi was sentenced to three months in prison for the same offence for which a Communist was sentenced to three years' ('Banai, Struzman, Farago,' *Hadashot*, 2 June 1986, quoted in Segev 1993: 410).

Avraham Shapira's *The Seventh Day* (1970), an oral history of the 1967 June War based on interviews, highlights the attitudes of the soldiers. The moral problematic was what the war did to the Israeli soldiers, rather than to the victims. The Israeli soldier, then, was the war's salient victim, and the one deserving of pity. Such exercises in self-extenuation and self-exculpation prevent the perpetrators from recognising themselves as murderers, and settle for presenting themselves as tragic figures and objects of pity. Such self-righteous and sanctimonious piety substitutes sentimental self-pity for genuine moral concern for the suffering which the self has inflicted on the other, all in the name of public duty (see N. Finkelstein 1995: 114–20). Invariably, when I question an Israeli soldier about his behaviour, and ask whether he experiences any moral perturbation about his activities, I get the answer, 'I am only doing my duty.'

Adjudicating between conflicting rights

From the beginning of the modern Jewish settlement in Palestine, Jews had to confront the reality that their Zionist zeal immediately precipitated conflict with the indigenous population. If convinced of their own claims to be there Jews had to contend with the Palestinian counterclaim. In theory, Jews could treat the Arab community either as relatives, or natives, Gentiles, Canaanites, an oppressed class, or, as engaged like themselves in a distinctive national movement (see Kimmerling 1983: 184–89). In the view of some early settlers, the Arabs as 'fellow semites' were worthy of respect. In practice, viewing them as 'natives' confirmed the Zionist tenet that a Jewish state could be achieved only by force.

Kimmerling's suggestion that many of the early Zionist settlers considered the Palestinian Arabs to be an oppressed class in the shackles of feudal, exploitative pre-capitalistic regimes does not square with the exclusivist policies of the JNF. Moreover, those who saw the growth of an Arab national movement as a challenge to the Jewish one determined to abort it as soon as possible. On the other hand, those who saw it as inevitable proposed various patterns of territorial division, and division of political authority (see Kimmerling 1983: 184–89). However, in the wake of the 1967 War and the rise of Gush Emunim, the (sole) 'descendants of the biblical children of Israel' portrayed the natives as 'Canaanites', thus bringing into the discourse the biblical paradigm justifying conquest of the land and the maltreatment of its population. Weighed against the divine right of the colonisers, the human rights of the local population carried no conviction.

The 'historical right' of Jews to *Eretz Yisrael* is considered to be so obvious as to require no demonstration. Today's Jews are presumed to be the descendants of the ancient people of Israel, while the Palestinian Arabs are interlopers. Historically, however, the Palestinian Arabs are likely to have been descendants of the inhabitants of the region from the earliest times. While it is well known that European historiography regarded the post-apostolic Christian and Islamic communities in Palestine as outsiders to its self-definition, more recently it is becoming obvious that it excludes also many of the peoples who inhabited the region from the Early Bronze Age to the end of the second century BC. The biblical narrative's 'ethnic markers' of the diverse inhabitants of Bronze or Iron Age Palestine ('Canaanite' during the Bronze Age, as contrasting with 'Israelite' and 'Philistine' of the Iron Age period) do not correspond to the social realities of those periods. Moreover, the concept of 'children of Israel' as a self-identifying metaphor of early Judaism was a concept that was created in the process of the Bible's formation. While population transfers were effected in the Assyrian, Babylonian and Persian periods, most of the indigenous population remained in place. Moreover, after Jerusalem was destroyed in AD 70 the population by and large remained *in situ*, and did so again after Bar Kochba's revolt in AD 135. When the vast majority of the population became Christian during the Byzantine period, no vast numbers were driven out, and similarly, in the seventh century, when the vast majority became Muslim, few were driven from the land. Palestine has been multi-cultural and multiethnic from the beginning, as one can read between the lines even in the biblical narrative (see Thompson 1998). Many Palestinian Jews became Christians, and in turn Muslims. Ironically, many of the forebears of Palestinian Arab refugees may well have been Jewish.

The Zionist appeal to Jewish forebears who were buried in *Eretz Yisrael*, and Jewish blood which had fertilised the land, etc., are of the order of the Nazi justification of their conquest of the East on the basis of it having been inhabited by Germans in primaeval times, and that it had been fertilised by the most noble ancient German blood. Finkelstein argues that Zionism's 'historical right' was neither historical nor a right: not historical because it denied 2,000 years of non-Jewish habitation of Palestine, and 2,000 years of Jewish habitation elsewhere, and not a right, except in terms of the Romantic mysticism of blood and soil (1995: 101).

The typical disjuncture we have noted between the public ideology of Zionism and its practice makes it more authentic to judge its attitudes by its practice than it rhetoric. If Ben-Gurion's ethical claim in 1928 that, in pursuit of the Zionist goal, Jews do not have the right to deprive even a single Arab child reflected his real views, his actions later witness to an accelerated moral collapse. It is more likely that they were only the public part of the double discourse of Zionism, which hid the sordid elements of its programme from public discussion. For his part, Jabotinsky attributed moral sensibilities to 'only those with crippled spirits, with a diaspora psychosis' (in Kimmerling 1983: 189).

The myth of ubiquitous and perennial diaspora longing

The status of the land of Israel in religious Jewish thought is integrally linked with the biblical narrative of the covenant between God and his people. However, the assumption that the diaspora condition of Jews resulted from expulsion, and that diaspora attachment to the land found its appropriate expression in political Zionism should not pass unchallenged.

Certainly there were forced expulsions and deportations, whether by the Assyrians (721 BC), the Babylonians (586 BC), Artaxerxes Ochus (345–343 BC?), or Tigranes (83–69 BC). The Romans carried off hundreds of prisoners of war to Rome after Pompey's conquest of Jerusalem 63 BC. Some deportation of Jews followed the defeat of the Jewish Rebellion of AD 70, but there was no mass exodus, and the community reorganised itself, under the leadership of the body of rabbis operating out of Yavneh (Gafni 1984: 28). Moreover, after the defeat of Bar Kochba's revolt (AD 135), Hadrian expelled Jews from the territory of Jerusalem only (Eusebius *His. Eccles.* 4: 6.3).

The general use of the term 'diaspora' establishes an artificial dichotomy between 'the land of Israel' and everywhere else. The polarity also suggests that conditions in the widespread 'diaspora' were consistent and uniform, and, invariably, altogether disadvantageous to Jews. In reality, in antiquity as today, not every Jew in 'the diaspora' experienced alienation. In the modern period, the Balfour Declaration was careful to insist that the drive to establish a Jewish homeland would not prejudice 'the rights and political status enjoyed by Jews in any other country'. In Britain itself at that time the leadership of the Jewish community, being in no mood to throw away its gains from assimilation into English culture for which it had been duly honoured by the establishment, had little time for Herzl's insistence that Jews could live authentically only in their own state (see Finklestone 1997: xvi–xvii).

The notion of Israel as separate has a long, but by no means uniform history. The famous prediction in Balaam's oracle, that Israel would not be reckoned among the nations (Num 23.9), was assessed variously by divers Jewish communities in the different areas of the widespread diaspora in the Hellenistic period alone. Philo, living contentedly in Alexandria in the first half of the first century AD, interpreted the oracle as indicative of demarcation on the basis of the exceptional ancestral customs of Jews, and 'not because their dwelling-place is set apart and their land severed from others' (*Mos.* I.278). The Jewish community had lived in Alexandria alongside Greeks and Egyptians for centuries, and he had no reason to doubt that it would continue to do so for centuries to come. For his part, Josephus, in commenting on Balaam's oracle, stressed not merely the social distinctiveness of Jewish customs but the ethical superiority of their virtue and their customs (*Antiquities* 4.114). The perspectives reflected in these two first-century Jews, one in Alexandria and the other in Rome, invites enquiry into the social and cultural strategies of Jews in the Mediterranean diaspora – not in an undifferentiated 'diaspora', but in the quite diverse geographical locations, and changing political fortunes that marked the conditions of Jewish communities scattered throughout the Mediterranean world.

Scholarship over the last hundred years has consistently undermined the earlier distorted portrayal of the real conditions of Jews in the diaspora by over-arching generalisations and extrapolations (see Barclay 1996: 1–9), heavily influenced by biblical texts, and the predominantly negative attitude of the (Palestinian) rabbis to the diaspora. While those with shallow roots in their environment bemoaned the conditions of their 'sojourn' away from home, others considered their diaspora position a real achievement, and, in the case of Josephus, for example, viewed the whole world as their eternal home (*Antiquities* 4.115–16). Hence, while 'the holy land' retained some religious significance for diaspora Jews, their attachment to Palestine reflected their social and political conditions (see Barclay 1996: 422–43).

From the perspective of the biblical authors the period in Babylon (586–538 BC) was one of unrelieved lament for the homeland (see e.g. Psalm 147). In reality, however, the evidence for the severity of the conditions in Babylon is by no means uniform – some implying no overt oppression or loss of identity – suggesting that it was not quite the catastrophe which the biblical authors intimate. Indeed, it is not easy to reconcile the view that Babylonian exile was an enormous 'physical, social, and psychological trauma' (see Smith-Christopher 1997: 36) with the reality that many Jews remained in Babylon after the return to Zion in 538 BC. In fact, it was held in antiquity that the 'ten tribes' had never returned (e.g. Josephus *Antiquities* 11.133; 4 Ezra 13. 39–47; *mSanh* 10.3 V). Documents from the Persian period show clearly that deported Judahites remained on in Babylon (see e.g. Bickerman 1984), and the region became the home of the majority of world Jewry from the exile to the end of antiquity. But even deportations were not altogether without their advantages, as attested by several of the rabbis (see Feldman 1997: 155). The terminology, also, is deserving of attention.

While the standard word for 'exile' in Greek is *phuge* ('banishment'), the Septuagint translators use the language of emigration or colonisation (*apoikia*) for the Hebrew *golah*. Indeed, the picture one gets is that of founding a colony, after the fashion of the Athenians founding colonies. Moreover, Philo uses the language of emigration and colonisation for Jews who settled outside of Palestine. Similarly, the Babylonian exile is referred to in Matthew's gospel (1.11, 12, 17) by *metoikesia*, a word signifying a change of abode, or a migration. Furthermore, Josephus never uses *phuge* with reference to the exiles of 721 BC or 586 BC. With respect to the developments after Nebuchadnezzar's capture of Jerusalem, Josephus uses the language of migration, colony and settlement, indeed settlement in the most suitable places in Babylonia (*Contra Apion* 1.138; see Feldman 1997: 145–48).

In addition, there was a widespread Jewish diaspora in the Hellenistic period altogether unrelated to expulsion. Voluntary emigration of Jews from Palestine into the cities of the so-called civilised world was widespread, and there is evidence of Jewish communities outside of Palestine long before Alexander the Great. Alexander encouraged the foundation of new cities, and invited new settlers on whom he bestowed various privileges and even citizenship. Jews answered the call in considerable numbers, going to Syria and Egypt, and to other newly founded Hellenistic cities. The *Ioudaioi* (Judahites) in Egypt included, as well as slaves, many who served in Ptolemy's army, and other *Ioudaioi* were adventurous economic migrants attracted to Egypt and particularly to Alexandria.[9]

Jewish voluntary emigration extended to Mesopotamia, Media, Babylonia, Dura-Europos, the Arabian Peninsula, Asia Minor, the North Coast of the Black Sea, Cyrenaica, the North African provinces of Africa proconsularis, Numidia and Mauretania, Macedonia and Greece, the Greek Islands, Cyprus, Crete, Rhodes, Delos, Euboea, Cos, the Balkans, Italy, Rome, and in the Christian period also to Spain, southern Gaul and

---

9   Originally, *Ioudaioi*, a term signifying Judaeans (i.e. from *Ioudaia*), referred to the inhabitants of Jerusalem and its surroundings. Later the geographical referent yielded in significance to the 'ethnic'.

Germany. An abundance of evidence witnesses to a widespread Jewish diaspora (1 Macc 15.22–23; the *Sibylline Oracles* iii: 271; Strabo, according to Josephus' *Antiquities* 14.115; Philo *Flaccus* 46 and *Legatio ad Gaium* 281–82; Josephus *Wars* 2.398; 7.43; Acts 2.5–11; etc.). There were colonies of Jews throughout most of the inhabited world, as known by people in the West. Salo Baron estimates that Jews in the middle of the first century AD numbered more than eight million, most of them living in the diaspora (Baron 1952, Vol I: 170). However acute the theoretical question of whether religious Jews could live other than in *Eretz Yisrael*, the communities of Jews who settled throughout Europe, North Africa, and east of Palestine gave a pragmatic answer. Whatever the degree of attachment to the homeland, there is no evidence for a longing sufficiently vigorous to induce more than a handful of Jews to 'return' even when the circumstances in the diaspora were difficult.

To the contemporary studies on individual locations, John Barclay has added a comprehensive survey of Jews living in five areas bordering on the Mediterranean Sea, from 323 BC to AD 117 (1996: 10). There were no 'typical' diaspora conditions, but each one reflected particular circumstances. Jewish comportment in these diverse diasporas, likewise, exhibited a wide spectrum, from total assimilation to near total isolation, and even within the same region, Jewish reactions reflected the different social levels of individual Jews, as well as their personal preferences. No single diaspora Jew, therefore, could be regarded as typical. Despite the diversity inherent in the Jewish communities, however, there was enough similarity to bind them together as coherent and enduring entities (see Barclay 1996: 399–400). The social and religious practices of diaspora Judaism (shared ancestral traditions, the Torah, circumcision, dietary distinctiveness, Sabbath and Jewish festival observance, the Temple tax, abstention from alien cults, and table-fellowship with non-Jews, etc.) provided a powerful unifying force within the Jewish communities, emphasising their common bonds, and distinguishing them from their environment. These distinctive elements, at times, bred resentment from other ethnic groups and the majority non-Jewish community, sometimes erupting into discrimination and violence.

Betsy Halpern-Amaru has shown convincingly how later writers adapted the biblical traditions of land to their own historical contexts and contemporary interests. In each of the four examples she examines, she shows how the author reconstructed the narrative in such a way that the land no longer functioned as the key signature of covenantal history, and developed new narratives which de-emphasised the theological significance of land. In *Jubilees* and *The Testament of Moses* the rewriting is eschatological, while in *Pseudo-Philo* and Josephus' *Antiquities* it is historically oriented. In each reworking of the tradition, the concept of the covenant is reformulated so that a promise other than land assumes the pivotal position (Halpern-Amaru 1994: 116–17).

Indeed, Josephus, writing in Rome some two decades after the fall of

Jerusalem, does so from the perspective of one fully committed to the diaspora. He has none of the poetic description of the biblical narrative ('land flowing with milk and honey, [etc.]', Deut. 8.7–9), and uses the normal word for land, *ge*. Whereas the Bible has Abraham sending away his sons by Keturah to the East (Gen 25.6), Josephus says that he did so to found colonies, implying that no real distinction existed between those regions and Canaan (*Antiquities* 1.239). For Josephus the diaspora is a blessing (*Antiquities* 1.282). Indeed, he, who consistently stresses the universal role of Jews (*Antiquities* 4.15), plays down the promise of land to the Patriarchs, and predicates the diaspora as Israel's destiny ordained by God, holding out no hope of an ingathering of Jews to their 'homeland'. Although it is quite possible that his altogether positive portrayal of the diaspora may have been influenced by his precarious position of being dependent on his Roman benefactors, there is little doubt that Josephus viewed diaspora living as eminently conducive to Jewish life, and never foresees an end to it (see Feldman 1997: 171–72).

It is important to assess the links between the Jewish diaspora and Palestine. In the centuries just before and after the inauguration of the Christian Era, travel of Jews, whether soldiers, slaves, refugees or economic migrants, between Palestine and Egypt is well documented (see e.g. Barclay 1996: 19–81), and physical proximity ensured easy contact between Syrian Jews and Palestine. Apart from the religious attachment to the Temple, and pilgrimage thereto, however, there is little evidence that there was any substantial link between Jews in the diaspora and in Palestine. The Jewish Scriptures and festivals, of course, reinforced the significance of the land, and the promised return to it, and diaspora Jews write in glowing terms about the beauties of Jerusalem and its temple (e.g. Aristeas 83–120; Philo *Legatio* 157; Josephus *Wars* 5.184–247).

It is not likely that diaspora Jews who chose to live therein would be very moved by the biblical promises of ingathering. There is, indeed, abundance of evidence of Jews being firmly and contentedly rooted in communities throughout the diaspora, and, as Philo expresses it (*Flaccus* 46), taking a certain pride in the ubiquity of Jews throughout Europe and Asia, encouraging them to see their 'new locations' as their fatherland. Philo does, however – against Josephus – anticipate a return to the homeland in accordance with the Scriptures (*Praem* 162–72) in the distant future (see *Quaest Exod* 2.76). Insofar as one may be permitted to generalise, it seems reasonable to assume that those who considered their roots in the diaspora to be shallow, or who found themselves there against their wills eagerly awaited return to the 'holy land' (e.g. *Sib Or* 5.260–85). Some may even have considered themselves to be 'perishing as foreigners in a foreign land', living lives that 'have become entangled in impieties in our exile' (3 Macc 6. 3, 10).

Philo, however, was not alone in viewing Jewish 'colonising' as a political achievement. Josephus considered the whole world as the *eternal* home of Jews (*Antiquities* 4.115–16), and nowhere does he express the hope that he would return to Jerusalem, his birthplace, or its Temple where he had served as a priest (*Vita* 2). Indeed, he seems to see the future of the Jews to be in the Western diaspora. For him, then, the land was not central to the Jewish people. He, like Philo, took pride in the diffusion of Jews throughout all the habitable world (*Wars* 6.442; 7.43; *Antiquities* 14.114), and in his accounts of the threatened dispersion, he omits any reference to the promise of return, such as is found in Deut 30.3, and veers away from the biblical notion that 'exile' was a punishment for sin. Moreover, he accords relatively little space to the contribution to Jewish history of the biblical heroes of the return from Babylon, Ezra and Nehemiah (see Feldman 1997: 146–49, 158–60).

Much of the attitude towards exile is strongly influenced by the biblical narrative, read in the synagogues of the diaspora, whether in the Hebrew original or in a Greek translation (e.g. Lev 26; Deut 28; 30; 2 Kgs 23–25; and Jer 32–45), which, in its turn, provided occasion for reflection by the rabbis and found its way into the rhythm of Jewish prayer. According to the biblical narrative, living outside the land was the result of sin, which insight was advanced as a threat (e.g. Lev 26.33; Deut 28.63–64; Jer 5.19). This theme found ready support later, precisely because of the authority of the biblical record. Jewish works of the Second Temple period written in Judea insisted that the diaspora was the result of sin (e.g. Sir 48.15, as well as the Apocrypha and Pseudepigrapha, e.g. the *Testament of Levi* 10.3–4; the *Testament of Asher* 7.2–7). Just as Adam had transgressed and was cast out of the Garden, so his transgressing descendants were exiled from Jerusalem (see 2 Esd 3.24–28). However, the equiparation of diaspora living with sin was challenged by rabbis living outside the land, for some of whom dispersion was seen as part of the universal mission of Jews (see Gafni 1997: 35–40).

Isaiah Gafni argues that the destruction of the Temple in AD 70 and the Bar Kochba debacle of AD 135 induced the Palestinian rabbis to demand even greater attachment to *Eretz Yisrael*. This was due in no small measure to the challenge to their authority which the Jews across the Euphrates presented. The two, rival centres of Jewish authority had different views on who was to guide the religious life of the Jewish people. For the Palestinian Jews, life outside the land was futile, while for those in Babylonia, the benefits of 'Zion' and 'the Land' were to hand: Davidic leadership, remnants of the Temple, links with the Patriarchs, etc.: 'We have made ourselves in Babylonia the equivalent of Eretz Israel from the day Rav came to Babylonia' (*b. Git.* 6a; *b.B. Qam.* 80a, in Gafni 1997: 116).

The Jews of Talmudic Babylonia (third to fifth century AD) displayed a distinctive, militantly pro-Babylonian 'local patriotism' and a definite sense of 'homeness' and familiarity with the Persian Empire. In fact, the Babylonian Talmud projects that particular diaspora as akin to a second Jewish homeland, with roots going back to the formative years of Israelite nationhood. This attitude, in turn, evoked censure from the rabbinic establishment in *Eretz Yisrael*, for whom not only the question of the significance of the land was at stake, but also its own position as constituting the central *halakhic* authority. These Palestinian rabbis, for the first time in Jewish history, produced an ideology of disdain for Jewish life in the diaspora (e.g. '*Abod. Zar.* 4.5). Nevertheless, despite the strain, the rabbis in the two regions reached an accommodation whereby the Jews of Babylonia could remain loyal to Palestine, while modifying patterns of behaviour to enable them to continue to thrive outside it. With respect to *halakhic* authority, the Babylonian sages show a preference for the foremost scholars of their generation, while their Palestinian counterparts refer to the authoritative status of those living in *Eretz Yisrael* (Gafni 1997: 13–18).

The myth of the 'right to return'

The 'Right to Return' is among the major claims to justify the establishment of the Jewish state. The 'Law of Return', enacted by the Knesset on 5 July 1950, permits any Jew to settle in Israel. This right of settlement is inherent in every Jew, simply by virtue of being a Jew, and precedes the state of Israel (Ben-Gurion, in Gilbert 1998: 270). However, in the wider world, the right of return operates only when an appropriately defined community has been subjected to recent expulsion. Such an understanding is a *sine qua non* of orderly international behaviour. In order to establish a right to return, all the Jews of the world would have to constitute a clearly defined community, which could demonstrate its recent collective expulsion. But there never was a unified Jewish community which was exiled at one time, or over a definite period. As we have seen, in addition to those forced into exile, Jews voluntarily emigrated from Palestine.

The moral case for return is undermined by the time-span between the act of expulsion and the determination to resettle. A right to return dissolves into desuetude as the time-span between expulsion and the determination to re-settle or reclaim the homeland exceeds reasonable limits. Without such limits international order would collapse. To concede the legitimacy of a Jewish Law of Return would open the floodgates for bizarre returns to ancestral homes at the expense of people in place for thousands of years.

The establishment of a Jewish state involved more than a mere return of Jews, and required the dislocation of the indigenous population. In customary international law, no group has a right to conquer and annexe the territory of another people, and expel its population. Moreover, a people's return to the land from which it has been expelled is a two-fold right under customary international law. The body of law on nationality requires a country to allow its nationals to reside within its territory, while the 'host' country has the right to demand that an expelled person be re-admitted to his/her own country. Moreover, individual rights require that each person has the right to reside in his/her own country: 'No one shall be arbitrarily deprived of the right to enter his own country' (International Covenant on Civil and Political Rights, art. 12), and the Universal Declaration of Human

Rights states that everyone has a right 'to return to his own country' (art. 13). This right has a universally valid moral quality, and obtains for all peoples which experience expulsion. The exiled Palestinians constitute a quintessential example of a people with a right to return, since, in 1948, a clearly identified population was expelled by their Zionist conquerors, and has never renounced its rights – many still possess their title-deeds to land, and even the keys of their homes. Yet, Israel maintains that the displaced Palestine Arabs have no right of return, on the basis that they are not nationals of Israel (see Quigley 1998: 84–85). Thus, by a legal subterfuge which lacks any semblance of morality, Israel exculpates itself from the crime of displacing another people.

The *Shoah* as legitimiser of the State of Israel

The systematic attempt by the Third Reich to wipe out European Jewry resulted in the murder of at least six million Jews (Gilbert 1982: 244–45), the first appearance in history of 'biological antisemitism' (Jacobs 1993: 4). Only some 1.6 million Jews who were in Europe in September 1939 survived until May 1945, and of these some 300,0000 endured the concentration camps (Gilbert 1982: 242–43). For some, the fact of the *Shoah* is sufficient to warrant the establishment of a Jewish state, which for many Jews is 'the phoenix literally arising out of the ashes of the *Shoah*' (Jacobs 1993: 4). Moreover, in some quarters Arab opposition to the establishment of the state is considered to be continuing the Nazi genocide (e.g. Manès Sperber's *Than a Tear in the Sea*, 1967: xiii), a sentiment which Emil Fackenheim quotes, apparently with approval (1987: 400).

Apologists commonly appeal to the *Shoah* to justify the establishment of the state of Israel: (a) The *Shoah* is an unique event in history, in that what happened to the Jews never happened to anyone else;[10] (b) not only did the Gentiles not aid the Jews, but they assisted in their mass murder – hence, Jews cannot ever rely on the *goyim* for protection; (c) a Jewish nation state is the only protection against another holocaust. One of the features of the *Shoah* as an *apologia* is that no attention is paid to the cost to the Palestinians. Indeed, since all the *goyim* are potentially antisemites, and even potential murderers of Jews, it might be necessary to cleanse Palestine ethnically, and expel the enemies within the gate. While linking the establishment of the state with the *Shoah* resonates with decent people's compassion and appeases Europe's guilt, it distracts attention from a core requirement of Zionism.

10 Some scholars point to a number of factors which justify the appellation 'unique' (e.g. its biological basis and its planned total annihilation; its use of technology and its 'assembly-line' efficiency), while others acknowledge the *Shoah's* difference in magnitude but not in kind from many other cataclysms in history. Fackenheim concludes that it is *unique* as well as *unprecedented* (1987: 400).

That movement, established some fifty years before the *Shoah*, mirrored European colonialists' disregard for indigenous populations.

The 'Holocaust Theology' of Elie Wiesel, Emil Fackenheim, Irving Greenberg, *et al.*, posits the perceived needs of Jews as constituting a moral absolute, without any reference to the legitimate needs of the Palestinian people, who function only in terms of their perceived threat to the survival of the Jewish people. Its absorption in 'what is good for the Jews' precludes a critical history of Zionism or of Israeli state policy. It is naïve to portray the establishment of the State of Israel as a haven for powerless Jews, victims of Nazi barbarism, particularly in the light of the fact that the mainstream ideologues of Zionism from the beginning were determined to expel the Arab population of Palestine, and did so to most of them when the first opportunity came in 1948.

In failing to deal meaningfully with the fact that Israel's success has been brought about by the humiliation of another people, Holocaust Theology eludes the moral imperative of confronting the realities of the formation of the Jewish state and its policies since 1948. The liberation of Jews has required the permanent dispossession of another people. Israel marks the end of Jewish innocence. The plight of the Palestinian people undermines the force of Holocaust Theology, with its portrayal of an innocent, suffering people in search of security and freedom. Auschwitz becomes for Jews a place where they can hide their accountability in the present, a symbol that makes them untouchable (Ellis 1994: 9, 12, 24, 32).

Conclusion

Consistent with the practice in virtually all nations and political movements, the historiographers of Zionism and the State of Israel fabricated a history of which a key element was the myth of a perennial Jewish longing to abandon the diaspora and establish a Jews-only state in the ancestral homeland. We have seen that there is little support from antiquity that the implementation of the goals of political Zionism fulfilled the ideals of world-wide Jewry from the earliest times to today. According to this reading of events, all Jews had been 'dispersed' (with all the negative implication of 'forcibly', and invariably carrying 'ethnocentric' attitudes to other peoples and their cultures) as if at one time, and that Zionism had rescued them, and brought them home. We have seen that many of the Jews living outside *Eretz Yisrael* did so voluntarily and with a noted level of contentment and even pride. To present matters otherwise is not only to distort the truth of history, but to pervert present-day Jews' perception of themselves, their origins and their destiny.

Colonisers seldom cared much about the impact of their enterprise on the indigenous population, and not infrequently corralled the natives in zones of exclusion. Distinctively in the case of Zionist colonisation a determined effort was made to rid the terrain altogether of the native population, since their presence in any number would frustrate the grand design of establishing a Jewish state. The necessity of removing the Arabs was recognised from the beginning of the Zionist enterprise, and was meticulously planned and executed in 1948 and 1967.

In their determination to present an unblemished record of the Zionist achievement, the fabricators of propagandistic Zionist history are among the most accomplished practitioners of the strange craft of source-doctoring, rewriting not only their history, but the documents upon which such a history was based – note the disjunctures between the hand-written diaries of Yosef Weitz and the sanitised published version, and the clear evidence of extensive self-censoring in Ben-Gurion's diaries. The propagandistic intent is evident, particularly in removing references to the 'transfer' intentions of the Yishuv, and all references to massacres, rapes and expulsions (Morris 1995: 44, 56–57). The aim was to hide things said and done, and to bequeath to posterity only a sanitised version of the past.

The argument from the compelling need of Jews to settle in a Jewish state does not constitute a right to displace an indigenous population. And, whether intended from the start, or not, the moral problematic arises most acutely precisely from the fact that Zionism has wreaked havoc on the indigenous population, and not a little inconvenience on several surrounding states. Nor can the *Shoah* be appealed to credibly to justify the destruction of an innocent third party. It is a dubious moral principle to regard the barbaric treatment of Jews by the Third Reich as constituting a right to establish a Jewish state at the expense of an innocent third party. Surely the victims of Auschwitz would not have approved. As we shall see, some other Jews, also, have the gravest reservations about the Zionist enterprise and achievement.

Part V

Critique of Zionism

8 Jewish critique of Zionism

Opposition to any particular form of Zionist achievement was inevitable given the variety of its aspirations. From the beginning Zionism was not a monochromatic ideology but one which expressed itself in a variety of colours: e.g. the political Zionism of Herzl, the cultural-historical Zionism of Ahad Ha'am, the religious Zionism of the Rabbis Kook, the syndicalist Zionism of Nahman Syrkin, the Marxist Zionism of Ber Borochov, the fascist Zionism of Jabotinsky and Labour Zionism, which dominated the Yishuv and prevailed for the first thirty years of the life of the state until the advent of a Likud-led government in 1977 (see Goldberg 1996). Yonatan Ratosh noted the lack of clarity:

> Zionism is essentially an attempt to provide an undefined answer (from a 'spiritual centre' to an empire) to an undefined problem (the Jewish question, all depending on the various attitudes towards the question of what Judaism is) of an undefined human grouping (all the Jews, according to the various conceptions of 'Who is a Jew?' – or portions thereof) in an undefined territory (from Western Palestine, or a portion thereof – to the borders of Egypt and the Euphrates).
>
> (in Diamond 1986: 23).

Nevertheless, despite the contrarieties at the core of the ideology, the majority of Jews delight in its achievement, and solidly support the state. For the Chief Rabbi of Great Britain and the Commonwealth the creation of the State of Israel is

> One of our greatest collaborative achievements. Many see in it the hand of Providence and the fulfilment of half of a great biblical prophecy. . . . Each prophet from Moses to Malachi foresaw a two-fold-return: to the land, and to the faith, of Israel. That is what 'return' in the biblical sense means. From the days of the Exodus to a century ago, Jews believed that they were inseparable. Only modern Jewry has separated them. The result has been that, for almost 2,000 years, we had the faith but not the land. Today, we have the land but we are beginning to lose the faith.
>
> (*Jewish Chronicle*, 22 September 1995, p. 29)

In the same *Rosh Hashanah* issue of the *Jewish Chronicle*, and by way of comment on the Chief Rabbi's pre-New Year message (1995), the late Chaim Bermant proposed that the question Rabbi Sacks should be asking is not whether Jews should return to the faith, but to what sort of faith they should return. He added, 'If it is the faith of the rabbis who are cursing the government of Israel and are preaching sedition to the Israeli Army, then give me the faithless, the godless and the feckless every time'. He lamented that there was a virtual consensus among Orthodox rabbis world-wide against the 'peace process': 'The modern Orthodox rabbis ... have no concept of democracy, equity or justice, and have never given a thought to the rights of the Palestinians'. A couple of months before the assassination of Rabin, confessing that while not given to composing his own prayers,

> I thank God every morning for making and keeping Israel secular, for had it – heaven forbid – been a religious society, it would have been hell-bent on destruction. ... It was Godless Jews who built Israel, and it is the Godless who are keeping it sane. ... And it was the religious, both within Israel and without, who have found a new force for their hatreds ... and who are calling down anathemas upon the heads of Messrs Rabin, Peres, and the entire government of Israel, and denouncing them as murderers and traitors.
>
> (*Jewish Chronicle*, 22 September 1995, p. 31)

In addition to return to an irredentist faith, that associated with the nationalist religious wing, there is also in Israel a return to a faith that, however politely expressed, is scarcely recognisable in terms of similarity with the Hebrew prophetic tradition, or with justice and common decency. During my year in Tantur Ecumenical Institute, in occupied Jerusalem, and surrounded by ubiquitous signs of the oppression of the Palestinians (1996–97), I was treated on a number of occasions to the special pleading of silver-tongued, invariably American Jews clothing Zionism in the garment of piety. In his Tantur Public Lecture (6 March 1997), having traced the theme of covenant in the biblical narrative and, secondly, in the rabbinic tradition, Professor David Hartman described Zionism as the high point of biblical spirituality, 'restoring the legacy of biblical spirituality in the modern world'. When pressed on the moral issue of the expulsion of the indigenous Arab population he sought the conventional refuge: Zionism never intended to disturb the Arabs; what happened was only the result of war; the problem was that the Arabs had not welcomed Jews back to their homeland, etc. To clinch his argument, he reminded the audience that great developments in history sometimes require initial destruction, instancing the USA's defeat of totalitarianism around the world, although this was preceded by the displacement of the Native Americans.

Yet, despite the acceptance of Zionism even within religious Jewish circles, the tradition of dissent continues to this day.

Religious critique

Although most of the opposition to the politics of Israel's 'far right' comes from altogether secular groups some religious ones maintain a non-, or anti-Zionist perspective. From the beginning opposition to Zionism was widespread in religious circles, both Orthodox and Reform. The Orthodox saw it as a demonic force which represented a betrayal of traditional beliefs. Agudat Israel, a broadly-based movement of Orthodox rabbis and laity, was formed in Germany in 1912 to oppose Zionism. It considered it to be a pseudo-Messianic, satanic conspiracy against God whose responsibility alone it was to gather in the Jews. Moreover, the enterprise was bent on removing from Jewish communal life the religious values which had united Jews down the ages. Zionism strove to protect Jewish life, while abandoning the values which had sustained it. The abandonment of what was most characteristically Jewish in the pursuit of purely secular, nineteenth-century European notions of nationhood, was the ultimate form of assimilation.

In Palestine, the ultra-Orthodox movement joined with Agudat in its struggle against Zionism. The conflict with Zionists led to the assassination in Jerusalem in 1924 by the Haganah of Jacob Israel de Haan, a member of the executive of the Agudat, and a vociferous critic of secular Zionism. According to Joseph Sonnenfeld, the spokesman of the ultra-Orthodox, the Zionists were evil men and ruffians: hell had entered Israel with Herzl. However, some opponents tempered their criticism in the wake of the massacre of Orthodox Jews during the Arab riots of 1929.

Nevertheless, even after the rise of the Nazis, Rabbi Isaac Brueur in 1934 appealed to Jews not to leave Jewish history to the Zionists. And even after the *Shoah*, Jacob Rosenheim, the political head of Central European Orthodoxy, maintained that the Zionist programme to evacuate Europe of Jews and bring them to Palestine was misguided, since it was impossible to ascertain God's plans in advance of the arrival of the Messiah (in Cohn-Sherbok 1992: 136). Nevertheless, between the end of the Second World War and the establishment of the State of Israel, the Agudat opposition to Zionism resulted in an unlikely liaison, consummated in the understanding with the Zionists on Sabbath observance, dietary laws and regulations concerning education and marriage. Orthodox theological opposition to the emerging state survives in such groups as Neturei Karta in Jerusalem, and among the followers of rabbis from Brisk and Satmar, who maintain their opposition to the Jewish state, regarding its supporters as apostates, and judging Agudat to be leading people away from Torah Judaism.

The polarity within Israeli Judaism can be seen at its most extreme by contrasting Gush Emunim with a movement at the opposite end of the spectrum. While the anti-Zionist, ultra-Orthodox Neturei Karta

('Guardians of the City') and the ultra-right religious nationalist Gush Emunim agree on central interpretations of Jewish life – that the *galut* is a punishment and that God promised to restore his people to the land, etc. – they differ fundamentally on the significance of the state:

Neturei Karta	Gush Emunim
The establishment of the State of Israel was a demonic event,	The establishment of the State of Israel was a redemptive event,
which is the result of sin.	which is the result of providence.
It defames the sanctity of *Eretz Yisrael*	It enhances the sanctity of *Eretz Yisrael*.

Diametrically opposed to the Kookist view of the mystical union of the political and the religious, Neturei Karta consider the fusion of Jewry's sacred past with its secular present to be a heinous intermingling of the hallowed with the profane. They consider the state to be a sacrilege, and a 'sell-out' to the spirit of the Enlightenment and the dictates of assimilation. Their head, Rabbi Hirsh, insists that the State of Israel should be replaced by a Palestinian state, in which the Jewish inhabitants would be 'Palestinian Jews'. Only the Messiah can regain the biblical homeland.

The ultra-orthodox Haredim of the Jerusalem district of Mea Shearim also hold that Israel was the work of Satan, and claim that the survival of the Jewish people rests on keeping Torah, stressing that a Torah society comes before considerations of a specific territory. Their concern is to ensure the land is worth protecting, and they adopt an attitude of indifference or hostility towards the state.

The influential Satmar Hasidim of Brooklyn, New York, also are virulently anti-Zionist. They judge the State of Israel to be the work of Satan, a sacrilege, and a blasphemy. Grand Rabbi Joel Teitelbaum (d. 1979) outlined his opposition in his *Veyoel Moshe* (1960), intimating that he would rather see his movement disappear than accept a Jewish state not brought to life by the Messiah. He blamed secularist Zionism for the divine visitation of the *Shoah*. His adviser and collaborator, Rabbi Sender Deutsch (d. 1998), a survivor of the *Shoah*, published many of his transcriptions of his master's lectures and speeches through the Deutsch Publishing House, founded in 1958. In 1958 also, Deutsch launched *Der Yid*, which became the largest Orthodox Yiddish weekly in the world, with a circulation exceeding 40,000, and continued to publish the organisation's vehement opposition to the existence of the state. Rabbi Deutsch became President of the United Talmudical Academy in 1973, which with over 18,000 students was the largest Jewish educational foundation in the USA. The Satmars maintain their anti-Zionism under the current leadership of Grand Rabbi Moshe Teitelbaum.

Recently Rabbi Moshe Schonfeld accused Zionism of reducing Judaism to a godless discourse, and of seducing young Orthodox children away from their religious roots. Secular Zionism was striking at the heart of Judaism to gain control of the Jewish people, and Zionists were using any means to secure that goal, including bribery, terrorism, antisemitism, and the violations of the basic right of religious freedom. The Zionist dream of establishing the State of Israel was based on manipulation of the antisemitism of Western leaders by Herzl (Schonfeld 1980: 7–8).

For their part, Liberal Jews considered Zionism to be a misguided utopian dream, offering a false solution to the Jewish problem, for which emancipation and assimilation were the true answers. For those committed to the ideals of meta-national socialism the determination to withdraw from among the nations to establish a Jewish national state was equivalent to substituting auto-segregation and cultural self-isolation for the despised ghetto-like existence which had characterised Jewry within European society in the bad old, pre-emancipation days. In the social programme envisaged by Marx and Engels, economic and social progress would transmute separate national states into a new world internationalist order based on socialist principles. Measured against the ideology of internationalist socialism, Zionism was a reactionary aberration.

In addition to the religious groups which do not attach significance to the nation state, and some which regard it as an apostasy, the religious constituency has seen the rise of several human rights groups (Oz veShalom, Netivot Shalom, Rabbis for Human Rights, Clergy for Peace, etc.), which emphasise the supremacy of the moral values of Judaism over the territorial ones stressed by Gush Emunim. In general, however, these groups bypass the foundational injustice associated with Zionism in 1947–49. As Zionist immigrants to the land, their consciences are perturbed only by the excesses of the post-1967 occupation and its attendant abuses of human rights. Whether the fervour of their observance of the Torah has been infected more by the values of the Enlightenment than moderated by the universalist perspectives of the Hebrew prophetic tradition is a matter for speculation.

The moral critique of Ahad Ha'am

If after the First Zionist Congress Herzl could boast, 'At Basle I founded the Jewish state', the Ukrainian cultural 'lover of Zion', Asher Zvi Ginzberg (1856–1927), who wrote under the pseudonym, Ahad Ha'am, and was present as an observer, lamented, 'At Basle I sat solitary among my friends, like a mourner at a wedding feast' (Goldberg 1996: 92). The Zionist programme, led by Jews with virtually no links to their religion strove to save the Jewish body but not its soul. He refused to attend another Congress until 1911.

Already in *Emet me-Eretz Yisrael* ('The Truth from *Eretz Yisrael*') published in 1891 after a three-month stay in Palestine – he visited again in 1893, in 1899 and in 1911 – he indicated the obstacles to large-scale Jewish colonisation:

We tend to believe abroad that Palestine is now almost completely deserted, a non-cultivated wilderness, and anyone can come there and buy as much land as his heart desires. But in reality this is not the case. It is difficult to find anywhere in the country Arab land which lies fallow; the only areas which are not cultivated are sand dunes or stony mountains, which can only be planted with trees, and even this only after much labour and capital would be invested in clearance and preparation.

(in Avineri 1981: 122)

He recognised the dilemmas the existence of an Arab population would pose for a Jewish state, emphasising that it showed no inclination to leave, and protesting against the ethnocentric behaviour of the Jewish 'pioneers':

We have to treat the local population with love and respect, justly and rightly. And what do our brethren in the Land of Israel do? Exactly the opposite! Slaves they were in their country of exile, and suddenly they find themselves in a boundless and anarchic freedom, as is always the case with a slave that has become king, and they behave toward the Arabs with hostility and cruelty, infringe upon their boundaries, hit them shamefully without reason, and even brag about it.

(in Avineri 1981: 123–24)

In a series of essays, and in the Hebrew monthly *Ha-Shiloah* which he edited after it first appeared in October 1896, he argued that it was neither realistic nor honest for Zionist leaders to envisage the establishment of a Jewish state. They should seek rather a Jewish settlement in Palestine, which would serve the cultural, spiritual and national needs of Jews everywhere, but which could not be established without harmonious relations with the indigenous population. In 'The Jewish State and the Jewish Problem', written soon after the First Zionist Congress as a rebuttal of Herzl's *Der Judenstaat*, Ahad Ha'am criticised the susceptibility of the masses to Messiah figures, contrasted the moral poverty of assimilated Jews with the material poverty of eastern Jewry, and, above all, distinguished between a truly Jewish state (*Jüdischer Staat*) and a mere state for Jews (*Judenstaat*). The most a purely Herzlian state, organised after the pattern of every other state with no distinctively Jewish culture and spirituality, could possibly deliver was material power and political dominion. It would remain adrift from the spiritual heritage of Judaism and sever bonds with diaspora Jews (Ahad Ha'am 1962: 78–80). Jewry's encounter with modernity required it to return to its historic centre, establish a sizeable settlement – a spiritual centre – in which Jewish culture could express itself, and radiate out into the diaspora, becoming at a favourable opportunity a truly Jewish state.

Ahad Ha'am was scathing on Herzl's *Altneuland*, which he reviewed in *Ha-Shiloah*. This utopian idyll lacked any semblance of Hebrew culture. It was the fulfilment of the assimilationist mentality. His concerns went beyond Jewish self-interest. Having criticised the boycott of Arab labour by Jewish settlers, he wrote to a settler in Palestine in November 1913:

> I cannot put up with the idea that our brethren are morally capable of behaving in such a way to humans of another people, and unwittingly the thought comes to my mind: if it is so now, what will be our relation to the others if in truth we shall achieve at the end of time power in Palestine? And if this be the 'Messiah': I do not wish to see his coming.
>
> (in Smith 1974: 31)

Ahad Ha'am settled in Tel Aviv in 1922, where he was fêted as the undisputed moral philosopher of Zionism. However, he soon succumbed to despair:

> I am broken, shattered, utterly and incurably depressed. And all this in Palestine, which has been my dream for years and years. And in the midst of all these blessings, I long for – London!
>
> (in Goldberg 1996: 111)

He died a broken-hearted man in Tel Aviv in 1927, outraged by the cycle of violence:

> My God, is this the end? ... Is this the dream of our return to Zion, that we come to Zion and stain its soil with innocent blood? It has been an axiom in my eyes that the people will sacrifice its money for the sake of a state, but never its prophets.
>
> (in Smith 1974: 36)

The bi-national critique of Zionism[1]

Jewish anti-Zionists in the universalist tradition of humanism rejected the particularism and enthnocentricism of the exclusivist nationalism of Zionism. The Reform Movement in the USA stressed that Judaism was fundamentally a religion, and that Jews derived their nationality status from wherever they lived. Professor Morris Cohen (1880–1947) saw Zionism as a rationalisation of the flawed proposition that Jews were unassimilable. Its end result was ghettoism: 'A national Jewish Palestine must necessarily mean a state founded on a peculiar race, a tribal religion, and a mystic belief in a peculiar soil'. Cohen charged that Zionism in America reflected the lack

---

1 See further Hattis 1970.

of confidence of Zionists in the ability of Judaism to 'hold its own in an open field', and that tribalism, whether it bears the label of Zionism, Anglo-Saxon America, or Pan-Islam, is a creed that leads to grief and massacre (in Smith 1974: 51–55). Already in 1919, Morris Jastrow, Jr, in an addendum to the (mostly) Reform Judaism's message to the Paris Peace Conference (1919), warned against the reactionary, segregationist nature of political Zionism. He called for the creation of a state in Palestine which would be based on all the nationalities living there (in Smith 1974: 40–41).

A bi-national entity was also the preferred option of Judah Magnes (1877–1948) and the *Brit Shalom* (Covenant of Peace) group, founded in 1925, under the leadership of Arthur Ruppin, ironically the father of Jewish settlement. *Brit Shalom* represented 'the one brief, genuine attempt to bridge the chasm between Zionism's aims and recognition of the indigenous population's rights'. It published its credo in *Sh'ifoteinu* ('Our Aspirations') in 1927, professing its commitment to 'a binational state, in which the two peoples will enjoy totally equal rights as befits the two elements shaping the country's destiny, irrespective of which of the two is numerically superior at any given time' (Goldberg 1996: 164). The status of people would no longer derive from their relative numerical strength.

Magnes, a Reform rabbi in the USA and disciple of Ahad Ha'am, resigned from the Zionist movement in 1915, preferring the international and the human to the new secular nationalism. Hailing the Balfour Declaration as 'imperialism's iniquitous gift to the Jewish people', he feared that Jews, in their efforts to create a political organism, would become devotees of brute force and militarism. He emigrated to Palestine in 1923, and became the first Chancellor of Hebrew University. He stressed the need for Jews to acquire an ease with Jewish nationalism, after which they could become internationalists. Their Jewish nationalism would be transcended, just as when a musician who has mastered his technique can devote himself to the higher art of playing. He appealed for an *entente cordiale* with the Arabs, and for consideration of their rights and needs, and of the need to live in peace with them (in Menuhin 1969: 316–17). In 1929, he wrote to Chaim Weizmann, warning against the creation of a Jewish state. There were two choices ahead for Zionism: statehood, with its attendant militarism and imperialism, and the creation of a Jewish majority, by force if necessary, or a pacific policy that focused on setting up a Jewish educational, moral and religious centre, with two nations, and three religions, all having equal rights and none special privileges: a country where nationalism was but the basis of internationalism, where the population was pacific and disarmed – in short, the Holy Land (in Ellis 1994: 45).

Magnes challenged Weizmann on whether Jews would conquer Palestine as in the time of Joshua, or whether it should take account of the religious developments of Judaism since Joshua, as reflected in the prophets, the psalmists and the rabbis. He wrote to Felix Warburg, a New York financier and philanthropist:

Palestine does not belong to the Jews and it does not belong to the Arabs, nor to Judaism or Christianity or Islam. It belongs to all of them together; it is the Holy Land. ... We must once and for all give up the idea of a 'Jewish Palestine' in the sense that a Jewish Palestine is to exclude and do away with an Arab Palestine. ... The fact is that nothing there is possible unless Jews and Arabs work together in peace for the benefit of their common Holy Land. It must be our endeavour first to convince ourselves and then to convince others that Jews and Arabs, Moslem, Christians and Jews have each as much right there, no more and no less, than the other: equal rights and equal privileges and equal duties. ... Judaism did not begin with Zionism, and if Zionism is ethically not in accord with Judaism, so much the worse for Zionism

(in Ellis 1990: 49).

In a pamphlet written in 1930 (*Like all the Nations?*, Jerusalem: Herod's Gate), Magnes avowed that if the prevailing option of creating a state were to obtain, involving force and the subjugation of the Palestinian Arabs, he would no longer define himself as a Zionist, but as a traditional *hibbat Zion* (lover of Zion).[2] He redefined, in order of importance, the three chief elements of Jewish life: the Jewish people around the world; the Torah (including the history, and ethical ideals of the Jewish people); and the land of Israel, where the people and the Torah can be creative as they were without the land.

In addition to aspiring to a binational Arab and Jewish Palestine Magnes argued for a union of Palestine, Transjordan, Syria and Lebanon in an economic and political federation, and, finally, a union of this federation with an Anglo-American union. He spent the last years of his life advocating his ideas, and in 1947 lobbied the USA State Department against the partition plan of the UN, and, only days before the declaration of the State of Israel, he spoke at length with Secretary of State George Marshall and President Truman, urging them to withhold recognition, but instead establish an American trusteeship to provide an umbrella for an eventual binational political settlement (Ellis 1994: 48–49). He produced in June 1948 a detailed plan, 'United States of Palestine: A Confederation of Two Independent States' after the declaration of the State of Israel. Magnes' work was carried on by Hannah Arendt.

Arendt, too, campaigned for the establishment of a renewed Jewish presence in Palestine, but opposed the establishment of a Jewish state. Even after victory in war,

2   Albert Einstein also emphasised the need to establish a reasonable agreement with the Arabs on the basis of living together in peace, an arrangement he preferred to the creation of a Jewish state. He feared the damage which a narrow nationalism would do to Judaism (in Menuhin 1969: 324).

The land that would come into being would be something quite other than the dream of world Jewry, Zionist and non-Zionist. The victorious Jews would live surrounded by an entirely hostile Arab population, secluded inside ever-threatened borders, absorbed with hysterical self-defence to a degree that would submerge all other interests and activities. The growth of a Jewish culture would cease to be the concern of the whole people; social experiments would have to be discarded as impractical luxuries; political thought would center around military strategy; economic development would be determined exclusively by the needs of war. And all this would be the fate of a nation that – no matter how many immigrants it could still absorb and how far it extended its boundaries...would still remain a very small people greatly out-numbered by hostile neighbours.

(Arendt 1978: 187)

The real goal should be the building up of a Jewish homeland, rather than the pseudo-sovereignty of a Jewish state. The independence of Palestine could be achieved only on a solid basis of Jewish-Arab co-operation. Local self-government and mixed Jewish-Arab municipal and rural councils were the only real political measures that could eventually lead to the political emancipation of Palestine. Arendt criticised Zionism's dependence on German nationalism which defined people in terms of 'biological superhuman personalities' rather than in terms of political organisations. She was critical of Herzl's definition of Jews as victims of the perennial and ubiquitous hostility of Gentiles, and of his failure to see Jewish liberation in broader, human terms. But there was still time to save the Jewish homeland (1978).

Magnes and Arendt believed in a renewed and augmented Jewish community in Palestine, and argued for a Jewish homeland, rather than a Jewish state, judging that a Jewish state would dominate the Palestinians and ultimately dominate the Jews. Although they shared some of the presumptions of the colonialist West, considering that the Palestinians needed Westerners, they believed in an equality that would be a litmus test for any Jewish community in Palestine.

The universalist critique of Zionism

Liberal Jews considered the goal of Zionism to be impossible since it would require the emigration of millions of Jews to a region already inhabited. Moreover, with Western society moving away from narrow nationalisms to a vision of a transnational global order, they considered the Zionist programme of constituting a national state to be reactionary and recidivist – I have already considered the opposition to Zionism of the American Council for Judaism, and of its Executive Director, the late Elmer Berger (Chapter 3). In their view, assimilation was the answer to the Jewish problem, a position countered by Zionists who insisted that assimilation was impossible, and that antisemitism was endemic wherever Jews were in a minority. Nevertheless, powerful liberal voices in Western European and American Jewry insisted that Jews belonged in the countries in which they lived.

William Zuckermann in 1934 accused Zionists of not escaping from the ghetto but of transplanting it, going to Palestine, not with idealism, but because it was the only country where they could have a fascism of their own (in Aruri 1989: 44–45). Like Arendt, Hans Kohn, the pioneering historian of nationalism (1946), considered Zionism to have grown out of German romanticism, with its glorification of the *Vaterland*, and its *Volk*, united by blood, chosenness and its manifest destiny. He lamented the degeneration of nationalism, a movement intended to protect the individual liberty and rights of citizens against their government, into a degenerative, depraved, and predatory aggressive political form.

Maxine Rodinson, a Jewish Marxist and Arabist, also criticised the ghetto-like character of the Jewish state, which was premised on the contention that Jews were aliens in all countries outside of Israel, a postulate similar to the charge of antisemitism. Far from solving the Jewish problem, the creation of the state produced another problem, that with the Palestinians, and in turn spread hatred of the Jews into the Arab countries where antisemitism was previously unknown. Moreover, the success of Zionism strengthened the most reactionary forces in the Arab countries, provided opportunities for the sale of arms from the imperialist countries, and encouraged a racist and chauvinistic mentality that impels society down the road of social regression (Rodinson 1983: 112).

I.F. Stone accused Israel of creating a kind of schizophrenia in world Jewry. Whereas outside, the welfare of Jews depends on the maintenance of secular, non-racial, pluralistic societies, in Israel, Jewry defends racist and exclusionist values and practices, which accord inferior status to non-Jews.

> Jews might fight elsewhere for their very security and existence – against principles and practices they find themselves defending in Israel. ...
> Those caught up in Prophetic fervour soon begin to feel that the light they hoped to see out of Zion is only that of another narrow nationalism.

He calls for a re-examination of Zionist ideology (in Aruri 1989: 45–46).

Jewish bi-nationalist and internationalist critics of Zionism feared that a Jewish state would be a 'fortress Israel', imposing upon the Jews of Palestine a ghettoised mentality, in continuity with the ghettos of Europe. In a trenchant critique of Zionism, Moshe Menuhin judged Jewish nationalism and the determination to establish a Jewish state to represent the decadence of Judaism, and to be 'A monstrous historical Crime and Curse' (1969: xi). As a conscientious Jew, he felt it necessary to pass judgement on the tragic and revolting perversion of the lofty and dignified Judaistic past of pure ethics, philosophy and religion into boisterous 'Jewish' nationalism:

'Judaism turned into rampant Israelism'. When others were aspiring to supranational unity 'the Jews of the world, through indoctrination with the regressive political Zionist philosophy, are being dragged back ideologically into the old, dark east European ghettos, where self-segregation and cultural isolation once reigned supreme' (1969: xi, xiv).

Other Jews, some fervently Zionist, insisted on a break with Jewry's (religious) past. The declaration of the Second Zionist Congress (1898) that Zionism had nothing to do with religion reflected the precedence of the secular aspect of the programme. Moreover, the Fifth Congress (1901), which brought to the fore the conflict between Herzl and the Russian 'cultural' Zionists, witnessed a walk-out by the *Demokratische Fraktion* in protest against Herzl's pragmatic accommodation with those advocating a religious element in the Zionist programme. This group, meeting at its own conference in Heidelberg in 1902, insisted that, 'The introduction of religion into the argumentation for, and (into) the programme of Zionism is inconsistent with the national character of Zionism' (Vital 1982: 191).

Likewise, the prevailing mood among those involved in the crucial second aliyah was secular.[3] For them, religion was irrational, non-empirical, imperialistic, and an altogether repressive and regressive force, from which no anthropological validity, social bonding, psychological insight, or existential illumination could be expected. Indeed, in the camp of strident anti-religious secularism one's way to salvation was to escape from the prison of the sacred (see Diamond 1986: 59, 154). Yosef Hayim Brenner declared, 'From the hypnotic spell of the twenty-four books of the Bible I have been liberated for some time now' (in Diamond 1986: 18), and in the estimation of Karl Kautsky, Judaism was a weight of lead attached to the feet of Jews who eagerly sought progress (see Laqueur 1972: 420). For such people, religion was a symptom of Jewry's sickness in exile. For a further minority, the break with the Jewish past should be not only with religion, but with Jewish history itself. Zionist Palestine would be new, secular, and qualitatively different from the past of the diaspora. Its Jewish nationalism would stand on its own feet, free of its religious modality.[4]

Nevertheless, despite the fact that various strands of Jewish thinking criticised the notion and actuality of a Jewish state, the reality of the *Shoah*, coupled with the embattled condition of the state has muted Jewish opposition to Zionism and the state, almost to the point of regarding it as

---

3   However, that the old wine of religious observance could be poured into the new bottles of secular nationalism was illustrated graphically in the adoption of religious symbols into the flag of the Zionist movement: the Star of David embedded within a prayer shawl.

4   Ratosh symbolised the new beginning by designing a flag for the new Hebrew nation that would emerge. Instead of the Zionist *tallit*, taken from the house of study to cover its nakedness, Ratosh chose the first letter of the alphabet, *Alef*, which was also the title of his movement's journal.

eccentric. A major factor in current assessments of Zionism is the victory in the 1967 War.

The 1967 War – for the Land and the Lord

The 1967 War was a watershed in Israeli history, and for many Jews who were indifferent to the state or even opposed to it it represented a conversion experience. From that time on, Jewish dissent was more costly (Ellis 1990: 64). The occupation of additional land, the immediate result of the war whether intended or not, precipitated an ideological crisis for old Zionism. Since the retention of land conquered in war violated international law, its justification would have to be sought beyond the parameters within which such legislation operates. It was in this context that appeal to the Bible and its traditions of the promise and gift of land were reinstated to the core of a self-identifying Israel. Not everyone subscribed to such a reformulating of national identity, and, as we shall see, the peace movement in particular dissented from it, calling for withdrawal from the territories occupied.

The newly-formed Gush Emunim stressed the religious basis of Jewish identity, and advocated settlement in the Occupied Territories for religious reasons. While its revolutionary New Zionism was not a core value for the whole of Israeli society it came to the fore at a time when the foundational ideology of the state had become routinised and jaded. The most distinctive feature of the new era of Zionism was the capacity of the religious zealots to collaborate with secular territorialist activists in settling the conquered territories. According to the all-embracing ideology of the elder Rav Kook, the secularists, even without realising it, were furthering the divine will.

Many of the secularists came from the Land of Israel Movement, also founded in the wake of the war, with a manifesto claiming that no government was entitled to give up any portion of *Eretz Yisrael*, the inalienable patrimony of the Jewish people from the beginning of its history. Gush Emunim provided the movement with pioneers to live in the Occupied Territories. The tendency of Israeli Jews to segregate on religious–secular criteria was reflected in the constitution of the earlier settlements: of the thirty-seven listed by Gush Emunim in 1983, twenty-nine were religious, three secular and five were mixed. The mix proved too explosive in Mizpe Jericho, which split into two, one religious and the other secular (Vered Jericho), and even the Beth El settlement had to divide into Beth El A and Beth El B, one religious and the other ultra-religious (Bauer 1985: 98).

If secular territorialists were prepared to co-operate with, and even join Gush Emunim, members of the latter reciprocated, and constituted an important ingredient in the founding of Tehiya, the party established to purify politics in the wake of the signing of the Camp David Accords. Tehiya proclaimed full Israeli sovereignty over all *Eretz Yisrael*, and determined to populate the Occupied Territories with Jews. The movement's 'back to basics' call invited individuals to reassess the importance of Judaism, with the result that religion was, once again, a respected ingredient of the national psyche.

The Israeli peace movement

But despite the euphoria within religious circles about the achievement of Zionism and the spectacular ('miraculous') military victory of 1967, for those with a concern for liberty, equality and fraternity, not to speak of justice, there was no escaping the realisation that the Zionist dream had been a nightmare for the indigenous population. While such humane concerns mattered little to those propelled by divinely inspired motivation, they could not be ignored by those who, while embracing political Zionism, residually subscribed to internationalist aspirations.

On the secular side, a plethora of human and civil rights groups appeared (Peace Now, ACRI, B'Tselem, Israeli Women Against the Occupation, Women in Black, Yesh Gevul, Parents against Moral Erosion, etc. – see e.g. Hurwitz (ed.) 1992: 197–208). However, unlike the Gush which has substantial facts on the ground, these organisations confine themselves to protest in words and demonstrations, most recently in processions from the grave of Yitzhak Rabin, whose murder has purified him of his crimes against humanity, and virtually canonised him as the patron saint of the peace camp.

The degeneration of the idealism associated with the foundation of the state – with its stress on the ideal of Jewish public service – into various expressions of egoism, symbolised by the corruption rampant in public life in the early 1970s, led to the formation of reform movements of various complexions. The 'Our Israel' movement advocated liberal democratic values as the remedy for the national malaise. Founded in February 1974 it disintegrated in the autumn of that year. The Dash party (Democratic Movement for Change) which won 11.6 per cent of the votes, and fifteen Knesset seats in the 1977 elections, advocated that the Jewish state should be based on enlightened democratic liberalism, and that Israel should withdraw from most of the Occupied Territories. However, it too disappeared from the scene very quickly.

The longer-lasting 'peace movement', a broad coalition of bodies which came into being in the wake of the 1967 War, considered that the ongoing occupation would erode the universalist values of socialist Zionism (understood in that uniquely exclusivist way which characterises even the most liberal Zionists), and replace them with particularist, chauvinistic and xenophobic tendencies. Responding to shifts in Israeli society in general it assumed a major role in confronting the growing racist ideology which was increasingly infecting the Israeli politic, and which manifested itself in its most extreme form in Kahanism.

The main membership and features of the two major strands within the peace movement in the period leading up to the 'peace process' may be represented as follows:

Mainstream Peace Camp	*Progressive Peace Camp*
Peace Now;	Women & Peace Coalition;
Mapam (old socialist);	Shanai;
Ratz (Citizens Rights Movement);	Women's Organization for Political Prisoners;
Shinui (centre party);	Human Rights Organizations;
Labour Party doves;	Physicians for Human Rights;
Kibbutz Peace Movement.	Hamoked/Hotline-Center for the Defence of the individual;
	Alternative Information Centre;
	Yesh Gvul;
	Rakah (Israeli Communist Party);
	Progressive List for Peace;
	Arab Democratic Party;
	Hadash (Democratic Socialist Front).
Fully Zionist;	Mixed (for/anti/neutral) Zionist;
Enlightened self-interest of Jewish state; strongly pro-USA, an 'honest broker'.	Primary concern for the human rights of the Palestinians.
The Occupation must end, because it is a corrupting influence.	The Occupation must end.
There must be territorial compromise, with divergence on a two-state solution.	There must be an independent Palestinian State negotiated with the PLO.

While the mainstream peace movement is thoroughly Zionist, the much smaller, but vocal minority left wing is mixed, with some groups non-, and others anti-Zionist (see Hurwitz 1992). The two tendencies diverge most clearly in their attitude to the occupation. The mainstream camp, driven by the enlightened self-interest of the Jewish state and its particularist values, sees it as precipitating the disintegration of democratic Israel, as well as being a drain on its economy. It rejects the traditional arguments concerning the security of the state, considering the West Bank to provide no protection against missile attacks, and avers that ruling it condemns Israel to subduing indefinitely an increasingly resistant Palestinian majority. It seeks refuge in a 'sane Zionism' which respects universalist principles, and for that reason insists on the necessity of ending the occupation.

Some segments of the peace movement see the establishment of a Palestinian state as a necessary condition for peace, even though such a move could precipitate a major conflict within Zionist circles, with the possibility of a civil war between those willing to make territorial 'compromises' and those for whom 'surrendering a square inch of sacred soil' would be a betrayal. Already by the mid-1990s, the virulence of the latter tendency led to the assassination of the Prime Minister, the 'traitor' who symbolised 'sane' Zionism.

Those motivated by principles of human rights and the dignity of the Palestinians are caught between upholding the universalist ideals of liberty, equality, justice, etc., and supporting the core Zionist ideal of maintaining Israel as a Jewish state (see Hall-Cathala 1990: 1–4). Since the occupation systematically violates the human and national rights of the Palestinians it must end. For many, the occupation accentuates the fundamental dilemma of Israeli society: how is it possible to honour universalist values, while insisting on the particularist Jewish quality of the state?

The peace movement reached the height of its popularity during the period of protests against the 1982 Israeli invasion of Lebanon. However, in the aftermath of that invasion its activities declined, coinciding with the participation of the Labour Party, with which many of its activists were associated, in the National Unity government of 1984. By the 1990s, however, it strongly supported the proposals for territorial concessions and has been to the fore in support of the 'peace process' and in opposition to the obstacles to its success which has been a feature of the Netanyahu government.

Few segments of the peace movement apply universalist principles to the 1948 context, which perpetrated the foundational injustice on the Palestinians, although some call for an enlargement of the particularist notion of a Jewish state, aspiring to a polity that would embrace all its citizens as equals. While some seek a semblance of justice for the Palestinians, few advocate the abandonment of the separatism and exclusivism that characterises Zionism.

Other secular and religious dissent

Even though the existence of the state and its expansion in 1967 have altered fundamentally the perspectives of many Jews *vis-à-vis* the state, there is a significant Jewish culture which is universalist rather than nationalist. I draw attention here only to a selection of authors. With few, but notable exceptions the criticism comes from secular perspectives.

Just as Zionism has much in common with the colonialist mentality of nineteenth-century Europe, anti-Zionism can be seen within the broad framework of anti-colonialist ideologies. Anti-Zionists view Zionism as essentially regressive, oppressive, and segregationist, inevitably creating a *Herrenvolk* and *Übermensch* mentality, which, above all, required the displacement of the indigenous culture of Palestine. The anti-Zionist literature of the last hundred years, while reflecting a broad spectrum of opinion, coalesces on the key question of opposition to the creation of a state exclusively for Jews, and on the perception that de-Zionisation is the key to co-existence with the Arab world. Despite the negativity of the term, anti-Zionism is proposed as a positive programme which aspires to the construction of a society which is free of the social malady which derives from Zionist philosophy.

In the opinion of the recently deceased Professor Yeshayahu Leibowitz, an Orthodox Jew and one of the foremost Jewish scholars of his day, 'Continued occupation and oppression of the Palestinians must eventually lead to a full fledged fascist regime inside Israel, and to the unification of the entire Arab world in a war against Israel' (in Hurwitz 1992: 9). Leibowitz regarded the entire religious establishment with contempt, and the mix of religion and politics as poisonous. In the immediate aftermath of the 1967 War, when the country was in the grip of religious euphoria, he warned: 'This brilliant victory will be a historical and political disaster for the State of Israel'. He denounced the Western Wall as a disco and said he would gladly return it to the Arabs (Chaim Bermant, in *Jewish Chronicle*, 26 August 1994, p. 21). He spared no Israeli leader, and considered Ben-Gurion to have hated Judaism more than any other man he had met. The Sabra and Chatila massacre, he insisted,

> was done by us. The Phalangists are our mercenaries, exactly as the Ukrainians and the Croatians and the Slovakians were the mercenaries of Hitler, who organised them as soldiers to do the work for him. Even so have we organised the assassins in Lebanon in order to murder the Palestinians.
>
> (in Chomsky 1983: 387)

Noam Chomsky is the best known Jewish diaspora critic of the State of Israel, for which he has suffered more vilification than most. He saw both Palestinian Arabs and Jews, each capable of making their case with a high degree of plausibility and persuasiveness, as locked into a suicidal policy – reflected at its sharpest in the designation of the 1948 war as a war of conquest (for Arabs) and the war of independence (for Jews). The only solution is the creation of a democratic, socialist Palestine that preserves for both some degree of communal autonomy and national self-government, wherein,

> People will be united by bonds other than their identification as Jews or Arabs. ... The society will not be a Jewish state or an Arab state, but rather a democratic multinational state.
>
> (Chomsky 1974: 34)

He was less optimistic after the Israeli invasion of Lebanon, which he judged to be manifestly aggressive. Operation 'Peace for Galilee' was a war of precision bombing against an unarmed civilian population. He held Israel culpable in the Sabra and Chatila massacre, seeing it as in line with the Deir Yassin and Qibua massacres, overseen by Begin and Sharon respectively, and architects of the Lebanese war. Nevertheless, he insisted that Israeli Jews and Palestinian Arabs were human beings with equal rights within the territory of former Palestine, and supported the Palestinian Arabs' right to national self-determination. The occupation of the West Bank, he argued, provided Israel with cheap labour, a controlled market for its goods, and badly needed water. He criticised the Allon plan of 1970 which called for the annexation of 30 to 40 per cent of the West Bank, excluding the areas of dense Arab population in order to contain the demographic problem. Chomsky's prognostication was that 'as long as the United States remains committed to an Israeli Sparta as a strategic asset ... the prospects are for further tragedy: repression, terrorism, wars, and possibly a conflict engaging the super-powers' (Chomsky 1983: 468–69).

For the Israeli peace activist, Israel Shahak, 'Israel as a Jewish state constitutes a danger not only to itself and its inhabitants, but to all Jews and to all other peoples and states in the Middle East and beyond' (1994: 2). He points out that the ideological defence of Israeli policies is usually based on Jewish religious beliefs or on the 'historical rights' of the Jews, which derive from those beliefs and retain the dogmatic character of religious faith (p. 8). He is scornful of the 'closed utopia' of the State of Israel, which can never become an open society:

> It can become a fully closed and warlike ghetto, a Jewish Sparta, supported by the labour of Arab helots, kept in existence by its influence on the US political establishment and by threats to use its nuclear power, or it can try to become an open society. The second choice is dependent on an honest examination of its Jewish past, on the admission that Jewish chauvinism and exclusivism exist, and on a honest examination of the attitudes of Judaism towards the non-Jews.
>
> (Shahak 1994: 13)

Shahak insists that the task ahead for Israeli and diaspora Jews must include a self-criticism of the Jewish past, particularly that related to the Jewish attitude to non-Jews. He concludes his study: 'Although the struggle against antisemitism (and of all other forms of racism) should never cease, the struggle against Jewish chauvinism and exclusivism, which must include a critique of classical Judaism, is now of equal or greater importance' (1994: 103).

The Israeli academic, Uri Davis, also is strongly critical of the 'apartheid State of Israel', and judges the mainstream of Israeli society to have been systematically deprived of its critical faculties to the point of barbarity, mainly through the religious indoctrination in its schools:

> Israeli society is subject to a process of escalating Nazification, as a result of which an increasing proportion of both the Israeli Jewish oriental population and the European and American Jewish populations are providing a solid base of support for Revisionist and National Religious parties.
>
> (Davis 1987: 85)

Motivated by conscience, by a sense of justice and by hatred of hypocrisy he struggles for the liberation of Palestine from Zionist colonial dispossession and Israeli apartheid legislation, preferring a united state of Palestine, with equal rights for Palestinian Arabs and Palestinian Hebrews. For this to happen, Zionist philosophy needs to be challenged, and Zionist practice to be dismantled (Davis 1991: 3, 55).

Reflecting more recently on the Holocaust, Davis makes a sharp distinction between the guilt of this generation for crimes committed by generations before it, and its moral responsibility to set matters right now, insofar as it can. He focuses on the question, 'How was it possible for the Jewish people, victims of Nazi genocide, to subject the Palestinian people to war criminal policies of mass deportation, transfer and ethnic cleansing during, and around the 1948–49 war?' He addresses the question by adducing examples from the practice of the Labour Zionist leadership which reflects its subjugation of everything to the Zionist goal. If the leadership could tolerate the annihilation of some of 'its own people' in Nazi-occupied Europe, in the interests of advancing its programme, what would deflect it from inflicting war crimes on 'another people' for the same purpose? The enormity of the Zionist crimes must be exposed, and owned up to. Because the war crimes were, and continue to be committed by the successive governments of Israel in their name, present-day Israelis have a responsibility to protest, to act in defence of the Palestinian Arab victim, and insist on due reparation for the war crimes (Davis 1999).

Akiva Orr considers that Zionism institutionalised a major schism in Jewish civilisation, between secular nationals and the religious Jews. 'It introduced an ethnocentric value system into a civilisation founded on theocentrism. It capitalised on the *de facto* divide between religious and non-religious Jews and established an organisation that aimed to create an ethnocentric state for Jews' (1994: 160).

Stanley Cohen, the South African-born Professor of Criminology at the Hebrew University, judged the level of state violence to which Palestinians were exposed in the Occupied Territories to be, person for person, more intense than that suffered by blacks in apartheid South Africa (S. Cohen 1992: 186). Whereas he was confident that social justice would be worked out there eventually in terms of people living as equals in one democratic, multiracial society, the most one hopes for in Israel, even in the peace movement, is an uneasy separation from the enemy in the form of a two-state solution. Cohen considered Israel to be 'a society becoming more closed, locked in fundamentalist delusions, full of doom and with a government and majority of the population profoundly antidemocratic and unwilling to even visualise any pragmatic solution acceptable to the international consensus'. Writing shortly before the 'peace process', he bemoaned that Israel was a society where shame cannot be mobilised, hearts have hardened, where the whole society was becoming brutalised, and where the immoral had become socially acceptable (S. Cohen 1992: 186–89). He acknowledged that the real source of change lies in the international arena, notably in the foreign policy interests of the USA, and wondered whether the indulgent rich uncle – out of a combination of strategic interest, sentimental support for the 'only democracy in the Middle East', residual Holocaust guilt, and pressure from the Jewish lobby – would continue to pay the bill of its client mercenary state, however crazily the niece continued to behave (p. 192). He lamented that Israel must be the only country in the world where people drawing attention to human rights violations are called 'informers' (p. 194).

Israel's invasion of Lebanon in 1982 was a catalyst for Jewish dissent (see Timerman 1982; Shorris 1982; Rubenstein 1984). It first interested Norman Finkelstein, one of the most radical and hard-hitting Jewish critics of Zionism in the USA, in the Israeli–Palestine conflict. The son of survivors of Maidanek and Auschwitz, his thesis is that Zionism is a kind of Romantic nationalism which is fundamentally at odds with liberal thinking. His major study (1995) is a systematic slaughter of several of the sacred cows of Zionist historiography (A Land Without a People, Abba Eban's 'Reconstruction' of the June 1967 War, etc.). He passes judgement on the solutions to 'the Jewish problem' proposed by political Zionism, Labour Zionism, and the cultural Zionists who saw the real enemy of Judaism to be not antisemitism but the increasingly secular civilisation that rendered it anachronistic. Dissidents who stood outside the ideological consensus of requiring a Jewish majority saw that the insistence on it would inevitably imply the domination and suppression of the Palestinian Arabs – the state would be the property of one people only. Zionist logic ran along the following lines: the Jewish right to a national state in Palestine was *sui generis*; the Palestinian Arabs were not a nation in themselves, but were part of the greater Arab nation for which Palestine had no unique resonances; Jews had an 'historical' right to Palestine, whereas the indigenous Arab population only had rights of residence. Total population transfer was for many the most attractive solution to 'the Palestinian problem' (Finkelstein 1995: 16, and 177 note 20). Finkelstein concluded his review of the Zionist enterprise with the judgement that,

> Israel has not resolved the Jewish Question; if anything, the enthralment of the self-described 'Jewish state' to Western imperialism and its local satraps has exacerbated it. Israel has not become the spiritual beacon for world Jewry. ... Israel has not remade the Jewish people into a 'working nation'; if anything, it is transforming Israeli Jews into a parasitic class – *pieds noirs* battening off cheap Arab labour and massive foreign subvention. The means have become the ends. What is the *raison d'être* of Zionism in the contemporary world save as an outpost of 'reactionary and imperialist forces upon a resurgent East'?
>
> (Finkelstein 1995: 20)

The war in Lebanon was a catalyst also for Henry Schwarzschild who saw it as a turning point in Jewish history and consciousness, exceeded in importance only by the end of the Second Commonwealth and the Holocaust. It crystallised for him the inference which he had resisted for thirty years that 'the resumption of political power by the Jewish people after two thousand years of diaspora has been a tragedy of historical dimensions', yielding a Jewish ethnic-religious nation-state, a human and moral disaster.

> The lethal military triumphalism and corrosive racism than inheres in the State and its supporters ... are profoundly abhorrent to me. So is the message that now goes forth to the nations of the world that the Jewish people claim the right to impose a holocaust on others in order to preserve its State. ... The price of the millennial survival of the Jewish people has been high; I do not think the point was to make others pay it.
>
> (in Ellis 1994: 33–34, 146 note 4)

It was military service in the army that precipitated the Israeli artist Gadi Gofbarg's 'divorce' from Zionism, whose ideology had shaped his education in Brazil. Having occupied a village in the Golan Heights in 1973 he could not bring himself to 'sleep in some else's bed'. He recalls spending a night in a bombed-out school, warming himself by a fire made with pupils' desks, 'watching the flames slowly consume that wood with children's names etched in it'. Such is the story of Zionism, which 'precipitated the creation of the Jewish state contingent on the destruction of Palestinian society':

> Everything that has a front has a back. ... And if in the front the desert was blooming, in the back Palestinian olive trees were being uprooted, and if in the front Israeli culture was flourishing, in the back Palestinian culture was withering, and if in the front Israelis had dignity, in the back Palestinians were humiliated. The Israelis have made their pleasure contingent on Palestinian suffering.
>
> (Gofbarg, in Ellis 1994: 34–35)

The volume, *Walking the Red Line*, edited by Deena Hurwitz (1992), illustrates that there is a broadly based critique of Israeli policy with respect to the Occupied Territories within Israeli Jewish society. This should contribute to the dissolution of the charge that critics of the inhumane behaviour of the State of Israel are motivated by racist dispositions akin to antisemitism, and since the writers are all Israeli Jews, they cannot all be conveniently branded 'self-hating Jews'.

> [The] refusal to collaborate with the apparatus of occupation is sometimes referred to as drawing a 'red line'. In other words, a red line marks the personal, moral, or psychological limit beyond which one is unwilling to transgress; or conversely, by which one is impelled to action, perhaps consciously, to incur risk.
>
> (Hurwitz 1992: 3)

However, while many Jews are embarrassed by the brutality of the post-1967 Israeli occupation and not least by the invasion of Lebanon – '*Al tagidu shelo yadatem*' ('Don't say you didn't know') is the slogan of the 'Women in Black' – few question the morality of the much more severe displacement of the Palestinians in 1947–49. For that reason, the existence of the peace camp in Israel inhibits the surfacing of a real critique of the Zionist enterprise and the policies of the State of Israel, namely one related to the foundational displacement of the indigenous Arab population of most of Palestine.

This is clear, for example, in the criticism of Michael Lerner, a proud Zionist, for whom, presumably, the foundational displacement of the Palestinians is above reproach: sin entered in only with the 1967 occupation. Reacting to the brutality of Defence Minister Rabin's policies of suppressing the *intifada*, as editor of the Jewish journal, *Tikkun*, Lerner wrote an editorial with the title, 'The Occupation: Immoral and Stupid', protesting,

> These activities [Israel's attempt to regain control of the refugee camps] are deplorable to any civilized human being. That they are done by a Jewish state is both tragic and inexcusable. We did not survive the gas chambers and crematoria so that we could become the oppressors of Gaza. . . . If Jewish tradition has stood for anything, it has stood for the principle that justice must triumph over violence. . . . We, who love Israel, who remain proud Zionists, are outraged at the betrayal of this sacred legacy by small-minded Israeli politicians who feel more comfortable with the politics of repression than with the search for peace.
>
> (*Tikkun* 3, March–April 1988: 7, reproduced in
> Ruether and Ellis 1990: 99–100)

He called for an end to repression, and for negotiations with the Palestinians. Lerner's critique is rooted in the self-interest of Jews. His patronising solution in 1988 was for a demilitarised and politically neutral Palestinian state in the West Bank and Gaza, guaranteed by the USA, USSR, with Israel joining in to protect it from outside attack. After a period of peaceful coexistence, Israel and Palestine would form an economic confederation. Reacting to the report of the killing of an Israeli policeman in Gaza, by January 1993, Lerner advocated unilateral Israeli withdrawal from Gaza, on the grounds that 'We've had enough', for a moment entertaining the fantasy of a different kind of population transfer as a solution to the 'Palestinian problem': 'How nice it would be for Israel if all the Palestinians were living in Los Angeles or Queens' ('Israel's Choice: Either Transfer a Million Palestinians or Get Out of Gaza', *Tikkun* 8 [January/February 1993]: 7).

Enlightened self-interest pervades the religious wing of Jewry also, where it is rare indeed to encounter any criticism of Israel. Rabbi Jeremy Milgrom, espousing what in Israeli religious life is an extreme position, represents a particular type of Zionism which, without righting the foundational injustice done to the indigenous population and making the restitution which universal justice demands, wants to live in peace. He views the Zionist intention to set up a homeland somewhat naively, considering it to have had neither an explicit nor a conscious program *vis-à-vis* the Arabs. Milgrom notes that the experience of the Holocaust, far from sensitising them to the abuse of power in the service of an inhumane ideology, has made Jews obsessed with only their own vulnerability. All threats to Jewish existence must be eliminated, at any cost, even, if necessary, at the cost of an entire nation of innocent bystanders. He views 'the release of the Palestinian people' as essential to the resurrection of Judaism, which, he claims, was the goal of Zionism. For Milgrom, 'the release of the Palestinian people' means no more than according them an expression of their nationalism, based on territorial compromise and mutual recognition. He hopes that in our post-imperialist era, world opinion, if not Jewish moral restraint, will not allow the genocide of the Palestinian people: the price of the occupation is too expensive, emotionally, morally and militarily (Milgrom 1992: 31–32).

Unusually for a Zionist, Milgrom acknowledges that the Israeli Palestinians have lost almost all their lands, are socio-economically disadvantaged and have become a minority in their own homeland. He laments the thorough, official whitewash of the injustice done to the Palestinian people and the systematic eradication of Palestinian roots, an erasure which is expressed fervently in the transformation of abandoned Arab homes into highly-sought-after real estate, and of destroyed villages into campsites and forest parks. He concedes that the redressing of the injustices inflicted on them would require the repatriation of the Palestinian refugees, the rebuilding of the four hundred villages destroyed after the war of 1948, and the restoration to Palestinians of agricultural lands expropriated 'for the public good' (i.e. for the good of Jewish farmers). He realises that such demands would entail a major restructuring of the Israeli society and economy, and, he might have added, would lead to the collapse of a Jewish state. However, neither his understanding of justice or liberty allows him to concede that the ultimate solution lies in the dismantling of the Jewish particularism of the state, the repatriation of refugees, and the generous compensation for past wrongs. Rather than advocating such foundational requirements for reconciliation, he stays on the safer, sentimental ground of supporting individual civil rights for Israeli Palestinians, and territorial independence for the Palestinians in the Occupied Territories (see Jeremy Milgrom 1992: 33–35).

But the critique of some stretches back to the 'original sin' of the foundational injustice of 1948. In a series of presentations – an ongoing sequence of public lectures, articles, and studies – the American Jewish theologian, Marc H. Ellis challenges Jewish moral and religious thinkers – who functioned brilliantly when confronting the oppression of Jews in Christian Europe, but are now quiescent in the service of Jewish state power – to speak before it is too late (1987; 1990; 1994; 1997; 1999). His experience of oppression and of various liberation theologies had made him sensitive to the miseries of oppressed peoples around the world, and the attempts to mitigate or eliminate them. His first visit to Israel, in 1973, assured him immediately that something was profoundly wrong, with Jews dominating Israel's unwanted Arab, second-class citizens. On subsequent reflection, and after a second visit in 1984, he agonised whether the Zionist determination to end the Arab presence in Palestine might spell the end of the Jewish tradition of suffering and struggle. Could Jews call the permanent dispossession of the indigenous Arab population their own liberation? (Ellis 1994: 9).

Ellis attempts to chart a way out for the Jewish people to create a moral future which respects the high moral traditions of Judaism. He sees his people today facing the greatest crisis of its history since the destruction of the Temple in AD 70. This time, the Jews have power, which they use to disperse, dislocate, maim, humiliate and destroy another people. The 1980s, he suggests, are perhaps the most shameful decade in the history of the Jewish people, clearly showing that the policy of the State of Israel was to end the indigenous Palestinian presence and culture in historic Palestine. He raises questions about how Jewish theology might either legitimate this oppression, or help Jews to face the reality of what they had become, with Jewish suffering in the Holocaust being seen as mandating its new empowerment, especially since 1967.

Ellis' visit to Auschwitz in 1991 as part of a delegation of Jewish intellectuals made him ponder whether 'Auschwitz', interpreted as the freezing of Jewish history in that catastrophe, had become a safe haven for Jews, where they can insistently demand accountability of others for past wrongs, while hiding from their own accountability in the present (1994: 24). Jews, having dirtied their hands in becoming Israelis, nevertheless continue with 'the old-time theodicy of victimage' (John Murray Cuddihy), and in fact resort to blaming the victims, the Palestinians, seeing nothing irrational in so doing. The portrayal of the Holocaust as a metaphysical evil beyond the possibility of human explanation, historically unique and without precedent, as if it were 'ontologically separate from human history' (Joan Ringelheim), puts it beyond all speech. Jews, he argues, employ 'Auschwitz' as a functional symbol to keep them untouchable. He calls on his fellow Jews to 'end Auschwitz', that is, to admit they are no longer innocent, that Israel is not their redemption, and that solidarity with the Palestinian people is the way forward for the Jewish people. He longs for his people to be healed of the tragedy of the Holocaust, even though this would minimise the special status of Jews as victims and make them accountable to the world for their present actions: 'Auschwitz' 'has created such anger, isolation, and a pretense of nonaccountability that it erodes the basic sensibilities and fundamental ethics of our existence'. Jews should use the suffering of 'Auschwitz' as a way of entering into the suffering of others, rather than as a blunt instrument against others, all the while protecting Jewish suffering as unique and incomparable (1994: 30–33, 39–41).

Ellis laments that, although the Israeli occupation and its policies are in their third decade, no major Jewish theologian has acknowledged the obvious: what Jews have done to the Palestinians since the establishment of the State of Israel is wrong; in the process of conquering and displacing them Jews have done to the Palestinians what was been done to them over two millennia, and have become almost everything they loathe about their oppressors; Jews can move beyond being victims or oppressors only by confronting state power in Israel, and through solidarity with the Palestinian people.[5] What, he asks, is the mission of the Jewish people? To build Israel as an exclusively Jewish state, and to serve it in the USA by lobbying for economic and military aid? Is such a choice faithful to a history filled with suffering and struggle? Can Jews continue to pretend to an innocence and redemption when actions of Israel closely replicate the history of suffering that Jews sought to escape? Failure to address these central questions threatens the very tradition of suffering and struggle that Jews inherit (Ellis 1990: xv–xvi).

From the perspective of a 'new exile' – of separation from the prevailing Zionist reading of Jewish identity and history – Ellis sees the ongoing destruction of Palestine as forcing a re-evaluation of the last fifty years, and of Jewish history in general. Just as Auschwitz revealed the reality of Jewish weakness and Europe, Palestinians proclaim the reality of Jewish power and Israel. How can a Jew feel at home when those who were once at home have been displaced? The displacement of Palestinians constitutes the central question that accompanies the journey from Auschwitz to Jerusalem. Palestinians, who suffer at the hands of some who survived the Holocaust, and of those who assert power in the name of its victims, are in fact the last victims of the Holocaust.

The ongoing survival of the Palestinian people stands over against the Jews who commemorate the Holocaust as if Palestinians do not exist, and as if Jews were innocent of the crimes against them. Forgetfulness, it appears, has displaced memory as a distinctive, constitutive aspect of Jewish identity and history. Nevertheless, the boundaries of Jewish destiny are being defined by Jews who have crossed over into a solidarity with the Palestinian people. What is called for is a new vision which will incorporate a shared future. The future should not be dictated by the desire to conquer and displace, but by a spirit of inclusiveness and reconciliation, suggested by some of the traditions within Judaism, as in Christianity and Islam, and in particular by that of the Jubilee (Ellis 1999).

---

5 Sharing a platform with Marc Ellis, Jacob Milgrom provided a striking example of the Jewish reluctance to face the reality of the displacement of the Palestinians. In dealing with the theme of Jubilee at the *Sabeel* International Conference in Bethlehem University in 1998, he confined himself to 'Third World' countries. The most he could offer his Palestinian friends was a prayer of consolation and hope from Job 14.7–9 (Jacob Milgrom 1999).

Ellis has a message for Christians in the West. Jews need neither a heightened silence nor a paternalistic embrace from Christians, but rather a critical solidarity. He demands that Christians treat Jews like adults rather than children, and confront them with their history, 'as Jews have confronted Christians'. The logic of Zionism, he insists, is no Palestinians. Jews alone will not be able to stop Israeli state power. They need the help of their former enemies, Christians in the West, who have transformed their tradition partly because of understanding what they did to Jews. Jews need a critical solidarity which does not 'let them off the hook'.

Ellis, more than any other thinker of his generation, is restoring to Jewish religious thinking the renowned tradition of dissent. While realising that prophetic critique has lost every battle with Jewish state power, he persists in his challenge to 'end Auschwitz' and to move beyond the pretence of victimage which suffuses Holocaust Theology. If much of his moral challenge to the abuse of power concentrates on Israel and the particular responsibility of Jews, his critique of the descent of Christianity into Christendom, and of the replacement of Christian rhetoric by the reality of state power and Christian praxis is no less piercing. His public espousal of his theses challenges Christians as it does Jews. His contribution to Jewish theology and the wider moral discourse will be remembered long after the names of the legitimisers of Jewish oppression are forgotten.[6]

Conclusion

We have examined a broadly based critique of Israeli policy both within Israeli Jewish society, and among Jews throughout the world. Much of the criticism of Israeli Jews is based on the criterion that the prevailing territorialist Zionism is 'bad for the Jews'. Even the most sensitive souls within this group restrict their moral concern to the indigenous population in the Occupied Territories only. As beneficiaries of the catastrophe inflicted upon Palestinians in the conquest of Palestine in 1947–49, they show little appetite for dismantling the particularist, discriminating structures of the state.

However, Jewish soul-searchers include also those who are anti-Zionist on straightforwardly moral grounds. They stress the foundational injustice

---

6 Four pamphlets of some of Ellis' essays have just been published (1998): (1) 'Edward Said and the Future of the Jewish People'; (2) 'A Reflection on the Jewish Exile and the New Diaspora' and 'Finding the Lost Agenda. A Jewish Lament in the Era of Netanyahu'; (3) 'The Boundaries of Our Destiny. Mapping Oslo and the Future of the Jewish People', 'Unholy Alliance. A Meditation on Religion, Martyrdom and Atrocity', and 'In the Holy Land. A Jewish Reflection on the Biblical Jubilee on the Fiftieth Anniversary of Israel'; (4) 'On the Fiftieth Anniversary of Israel. A Jewish Vision of Justice and Reconciliation', and 'Reading Goldhagen in the Time of Netanyahu'. They are available for £2 each from Friends of *Sabeel* UK, 46 Timms Lane, Formby, Liverpool L37 7DN, United Kingdom.

which the creation of a Jewish state perpetrated on the Palestinians, and the impossibility of repairing the damage on purely Zionist terms. They call for a restructuring of society, in terms which respect the universal rights of liberty and equality. They stress the imperative of acknowledging the injustice done to the Palestinians, and advocate a variety of models in which future political arrangements would remove the present injustices (for example, a unitary state of Jews, Muslims and Christians, or two states in a confederation). The contribution to the critique of the religious Jewish establishment is not impressive. On the contrary, a rejuvenated religiosity has become the major ideological support for the ongoing injustice towards the Palestinian people.

9 Conclusion

From vision to realisation

That the vision of Theodor Herzl of establishing a Jewish state was realised fifty years after the First Zionist Congress (1897) witnesses to the remarkable dedication and sense of purpose of his followers. Political Zionism insisted that equality and emancipation for Jews would be achieved only within the framework of an independent Jewish state, whether in Uganda, northern Sinai, Argentina, Biro Bidzhan or Palestine. Whatever the popularity of his analysis of the condition of European Jews – that anti-Jewish racism in Europe was ineradicable – Herzl's solution was espoused by only a tiny fraction of world Jewry, and was bitterly opposed by both major wings of the religious establishment. The Orthodox rejected emancipation, considering diaspora living to be the divinely ordained fate of Jews until the advent of the Messiah. Reform Jews who regarded the place of their citizenship as their fatherland rejected the re-establishment of Jewish sovereignty, and saw their diaspora condition as facilitating the world mission of Judaism.

However, in the process of securing their own homeland, Zionists uprooted another people:

> The Palestinian Nakba is unsurpassed in history. For a country to be occupied by a foreign minority, emptied almost entirely of its people, its physical and cultural landmarks obliterated, its destruction hailed as a miraculous act of God and a victory for freedom and civilised values, all done according to a premeditated plan, meticulously executed, financially and politically supported from abroad, and still maintained today, is no doubt unique.
>
> (Abu-Sitta 1998: 5)

The determination to create a state for Jews abrogated any possibility of its being guided by universalist values, guaranteeing equality to all its people. Despite the rhetoric of the Preamble to its Declaration of Independence (14 May 1948), the State of Israel does not foster the development of the country for the benefit of all its inhabitants, nor is it based on freedom, justice and peace. There is not equality of social and political rights for all its inhabitants irrespective of religion, etc. Israel is essentially a state for the Jews, dramatically demonstrated by the Zionist expulsion of the majority of the indigenous Arab population and the levelling of their villages to ensure they could not return.

From the beginning the Zionist leadership realised that Palestine had a sizeable indigenous population, that there was no free cultivable land, and that the Arabs working the land had a developed sense of ownership. Despite his public protestations to the contrary, Herzl envisaged expelling the Arab population, and this obvious goal was subscribed to by all significant Zionist leaders, who planned accordingly. Already in 1905, Zangwill had a Bible-based solution: 'We must be prepared either to drive out by the sword the tribes in possession as our forefathers did, or to grapple with the problem of a large alien population, mostly Mohammedan and accustomed for centuries to despise us' (1937: 201). While Ben-Gurion disingenuously protested in 1928 that Jews did not have the right to deprive even a single Arab child in pursuit of the Zionist goal, his rival Jabotinsky attributed moral sensibilities to 'only those with crippled spirits, with a diaspora psychosis' (in Kimmerling 1983: 189).

At the first opportunity (1947–49), the Zionists dispossessed and dispersed some three-quarters of a million Palestinian Arabs. The 'transfer' of the Arab population was promoted by virtually the whole pantheon of Zionist ideologues, albeit mostly in strict secrecy, thereby comprehensively unmasking the myth of the benevolent and peaceful intentions of Zionism. Furthermore, Israeli appeal to an exclusively 'defensive ethos' is merely a public relations device, as well as an exercise in conscious self-deception, assuaging both world opinion and the consciences of Zionists. Moreover, the consistency with which the State of Israel is excused from having to conform to decent behaviour is one of the great eccentricities of twentieth-century political ethics. Most alarmingly from a moral perspective, the injustice to the indigenous population is passed over in most Western discourse, including biblical and theological scholarship, and in some religious circles is even clothed in the garment of piety.

Religious revivalism 1967

Labour and Revisionist (Likud) Zionism have dominated the polity of Israel since its foundation. While 'Labour Zionism' pretends to a Jewish version of a European-style democratic socialist republic (but retaining only as many Arabs as are necessary to 'hew wood and draw water'), 'revisionist Zionism' is more concerned with expanding territorial boundaries. Despite its socialist and democratic rhetoric, the Labour establishment was the architect of the foundational displacement of the Palestinian Arabs in 1948, and again in 1967. It resolved the inevitable contradiction between universalist socialism and particularistic nationalism by abandoning the former in favour of the latter (Sternhell 1998: 32–34). It has differed from the more vulgarly racist ideology of the Israeli right only in its success in deceiving Western opinion about its intentions. Both left and right have settled Jews in the Occupied Territories, one acting with more stealth, and the other in a world-defying brazenness. With respect to cleansing the land of Arabs, there is a continuum from Herzl through Weizmann, Ben-Gurion, Eshkol, Meir, Rabin, Begin, Shamir, Peres and Netanyahu.

A third strand, 'Religious Zionism' grew out of the war of 1967. 'Labour Zionism' had altogether secularised and reduced the 'Messianic age' of Jewish eschatology to the three-fold deliverance of 'national' liberation, social development and individual salvation. The establishment of the state having virtually achieved these aspirations, 'Labour Zionism' did not have a vision to carry the revolution much further. The 1967 conquest of the heartland of 'biblical Israel', however, brought a profound change at the ideological level, inserting religious values into the heart of at least some segments of Israeli society. In identifying a new set of priorities 'Religious Zionism' came to the rescue of a jaded secular Zionism.

The thoroughly secular Zionist enterprise was invested with distinctively (Messianic) redemptive significance. What others might perceive as old-fashioned, nineteenth-century colonialist plunder was metamorphosed into the eschatological 'redemption of the land'. The civic religion of Jewish nationalism was refracted into a Jewish religious nationalism, displacing secular, universalist democratic values, and substituting a distinctive religious nationalism more reminiscent of fascism and totalitarianism. 'Idolatry of the land' had superseded the triadic relationship of People–God–Land, reducing it to a bipolar one of Land–People, with all the consequences for Jewish settlement in, and reluctance to withdraw from the Occupied Territories. The catastrophe of the enterprise for the indigenous Arab population was a small price to pay for the benefits of Messianic redemption – especially when someone else was paying.

There is no shortage of utopian idealisations of the catastrophe: 'The union of people and land is intended to contribute to the perfecting of the world in order to become the Kingdom of God' (Buber 1985: 48). Whereas other nations who dispossessed indigenous people can legitimately be accused of robbery,

> Their charge against Israel is totally unjust for it acted under authority and in the confident knowledge of its authorization. ... No other people has ever heard and accepted the command from heaven as did the people of Israel. ... So long as it sincerely carried out the command it was in the right and is in the right in so far as it still carries it out. Its unique relationship to its land must be seen in this light. ... Where a command and a faith are present, in certain historical situations conquest need not be robbery.
>
> (Buber in 1944, in 1985: 49–50).

For André Neher, too, Palestine holds the key to Jewish existence. He writes of a 'geo-theology' and its charm, and supports the view that aliyah will speed up the redemption of the whole world, and the coming of the Messiah (1992: 22–23). The language of morality is applied liberally: Liebman and Don-Yehiya describe the State of Israel as 'a moral community' and 'a moral state' (1983: 214–17), even though the expulsion of the indigenous population was required, planned and executed.

The Jewish religious establishment, although late in embracing Zionism, today fully supports its achievement and has been at the forefront of its expansionist intentions since 1967, and denounces the entire 'peace process'. On the occasion of the signing of the Declaration of Principles (13 September 1993) Hasidic Jews gathered opposite the White House gates, and, having said their morning prayers, protested against the peace agreement, chanting 'Rabin is a Traitor' (*Washington Post*, 14 September A13). Shortly before Rabin's assassination, Britain's former Chief Rabbi, Lord Jakobovits had written to him: 'As one of the very few Orthodox rabbis broadly supporting your peace efforts, I thought I might render some assistance in moderating the bitter hostility of the two principal opposition groups: the settlers and the various religious factions' (*Jewish Chronicle*, 18 August 1995, p. 17). While for much of the world the signing of the Declaration of Principles symbolised a new hope and a new beginning, for the religious Messianists and ultranationalists it spelled disaster, and the end of the dream of an undivided, full-blooded Jewish state on the west of the Jordan. Rabin the traitor, the obstacle to the divine schema, had to be removed.

The alignment of religious mythology with militant nationalism has resurrected a type of Jewish piety that had been dormant since the Bar Kochba revolt of AD 135, bringing into the body politic a new type of holiness, propelled by some of the more ignoble elements of the religious tradition, particularly those underpinned by a naïve-literalist reading of the land traditions of the Bible (especially of the book of Joshua), and of some of its Messianic texts. The potentially humanising function of religion has been corrupted through its association with a form of nationalism that is ineradicably colonialist and imperialist, to the extent that it is scarcely distinguishable from the most reprehensible forms of totalitarianism. This new expression of parochial, self-indulgent, and self-seeking religion secludes the holy, canonises prejudices and petrifies the sacred rather than sanctifying the secular (see Heschel 1987: 414).

Zionism and Western Christianity

It is one of the anomalies of recent Church history that while Christians have supported oppressed peoples everywhere else, there has been little protest against the injustice perpetrated on the Palestinians. The pro-Zionist lobbies in the West have ensured that the guilt felt by Western Christians in the wake of the *Shoah* would be paid for by an uncritical support of Israel: 'An affirmative attitude to Israel is essential to the healing of the Churches' misery' (Littell 1987: 521). It is as if the horror of the *Shoah* sanctioned the oppression of an innocent third party. However, 'Right and wrong are the same in Palestine as anywhere else. What is peculiar about the Palestine conflict is that the world has listened to the party that committed the offence and has turned a deaf ear to the victims' (Arnold Toynbee in Kayyali 1979: 5).

Western Christian support for Zionism is facilitated by the direction frequently adopted in the Jewish–Christian dialogue. With a virtual Orthodox Jewish veto on discussion of theological matters, much of the dialogue's energy focuses on support for Israel. It does this by fuelling guilt in contemporary Christians for sins for which they themselves have no responsibility, while ensuring that they will not intervene in a contemporary question for which they have some. Typically the modern penchant for apology is restricted to events of the past, for which the apology costs nothing. Such a disposition is consistent with obduracy concerning matters in which one has a clear responsibility. The imperative seems to be to confess only those things for which one has no responsibility. Collective inherited guilt is neither reasonable nor productive. The remedy for true guilt is to confess, seek the pardon of the offended party, and make appropriate restitution. The horror of the Nazi *Shoah* must never be allowed to sanction the oppression of an innocent people: 'We did not survive the gas chambers and crematoria so that we could become the oppressors of Gaza' (Lerner 1988: 7). Yet, silence on the oppression of the Palestinians appears to be a compulsory element in maintaining good relations in the dialogue between Jews and Christians.

Invariably in such circles, consideration of the origins of Zionism and the birth of Israel betrays either ignorance, naïveté or dishonesty, and contradicts both the theory of Zionism and the reality of the expulsion of the Palestinians. Reflecting an irredentist benevolent Zionist interpretation of events, it distorts facts of history, omits core elements of the discourse, and makes claims that lack substance. Such a discourse does little to advance truth and justice. Silence in the face of contemporary violations of human dignity is unworthy of adherents of any religion. Those who allow others to suffer without protesting become 'accomplices by omission'.

However, exposure to the oppression of the Palestinian people has required segments of the Christian Church to reconsider its position, although parts of the fundamentalist evangelical wing, locked into a naïve interpretation of biblical and other apocalyptic texts remain unperturbed by such human suffering. The extent of the Nakba and the intransigence of Israel have gradually been recognised, and people's consciences have been roused accordingly. There are now sufficient numbers of concerned Jews and Christians who know the extent of the Palestinian catastrophe. Christians and Jews in the West must not be silent now about the plight of the Palestinians as Christians were about the plight of the Jews in the period leading up to the *Shoah*.

The rights of Jews

The Zionist appeal to the rights of Jews elevates the perceived needs of Jews to an imperative that does not have to contend with the demands, needs or rights of any other people. In that unique discourse, Zionism defines universal morality exclusively in its own terms. In reality, of course, Zionists cannot engage comfortably in moral discourse. The establishment of the State of Israel was possible only on the basis of massive expulsion of the Arab population, and the expropriation of its land. No amount of legal acrobatics could ever justify such behaviour. From that point on, the exercise of legal power could only consolidate and amplify the foundational immorality, thereby corrupting the normal discourse of jurisprudence, which, instead of being an instrument of morality, merely compounds the original crime. The Jewish claims of a 'right to return' have no measure of justice and morality, and rely only on assertions and legislation which lack moral coherence, receiving their force exclusively from conscienceless power. While conquest and war are effective agents of annexation, they are not instruments of legitimacy in the moral world. Moreover, Israel's attempt to present itself as an innocent victim of Arab aggression serves only to perpetuate its self-deception, and falsely exonerate itself of responsibility for its conquest.

One of the most significant effects of a pan-Zionist reading of Jewish history – that Jews everywhere and at all times longed to control their own homeland (state) – is the reduction of the rich diversity of Jewish historical experience to one kind of ideological drive which emphasises some of the most ignoble and regressive elements of Jewish tradition, namely those which glory in a separation from the nations, and a determination to carve out the destiny of a Jewish state, irrespective of the cost to others. These dispositions which derive from an ethnicist and xenophobic nationalism, and are premised on attitudes of racial dominance and exclusion do not advance the goal of other traditions within Judaism, such as that inviting the Jewish community to be a light to the nations.

This rewriting of Jewish history has gone hand in glove with the myth which propels Zionism, and catapults to the zenith of Jewish aspirations a single phase of its history that is very recent, and one that in all likelihood will not endure. It will not endure, in the same way that tyrannies collapse eventually, usually under the weight of a combination of internal tensions which spring from ideological contradictions, and external ones which will not tolerate or support such oppression indefinitely. Pre-Zionist Judaism deserves to be assessed on its own terms, and the whole of Jewish history must not be allowed to be dominated by the combined forces of nineteenth-century imperialist and colonial-nationalist tendencies and the disaster inflicted on European Jewry by the racist policies of the Third Reich. Establishing a state by making an innocent people homeless is not a fitting monument and memory for the victims of the *Shoah*.

Many of the most important Jews in the formative period of Zionism were opposed to the creation of a Jewish state. The tradition of dissent continues. Some of it is Zionist, opposing only parts of Zionist policy. Non-Zionist, or anti-Zionist criticism opposes the enterprise more generally, whether on matters of principle or in terms of its cost. But often, even the most urbane discussions are driven more by the enlightened self-interest of the Jewish state and its particularist values, betraying that kind of insensibility to natives that characterised the whole nineteenth- to twentieth-century European colonialist enterprise. The ultimate moral question in such a discourse is not whether such and such a policy violates the rights of others, but only whether it is 'good for the Jews'. Despite the euphoria in the religious camp, the moral problematic posed by the sacralisation of colonial theft has not been submerged altogether. But here also, the prevailing preoccupation is with the impact of the Zionist enterprise on Jewish interests.

The future

While Zionism triumphed in the formation of a Jewish state, the prognostications of anti-Zionists also have been fulfilled. Whereas Zionists predicted that Israel would become a normal state, and a light to the nations, it has become a garrison, ghetto state, with an inordinately high level of dependence on the USA. Hannah Arendt's prescient fears have been fulfilled. Militarily triumphant Israel is now surrounded by virtually entirely hostile Arab neighbours, and is absorbed with hysterical self-defence which submerges virtually everything else. Political thought and economic development are focused on military strategy and the needs of war. No matter how many immigrants it can absorb and how far it extends its boundaries Israel will forever remain a very small people greatly outnumbered by hostile neighbours (1978: 187).

After fifty years, much of the rationale which provided the major plank for Herzlian Zionism (e.g. that Jews could not live except in a Jewish state) is confounded by the reality of Jewish demography. While Zionist success has brought about a national revolution in establishing a state and fostering the immigration of millions of Jews – albeit in some cases with the gentle persuasion of Zionist bombs[1] – it has succeeded in attracting only some 33 per cent of world Jewry. The present world population of Jews is

---

1 In 1950–51, Ben-Gurion sanctioned the bombing of synagogues and other Jewish buildings in Baghdad to engineer the *aliyah* of Jews from Iraq – an immensely successful campaign, which drove some 105,000 Jews to flee the country with no choice of destination other than Israel, leaving only some 4,000 behind. Agents of the Israeli government spread the fear of antisemitism into the Iraqi Jews by blowing up synagogues, and other places frequented by Jews, as well as the US Information Centre in Baghdad (March 1951), in order to gain support for the Zionist cause in the USA. 'Every time fears would abate, a new bomb shattered the feeling of security, and the prospect of staying on in Iraq seemed gloomier' (Shiblak 1986: 127, 124).

c. 14,343,910, of which 4,420,000 live in Israel and the Occupied Territories of East Jerusalem, the West Bank and Gaza. Some 5,800,000 live in the USA, one of the ninety-eight principal countries where Jews live (Massil (ed.) 1997: 187–90). Moreover, half a million Israelis live outside the country (Gilbert 1998: 618).

Contrary to the expectations at the time of the Declaration of Principles (September 1993) there is growing Palestinian disaffection. Living conditions have got worse, and the Netanyahu government shows no appetite to accommodate Palestinian aspirations. The absence of any significant peace dividend for the Palestinians, and the counter-signs of the growth in Israeli settlement activity, fuel Palestinian resentment, while it needs only an extra-judicial assassination followed by a suicide-bomb in Jerusalem to change the atmosphere profoundly. Meanwhile, north of its own border, Israel pays a higher price than is politically permissible for its occupation of the self-declared security zone in Lebanon – ironically the most insecure place in the Middle East for Israeli soldiers. Altogether, then, the earlier optimism that things would change for the better has suffered protracted reverses.

Historians will look back with some bewilderment at how the Zionists in 1948 callously destroyed the lives and heritage of the innocent indigenous population of Palestine, and systematically imposed an apartheid structure on the land. 'The classic victims of years of antisemitic persecution and Holocaust have in their new nation become the victimisers of another people, who have become therefore the victims of the victims' (Said 1992: xxiv).

While the future is obscure, there are some things about which one can be relatively certain. Zionist Jews will be exposed as having engineered an outrageous act of population displacement. History will not judge benevolently those who systematically planned the dislocation of almost the entire indigenous population of that part of Palestine which became the State of Israel, nor will it honour those who executed the deed so callously and with a level of pretence to legitimacy and appropriateness that confounds all rationality and moral discourse. Most of the practitioners of Western intellectual life and virtually all of Western theology have become, in Antonio Gramsci's phrase, 'experts in legitimation' for Zionism. Historians of the future will be particularly critical of the Western Churches and theologians who at best have been complicit by silence, or even supportive by encouragement and aid of the dislocation of an innocent people.

The foundational injustice done to the indigenous Palestinian people by the Zionist venture will not be righted, at least at this stage. A just solution to the problem would require a rolling back of the achievement of Zionism, and the abandonment of its ideology, including that the displaced Palestinians be allowed return to their former homes, or be adequately compensated in accordance with international law. It is not likely that the State of Israel will acknowledge the injustice Zionism has perpetrated on the Palestinians, will beg their forgiveness and will make commensurate reparation. There can, of course, be a pragmatic solution, based on compromise by the parties concerned. But justice will have to wait another day.

It is inevitable that a generation of Jews will arise, which will acknowledge the injustice that Zionism has perpetrated on the indigenous Arab population, as well as the moral damage which the enterprise has done to the Jews. Despite the modern fashion of apologies for the crimes of others, perpetrators of injustice seldom acknowledge their deeds, express sorrow and make some, however inadequate, restitution. And yet, no lasting peace can proceed without telling the truth and being reconciled by the injured party. The Truth and Reconciliation Commission in South Africa and the much more widespread local equivalents, facilitated in many cases by the Churches, provide a precedent. Moreover, the traditional Arabic practice of *sulha* offers a semitic paradigm for progress.

The two parties, the aggrieved and the perpetrators make the first move towards reconciliation by independently consulting a facilitator in whom both sides have the utmost confidence, and who is experienced in 'conflict resolution'. At the appropriate time the two sides are brought together. The perpetrator of the damage takes the first step, acknowledging responsibility and expressing profound sorrow for causing the suffering. The confession invariably transforms the encounter, converting any residual emotions for revenge into a desire for restoration to good order. The details of the restitution are fixed after the customary ritual of 'bartering' – the terms of which have already been 'sounded out' privately with each party by the facilitator, and the pardon is pronounced. The parties, then, share a common meal.

Several factors point to a bleak future for the State of Israel as a Zionist entity. History assures us that political hegemony based on military pre-eminence does not survive indefinitely. Unless it deviates from its aggressive posture and establishes a *modus vivendi* with its Arab neighbours Israel has every reason to fear retribution from the surrounding states when they become sufficiently powerful. Moreover, the ideological drive for separatism, which propelled Zionism from minority to widespread Jewish support, appears somewhat out of place in a world in which multiracialism and multiculturalism are taken for granted. Moreover, the demographic factor alone bodes ill for its maintenance as a Jewish state. For the period 1967–92, the population growth rate for the West Bank and the Gaza Strip, respectively 4.2 and 5.3 per cent, has yielded Arab populations of 1.05 million in the West Bank, 155,500 in East Jerusalem, and 716,800 in the Gaza Strip in 1992. Population increases of that order will ensure that the Jewish majority in Mandated Palestine will soon be overturned (see Sabella 1996).

In the short term, Israel has three options. The Likud-led government reluctantly will allow some extension of Palestinian autonomy over the high-density populations of the Occupied Territories, with Israel retaining overall control. The second would allow for the formation of a Palestinian state in the Occupied Territories alongside the State of Israel, with modifications to the pre-1967 War boundaries. This solution could gain the support of a Labour-led administration. The third would lead to the formation of a unitary, secular, non-racial state in Mandated Palestine, with equal rights for both peoples and all religions, as in other democracies. At present this would not win the support of any substantial Zionist grouping within the Israeli body politic, since it would require a national vision contrary to the core separatist aspiration of Zionism from its inception. Writing in 1986, James Diamond considered it as unlikely that Israel would disavow or move beyond Zionism as that the USA would renounce democracy or capitalism, or Russia would forsake Marxism or communism (1986: 126–27). Although it appears to be the least desirable option from an Israeli perspective, the evolution of Israel into a pluralistic secular democracy represents the best prospect in the short term for the maintenance of Jewish interests in the region.

From a purist Palestinian perspective, what the Oslo and subsequent agreements call 'compromise' is 'a massive abandonment of principles, the main currents of Palestinian history, and national goals' (Said's 'Preface', in Mikhail 1995: vii). The peace process is sure to end in a defection from the ideals of Palestinian national liberation. The immediate future will not result in the establishment of a unitary, secular state in all of Palestine – the aspiration of the PLO until 1988 – nor in the creation of a Palestinian state alongside the State of Israel – the aspiration since 1988. Nor is there a viable alternative to the capitulation of the PLO, since the secular Palestinian opposition is impotent, while Hamas has little to offer beyond grandiloquence and the anaesthetising rhetoric of a religious solution for a secular situation. And those outside Palestine, particularly in the refugee camps, have a strong sense of having been abandoned by the Palestinian leadership.

For any long-term future, Israeli Jews will have to secure a just peace with the people it has displaced, rather than the reluctant and minuscule concessions exemplified by the miserly 'further redeployment' of the Wye Agreements.[2] For an agreed future, the national goals of both people must become inclusive. For that reason, the biblical paradigm of the displacement by one people of the indigenous population is no help. An obvious solution is to create a single state which respects the right of citizenship of all inhabitants (including returned expulsees), irrespective of religion. The obstacle to such a programme, of course, is the Zionist principle of chauvinistic separatism. To achieve a unified state, with equality of rights for all citizens, the basis intentions of Zionism would have to be re-evaluated,

---

2 The 'speech' by the British chieftain Calgacus to rouse his army to resist the Roman invaders, comes to mind: *Auferre, trucidare, rapere falsis nominibus imperium, atque ubi solitudinem faciunt, pacem appellant* ('Theft, slaughter and plunder [rape] they call by the false name of government, and where they make a wasteland they call it peace') (Tacitus, *Agricola* 30).

and its essentially discriminatory, complex base and structure would have to be dismantled. A federation of two states, with permeable borders, and a wide range of collaboration is the preferred option, and could serve as an intermediate stage to a unified state. Perhaps the dismantlement of apartheid South Africa and the movements towards an agreed settlement in Northern Ireland encourage one to believe that such a future might just be possible. In any case, some solution must be devised which will be an improvement on throwing the Jews into the sea, or throwing the Palestinian Arabs into the desert.

Epilogue

I have long been impressed by the volatility of Israel–Palestine, a phenomenon which makes it singularly difficult to ensure that a book takes account of the most recent developments. The period between the completion of the manuscript and its publication allows me to note a number of significant events.

Soon after the signing of the Wye Plantation Agreement in November 1998, President Clinton visited Gaza (13 December), an event marked by unprecedented Palestinian euphoria celebrating the first arrival of a US President on territory of the Palestinian Authority. The Palestine National Council, or some metamorphosed version of it, duly 'reaffirmed' the repeal of anti-Israeli clauses in the Palestinian Charter, and Clinton applauded the Palestinian leadership for choosing peace, calling on the Israelis to follow its example. As if to mark his own embrace of peace, and while singing 'Joy to the World' with a choir in Bethlehem's Manger Square, the President ordered a four-day blitz on Iraq – symbolically supported by Britsh Prime Minister Tony Blair's Tornados to prove that the USA was not acting alone, and that its action was not governed by the President's domestic problems – much to the chagrin of the Arab world.

A few days later (21 December), under the strain of the inner contradiction of the government's rhetorical commitment to the 'peace process' and the implacable opposition of some of its members thereto, the Israeli Knesset voted for early elections. Prime Minister Netanyahu's troubles were only beginning. Being sure that his Defence Minister, Yitzhak Mordechai, would resign from the Likud party to lead a 'centrist' one, the Prime Minister sacked him from the cabinet on 23 January. Mordechai arrived at his last cabinet meeting wearing a black skullcap, and, armed with a Bible, read from Psalm 120: 'Deliver me, YHWH, from lying lips, from a deceitful tongue. ... Too long have I had my dwelling among those who hate peace. I am for peace; but when I speak, they are for war'. Mordechai visited Jerusalem's (Wailing) Western Wall, where he received a blessing from Rabbi Ovadia Yosef, the spiritual leader of Shas. Mordechai suggested that the Prime Minister should read from the Book of Samuel: 'Samuel said to Saul, "I will not return with you; for you have rejected the word of

YHWH, and YHWH has rejected you from being king over Israel" ' (1 Sam 15.26).

The death of King Hussein of Jordan on 7 February 1999 threw the region into further uncertainty for the future. The withdrawal of three of the five candidates for the election of Israel's Prime Minister on 17 May, including a Palestinian Member of the Knesset, left the contest between Ehud Barak, leader of the Labour Party, and Binyamin Netanyahu. Barak's convincing victory promises 'a new path of unity, of change, of a new hope for Israel'.

Meanwhile, the television coverage of the Serbian expulsion of the Albanian Kosovars (March–May 1999) – the threats, massacres, destruction of homes and villages, and the interminable lines of displaced people – assure viewers that the spirit and tactics used by the Zionists in Palestine in 1948 are very much alive today. This time, however, it appears that external forces are determined to reverse the expulsion. Whether Ehud Barak will restore some element of justice for the Palestinians remains to be seen.

Bibliography

Only those works referred to in the text are included here.

Abu Lughod, Ibrahim (ed.) (1987) *The Transformation of Palestine. Essays on the Origin and Development of the Arab–Israeli Conflict*, 2nd edn, Evanston, IL: Northwestern University Press.

Abu Lughod, Janet (1987) 'The Demographic Transformation of Palestine', in Ibrahim Abu Lughod (ed.) 1987: 139–63.

Abu-Sitta, Salman H. (1998) *The Palestinian Nakba 1948. The Register of Depopulated Localities in Palestine* (with accompanying Map, *Palestine 1948, 50 Years after Al Nakba. The Towns and Villages Depopulated by the Zionist Invasion of 1948*), London: The Palestine Return Centre.

Adams, Michael and Mayhew, Christopher (1975) *Publish it not . . . The Middle East Cover-Up*, London: Longman; repr. 1989.

Adler, Marcus N. (1894) 'Jewish Pilgrims to Palestine', in *Palestine Exploration Fund Quarterly Statement*, October: 288–300.

Ahad Ha'am (1962) *Nationalism and the Jewish Ethic*, ed. H. Kohn, New York: Herzl Press.

Ahlström, Goesta W. (1993) *The History of Ancient Palestine from the Palaeolithic Period to Alexander's Conquest*, Sheffield: Sheffield Academic Press.

Ahmad, Hisham H. (1994) *From Religious Salvation to Political Transformation: The Rise of Hamas in Palestinian Society*, Jerusalem: PASSIA.

Albright, William F. (1942) 'Why the Near East needs the Jews', in *New Palestine* 32: 12–13.

—— (1957) *From the Stone Age to Christianity: Monotheism and the Historical Process*, New York: Doubleday.

Aldeeb, Sami (1992) *Discriminations contre les non-juifs tant chrétien que musulmans en Israël*, Lausanne: Pax Christi.

Alfaro, J. I. (1978) 'The Land – Stewardship', in *Biblical Theology Bulletin* 8: 51–61.

Appleby, R. Scott (1997) *Spokesmen for the Despised. Fundamentalist Leaders of the Middle East*, Chicago, IL and London: University of Chicago Press.

Aran, Gideon (1997) 'The Father, the Son, and the Holy Land: The Spiritual Authorities of Jewish-Zionist Fundamentalism in Israel', in Appleby 1997: 294–327.

Archbold, Norma (1993) *The Mountains of Israel. The Bible and the West Bank*, 2nd edn, Phoebe's Song.

Arendt, Hannah (1978) 'To Save the Jewish Homeland: There is Still Time', in R.H. Feldman (ed.) *Hannah Arendt: The Jew as Pariah*, New York: Grove Press, 178–92.

Ariel, Yaakov (1992) 'In the Shadow of the Millennium: American Fundamentalists and the Jewish People', in Wood (ed.) 1992: 435–50.

—— (1997) 'A Christian Fundamentalist Vision of the Middle East. Jan Willem van der Hoeven and the International Christian Embassy', in Appleby 1997: 363–97.

Aronoff, Myron J. (1985) 'The Institutionalisation and Cooptation of Charismatic, Messianic, Religious-Political Revitalisation Movement', in Newman (ed.) 1985: 46–69.

Aronson, Gaza (1987) *Creating Facts: Israel, Palestinians and the West Bank*, Washington: Institute for Palestine Studies.

Aruri, Naseer H. (1989) 'Anti-Zionism: A Democratic Alternative', in Tekiner, Abed-Rabbo and Mezvinsky (eds) 1989: 33–61.

Ateek, Naim Stifan (1989) *Justice and Only Justice. A Palestinian Theology of Liberation*, Maryknoll, NY: Orbis.

—— (1991) 'A Palestinian Perspective: The Bible and Liberation', in Sugirtharajah (ed.) 1991: 280–6.

Ateek, Naim Stifan, M.H. Ellis, and R.R. Ruether (eds) (1992) *Faith and the Intifada. Palestinian Christian Voice*, Maryknoll, NY: Orbis.

Ateek, Naim, Cedar Duaybis and Marla Schrader (eds) (1997) *Jerusalem: What makes for Peace?* London: Melisende.

Ateek, Naim S. and Michael Prior (eds) (1999) *Holy Land – Hollow Jubilee: God, Justice and the Palestinians*, London: Melisende.

Avineri, Schlomo (1981) *The Making of Modern Zionism. The Intellectual Origins of the Jewish State*, New York: Basic Books.

Bainton, Roland H. (1960) *Christian Attitudes Toward War and Peace*, Nashville, TN: Abingdon.

Barclay, John M.G. (1996) *Jews in the Mediterranean Diaspora from Alexander to Trajan (323 BCE–117 CE)*, Edinburgh: T&T Clark.

Baron, Salo W. (1952) *A Social and Religious History of the Jews*, 2nd edn, vol. 1, *To the Beginning of the Christian Era*; vol. 2, *Christian Era: The First Five Centuries*, New York: Columbia University Press; Philadelphia, PA: The Jewish Publication Society of America.

Barr, James (1993) *Biblical Faith and Natural Theology: The Gifford Lectures for 1991*, Oxford: Clarendon.

Bass, Clarence (1960) *Backgrounds to Dispensationalism*, Grand Rapids: Eerdmans.

Bauer, Julien (1985) 'A New Approach to Religious-Secular Relationships?', in Newman (ed.) 1985: 91–110.

Bein, Alex (1961) 'Von der Zionsehnsucht', in *Robert Weltsch zum Geburtstag*, Tel Aviv: Irgun Olej Merkas Europa.

Ben-Gurion, David (1954) *The Rebirth and Destiny of Israel*, New York: Philosophical Library.

—— (1971–2) *Zichronot* (Memoirs), vols 1–4, Tel Aviv: 'Am 'Oved.

Benvenisti, Meron (1984) *The West Bank Data Project: A Survey of Israel's Policies*, Washington DC/London: American Enterprise Institute of Public Policy Research.

Benvenisti, Meron, and Shlomo Khayat (1988) *The West Bank and Gaza Atlas*, Jerusalem: The West Bank Data Base Project.

Berger, Elmer (1989) 'Zionist Ideology: Obstacle to Peace', in Tekiner, Abed-Rabbo and Mezvinsky (eds) 1989: 1–32.

—— (1993) *Peace for Palestine. First Lost Opportunity*, Gainsville, FL: University Press of Florida.

Bickerman, E.J. (1984) 'The Babylonian Captivity', in Davies, W.D. and L. Finkelstein, eds. *The Cambridge History of Judaism*, vol. 1: 342–58.

Blackstone, William E. (1908) *Jesus is Coming*, 3rd edn; 1st edn 1878, New York: Fleming Revel.

Bokser, Ben Zion (1988) *Abraham Isaac Kook*, New York and Toronto, Ont.

Boyden, Michael (1996) 'The Challenge for Reform Judaism in a Jewish State', in Romain 1996: 202–11.

Brettler, Marc Zvi (1995) *The Creation of History in Ancient Israel*, London and New York: Routledge.

British Council of Churches (1989) *Impressions of Intifada. Report of a British Council of Churches Delegation to Israel and the Occupied Territories, March 1989*, London: BCC.

Brody, H. (ed.) (1924) *Selected Poems of Jehudah Halevi*, trans. N. Salaman, Philadelphia, PA: Jewish Publications of America.

Brown, R.E., J.A. Fitzmyer, and R. Murphy (eds) (1990) *The New Jerome Biblical Commentary*, London: Chapman.

Brown, Robert McAfee (ed.) (1990a) *Kairos: Three Prophetic Challenges to the Church*, Grand Rapids: Eerdmans.

—— (1990b) 'Christians in the West Must Confront the Middle East', in Ruether and Ellis (eds) 1990: 138–54.

Brueggemann, Walter (1977) *The Land. Place as Gift, Promise, and Challenge in Biblical Faith* (Overtures to Biblical Theology), Philadelphia, PA: Fortress.

Buber, Martin (1985) *On Zion: The History of an Idea*, trans. by Stanley Godman, new Foreword by Nahum N. Glatzer, Edinburgh: T&T Clark.

Burrell, David and Y. Landau (1992) *Voices from Jerusalem. Jews and Christians Reflect on the Holy Land*, New York: Paulist.

Byrne, James M. (1996) *Glory, Jest and Riddle: Religious Thought in the Enlightenment*, London: SCM; American edn (1997) *Religion and the Enlightenment. From Descartes to Kant*, Louisville, KY: Westminster John Knox.

Carmesund, Ulf (1992) *Two Faces of the Expanding Jewish State. A Study of how Religious Motives can legitimate two Jewish Groups trying to dominate Mount Moriah in Jerusalem*, Uppsala: Uppsala Universitet.

Carmi, T. (1981) *The Penguin Book of Hebrew Verse*, ed. and trans. by T. Carmi, Harmondsworth: Penguin.

Chacour, Elias (1985) *Blood Brothers. A Palestinian's Struggle for Reconciliation in the Middle East*, Eastbourne: Kingsway Publications

—— (1992) *We Belong to the Land*, San Francisco: Harper.

Childers, Erskine B. (1987) 'The Wordless Wish: From Citizens to Refugees', in Abu-Lughod (ed.) 1987: 165–202.

Childs, Brevard S. (1976) *Introduction to the Old Testament as Scripture*, London: SCM.

Chomsky, Noam (1974) *Peace in the Middle East: Reflections on Justice and Nationhood*, New York: Vintage.

—— (1983) *The Fateful Triangle: The United States, Israel and the Palestinians*, London: Pluto Press.

Coggins, Richard J. and J.L. Houlden (eds) (1990) *A Dictionary of Biblical Interpretation*, London: SCM.

Cohen, Arthur A. and Paul Mendes-Flohr (eds) (1987) *Contemporary Jewish Religious Thought. Original Essays on Critical Concepts, Movements and Beliefs*, New York: The Free Press and London: Collier Macmillan.

Cohen, Erik (1995) 'Israel as a Post-Zionist Society', in Wistrich and Ohana (eds) 1995: 203–14.

Cohen, Stanley, 'Resuming the Struggle', in Hurwitz (ed.) 1992: 184–95.

Cohn-Sherbok, Dan (1992) *Israel: the History of an Idea*, London: SPCK.

Coote, Robert B. and Keith W. Whitelam (1987) *The Emergence of Early Israel in Historical Perspective*, Sheffield: Almond.

Cragg, Kenneth (1992) *The Arab Christian. A History of the Middle East*, London: Mowbray.

—— (1997) *Palestine. The Prize and Price of Zion*, London and Washington: Cassell.

Croner, Helga (compiler) (1977) *Stepping Stones to Further Jewish-Christian Relations*, London & New York: Stimulus.

—— (compiler) (1985) *More Stepping Stones to Further Jewish-Christian Relations*, Mahwah, NJ: Paulist Press.

Darby, John Nelson (1962) *The Collected Writings*, edited by William Kelly, Kingston on Thames: Stow Hill Bible and Trust Depot.

—— (nd) *Synopsis of the Books of the Bible*, London: G. Morrish.

Davies, Philip R. (1995) *In Search of 'Ancient Israel'*, Sheffield: Sheffield Academic Press.

Davies, W.D. (1974) *The Gospel and the Land. Early Christianity and Jewish Territorial Doctrine*, Berkeley, CA: University of California Press

—— (1981) 'The Territorial Dimensions of Judaism', in *Intergerini Parietis Septum (Eph. 2:14). Essays Presented to Markus Barth on his Sixty-fifth Birthday*, ed. Dikran Y. Hadidian, Pittsburgh, PA: The Pickwick Press.

—— (1982) *The Territorial Dimensions of Judaism*, Berkeley, CA: University of California Press.

—— (1991) *The Territorial Dimensions of Judaism. With a Symposium and Further Reflections*, Minneapolis, MN: Fortress.

Davis, Uri (1987) *Israel: An Apartheid State*, London and New Jersey: Zed.

—— (1991) *The State of Palestine*, London: Ithaca.

—— (1999) 'Re-Examining History: Israel and the Holocaust', in Ateek and Prior (eds) 1999, pp. 97–104.

Dayan, Moshe (1977) *Story of My Life*, London: Sphere Books.

De Ste. Croix, G.E.M. (1981) *The Class Struggle in the Ancient Greek World from the Archaic Age to the Arab Conquest*, London: Duckworth.

De Vaux, Roland (1965) 'Les Patriarches hébreux et l'histoire', in *Revue Biblique* 72: 5–28.

Dever, William G. (1996) 'The Identity of Early Israel: A Rejoinder to Keith W. Whitelam', in *Journal for the Study of the Old Testament* 70: 3–24.

—— (1997) 'Philology, Theology, and Archaeology: What Kind of History Do We Want, and What Is Possible?', in Silberman and Small 1997: 290–310.

Diamond, James S. (1986) *Homeland or Holy Land? The 'Canaanite Critique of Israel'*, Bloomington, IA: Indiana University Press.

Drinan, Robert F. (1977) *Honor the Promise: America's Commitment to Israel*, Cape Town, N.Y.: Doubleday.

Dyer, Charles H. (1993) *World News and Biblical Prophecy*, Wheaton, IL: Tyndale House.

Eban, Abba (1957) *Voice of Israel*, New York: Horizon Press.

Eckardt, Alice and Roy Eckardt, (1970) *Encounter with Israel: A Challenge to Conscience*, New York: Association Press.

El-Assal, Riah Abu (1994) 'The Birth and Experience of the Christian Church: The Protestant/Anglican Perspective. Anglican Identity in the Middle East', in Prior and Taylor (eds) 1994: 131–40.

Ellis, Marc H. (1987) *Toward a Jewish Theology of Liberation*, Maryknoll, NY: Orbis.

—— (1990) *Beyond Innocence and Redemption. Confronting the Holocaust and Israeli Power. Creating a Moral Future for the Jewish People*, San Francisco, CA: Harper & Row.

—— (1994) *Ending Auschwitz. The Future of Jewish and Christian Life*, Louisville, KY: Westminster/John Knox.

—— (1997) *Unholy Alliance: Religion and Atrocity in Our Time*, London: SCM.

—— (1999) 'The Boundaries of Our Destiny. A Jewish Reflection on the Biblical Jubilee on the Fiftieth Anniversary of Israel', in Ateek and Prior (eds) 1999, pp. 236–46.

Elon, Amos (1997) 'Politics and Archaelogy', in Silberman and Small 1997: 34–47.

Ernst, Morris L. (1964) *So Far so Good*, New York: Harper.

Evron, Boas (1981) 'The Holocaust: Learning the Wrong Lessons', in *Journal of Palestine Studies* 10 (Spring): 16–26.

—— (1995) *Jewish State or Israeli Nation?* Bloomington and Indianapolis, IA: Indiana University Press.

Exum, Cheryl and David J.A. Clines (1993) *The New Literary Criticism and the Hebrew Bible*, Sheffield: JSOT Press.

Fackenheim, Emil (1987) 'Holocaust,' in Cohen and Mendes-Flohr (eds) 1987: 399–408.

Feldman, Louis H. (1997) 'The Concept of Exile in Josephus', in Scott 1997: 145–72.

Finkelstein, Israel (1997) 'Pots and People Revisited: Ethnic Boundaries in the Iron Age I', in Silberman and Small 1997: 216–37.

Finkelstein, Norman G. (1995) *Image and Reality of the Israel Palestine Conflict*, London and New York: Verso.

Finklestone, Joseph (1997) 'Zionism and British Jews', in Massil (ed.) 1997: ix–xxx.

Fisher, Eugene J. and Leon Klenicki (eds) (1995) *Spiritual Pilgrimage: Texts on Jews and Judaism, 1979–1995 by Pope John Paul II*, New York: Crossroad.

Fisher, Eugene J., A. James Rudin, and Marc H. Tanenbaum (1986) *Twenty Years of Jewish-Catholic Relations*, Maywah, NY: Paulist.

Flannery, Edward H. (1986) 'Israel, Jerusalem, and the Middle East', in Fisher, Rudin and Tanenbaum 1986: 73–86.

Flapan, Simha (1979) *Zionism and the Palestinians 1917–1947*, London: Croom Helm.

—— (1987) *The Birth of Israel: Myths and Realities*, London and Sydney: Croom Helm.

Fox, Richard Wrightman (1987) *Reinhold Niebuhr: A Biography*, New York: Harper & Row.

Friedman, Robert I. (1990) *The False Prophet: Rabbi Meir Kahane – From FBI Informant to Knesset Member*, London and Boston, MA: Faber & Faber.

Friedman, Robert I. (1992) *Zealots for Zion. Inside Israel's West Bank Settlement Movement*, New York: Random House.

Gafni, Isaiah M. (1984) 'The Historical Background', in Michael E. Stone (ed.) 1984, pp. 1–31.

—— (1997) *Land, Center and Diaspora. Jewish Constructs in Late Antiquity*, Sheffield: Sheffield Academic Press.

Garbini, Giovanni (1988) *History and Ideology in Ancient Israel*, London: SCM.

Gee, John R. (1998) *Unequal Conflict. The Palestinians and Israel*, London: Pluto Press.

Geraisy, Sami (1994) 'Socio-Demographic Characteristics: Reality, Problems and Aspirations within Israel', in Prior and Taylor (eds) 1994: 45–55.

Gilbert, Martin (1975) *Winston S. Churchill*, vol. 4, *1916–1922*, London: Heinemann.

—— (1982) *Atlas of the Holocaust*, London: Michael Joseph in Association with the Board of Deputies of British Jews.

—— (1998) *Israel. A History*, London and New York: Doubleday.

Goldberg, David J. (1996) *To the Promised Land. A History of Zionist Thought from Its Origins to the Modern State of Israel*, London: Penguin.

Gorny, Yosef (1987) *Zionism and The Arabs 1882–1948. A Study of Ideology*, Oxford: Clarendon Press.

Greenstein, Howard R. (1981) *Turning Point: Zionism and Reform Judaism* (Brown Judaic Studies 12), Chico, CA: Scholars Press.

Gunner, Göran (1999) 'Christian Zionism in Scandinavia', in Ateek and Prior (eds) 1999, pp. 180–88.

Hadawi, Sami (1988) *Palestinian Rights and Losses in 1948. A Comprehensive Study* (with Part V, 'An Economic Assessment of Total Palestinian Losses' written by Dr Atef Kubursi), London: Saqi Books.

Hagee, John (1996) *The Beginning of the End: The Assassination of Yitzhak Rabin and the Coming Antichrist*, Tennessee: Thomas Nelson.

Halabi, Usama (1985) *Land Alienation in the West Bank, A Legal and Spatial Analysis*, Jerusalem.

Hall-Cathala, David (1990) *The Peace Movement in Israel, 1967–87*, London: Macmillan.

Halperin, Samuel (1961) *The Political World of American Zionism*, Detroit, MI: Wayne State University Press.

Halpern, Ben (1969) *The Idea of the Jewish State*, 2nd edn, Cambridge, MA and London: Harvard University Press.

Halpern-Amaru, Betsy (1994) *Rewriting the Bible: Land and Covenant in Post-Biblical Jewish Literature*, Valley Forge: Trinity Press.

Handy, Robert T. (ed.) (1981) *The Holy Land in American Protestant Life 1800–1948. A Documentary History*, New York: Arno.

Harrelson, Walter and Randall M. Falk (1990) *Jews and Christians: A Troubled Family*, Nashville, TN: Abingdon.

Harris, William (1980) *Taking Root: Israeli Settlement in the West Bank, the Golan and Gaza-Sinai 1967–1980*, Chichester: Research Studies Press.

Hattis, Lee (1970) *The Bi-national Idea in Palestine During the Mandatory Times*, Haifa: Shikmona.

Hayes, John H. and J. Maxwell Miller (eds) (1977) *Israelite and Judaean History*, London: SCM.

Heilman, Samuel C. (1997) 'Guides of the Faithful: Contemporary Religious Zionist Rabbis', in Appleby 1997: 328–62.

Hertzberg, Arthur (1996) 'The End of the Dream of the Undivided Land of Israel', in *Journal of Palestine Studies* 25 (2): 35–45.

Herzberg, Arthur (ed.) (1959) *The Zionist Idea. A Historical Analysis and Reader*, New York: Doubleday & Co. and Herzl Press.

Herzl, Theodor. (1896) *Der Judenstaat. Versuch einer Modernen Lösung der Judenfrage*, Leipzig and Vienna: M. Breitenstein's Verlags-Buchhandlung; trans. Sylvie d'Avigdor, *A Jewish State*, 1896; repr. *The Jewish State*, American Zionist Emergency Council, 1946; repr. New York: Dover, 1988 (citations are taken from the Dover edition).

—— (1960) *The Complete Diaries of Theodore Herzl*, 5 vols, (ed.) Raphael Patai, trans. Harry Zohn, New York: Herzl Press.

—— (1983–96) vol. 1 (1983) *Briefe und Autobiographische Notizen. 1886–1895*, vol. 2 (1983) *Zionistiches Tagebuch 1895–1899*, vol. 3 (1985) *Zionistiches Tagebuch 1899–1904* (vols 1–3 ed. Johannes Wachten *et al.*), vol. 4 (1900) *Briefe 1895–1898*, vol. 5 (1993) *Briefe 1898–1900*, vol. 6 (1993) *Briefe Ende August 1900-ende Dezember 1902*, vol. 7 (1996) *Briefe 1903–1904* (vols 4–7 ed. Barbara Schäfer *et al.*), Berlin: Propylaen Verlag.

Heschel, Abraham (1987) *God in Search of Man*, Northvale, NJ: Jason Aronson.

Hesse, Brian and Wapnish, Paula (1997) 'Can Pig Remains Be Used for Ethnic Diagnosis in the Ancient Near East?' in Silberman and Small 1997: 238–70.

Higgins, George G. (1986) 'Twenty Years of Catholic–Jewish Relations: Nostra Aetate in Retrospective', in Fisher, Rudin and Tanenbaum 1986: 19–38.

Hilliard, Alison and Bailey, Betty Jane (1999) *Living Stones. Pilgrimages with the Christians of the Holy Land*, London: Cassell.

Hirst, David (1983) *The Gun and the Olive Branch*, London: Futura, McDonald & Co.

Hitchens, Christopher (1988) 'Broadcasts', in Said and Hitchens (eds) 1988: 73–83.

Hobbs, T.R. (1989) *A Time for War: A Study of Warfare in the Old Testament*, Wilmingtom, DE: Michael Glazier.

Hoffman, Lawrence A. (ed.) (1986) *The Land of Israel: Jewish Perspectives*, Notre Dame, IA: University of Notre Dame Press.

Hummel, Ruth and Thomas Hummel (1995) *Patterns of the Sacred. English Protestant and Russian Orthodox Pilgrims of the Nineteenth Century*, London: Scorpion Cavendish.

Hunt, E.D. (1984) *Holy Land Pilgrimage in the Later Roman Empire AD 312–460*, Oxford: Clarendon Press.

Hurewitz, J.C. (1956) *Diplomacy in the Near and Middle East*, vol. 2, Princeton, NJ: D. Van Nostrand.

Hurwitz, Deena. (ed.) (1992) *Walking the Red Line. Israelis in Search of Justice for Palestine*, Philadelphia, PA: New Society Publishers.

—— (1992) 'Introduction', in Hurwitz (ed.) 1992: 3–19.

Ingrams, Doreen (1972) *Palestine Papers 1917–1922: Seeds of Conflict*, London: John Murray.

Jacobs, Steven L. (ed.) (1993) *Contemporary Jewish Religious Responses to the Shoah*, Lanham, New York and London: University Press of America.

Jeffries, J.N. (1976) *Palestine: The Reality*, Westport, CT: Hyperion Press.

Karmi, Ghada and Eugene Cotran (eds) (1999) *The Palestinian Exodus 1948–1998*, Reading: Ithaca.

Karsh, Efraim (1997) *Fabricating Israeli History: The 'New Historians'*, London: Frank Cass.

Kayyali, Abdul Wahhab Al (1979) 'The Historical Roots of the Imperialist-Zionist Alliance', in Al Kayyali (ed.) 1979: 9–26.

—— (ed.) (1979) *Zionism, Imperialism and Racism*, London: Croom Helm.

Khalidi, Rashid (1988) 'Palestinian Peasant Resistance to Zionism Before World War I', in Said and Hitchens (eds) 1988: 207–33.

Khalidi, Walid (1984, 1991) *Before their Diaspora: A Photographic History of the Palestinians 1876–1948*, Washington, D.C.: Institute for Palestinian Studies.

—— (1992) *Palestine Reborn*, London and New York: Tauris.

—— (ed.) (1992) *All that Remains. The Palestinian Villages Occupied and Depopulated by Israel in 1948*, Washington D.C.: Institute for Palestine Studies.

—— (1998) 'Selected Documents on the 1948 Palestine War', in *Journal of Palestine Studies* 27: 60–105.

Khoury, F.J. (1985) *The Arab–Israeli Dilemma*, 3rd edn, Syracuse: Syracuse University Press.

Kidron, Peretz (1988) 'Truth Whereby Nations Live', in Said and Hitchens 1988: 85–96.

Kimmerling, Baruch (1983) *Zionism and Territory. The Socio-Territorial Dimensions of Zionist Politics*, Berkeley, CA: University of California, Institute of International Studies.

Koestler, Arthur (1949) *Promise and Fulfilment. Palestine 1917–1949*, London: Macmillan.

Kohn, Hans (1946) *The Idea of Nationalism*, New York: Macmillan.

Kolsky, Thomas A. (1990) *Jews Against Zionism: The American Council for Judaism 1942–1948*, Philadelphia, PA: Temple University Press.

Kook, Abraham Isaac (1979) *The Lights of Penitence, the Moral Principles, Lights of Holiness, Essays, Letters, and Poems*, translation and introduction by Ben Zion Bokser, London: SPCK.

Kook, Zvi Yehuda (1991) *Torat Eretz Yisrael. The Teachings of HaRav Tzvi Yehuda HaCohen Kook*, commentary by HaRav David Samson, based on the Hebrew *Sichot of HaRav Tzvi Yehuda*, English translation by Tzvi Fishman, Jerusalem: Torat Eretz Yisrael Publications.

Kraabel, A.T. (1987) 'Unity and Diversity among Diaspora Synagogues', in L.I. Levine (ed.) 1987: 49–60.

Kreutz, Andrej (1990) *Vatican Policy on the Palestinian-Israeli Conflict. The Struggle for the Holy Land*, New York, Westport, London: Greenwood Press.

—— (1992) 'The Vatican and the Palestinians: A Historical Overview', *Islamochristiana* 18: 109–25.

Kulka, Otto Dov and Paul R. Mendes-Flohr (eds) (1987) *Judaism and Christianity under the Impact of National Socialism*, Jerusalem: The Historical Society of Israel and the Zalman Shazar Center for Jewish History.

Kwok, Pui-lan (1995) *Discovering the Bible in the Non-Biblical World*, Maryknoll, NY: Orbis Books.

Laqueur, Walter (1972) *History of Zionism*, New York, Chicago, IL and San Francisco, CA: Holt, Rinehart & Winston.

—— (1976) *The Israel-Arab Reader*, New York: Bantam.

Lehn, Walter (in association with Uri Davis) (1988) *The Jewish National Fund*, London and New York: Kegan Paul International.

Lemche, Niels Peter (1985) *Early Israel: Anthropological and Historical Studies on the Israelite Society before the Monarchy. Vetus Testamentum Supplements* 38, Leiden: Brill.

—— (1995) *Ancient Israel. A New History of Israelite Society*, Sheffield: Sheffield Academic Press.

Lerner, Michael (1988) 'The Occupation: Immoral and Stupid', editorial in *Tikkun* 3, March–April; repr. in Ruether and Ellis 1990: 99–100.

Levine, L.I. (ed.) (1987) *The Synagogue in Late Antiquity*, Philadelphia, PA: American Schools of Oriental Research.

Liebman, Charles S. and Eliezer Don-Yehiya (1983) *Civil Religion in Israel: Traditional Judaism and Political Culture in the Jewish State*, Berkeley, CA and London: University of California Press.

Lilienthal, Alfred M. (1982) *The Zionist Connection II: What Price Peace?*, New Brunswick, NJ: North American (revised from 1978 edition).

Lind, Millard C. (1980) *Yahweh is a Warrior. A Theology of Warfare in Ancient Israel*, Scottdale, PA and Kitchener, Ont: Herald.

Lindsey, Hal (1970) *The Late, Great Planet Earth*, London: Lakeland.

—— (1983) *Israel and the Last Days*, Eugene, OR: Harvest House.

Littell, Franklin H. (1987) 'Christian Antisemitism and the Holocaust', in Kulka and Mendes-Flohr (eds) 1987: 513–29.

Lohfink, Norbert (1996) *The Laws of Deuteronomy. A Utopian Project for a World without any Poor?* Cambridge: Von Hügel Institute, and in 'The Laws of Deuteronomy. A Utopian Project for a World without any Poor' (without the question), *Scripture Bulletin* 26 (1996): 2–19.

Lüdemann, Gerd (1997) *The Unholy in Holy Scripture. The Dark Side of the Bible*, translated and with an Appendix by John Bowden, London: SCM.

Lustick, Ian S. (1988) *For the Land and the Lord*, New York: Council on Foreign Relations Press.

MacBride, Seán (Chairman) (1983) *Israel in Lebanon. The Report of the International Commission to enquire into Reported Violations of International Law by Israel during its Invasion of the Lebanon*, London: Ithaca Press.

Mahoney, John F. (1992) 'About This Issue', in *The Link* (Americans for Middle East Understanding) 25 (4): 2.

March, W. Eugene (1994) *Israel and the Politics of Land. A Theological Case Study*, Foreword by Walter Brueggemann, Louisville, KY: Westminster and John Knox Press.

Masalha, Nur (1992) *Expulsion of the Palestinians: the Concept of 'Transfer' in Zionist Political Thought, 1882–1948*, Washington, DC: Institute for Palestine Studies.

—— (1997) *A Land without a People. Israel, Transfer and the Palestinians 1949–96*, London: Faber & Faber.

—— (1999) 'The 1967 Palestinian Exodus', in Karmi and Cotran (eds) 1999: 63–109.

Massil, Stephen W. (ed.) (1997) *The Jewish Year Book*, London: Vallentine Mitchell.

Matar, Ibrahim (1992) 'Exploitation of Land and Water Resources for Jewish Colonies in the Occupied Territories', in Playfair (ed.) 1992: 443–57.

McCarthy, Justin (1991) *The Population of Palestine: Population History and Statistics of the late Ottoman Period and the Mandate*, New York: Columbia University Press.

McDowall, David (1989) *Palestine and Israel. The Uprising and Beyond*, London: Tauris.

—— (1994) *The Palestinians. The Road to Nationhood*, London: Minority Rights.

Menuhin, Moshe (1969) *The Decadence of Judaism in our Time*, Beirut: The Institute for Palestinian Studies.

Mergui, Raphael and Philippe Simonnot (1987 Eng. trans.) *Israel's Ayatollahs. Meir Kahane and the Far Right in Israel*, London: Saqi Books.

Mezvinsky, Norton (1989) 'Reform Judaism and Zionism: Early History and Change', in Tekiner, Abed-Rabbo and Mezvinsky (eds) 1989: 313–39.

Mikhail, Hanna (1995) *Politics and Revelation. Mwardi and After*, Edinburgh: Edinburgh University Press.

Milgrom, Jacob (1999) 'Jubilee: A Rallying Cry for Today's Oppressed', in Ateek and Prior (eds) 1999, pp. 233–35.

Milgrom, Jeremy (1992) 'The Responsibility of Power', in Hurwitz (ed.) 1992: 27–36.

Millard, A.R. (1992) 'Abraham', in *The Anchor Bible Dictionary*, vol. 1 (A–C): I.35–41.

Miller, J. Maxwell and Hayes, John H. (1986) *A History of Ancient Israel and Judah*, Philadelphia, PA: Westminster; and London: SCM.

Minerbi, Sergio I. (1990) *The Vatican and Zionism: Conflict in the Holy Land, 1895–1925*, New York and Oxford: Oxford University Press.

Mo'az, Moshe (1992) 'The Jewish-Zionist and Arab-Palestinian National Communities: The Transposing Effect of a Century of Confrontation', in Spagnolo (ed.) 1992: 151–68.

Moltmann, Jürgen (1967) *The Theology of Hope. On the Ground and the Implications of a Christian Eschatology*, London: SCM.

Morgan, Robert with Barton, John (1989) *Biblical Interpretation*, Oxford: Oxford University Press.

Morris, Benny (1987) *The Birth of the Palestinian Refugee Problem, 1947–1949*, Cambridge: Cambridge University Press.

—— (1990a) *1948 and After: Israel and the Palestinians*, Oxford: Oxford University Press.

—— (1990b) 'The Eel and History', in *Tikkun*, January–February: 20–21.

—— (1993) *Israel's Border Wars*, Oxford: Oxford University Press.

—— (1995) 'Falsifying the Record. A Fresh Look at Zionist Documentation of 1948', in *Journal of Palestine Studies* 24: 44–62.

—— (1998) 'Refabricating 1948' (Review Essay), in *Journal of Palestine Studies* 27: 81–95.

Mosse, George L. (1992) 'The Jews and the Civic Religion of Nationalism', in Reinharz and Mosse 1992: 319–28.

Neff, Donald (1991) 'The Differing Interpretation of Resolution 242', in *Middle East International* 404 (*sic*, for 408, 13 September): 16–17.

Neher, André (1992) 'The Land as Locus of the Sacred', in Burrell and Landau (eds) 1992: 18–29.

Nemoy, Leon (ed.) (1952) *The Karaite Anthology: Excerpts from the Early Literature*, New Haven, CT: Yale University Press.

Neusner, Jacob (1990) 'The Role of History in Judaism: The Initial Definition', in Neusner (ed.) 1990: 233–48.

—— (ed.) (1990) *The Christian and Judaic Invention of History*, Atlanta, GA: Scholars Press.

Nevo, Naomi (1985) 'Religiosity and Community: A Case Study of a *Gush Emunim* Settlement', in Newman (ed.) 1985: 221–44.

Newman, David (ed.) (1985) *The Impact of Gush Emunim. Political Settlement in the West Bank*, London and Sydney: Crook Helm.

Newton, B.W. (1838) *The Christian Witness*, vol. 5, Plymouth: The Christian Witness & Tract Depot.

Niditch, Susan (1993) *War in the Hebrew Bible. A Study of the Ethics of Violence*, Oxford: Oxford University Press.

O'Mahony, Anthony, with G. Gunner and K. Hintlian, (1995) *The Christian Heritage in the Holy Land*, London: Scorpion Cavendish.

O'Neill, Dan and Don Wagner (1993) *Peace or Armageddon? The Unfolding Drama of the Middle East Peace Accord*, Grand Rapids: Zondervan Publishing House.

Orlinsky, Harry M. (1985) 'The Biblical Concept of the Land of Israel: Cornerstone of the Covenant between God and Israel', in *Eretz-Israel* 18: 43–55.

Orr, Akiva (1994) *Israel: Politics, Myths and Identity Crises*, London: Pluto Press.

Pappé, Ilan (1992) *The Making of the Arab–Israeli Conflict, 1947–51*, New York: Macmillan and St Anthony's Press.

PASSIA (1996) *Documents on Jerusalem*, Jerusalem: Palestinian Academic Society for the Study of International Affairs.

Pawlikowski, John T. (1990) 'Ethical Issues in the Israeli-Palestinian Conflict', in Ruether and Ellis (eds) 1990: 155–70.

Peleg, Muli (1997) *Lehafitz et Za'am Hael* ('Spreading the Wrath of God'), Hakibbutz Hameuchad.

Peretz, Don and Gideon Doron (1996) 'Israel's 1996 Elections: A Second Political Earthquake', in *The Middle East Journal* 50: 529–46.

Peters, Joan (1984) *From Time Immemorial*, New York: Harper & Row

Petuchowski, Jakob (1966) *Zion Reconsidered*, New York: Twayne.

Pikkert, Peter (1992) 'Christian Zionism: Evangelical Schizophrenia', in *Middle East International* 439: 19–20.

Plaut, W. Gunther (1963) *The Rise of Reform Judaism: A Sourcebook of its European Origins*, New York: World Union of Progressive Judaism.

—— (ed.) (1965) *The Growth of Reform Judaism; American and European Sources until 1948*, New York: World Union of Progressive Judaism.

Playfair, Emma (ed.) (1992) *International Law and the Administration of Occupied Territories. Two Decades of Israeli Occupation of the West Bank and Gaza Strip*, Oxford: Clarendon Press.

Pontifical Biblical Commission (1993) *The Interpretation of the Bible in the Church*, Boston, MA: St Paul Books & Media.

Ponting, Clive (1994) *Churchill*, London: Sinclair-Stevenson.

Prior, Michael (1989) *Paul the Letter Writer and the Second Letter to Timothy*, Sheffield: Sheffield Academic Press.

—— (1990) 'A Christian Perspective on the *Intifada*', in *The Month* 23: 478–85.

—— (1993) 'Palestinian Christians and the Liberation of Theology', in *The Month* 26: 482–90.

—— (1994a) 'Pilgrimage to the Holy Land, Yesterday and Today', in Prior and Taylor (eds) 1994: 169–99.

—— (1994b) 'Clinton's Bible, Goldstein's Hermeneutics', in *Middle East International* 16 December: 20–1.

—— (1995a) *Jesus the Liberator. Nazareth Liberation Theology (Luke 4.16–30)*, Sheffield: Sheffield Academic Press.

—— (1995b) 'The Bible as Instrument of Oppression', in *Scripture Bulletin* 25: 2–14.

—— (1996) 'The Future of the Christian Community in the Holy Land', in *The Month* 29: 140–5.

—— (1997a) *The Bible and Colonialism. A Moral Critique*, Sheffield: Sheffield Academic Press.

—— (1997b) 'A Perspective on Pilgrimage to the Holy Land', in Ateek, Duaybis and Schrader 1997: 114–31.

—— (1997c) *A Land flowing with Milk, Honey, and People*, Cambridge: Von Hügel Institute, and in *Scripture Bulletin* 28 (1998): 2–17.

—— (1998a) 'The Moral Problem of the Land Traditions of the Bible', in Prior (ed.) 1998: 41–81.

—— (ed.) (1998b) *Western Scholarship and the History of Palestine*, London: Melisende.

Prior, Michael and William Taylor (eds) (1994) *Christians in the Holy Land*, London: WIFT/Scorpion.

Quigley, John (1990) *Palestine and Israel. A Challenge to Justice*, Durham and London: Duke University Press.

—— (1998) 'The Right of Return of Displaced Jerusalemites', in Prior (ed.) 1998b: 83–90.

Rabin, Leah (1997) *Rabin: Our Life, His Legacy*, New York: G.P. Putnam's Sons.

Raheb, Mitri (1995) *I am a Palestinian Christian*, Minneapolis: Fortress Press.

Rantisi, Audeh (1990) *Blessed are the Peacemakers. The Story of a Palestinian Christian*, Guildford: Eagle.

Raviv, Moshe (1998) *Israel at Fifty: Five Decades of Struggle for Peace*, London: Weidenfeld & Nicolson.

Redford, Donald B. (1992) *Egypt, Canaan, and Israel in Ancient Times*, Princeton, NJ: Princeton University Press.

Reinharz, Jehuda and Mosse, George L. (eds) (1992) *The Impact of Western Nationalisms. Essays dedicated to Walter Z. Laqueur on the occasion of his 70th birthday*, London: Sage Publications.

Rodinson, Maxine (1983) *Cult, Ghetto, and State: The Persistence of the Jewish Question*, London: Al Saqi.

Rokach, Livia (1980) *Israel's Sacred Terrorism: A Study based on Moshe Sharett's Diaries*, Belmont, MA: Association of Arab-American University Graduates

—— (1987) *The Catholic Church and the Question of Palestine*, London: Saqi Books.

Romain, Jonathan A. (ed.) (1996) *Renewing the Vision. Rabbis Speak Out on Modern Jewish Issues*, London: SCM.

Rosenak, Michael (1987) 'State of Israel', in Cohen and Mendes-Flohr (eds) 1987: 909–16.

Rubenstein, Amnon (1984) *The Zionist Dream Revisited: From Herzl to Gush Emunim and Back*, New York: Schocken.

Rudin, A. James (1986) 'The Dramatic Impact of Nostra Aetate', in Fisher, Rudin and Tanenbaum 1986: 9–18.

Ruether, Rosemary Radford (1974) *Faith and Fratricide: The Theological Roots of Anti-Semitism*, New York: Seabury.

—— (1990) 'The Occupation Must End', in Ruether and Ellis (eds) 1990: 183–97.

—— (1999) 'Justice and Reconciliation', in Ateek and Prior (eds) 1999: 116–21.

Ruether, Rosemary and Ruether, Herman (1989) *The Wrath of Jonah: The Crisis of Religious Nationalism in the Israeli-Palestinian Conflict*, New York: Harper & Row.

Ruether, Rosemary and Marc Ellis (eds) (1990) *Beyond Occupation: American Jews, Christians and Palestinians Search for Peace*, Boston: Beacon Press.

Runciman, Steven (1951) *A History of the Crusades*, vol. 1, *The First Crusade and the Foundation of the Kingdom of Jerusalem*, Cambridge: Cambridge University Press; repr. 1991, London: Penguin.

Ruppin, Arthur (1913) *The Jews Today*, trans. Margery Bentwich, London: G. Bell & Sons.

Sabbah, Michel (1993) *Reading the Bible Today in the Land of the Bible*, Jerusalem: Latin Patriarchate.

Sabella, Bernard (1994) 'Socio-Economic Characteristics and the Challenges to Palestinian Christians in the Holy Land', in Prior and Taylor 1994: 31–44.

—— (1996) 'Demographic Trends in Jerusalem and the West Bank', in *Arab Regional Population Conference. 8–12 December 1996, Cairo*, Liège: International Union for the Study of Population: 177–96.

Said, Edward W. (1988) 'Michael Walzer's *Exodus and Revolution*: A Canaanite Reading', in Said and Hitchens (eds) 1988: 161–78.

—— (1994) *The Politics of Dispossession. The Struggle for Palestinian Self-Determination, 1969–1994*, New York: Pantheon Books.

—— (1992, second edn) *The Question of Palestine*, London: Vintage.

Said, Edward W. and Christopher Hitchens (eds) (1988) *Blaming the Victims. Spurious Scholarship and the Palestinian Question*, London and New York: Verso.

Schlink, Basilea (1991) *Israel at the Heart of World Events*, Darmstadt-Eberstadt: Evangelical Sisterhood of Mary.

Schonfeld, Moshe (1980) *Genocide in the Holy Land*, Brooklyn New York: Bnei Yeshivos.

Schürer, E. (1979) *The History of the Jewish People in the Age of Jesus Christ (175 B.C.–A.D. 135)*, vol. II, revised and edited by G. Vermes, *et al.*, Edinburgh: T&T Clark.

Schweid, Eliezer (1987) 'Land of Israel', in Cohen and Mendes-Flohr (eds) 1987: 535–41.

Scott, James M. (1997) 'Exile and the Self-understanding of Diaspora Jews in the Greco-Roman Perior', in Scott (ed.) 1997: 173–218.

—— (ed.) (1997) *Exile: Old Testament, Jewish and Christian Conceptions*, Leiden: Brill.

Segev, Tom (1993) *The Seventh Million. The Israelis and the Holocaust. (trans. by Haim Watzan)*, New York: Hill & Wang.

Seikaly, May (1999) 'Justice and Reconciliation – Living with the Memory. Legitimacy, Justice and Nationhood', in Ateek and Prior (eds) 1999: 105–10.

Seward, Desmond (1995) *The Monks of War. The Military Religious Orders*, London: Penguin Books.

Shahak, Israel (1994) *Jewish History, Jewish Religion. The Weight of Three Thousand Years*, London: Pluto.

—— (1975) *Report: Arab Villages destroyed in Israel*, 2nd edn, Jerusalem: Shahak.

—— (1994) 'New Revelations on the 1982 Invasion of Lebanon', in *Middle East International* 485 (7 October): 18–19.

Shapira, Anita (1992) *Land and Power. The Zionist Resort to Force*, Oxford: Oxford University Press.

Sharif, Regina S. (1983) *Non-Jewish Zionism. Its Roots in Western History*, London: Zed Press.

Sharot, S. (1976) *Judaism: A Sociology*, New York: Holmes & Meier.

Shavit, Yaacov (1997) 'Archaelogy, Political Culture and Culture in Israel', in Silberman and Small 1997: 48–61.

Sheffer, Gabriel (ed.) (1997) *U.S.-Israeli Relations at the Crossroads*, London and Portland, OR: Frank Cass.

Shiblak, Abbas (1986) *The Lure of Zion. The Case of the Iraqi Jews*, London: Al Saqi Books.

Shorris, Earl (1982) *Jews without Mercy: A Lament*, Garden City, NY: Doubleday.

Silberman, Neil Asher and David Small (1997) *The Archaeology of Israel. Constructing the Past, Interpreting the Present*, Sheffield: Sheffield Academic Press.

Simon, Leon (1962) *Selected Essays of Ahad Ha-'Am*, trans. (from Hebrew) and ed. Leon Simon, New York: Atheneum (reprint of 1912 edition).

Simonetti, Manlio (1994) *Biblical Interpretation in the Early Church. An Historical Introduction to Patristic Exegesis*, Edinburgh: T&T Clark.

Sizer, Stephen R. (1994) *Visiting the Living Stones*, unpublished MTh Thesis, University of Oxford.

—— (1999) 'Christian Zionism: A British Perspective', in Ateek and Prior (eds) 1999: 189–98.

Small, David B. (1997) 'Group Identification and Ethnicity in the Construction of the Early State of Israel: From the Outside Looking in', in Silberman and Small 1997: 271–88.

Smith, Gary (1974) *Zionism, the Dream and the Reality*, New York: Harper & Row.

Smith-Christopher, D.L (1997) 'Reassessing the Historical and Sociological Impact of the Babylonian Exile (597/587–539 BCE)', in Scott (ed.) 1997: 7–36.

Soggin, J. Alberto (1984) *A History of Israel. From the Beginnings to the Bar Kochba Revolt, A.D. 135*, London: SCM.

Spagnolo, John P. (ed.) (1992) *Problems of the Modern Middle East in Historical Perspective. Essays in Honour of Albert Hourani*, Reading: Ithaca.

Sprinzak, Ehud (1985) 'The Iceberg Model of Political Extremism', in Newman (ed.) 1985: 27–45.

—— (1991) *The Ascendance of Israel's Radical Right*, New York and Oxford: Oxford University Press.

Stein, Leonard (1961) *The Balfour Declaration,* London: Valentine, Mitchell.

Sternhell, Zeev (1998) *The Founding Myths of Israel. Nationalism, Socialism and the Making of the Jewish State*, trans. David Maisel, Princeton, NJ: Princeton University Press.

Stone, Michael E. (ed.) (1984) *Jewish Writings of the Second Temple Period. Apocrypha, Pseudepigrapha, Qumran Sectarian Writings, Philo, Josephus*, Assen: Van Gorcum and Philadelphia, PA: Fortress Press.

Sugirtharajah, R.S. (ed.) (1991) *Voices from the Margin: Interpreting the Bible in the Third World*, London: SPCK.

Sykes, Christopher (1953a) *Two Studies in Virtue*, New York: Knopf.

—— (1953b) 'The Prosperity of his Servant: A Study of the Origins of the Balfour Declaration', in Sykes 1953: 107–235.

—— (1965) *Crossroads to Israel. Palestine from Balfour to Bevin*, London: Collins.

Tamarin, Georges R. (1973) 'The influence of ethnic and religious prejudice on moral judgement', in Tamarin 1973: 183–90 (first edition 1963).

—— (1973) *The Israeli Dilemma. Essays on a Warfare State*, ed. Johan Niezing, Rotterdam: Rotterdam University Press.

Tanenbaum, Marc H. (1986) 'A Jewish Viewpoint on Nostra Aetate', in Fisher, Rudin and Tanenbaum 1986: 39–60.

Tastard, Terry (1998) 'Perspectives on the Palestine crisis in some of the UK Press 1946–1948' (MA Dissertation, The University of Hertfordshire, UK)

Tekiner, Roselle, Samir Abed-Rabbo and Norton Mezvinsky (1989) *Anti-Zionism. Analytic Reflections*, Battleboro, VT: Amana Books.

Teveth, Shabtai (1985) *Ben-Gurion and the Palestinian Arabs*, Oxford: Oxford University Press.

Thiselton, Anthony C. (1992) *New Horizons in Hermeneutics. The Theory and Practice of Transforming Biblical Reading*, London: HarperCollins.

Thompson, Thomas L. (1974) *The Historicity of the Pentateuchal Narratives. The Quest for the Historical Abraham*, Berlin and New York: de Gruyter.

—— (1987) *The Origin Tradition of Ancient Israel. 1. The Literary Formation of Genesis and Exodus 1–23*, Sheffield: JSOT Press.

—— (1992) *Early History of the Israelite People from the Written and Archaeological Sources*, Leiden: Brill.

—— (1995) 'A Neo-Albrightean School in History and Biblical Scholarship', in *Journal of Biblical Literature* 114: 685–98.

—— (1998) 'Hidden Histories and the Problem of Ethnicity in Palestine', in Prior (ed.) 1998b: 23–39.

Timerman, Jacobo (1984) *The Longest War. Israel in Lebanon*, New York: Simon & Schuster.

Toubbeh, Jamil I. (1998) *Day of the Long Night. A Palestinian Refugee Remembers the Nakba*, Jefferson, NC and London: McFarland.

Van Buren, Paul (1980) *Discerning the Way: A Theology of Jewish Christian Reality*, New York: Seabury.

Van der Hoeven, Jan Willem (1993) *Babylon or Jerusalem*, Shippensburg PA: Destiny Image.

Van Seters, John (1975) *Abraham in History and Tradition*, New Haven, CT and London: Yale University Press.

—— (1992) *Prologue to History: The Yahwist as Historian in Genesis*, Louisville, KY: Westminster/John Knox.

van Unnik, W.C. (1993) *Das Selbstverständnis der jüdischen Diaspora in der hellenistisch-römischen Zeit*, ed. P.W. van der Horst, Leiden: Brill.

Vital, David (1975) *The Origins of Zionism*, Oxford: Clarendon.

—— (1982) *Zionism: The Formative Years*, Oxford: Clarendon.

—— (1990) *The Future of the Jews: A People at the Crossroads*, Cambridge: Harvard University Press.

Von Rad, Gerhard (1966) 'The Promised Land and Yahweh's Land in the Hexateuch', in *The Problem of the Hexateuch and Other Essays* (repr. 1984), London: SCM and Philadelphia, PA: Fortress, pp. 79–93.

Wagner, Don (1992) 'Beyond Armageddon', in *The Link* (Americans for Middle East Understanding) 25 (4): 1–13.

—— (1995) *Anxious for Armageddon: A Call to Partnership for Middle Eastern and Western Christians*, Scottdale & Waterloo: Herald Press.

—— (1999) 'Reagan and Begin, Bibi and Jerry: The Theopolitical Alliance of the Likud Party with the American Christian "Right" ', in Ateek and Prior (eds) 1999, pp. 199–215.

Walker, Peter W.L. (1996) *Jesus and the Holy City. New Testament Perspectives on Jerusalem*, Grand Rapids & Cambridge: Eerdmans.

Walzer, Michael (1985) *Exodus and Revolution*, New York: Basic Books.

Warrior, Robert Allen (1991) 'A North American Perspective: Canaanites, Cowboys, and Indians', in Sugirtharajah (ed.) 1991: 287–95.

Watson, Francis (1994) *Text, Church and World. Biblical Interpretation in Theological Perspective*, Grand Rapids: Eerdmans.

WCC (1988) *The Theology of the Churches and the Jewish People. Statements by the World Council of Churches and its Member Churches*, with commentary by Allan Brockway, Paul van Buren, Rolf Rendtorff and Simon Schoon, Geneva: World Council of Churches.

Weitz, Yosef (1965) *Yomani Ve'igrotai Labanim* (My Diary and Letters to the Children), vols 1–4, Tel Aviv: Massada.

Weizmann, Chaim (1929–30) 'The Position of Palestine', in *Palestine Papers 2*, London: Jewish Agency for Palestine.

—— (1949) *Trial and Error: The Autobiography of Chaim Weizmann*, New York: Harper & Row.

Whitelam, Keith W. (1996a) *The Invention of Ancient Israel. The Silencing of Palestinian History*, London and New York: Routledge.

—— (1996b) 'Prophetic Conflict in Israelite History: Taking Sides with William G. Dever', in *Journal for the Study of the Old Testament* 72: 25–44.

—— (1998) 'Western Scholarship and the Silencing of Palestinian History', in Prior (ed.) 1998b: 9–21.

Whybray, R. Norman (1995) *Introduction to the Pentateuch*, Grand Rapids: Eerdmans.

Widoger, Geoffrey (1988) *Jewish-Christian Relations since the Second World War*, Manchester and New York: Manchester University Press.

Wise, Isaac Mayer. (1899) 'Zionism', in *The Hebrew Union College Journal* 4: 445–47.

Wistrich, Robert (1995) 'Theodor Herzl: Zionist Icon, Myth-Maker and Social Utopian', in Wistrich and Ohana (eds) 1995: 1–37.

Wistrich, Robert and David Ohana (eds) (1995) *The Shaping of Israeli Identity: Myth, Memory and Trauma*, London: Frank Cass.

Wood, Diana (ed.) (1992) *Christianity and Judaism. Studies in Church History*, vol. 29, Oxford: Blackwells.

Wright, George E, in Wright, G.E. and R.H. Fuller (eds) (1960) *The Book of the Acts of God: Christian Scholarship Interprets the Bible*, London: Duckworth.

Yaron, Zvi (1991) *The Philosophy of Rabbi Kook*, Jerusalem: Eliner Library.

Zangwill, Israel (1920) *The Voice of Jerusalem,* London: Heinemann.

—— (1937) *Speeches, Articles and Letters of Israel Zangwill*, ed. Maurice Simon, London: Soncino Press.

Zureik, Elia (1994) 'Palestinian Refugees and Peace', in *Journal of Palestine Studies* 93: 5–17.

Index

The terms 'Zionism' and 'the State of Israel' occur so frequently in the text that they have not been singled out here.